A. TYULIN, A. CHURSIN

ADVANCED DEVELOPMENT AND SUSTAINABILITY OF A COMPANY IN THE CONDITIONS OF CRISES AND TRANSFORMATION OF GLOBAL ECONOMIES

Monograph

EurAsian
Scientific Editions Ltd

Tallinn, 2021

UDC 330.101.542:004
LBC 65.012.1я73
B 71

ISBN 978-9949-7485-9-4

Acknowledgments:
The reported study was funded by RFBR,
project number 20-010-00788.

A. Tyulin, A. Chursin. Advanced development and sustainability of a company in the conditions of crises and transformation of global economies. – Talinn: EurAsian Scientific Editions Ltd, 2021 – 428 p.

ISBN 978-9949-7485-9-4

www.eurasian-scientific-editions.org

Translation from Russian: Balasanyan Arus
Cover photo: Ramon Salinero

INTRODUCTION

In the modern world, the trends of the world's economies do not just affect each other, but also enter into insoluble contradictions. We can see their transformation, the redistribution of the roles of the leading countries and macro-regions in the global economic and geopolitical arena, and the redistribution of spheres of influence in significant market segments driving the economy. At the same time, multinational corporations, which are becoming increasingly important, are beginning to dictate the rules of the game in global markets, leveling country opportunities and development priorities. In this regard, national companies are, on the one hand, under the strong influence of large business giants, and on the other, they are forced to survive in the current economic situation in their country. In these conditions, one of the challenges for the organization of economic activity and the solution of one of the most important tasks facing the company is not just to maintain and increase its competitiveness, but to implement the model of advanced development, growth of stability in the conditions of crises and transformation of world economies.

The solution of such a multi-factor dynamic task requires the formation of effective mechanisms for anticipating future needs, anticipating entering an economic crisis, tools for an early exit from the crisis and ensuring advanced economic growth.

The history of the development of the world industrial society in the economy of many countries shows periodically emerging crises, during which there was an increasing decline in production, the accumulation of unrealized goods on the market, falling prices, the collapse of the system of mutual settlements, the collapse of banking systems, the ruin of industrial and commercial firms, and a sharp jump in unemployment.

At the same time, economic crises until the 20th century were limited to one, two or three countries. With the acceleration of the pace of innovation development, the crises have become a global issue.

Despite the fact that in recent decades the world community has formed certain mechanisms to minimize the consequences of global crises, as the history of the world economy testifies, it is impossible to accurately predict, much less avoid them.

In these conditions, business structures are forced to balance and look for new effective mechanisms to ensure sustainable development in the context of ongoing economic structural shifts. The basis of such mechanisms should be a system of building, continuous improvement and development of radical competencies, and their dissemination at the intersectoral level, as well as the construction of models of economic development based on the algorithm «competencies – industry –personalized needs». Such a system creates the preconditions for a multiple increase in labor productivity and profound economic changes, leading to sustainable economic growth. The progress observed today in the management of economic systems, of course, allows us to develop the most reasonable directions of economic development, to create an effective model of operational management of economic processes as a result of the creation of intersectoral radical competencies.

The need for such changes is related to the formation of new systemic approaches to management arising from increasing the growth and development of global industry on the basis of the transformation of organizational and economic relations in the management of the development and manufacture of promising radically new products that in the future will have a high market potential, can take a high market share or create a new consumer segment.

As a result, an important competitive advantage of every industrial organization is the ability not only to organize product life-cycle management in such a way that it is developed and produced in the shortest possible time at an optimal cost level, but to build its competitive potential, a business environment for creating a radically new product that provides global technological leadership of the company in the market.

Global technological leadership allows to significantly increase the volume of profit from the sale of products in a short time and direct it in large quantities compared to competitors to solve the fundamental and applied problems of creating other products that have a new personalized unique value for society and are able to meet the needs in a short time. The radical competence of the «rapid» response and the anticipation of the future personalized needs of society in unique products provide conditions that significantly increase the dynamism of the processes of economic development.

Based on the economic processes studied in the monograph, the economic law of advanced satisfaction of prospective needs is formulated. On its basis, the axiomatic foundations of the theory of advanced development and economic growth of the company are created, which allow us to describe the economic mechanisms and tools for creating unique products that can be developed as an applied software solution with high practical significance for industrial companies.

Innovative development objectively shapes the trends of society's development. Achieving success in competition in the context of crises and transformation of world economies means being ahead in forecasting the development vectors of market demand on the basis of knowledge of the economic law of advanced satisfaction of long-term needs formulated in the book and the basics of the theory of advanced development and economic growth of the company. For the sustainable development of the company, the monograph describes the basics of the transformation of scientific and technological capacity and the mechanisms for building unique technological competencies into a radically new product. At the same time, flexibility and relative stability are achieved through the transformation of activities based on service models and advanced development management mechanisms based on technology platforms.

The systematic approach to describing the processes of advanced development is based on the use of intelligent methods in solving management tasks throughout the cycle of creating radically new products.

The formulated decision-making rules contain the main methods, tools and mechanisms and allow to ensure technological leadership in the real economy in the face of the challenges of the XXI century.

The monograph will be of interest to scientists, theoretical economists dealing with the problems of microeconomics, industrial technologists, heads of industrial organizations, as well as researchers interested in the described issues.

5

CHAPTER 1.
DEVELOPMENT OF RADICAL COMPETENCIES: RECOVERY FROM THE CRISIS AND RAPID ECONOMIC GROWTH

1.1. RADICAL COMPETENCIES AS A DRIVER FOR OVERCOMING ECONOMIC CRISES AND ENSURING ECONOMIC GROWTH

For almost two centuries of the formation and development of the world industrial society, the economies of many countries experienced crises, during which there was a growing decline in production, theaccumulationofunsoldgoodsonthemarket,fallingprices,thecollapse of the mutual payment system, the collapse of banking systems, the ruin of industrial and trading firms, and a sharp jump in unemployment. Economic crises until the twentieth century were limited to one, two or three countries, then began to assume an international character. Despite the fact that in recent decades the international community has created mechanisms to prevent world crises (strengthening state regulation of economic processes, creating international financial organizations, monitoring, etc.), the history of world economic cataclysms shows that it is impossible to accurately predict, let alone avoid crises. In Eurasia and America during the XX and XXI centuries, large-scale economic crises have occurred more than 10 times, while in the XXI century in twenty years there have already been five large-scale crises and the sixth one is growing. These data indicate that the world has already experienced as many major economic crises in the early twenty-first century as in the entire twentieth century, which shows an increase in the frequency of their occurrence.

The periodic occurrence of crises in economic life of a number of countries makes it necessary to analyze the causes and factors that determine their occurrence. Many negative phenomena in the development of the economy – the strengthening of crisis recessions, the decrease in economic growth and labor productivity, etc. – as a deep and decisive reason have scientific and technological development, more precisely, fluctuations in its performance in various fields of activity, leading to a change in marginality in the context of economic sectors. At the same time, there is a redistribution of financial resources between segments and individual industries, as well as their accumulation in the economy. A country accumulates a sufficient amount of financial resources that have nowhere to direct. In these conditions, there is a decrease in deposit rates, which indicates the sufficiency of the money supply in a country and industry. An Industry independently ensures its own development in proportion to the rate of consumption, while it mainly works to improve outdated product samples and give them new characteristics that meet consumer expectations.

At the same time, the income of the population often ceases to grow, since there is no scientific and technological breakthrough; the volumes of consumption decrease, and money, being a kind of commodity, is not consumed. Due to the decrease in rates on deposits, their volume is also decreasing. All these conditions together boost the crisis phenomena.

The relationship between the rates on dollar deposits and crises, shown in Fig. 1.1, indicates that the lack of demand for the money

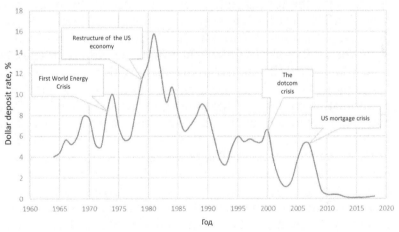

Figure 1.1. Dynamics of interest rates on USD deposits

supply, confirmed by minimum rates, leads to a crisis and a sharp jump in rates in order to attract financial resources to improve the economy and search for new sources of economic growth.

Another reason for the onset of crises is the problem of over-production of goods due to the saturation of existing markets and the lag in the creation and conquest of new markets, which leads to commodity crises. If in the industrial era it took many years and decades from the moment of building new types of products to the creation of stable consumer markets, now this period has been reduced to several months. Competition in the field of high technologies and unique competencies has different mechanisms in contrast to traditional industry. These mechanisms respond much more quickly to changes of competitors, which forces companies to adapt to a rapid and effective change in their behavior. When the possibilities of existing competencies and technologies are exhausted, a crisis arises, the way out of which is connected to the emergence of "goods of advanced satisfaction of prospective needs", stimulating society to form new demand.

Overcoming the crises of the end of the XX century is related to the use of the scientific and technological reserve of the first post-war decades. For example, microelectronics served as the framework for the economic rise: computers, mobile phones, portable devices, etc., the increasingly important Internet. Even for more "traditional" industries, it was microelectronics that became the tool that gave them a new life for a while. Thus, the automotive industry in the 1990s completely switched from the carburetor engines, which dominated the industry since its inception, to models with electronically controlled injection; in aviation the development of automation has reduced the number of crews to two pilots. Even household appliances in the 1990s got electronic control instead of electromechanical. However, this rise was based on investments made in previous decades. The potential of post-war technologies was exhausted by the beginning of the XXI century. As a result, the subsequent overcoming of crises was, to a large extent, fictitious – new markets were not created, but the "old" ones were used more effectively (for example, the "smartphone era" of the 2000s was only a slight development of ideas proposed in the 1990s).

In terms of structural factors that currently restrain economic growth in countries traditionally divided into two large groups, in a number of countries with emerging market economies such factors are low productivity growth and low investment attractiveness of business, while in advanced economies the aging of the population is the limiting factor. According to the analytical agency Morgan Stanley this problem affects economies with a combined share of 78% of world GDP (64% – GDP at purchasing power parity). The growth of the working-age population is slowing down, which leads not only to an increase in the demographic load (the number of retirees and children in relation to the employed), but also to the aging of the labor force itself, which, in turn, reduces labor productivity. Moreover there is a paradigm shift of the world development characterized by the configuration change of interests of major global players as well as undermining the traditional rules of the game in international relations. Bypassing the UN order, some states impose "sanctions" against others, turning them into trade wars.

With the deterioration of the epidemiological situation in the world in 2020, more signs of a crisis are showing up: a dual shock of supply and demand, a fall in stock prices on world exchanges, a rise in gold prices and a fall in oil prices, etc. All the world's economies are forced to confront the growing crisis, which leads to the adoption of decisions at the state level that can change the established paradigms in many areas of economic relations. Even now scientists predict a serious transformation that will allow the world economy to get out of the crisis, including in the field of work organization (organization of remote work, which can lead to a reduction in employers' expenses for rent and maintenance of office spaces); further development of e-commerce will lead to a drop in demand for office and retail real estate by 25-50%; service models of the economy will receive a boost for rapid development[1]. The current crisis is a serious incentive for the development

---

[1] A. Nekipelov «We know that we are on the verge of creating a new world financial and economic system»
Kuzminov Ya. Viral Revolution: How the Pandemic Will Change Our World (*https://www.rbc.ru/opinions/society/27/03/2020/5e7cd7799a79471ed230b774*)

of medicine and medical education, as well as industries related to the production of medicines and the development of new equipment. All this will lead to the accumulation and creation of new radical competencies in this area that can «extinguish» the source of crisis phenomena.

The slowdown in economic development and the transition of the economy to a crisis state is well described by well-known economic laws, such as the law of management of competitiveness and the law of advanced development of a manufacturer. Under these laws, to maintain the ability to economic development and competitiveness at a given level, constant control actions are needed to stimulate innovation through the creation of radical innovations and the accumulation of radical competencies[2] or, more generally, to meet the needs of society in advance.

All these phenomena are largely due to the fact that before the onset of an economic downturn society does not have time to update and create new radical competencies that are the source of economic development and growth, followed by a crisis that manifests itself in various forms, including in the form of wars (political, economic, information, technological, etc.). N. D. Kondratieff also noted that " ... wars and revolutions arise on the basis of real, and above all economic conditions... on the basis of an increase in the pace and tension of economic life, intensification of economic competition for markets and raw materials… Social upheavals occur most easily during the period of the onslaught of new economic forces."

The processes of growing crisis phenomena can be demonstrated by the example of long economic waves (see Fig. 1.2). The first upward phase of a long economic wave is characterized by intensive scientific and technological development, when significant changes take place in engineering and technology based on the advanced achievements of fundamental science. The created technologies are focused on meeting the long-term needs, which are fully

---

[2] Radical competences are understood as competencies in various fields, the appearance of which is interconnected with the emergence of new scientific discoveries and the set of which is capable of creating a new technology platform for the development of society and the world economy, creating new opportunities for industrial business organizations to achieve advanced satisfaction of promising market needs

manifested at the peak of the long wave. Moreover, historically, the peak phase is synchronized with the manifestation of the effect of socio-economic transformations, when a significant increase in government demand is observed against the background of high consumer demand.

At the post-peak phase of a long economic wave, there is an increasing economic turbulence, leading to the emergence of local crises, the overcoming of which is related to the use of existing competencies and a slight improvement of existing technologies and their widespread introduction into products with stable demand. However, the products created using these technologies and competencies can no longer be oriented towards future needs. During this period, the intensity of local economic crises increases, and a global economic crisis sets in (the depression phase of a long economic wave), accompanied by a significant slowdown or a complete stop in world GDP growth. However, during this period, the global socio-economic paradigm that underlies the upward phase of the new wave is formed. According to the theory of Kondratieff 's economic cycles, the upward phase of an economic wave begins from the moment of the application of new technological solutions and competencies, the groundwork for which was formed

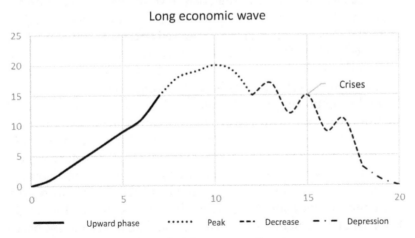

Figure 1.2. A long economic wave

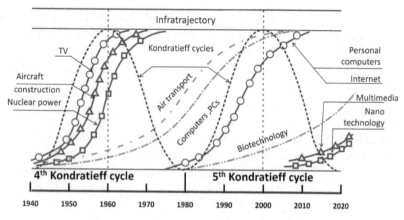

Figure 1.3. The interrelation between waves
of innovation and Kondratieff waves

during the economic recession, when the subjects of economic relations are active in the direction of mastering radical competencies and innovations. Figure 1.3 shows that economic waves reach their peak during the development of the pool of competencies in various technological areas, resulting in the development of a new technology platform.

The latest iterations of the crisis have shown that the "technological method" of overcoming the recession, which has worked for many decades, no longer gives the desired effect, and fundamentally new mechanisms for overcoming crises are needed to avoid military scenarios of restarting economic systems, since the currently existing and actively used tools (stimulating demand and creating new jobs, supporting small businesses, improving the institutional environment, improving the system of technical regulation in order to strengthen incentives for organizations to improve the technological level of their products; modernizing the regulatory system in financial markets, which will ensure the reliability of the financial services sector) are becoming less and less effective. In this regard, the efforts of individual countries should be combined to establish a single interstate mechanism to stabilize the economy, based on the integration of radical competences, stimulating the creation of a new technology platform for further economic development and growth.

In this regard, the agenda should include new tools and measures: financial measures and instruments that stimulate subjects of economic relations to develop radical innovations, and instruments that contribute to the accumulation of human capital in various fields, the development of competencies in various fields and the creation of radical competencies that will lead to a breakthrough in science, new discoveries and achievements providing a technology platform for the development and production of radically new products and services for the future needs of the market, capable of steering the economy on the advanced development path.

As part of the financial instruments, one of the important tasks is to develop a system of measures at the level of national economies, aimed primarily at eliminating the negative feedback between the financial and economic subsystems, understanding the economic subsystem as production, scientific, technical and innovative, where resources should first be directed in order to improve these areas.

However, improvement should be carried out not on the basis of outdated equipment, but with the help of new radical competencies, a new technology platform that allows creating a popular product on the market.

As part of tools contributing to the accumulation of human capital and radical competencies, it is necessary to solve the problem of management of advanced development and the accumulation of knowledge and competencies not as individual competing objects, but within certain state regulation of the competitive system in order to create quasi-perfect competition, which, ultimately, will increase the competitiveness of individual objects, their ability to advance development and the economic efficiency and balance of the entire system.

Herewith, our studies show that in modern economic conditions, trends in the structure of GDP continue to change (see Figure 1.4), and in view of the progressive transformation of the world economy (including digital transformation), the shares of segments

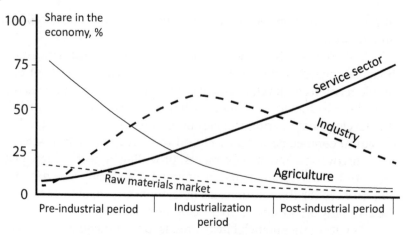

Figure 1.4. Changes in the structure of GDP

are redistributed towards the continuing rapid growth of the service sector, the profitability of which continues to grow rapidly, since digitalization leads to a more dynamic development of this segment in comparison with the rest.

The processes taking place in the economies of technologically developed countries indicate the particular relevance of solving the problem of overcoming economic crises by ensuring the growth of innovative potential and creating radically new competencies, that, in the process of accumulation and integration, form a new technology platform for creating products and services that meet market needs. The identification of this kind of stable and regular links between technical and technological innovations and economic fluctuations creates the necessary grounds for developing effective mechanisms to overcome or mitigate the influence of the negative consequences of cyclicality on the development of the economic life of countries by consistently implementing innovative changes.

The main factor in creating radically new products aimed at meeting future needs is the continuous growth of innovative potential related to the development of a set of radical competencies of technologies and equipment, and the improvement of management methods. This is achieved by improving the quality of products, reducing their cost, as well as the emergence of new types of products and services.

Such processes should affect all key sectors of the economy, the dynamic development of which has a greater impact on a country's economic growth, measured by the GDP growth rate.

Radical new products are usually created on the basis of new technology platforms, the dynamic development of which leads to their more frequent changes as a result of the accumulation of intellectual potential by society, which can lead to an «intellectual explosion» and a pool of scientific discoveries that contribute to changing needs and manufactured products and services according to these needs.

The acceleration of the processes of accumulation of intellectual potential in the world, its implementation in the form of radically new products and services that change markets and their needs, leads to an acceleration of the pace of development of technology platforms. These processes are stimulated due to the following main factors:

- a slowdown in economic growth, since, on the one hand, a number of macroeconomic and geopolitical factors rapidly restrain the progressive development of a country's economy, and on the other hand, traditional drivers give the desired effect to ensure the dynamic development of a economy for an ever shorter period of time, and therefore there is a need to find new sources of growth stimulation;

- the acceleration of the pace of development of new technologies results in a reduction in the life cycle of innovations that underlie the competitiveness of goods produced and sold on the market, which leads to increased competition and forces manufacturers to qualitatively improve or create fundamentally new products through the development of radical innovations and the use of gained and developed competencies.

Slowing economic growth as an incentive for rapid development and changing technology platforms

With the development, improvement and fundamental change of technology platforms, a country's economic growth is ensured, since the economy and technology are inextricably linked. In this regard, the slowdown in the growth of the world economy and the economies of individual countries indicates the need for accelerated development of radical competencies that create the opportunity to develop new technologies and products that can stabilize the economic situation in the field of production and consumption, while increasing the pace of economic development.

Economic growth occurs under the influence of certain drivers that stimulate development and, in some cases, are able to compensate to some extent for the effect of constraints.

The traditional drivers of economic development are innovative changes, transformations in the field of economic policy of a State, support and development of science, education, building up human capital, increasing productivity, increasing wages, investment in business and production.

Development drivers act as catalysts for economic growth, creating the basis for economic stability in all its industries and segments by building multi-level ties and effective intersectoral cooperation.

We systematize all the traditional drivers for achieving long-term economic progress into five main groups (Figure 1.5): structural; socio – political; intersectoral; intra-sectoral; resource-based, which we will distribute by management levels.

This systematization makes it possible to delineate the role of the state, industry and business structures in ensuring economic

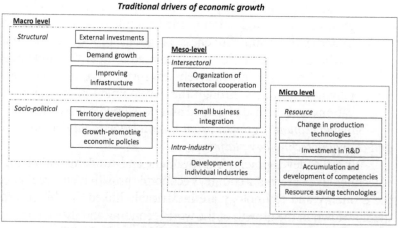

Figure 1.5 – Traditional drivers of economic growth

growth in the country and at each level of management to ensure the implementation of appropriate measures for the development of certain areas that can lead to advanced development and further accumulation of scientific groundwork for new scientific discoveries that in the future will allow to produce radically new products and create economic systems of a new type.

Drivers of economic growth at the micro level are connected to ensuring the strategic competitiveness of companies that manufacture products in demand, represented by a constantly upgraded or updated line of products that allow meeting and creating market demand.

In the conditions of intense competition and accelerated transfer of scientific knowledge, the strategic competitiveness of individual companies that have a great impact on economic growth cannot be achieved by individual successful R&D results or targeted management actions. A temporary increase in profitability under the influence of certain achievements will attract competitors, the experience will be replicated or reworked, as a result of which the average profit rate in this market segment will fall, and a company will lose profit and investment attractiveness, thereby reducing its growth potential and economic stability, which in turn will negatively affect the economic growth of the industry and a country's economy as a whole.

In these conditions, traditional sources of ensuring economic sustainability and competitiveness start to lose their effectiveness. A company faces an urgent need not only to develop existing competencies, but also to create new radical competencies that can provide high competitive advantages of the developed products due to their uniqueness and the ability to meet the needs that were not met before their appearance on the market. Such new competencies should form the basis of R&D aimed at the development of radical innovations that qualitatively modernize the production and technological base of an industrial business structure and production processes and change the entire production and management system of a company's economic activities due to changes in the principles of building such systems.

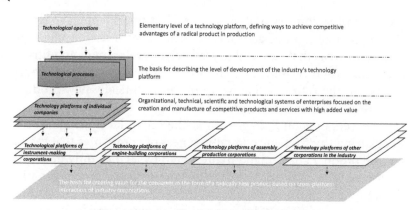

Figure 1.6 – Industrial Technology Platform

In these circumstances, the main driver of overcoming the crisis is the creation of new technology platforms [3] (industrial and company levels), enabling the application of radical competencies to create unique products that can generate new markets or to be dominant in the existing ones.

The basic approach to creating an industrial technology platform from smaller-level platforms is presented in Figure 1.6.

The creation and development of a technology platform at the industry level solves the problems connected with the organization of interaction of all industry participants within a single scientific and production system, with the main goal of creating value for the consumer in the form of a radically new product based on cross-platform interaction of an industry's business structures. As shown in Figure 1.6, various sub-platforms (technology platforms of companies) are involved in the industry technology platform, depending on their multidirectional activities and opportunities for cooperation to create radically new products.

Industry technology platforms are formed in accordance with the following principles that have developed in the world practice:

---

[3] A technology platform is a set of interrelated processes for creating value for the consumer in various sectors of the economy, based on radical competencies and key technologies of the product life cycle and the basic principles of cooperation of participants.

- clear definition of scientific and technical tasks and the validity of their significance for the development of the relevant sectors of the economy. For the success of the platform, it is especially important from the very beginning to clearly define the tasks of its creation. Strategic tasks that are significant for the development of the economy sector as a whole, as well as specific tasks in the field of science, technology and innovation arising therefrom, can be identified;
- ultimate market orientation, not just technology development. It is assumed that it is the manufacturer who should set the vector of the technology platform, determining the strategic agenda for the development of a given sector of the economy. The key benchmarks are business interests, future consumer preferences and, ultimately, a strategic vision of the future state of the economy sector;
- compliance with the definition of a technology platform ("platform, not a project"). It is important that a technology platform does not degenerate into separate projects in the interests of one or more participants. A platform is rather a system of actions, the implementation of which will allow a sector as a whole to reach a new technological level;
- the impossibility of solving the assigned tasks without the coordination of a wide range of participants. This may be due to the high cost of research and development, significant technological risks, etc;
- the interaction of key scientific and educational organizations working with this technology is necessary to work out all possible scientific and technological alternatives and select the most effective solutions;
- eliminating the dominance of monopolists-technological and market-based: technology platforms should be open to new entrants at all stages of their life cycle;
- the significance of the positive effects achieved through the creation of a technology platform in comparison with the current situation.

Elaboration of priority actions within a technology platform: at the first stage of creating the platform, it is necessary to take steps mostly of an organizational nature, and the participants must show the ability to negotiate, which is not always possible due to the competitive relations between many of them.

If we turn to the issue of creating a platform, then it should organically fit into the industry technology platform. Its main goal is to ensure the advanced development of a company, to reach a leading position in key areas of activity, to develop radically new products focused on meeting the long-term needs of a country and society.

The elements of a company's technology platform are shown in Figure 1.7.

The results of the effective functioning of a company's technology platform are:

– improving the competitiveness of products and companies;
– development of new key competencies of a company;
– leading positions in existing markets and creating completely new markets with radically new products;
– emergence of new high-tech products focused on meeting future needs;

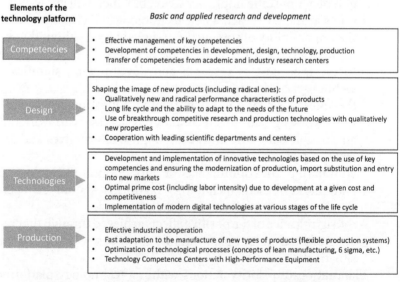

Figure 1.7 – The elements of a company's technology platform

The number of "things" connected to the Internet exceeded the number of computers and smartphones by 2020

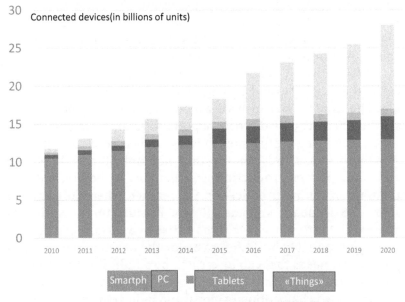

Figure 1.8 – Dynamics of the spread of IoT

– creation of a diversified and multidirectional product line;
– achieving global competitiveness;
– creating conditions for advanced development through building radical competencies and innovations and their transformation into a radically new product.

Radical competencies, as well as radical innovations, ensure the rapid development and growth of the economy until these competencies become widespread, when a large proportion of market actors master them and apply them in products and services. For example, the modern technology of the Internet of things (IoT) (emerged as a result of radical innovations – the Internet) that change the organization of labor and production in industrial companies, providing productivity growth as a stimulus for economic development.

There is a significant increase in the spread and adoption of IoT technologies over the years, (Figure 1.8).

The fact that the number of "things" connected to the Internet already in 2020 exceeds the number of connected computers and smartphones used by the mass consumer is of particular interest. The technology is used both in the production segment (building "smart factories", which is already widely used in the world), and in the consumer segment (creating a "smart home" system).

Similar growth trends are observed, for example, in the spread of cloud technologies and big data analytics, which are growing rapidly. The use of these elements of a modern technology platform (also via the Internet) provides new opportunities for forecasting future needs, identifying the first prerequisites for their development.

In this case, we can say that not only the technologies and principles of production are changing as before, but also the ways of selling products on the market, when the products sold with feedback systems allow a manufacturer to identify and predict future needs that may arise in a certain market segment and, possibly build forecasts for the development of completely new needs that can be created by a radical innovation.

Accelerating the pace of radically new product development

Increased competition in global and industry markets encourages manufacturers to develop or gain new competencies, which are then implemented in the form of radical innovative ideas that allow them to create products that bring value to the consumer and are able to meet promising market demand. One of the factors that significantly affects the maintenance and growth of competitive positions is the time it takes to enter the market with a new product (the first manufacturer to introduce a new product on the market that differs from existing offers has a chance to capture a high market share, at least until there is another able to create a similar product).

In order to increase their competitive positions, including by reducing the time period for product launch to the market, manufacturers are rapidly developing their technology platforms.

Currently radical competencies embodied in new technology platforms are becoming the basis for creating competitive products, which contributes to economic growth through the development of the industrial and consumer segments.

Experience in many countries shows that such a task can be solved only on the basis of an integral system of Government incentives and increasing the investment attractiveness of science-based industries, with the creation of breakthrough technologies. Innovation economy is not limited to the selection of priority areas for development, and any knowledge-based activity should be viewed as a component of a single national innovation system in which innovative clusters and public-private partnerships arise with integration of large, medium and small high-tech business and the introduction of other mechanisms that allow to get a significant synergistic effect.

The constant introduction of new technologies, the search for new solutions and the creation of unique radically new competencies form its innovative and intellectual potential, which is continuously increased at an accelerated pace for further economic development, growth and achieving global competitive leadership.

Creating and enhancing intellectual potential is becoming one of the most important tasks towards the transformation of a company and its adaptation to the existing new technology platform. Primarily the rapid development of intellectual potential occurs as a result of the acquisition and development of radical competencies and the dynamic introduction of modern digital solutions in practice, creating conditions for the development of competitive products, which form the basis for further innovative development at a high rate by creating new discoveries and developments in the field of science, technology and technology through these technological solutions.

The accelerated development of new competencies in order to form a new technology platform and increase innovation potential is a natural process taking place in the global economy. Companies are forced to meet or be able to flexibly adapt to global transformations at the macroeconomic level, to use new tools and methods to improve their economic efficiency and business margins by creating and accumulating their innovative and competent potential. Otherwise, they will lose their market shares and become unprofitable, which will lead to their closure.

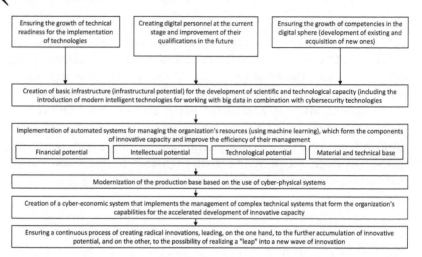

Figure 1.9. Scheme of achieving conditions for ensuring rapid economic development and development of a technology platform

In order to avoid losses and bankruptcy, as well as to provide innovative capacity and adapt to the new technology platform in the modern environment, companies need to implement a comprehensive approach to the development of radical competence, provide transformation principles in all spheres of activity. In this regard, the following scheme is proposed for creating conditions for ensuring the accelerated growth of innovative potential and the development of a technology platform, shown in Fig.1.9.

Taking steps shown in Fig. 1.9, will provide companies with opportunities for the rapid growth of their innovative potential, which allows them to develop radical competencies and products based on them, to ensure continuous updating of the product line, taking into account the emerging consumer expectations in the market, thereby, maintaining long-term competitive leadership in market and stimulating other market players to progressively develop towards acquiring technological capabilities and creating their own innovative products, which in turn will further accelerate the advanced transition of industries and economies of individual countries to the creation of new technology platforms.

Companies need to constantly monitor the technological development of all market players and industries in order to maintain the competitiveness of existing products and create radically new products that can lead the company to long-term competitive leadership.

Long-term leadership is possible only in the case of constant superiority over competitors through advanced and continuous innovative development, taking into account changing needs. The development goal of a modern company is to build an economically sustainable, innovative, competitive, and diversified company, able to solve strategic tasks of improving and developing both innovations and radical competencies that can qualitatively change the future needs of the markets.

The implementation of these strategic tasks requires a company to form a certain basis, competence and innovation potential for development, which is expressed in achieving the required level of development of management and planning systems, the establishment of a scientific, technical, technological base. In this case, the creation, development and accumulation of radical competencies can be viewed as a continuous process of forming the necessary conditions through which the strategic innovative tasks of the economy will be solved.

Since radically new technologies create the potential for a new technology platform, which can further lead to the creation of a new technological order, it is possible to form a chain of development growth of innovative potential and competences accumulated by the world community on the change of technological orders (Figure 1.10).

Based on the foregoing, it can be noted that the growth of innovative potential and the accumulation of radical competencies of the world community creates conditions for an accelerated change of waves of innovation by stimulating the development of radically new technologies and this process is becoming more and more dynamic, new solutions appear within a shorter timeframe.

The rapid emergence and development of radical innovation is ensured, as shown in Fig. 1.10, as a result of the accumulation of intellectual potential, formed by developing and emerging knowledge and competencies, stimulating, both a faster achievement of the point of intellectual explosion, in which new technologies are emerging, and the creation of resource support for their rapid

25

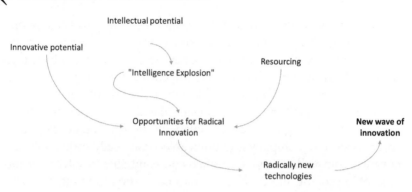

Figure 1.10 – The relationship between the growth of the intellectual and innovative capacity of the world community and the change of waves of innovation

implementation which will result in a more dynamic development of the innovative capacity.

The growth of these investments, development of competences, accumulation of intellectual and innovation capacity is accelerating innovation, which entails the smoothing of waves of economic development by increasing the pace of development and innovation efficiency while reducing the period of their implementation.

In this regard, it is possible to formulate the axiom that **"starting from a certain period of time, the wave-like process of economic cycles with high fluctuations (a long period of reaching the development peak of a new wave of innovation and a long phases of recovery, recession and depression) can be transformed into a linear process by reducing the development time of technologies of a new wave and leveling the phases of economic recession and depression due to the effect, that new radical innovations managed to achieve their development at the initial points of economic recession of the previous wave as a result of the exhaustion of the potential of existing technologies. This will take place under the influence of radically new scientific and technological advances, since there will be a continuous dynamic development of technologies and a change in their generations in the face of a constant growth of innovative potential and the accumulation of competencies, incl. radical ones ".**

Such a constant development of technologies and advanced science can smooth out fluctuations in the economy, and the slow-down in economic growth will lead not to acute crises, but to small economic downturns, which can be overcome in a short time due to the emergence of radical innovations that stimulate the development of both the industrial and consumer segments.

This formulated postulate can serve for the further development of the theory of economic growth and development, ensured through the advanced satisfaction of needs by creating radically new products and services through the rapid growth of innovative potential and the development of radical competencies.

The theory of economic growth and development will be developed in this monograph, both in relation to a country's economy and in relation to individual companies involved in the creation of this growth, and will be described by the corresponding mathematical models that have practical value for companies implementing activities of development radically new products and services capable of creating new markets and meeting the growing and evolving needs of society.

This radical competence, which is the main driver for overcoming economic crisis and providing economic growth in modern conditions of digitalization, is the main source of economic growth in the world economy, while the economic growth of individual countries and organizations of these countries involved in foreign economic activity can be limited by geopolitical factors and economic barriers to its achievement. The globalization processes force countries to build their economic systems in accordance with the world economic order.

1.2. ENSURING THE COMPETITIVE CAPACITIES OF PRODUCTS AND SERVICES IN THE MARKETS

The economic development and growth achieved through the development and accumulation of radical competencies takes place when these competencies are realized as radically new products and services that have a high competitive capacities in the markets.

In this case, the competitive capacity of a product is defined as a set of product characteristics that form its uniqueness, competitive advantages created as a result of a qualitative transformation of the process of development and production of these products, as well as opportunities for the sale of goods and services in markets created at the national and international level, thanks to which products can occupy a significant market share.

The specific of creating competitive capacities of products is its two level nature.

Firstly, it is the macro level, since markets function at the macro level, and players with their products and services are have to compete, trying to meet the prospective needs of customers in their market segment, as well as plan to capture new market segments that will increase their profitability. Economic conditions and factors at the macro level affect the markets to varying degrees (by regulating the relations of economic entities), which determines the special role of economic policy and the situation in a country in ensuring the high competitive capacities of products in the markets. Secondly, the competitive capacities of products and services is created at the micro level (directly from the manufacturer), where promising needs are identified, unique products are created, the processes of their implementation on the market are monitored, timely updates are made by increasing competitive advantages, etc.

The main directions of building the competitive capacities of products in the markets at both levels are shown in Figure 1.11.

Below we will reveal in more detail the main provisions of creating the competitive capacities of products and services at both levels.

Ensuring the competitive potential of products at the macro level

The role of the macro level in building competitive potential of products is that it determines the priority areas of development, creates a country's economic and political image in the world arena, approves the Government economic, financial, tax, customs, and foreign trade policies which establish the "rules of the game" for both national and foreign market participants. Thus, countries use restrictive instruments as various barriers (duties, fees, import bans, etc.) that prevent the import of foreign goods, protecting their markets.

Macro-level (national and international)

- ensuring the financial stability of a state
- the level of economic and military potential of a country
- participation in international intergovernmental organizations
- state support and investment in the development of fundamental science and ensuring the well-being of the population

Micro-level (enterprise and products)

- using the benefits of digitalization as a means of increasing the efficiency of management and production
- development of radical competencies and their application in the creation of unique products that can provide a temporary monopoly on the market

Figure 1.11. Levels of building competitive capacities of products

In this case, building the competitive capacities of products and success in the conquering markets is determined by the following components:

The first component is determined by the financial potential of a country, based on the stability and efficiency of the development of subjects of economic relations, primarily industries, large corporations and holding structures that are able and seek to enter foreign markets of other countries, creating there their own industries and companies that provide high profitability. For example, a number of Russian metallurgical companies are moving their subsidiaries to foreign European countries, moving abroad the production of high value added products that are in demand. Similar mechanisms are being implemented in the banking sector. The same practice appears in the oil sector, when oil is refined at enterprises established abroad, thereby providing the highest profitability.

The second component is establishing a powerful economy and strengthening the military potential, which provides the conditions for putting political and economic pressure on other countries by providing loans, concluding deals for the construction of facilities on the territory of these countries, etc. Political pressure is aimed at achieving loyalty on the part of the governments of third countries towards an economically and politically more developed

29

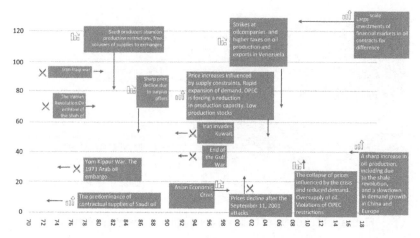

Figure 1.12. Dynamics of world oil prices

country that can provide various opportunities and benefits for business development in these countries.

Political events and political decisions made by individual market players, including the most influential ones in specific segments of the market, also have an impact on the global economy and the world market. The most obvious example in this case would be the oil market, where prices are closely linked to political decisions (see Figure 1.12).

The third component involves participation in the activities of joint large international intergovernmental organizations that manage market segments to some extent and dictate their terms due to their power. The activities of interstate unions, which in principle create conditions in their market segment to support producers-members of the groupings in order to ensure their competitiveness in the market, leads to certain obstacles for all other players. Among such unions that dictate market conditions, the following ones can be identified: Organization of Petroleum Exporting Countries (OPEC), Gas Exporting Countries Forum (GECF), Countries Association of Iron Exporting Countries (APEF), etc.

Thus, the above Figure 1.12 reflects the impact of OPEC decisions on the change in oil prices in different years.

The fourth, equally important component should be the implementation of state support and investment in the development of basic science and priority areas of scientific and technological development, the creation of radically new products and services, as is the case in countries with developed economies.

In this case, the State plays an important role in creating resources and infrastructure for the development of manufacturers of radically new products. This is confirmed by the close interdependence of global competitive potential and, for example, the level of development of information technologies, keeping in mind that these technologies and infrastructure are considered as auxiliary tools that form a basis for the manufacture of products with high competitive capacities and are widely represented in the markets (see Figure 1.13).

The figure shows that countries with developed economies, while stimulating the development of informatization at the state level, provide a high index of global competitiveness, one of the components of which is products with high competitive capacities.

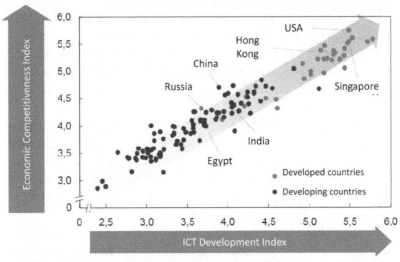

Figure 1.13. The relationship between the ICT development index
and competitiveness

31

All the above conditions offer advantages when forming the competitive potential of products, which cannot be fully realized without taking into account the factors of the external environment of a company and the global market, due to the current economic and geopolitical situation in the world and the image of a manufacturing country on the world stage.

In this regard, an important task of the first level is to form not just a powerful potential (financial, economic, political, military, etc.), but an attractive image of a country in the world, actively involved both in the international economy and politics and known due to the wide distribution of unique products on the market, manufactured given opportunities of the new technology platform. Accordingly, at the macro level, conditions have been created for the functioning of the micro level, where the development and production of unique goods is directly carried out.

Ensuring the competitive capacity of products at the micro level

At the micro level, the competitive capacity-building of each specific type of product or service created by companies is carried out. Currently, the competitive capacities created at the micro level depend both on the development of radical competencies and their use in creating unique products that can provide a temporary monopoly on the market due to the advanced satisfaction of needs, and on the use of the advantages of digitalization as a means of improving the efficiency of management and production of this unique product.

Currently, the center of most modern technology platforms is digitalization, which acts as a means of organizing management and production, increasing the economic efficiency of a company and building the competitive capacities of products by optimizing costs and accelerating the pace of their development through new competencies and radical innovations.

The following components can be considered as elements of digitalization, summarized in Table. 1.1. They are listed with their contribution to building the competitive capacities of unique products.

Table 1.1. Elements of digitalization

Digitalization element	Opportunities created to build the competitive capacities of unique products
Supercomputer	Allows to effectively solve specialized tasks by using high-performance interconnected supercomputers. This interconnection allows to divide the task into a number of subtasks, each of which is solved by a specific supercomputer
Identification technologies	Allows automatic identification and efficient collection of data on specific objects
Simulation modeling. 3D technologies	Construction and study of an auxiliary model that corresponds to the characteristics of a real object. Allows to get data on the likely changes in the real object due to a particular impact. Allows to create solid three-dimensional objects based on a digital model by layering. Fundamentally opposite to traditional mechanical production methods
Intelligent methods	Based on the implementation of machine learning algorithms. Enables effective decision making
End-to-end technologies	Methods of automated information processing, preparing the basis for making an effective management decision
Blockchain technologies	Multifunctional information technologies that allow for objective and reliable accounting of company assets
Cyber-physical systems	They consist of a number of natural objects and artificial subsystems controlled by controllers. Allows to automate the control of technological equipment of a production enterprise, considering the changes in the external environment, continuous self-learning and adaptation of the cyber-physical system.
Robotization	The use of intelligent robots in manufacturing can significantly increase production speed and eliminate human errors
Brain-computer technology	A neurocomputer interface that allows direct exchange of information between the human brain and an electronic device. Allows to significantly speed up the process of information exchange

It's a fair assumption that the elements of digitalization listed in the table will stimulate the transformation of the economy as a whole, which will affect the principles of activity of industrial business structures.

Speaking about the development of digitalization, let us turn to such an index as labor productivity, which affects the efficiency of any company. Labor productivity is currently formed based on the productivity of human labor; it changes under the influence of technologies that allow speeding up many processes, and even eliminating some of them due to automation. This leads to an increase in product output and an increase in their consumption, if the products are valuable for the consumer. As a result, the economic development and growth of a manufacturer is ensured, which leads to an increase in the economic welfare of employees of individual business structures, as well as to an increase in GDP, accompanied by economic development. Moreover, the higher the rate of economic development, the higher the level of welfare in a country.

An increase in labor productivity increases in employees' wages, which in turn boosts ability to meet a wider range of needs. In connection with the growth of effective demand, the requirements for purchased goods and services are also increasing, both in terms of quality and functional characteristics, that is, there is a transformation of needs, causing the need to develop and produce new products using new competencies and technologies that can meet these new needs and lead to economic growth and development.

Thus, the following hypothesis can be put forward: **"the growth of labor productivity leads to economic development and increases the level of socio-economic condition (welfare) of the population, primarily due to wage growth, which offers opportunities to meet growing and newly emerging needs, which implies the need to create new products and services that can satisfy effective demand».** In this case, the main indicator of human well-being will be the level of satisfaction of needs as a result of the ongoing changes in consumer demand, leading to the fact that buyers will consume more personalized and high-quality products.

Despite the fact that many researchers consider automation and robotization to be a negative factor leading to a decrease in the welfare of the population, here are a number of examples that demonstrate the opposite.

For example, Germany, thanks to the introduction of advanced technologies, has a legally fixed working week of 38 working hours; the minimum hourly rate is 8.5 €, and the average is about 25 €.

In Denmark, the working week is 35-37. 5 hours; labor productivity is high due to the introduction of advanced methods of organizing production and labor, and the average Dane earns 37.5 €, per hour, which is a third more than the EU average.

The working week in Finland is also quite short and can be as low as 32 hours due to high labor productivity. Finnish economists believe that short working hours negatively affect the economy and competitiveness of the country, but the average hourly wage is $ 33, which indicates a fairly high level of welfare of the population. In addition, the high productivity of labor in these countries is also ensured by a high level of social development, provided by the growth of the welfare of the population. Thus, there are several interrelated effects shown in Fig. 1.14.

However, as noted above, the labor productivity index is influenced by modern promising technologies that positively affect

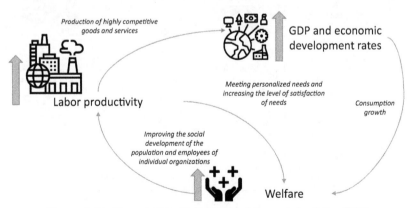

Figure 1.14. The relationship between labor productivity, GDP and population welfare

the processes at various levels of company management. All these technologies contribute to the creation of digital production, characterized by a high ability to transform and adapt, resource efficiency and ergonomics, as well as the integration of all subjects of economic relations (consumers, investors, partners, etc.) into business processes and value creation processes (Figure 1.15). The digital industry is focused on promising consumer expectations and is based on trends in scientific and technological development, which is achieved through the extensive use and intelligent analysis of available data from the global information space in real time.

The technological basis of the digital industry is cyber-physical systems, in which software components are connected to the mechanical and electronic components of the infrastructure through the data infrastructure, as well as the Internet of Things, in which physical objects such as devices, sensors and systems can send and receive data over the Internet. Cyberphysical systems represent distributed intelligent systems-microsystems or micro-electromechanical systems that include electronic, mechanical,

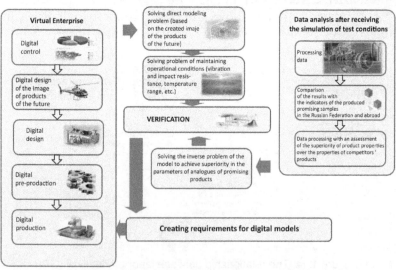

Figure 1.15. Organization of digital production

optical, and other, primarily digital components. Usually they also have the functions of recognition, information processing and are connected to communication networks. They are able to perform processes of perception and cognition, as well as actions that are becoming closer to human actions. The intellectual capabilities of cyber-physical systems are usually manifested in the process of more or less flexible interaction of distributed systems.

One of the main factors for increasing the economic efficiency of a company's activities is the improvement of the management system for the development and manufacture of new products. By improving it, it is possible to significantly improve the techno-economic characteristics of the developed products, arouse the economic interest of companies and developers in creating equipment that meets the needs of domestic and international markets, achieve a significant increase in economic performance in production to ensure the advanced development of a company and eliminate the prerequisites for the development of unprofitable products. There are certain trends in reducing the production cycle in terms of the impact of digitalization tools on the processes of creation and manufacture of products.

For example, the use of 3D printing allows you to reduce the pre-production stage, thereby reducing the time to create a more competitive product. As a result of reducing the development and production period, a manufacturer has an additional chance to achieve advanced development and become the leader of a newly created market or market segment meeting the newly created needs.

Moreover, the technology of creating digital twins of products has a high economic effect for a company. Thanks to modern technologies and programs a company is able to receive ready-made design documentation after creating a digital twin of a product (a virtual image with all the physical and techno-economic properties of the planned product and allowing for virtual testing of the product).

The economic benefits of using a digital twin are defined as follows:

– a digital twin improves the results of the teamwork of designers and technologists. At the moment, it is common for designers and technologists working in different computer systems face difficulties when working together. Designers transfer their developments to technologists who try to create technological processes in usual technological systems, as a result of which information is out of sync and the probability of errors increases. Using a digital twin the risk of error due to misunderstandings between designers and technologists is minimized;

– a digital twin of the product allows to optimize the choice of location and manufacturing technology, as well as the allocation of the necessary resources;

– with the use of digital design and modeling, a company avoids situations in which, due to errors or receiving new information that was not previously taken into account, it is necessary to make changes to the product characteristics. Making changes to the developed image of the product implies significant costs that are distributed throughout the development stage. At the same time, the later the development stage at which changes are made, the higher the level of costs that a company will incur. A digital twin allows to focus the main changes (and associated costs) at the initial stages of product development and thereby significantly minimize total costs, reduce costs, and ensure the creation of high-tech products of the future in the shortest possible time;

– testing on a digital twin saves money on the construction of expensive devices used to test the physical properties of a product sample.

Let us consider the experience of the Pratt and Whitney engine building company as an example of using the technology of building a digital twin, which changed the principles of organizing the activities of an industrial company. The company had the technology to create the most advanced jet propulsion system in the world, but it lacked the most advanced process management systems that would support production using this technology. In 2017, the company began to actively implement technologies for building a digital twin and big data, and a year later doubled its engine production, based on consumer expectations.

Thus, the company, having adopted a digital transformation strategy, eliminated 20-year production processes. Digital transformation has allowed for a restructuring and building a complete value chain. This means that four key planning principles have been consolidated: strategic, corporate, operational and executive. This approach allows each component of the supply chain and value chain to provide a synchronous solution to the given task. It links the planning and monitoring of goal achievement indicators, and the analysis of interim results is supported by interactive tools in real time.

All these trends indicate that the deepening of the processes of informatization in all spheres inevitably entails the development of technologies and the needs of society, and therefore the priority directions in the development of science and technology in the world are changing.

The elements of digitalization described above and their application in industry and all spheres of society lead to significant changes in the configuration of markets. Many traditional industries are losing significance in the structure of the world economy amid the rapid growth of new sectors that generate radically new needs. In these conditions, management decisions made in industrial companies seeking to occupy a competitive position in the market should be aimed at forming areas and projects, as a result of which unique products can be created able to dominate the market.

The digital transformation of a company is a complex process, before the implementation of which it is necessary to carry out certain preparatory measures related primarily to forecasting its technological development, transforming corporate culture and rethinking the organization and management of business processes.

First of all, a company faces the important issue of predicting the maximum efficiency of the applied methods and production technologies. In this case, the decision lies in determining costs and results, while identifying the point of decreasing the effectiveness of existing approaches in production and management, when it is necessary to stimulate the development of radically new competencies that create potential for the development of a company and build the competitive capacities of products.

As an example, we can give the effect of reducing the production cost when using digital design.

The cost of products is directly linked to on the number and size of the costs of their development. In this regard, we will consider the dynamics of production costs with the traditional approach (Figure 1.16) and with the use of digital design (digital approach) (Figure 1.17). Both graphs show the cost structure and the shaded area that characterizes the total cost of product development until its mass production moment.

When comparing the two graphs, it can be seen that with the traditional approach, a company bears the most significant costs connected with the production at the stage of transferring design and technical documentation to production (due to insufficient interaction between designers and technologists, which was described in detail earlier) and at the stage of production of a prototype (due to obtaining new, previously ignored information). With the digital approach to manufacturing, most of the costs are spent in the stages connected with product development. This feature is justified by the use of a virtual prototype of a product, which allows to make the necessary changes and correct errors before the direct production of a physical sample of a product.

The amount of production costs in the traditional approach is significantly higher than the costs in the digital approach S1>S2. Among other things, the difference in the time required to launch products should be taken into account: with the digital approach, no significant time is required to prepare tests, since they are carried out virtually on a digital twin, while with the traditional one – all tests are carried out on a physical sample of a product, and, accordingly, it takes more time not only to prepare and conduct the test, but also to produce a prototype. When using a digital twin, the time of full-scale tests can be shortened by conducting virtual tests on a digital twin of a product.

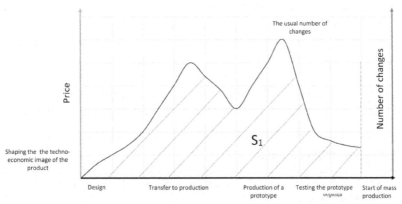

Figure 1.16. Dynamics of costs for product development
and production with the traditional approach

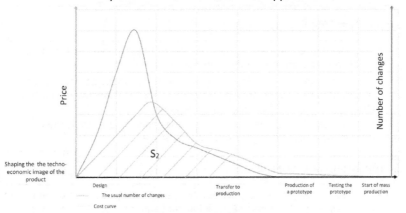

Figure 1.17. Dynamics of costs for product development
and production with the digital approach

It also follows that the digital approach reduces the costs of manufacturing and testing a prototype of a product, since when conducting virtual tests on a digital twin of a product, it is possible to improve many techno-economic characteristics of a product without the cost of manufacturing a physical sample.

Thus, we can say state the fact that the effectiveness of the traditional approach has decreased, while digitalization has created new sources of economic activity development and cost optimization.

However, digitalization cannot and should not be carried out simultaneously. The measures proposed to be implemented in preparation for the digital transformation of a company are shown in diagram 1.18.

In order to ensure the implementation of these activities, companies need to develop new unique competencies not only in the field of economics, but also in the use of digitalization tools,

---

Information preparation

- collection and analysis of best practices in the digital transformation of enterprises
- organization of cooperation with specialized companies that support the transition to a digital enterprise or develop the competencies of management

Employee training

- Creating orate culture focused on the interest of personnel in creating products with high competitive potential
- organization of retraining and training of personnel in the development of competencies necessary for a qualitative change in the organizational and managerial approaches used in the organization
- organization of retraining and training of personnel in the development of competencies necessary for a qualitative change

Preparation of processes

- classification of business processes into basic (creating added value and value for the consumer), supporting, development and management processes
- allocation and description of business processes at the top level of the organization. Building a top-level business process model
- development of a model for assigning responsibility for business processes
- detailing of business processes. Modeling and normative

Preparing for software implementation and starting digital transformation

- purchase of necessary equipment, licenses, installation of software
- transfer of business processes to digital representation
- training of personnel to work in the conditions of a digital enterprise

Figure 1.18. Preparing an enterprise for digital transformation

methods and related management techniques. Relevant competencies and their effective use can lead to:

- improving competitiveness through weak signal risk management;
- increasing labor productivity;
- creation of new product markets;
- improving the efficiency of the use of resources (assets, capital, competencies);
- creating new jobs to meet future needs and meet consumer expectations;
- increasing the transparency of economic activity and the objectivity of decisions made by introducing expert analytical systems based on intelligent methods that minimize human participation in economic processes that may be connected with subjective decision-making.

Companies can ensure shaping the above positive trends by creating (using the advantages of modern information technologies) integrated systems to support the adoption of effective management decisions aimed at achieving goals and solving problems of dynamic sustainable development of a company, increasing its competitiveness in the market by introducing advanced innovative ideas, primarily related to ensuring the functioning of digital production at a high level with the introduction of automated expert systems, improving the technical characteristics of products, the quality of operational services, etc.

The main task to be solved by a decision support system, created using the advantages of digitalization, is to objectively substantiate effective management decisions in the course of project management to create highly competitive products that can take a high market share (including by excluding competitors) or create new markets that meet the newly emerging needs of companies and society as a result of their development and the accumulation of intellectual and innovative potential. Moreover, effective decision support systems that need to be built by organizations seeking to succeed in the competition should provide the following results. The decision support systems:

- allow to identify customer expectations the most efficient way, highlight key (in terms of achieving competitive leadership) requirements and translate them into products;
- provide assurance that consumers will accept and use new (upgraded) products even before they are manufactured and placed on the market, i.e. at the pre-investment stage of the project;
- dramatically reduce the cycle time «market research-design-production-sales»;
- reduce the cost of producing a pilot batch of products and the cost of preliminary product development;
- provide an increase in a company's market share due to the earlier launch of products with a higher level of quality;
- more clearly define the processes that need to be transformed by the time a product is put into production;
- optimally distribute, and therefore most effectively use, a company's limited resources to ensure its global competitive leadership.

An example of the structure of an integrated decision support system based on the benefits of digitalization is shown in Figure 1.19.

Such an integrated management decision support system will create a competitive advantage for a company by:

- shorter decision-making time: the time spent on examining data and comparing possible courses of action is significantly reduced. The decision-making cycle is getting shorter, which allows enterprises to speed up the production process, ultimately shortening the time to market the products;
- increasing the objectivity of data: minimizing the human factor in the decision-making process;
- improving the quality of strategic management: the decision support system changes the way enterprises operate. «Value chain management» is an important concept that reveals the role of computerized decision making The decision support system takes into account economic factors and past and current trends to determine costs and benefits, as well as the total cost;

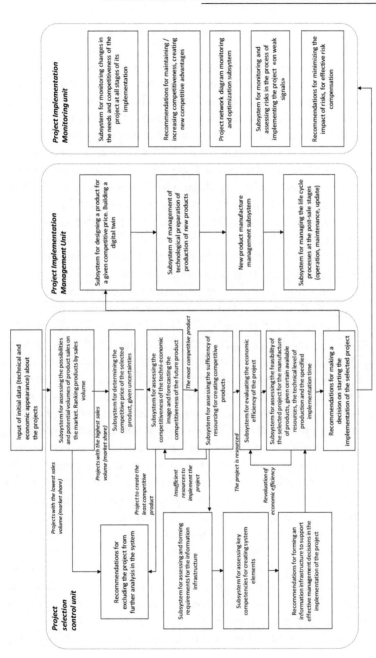

Figure 1.19. An example of the structure of an integrated management decision support system

– flexible response to market changes: adapting to changing market conditions and needs helps enterprises stay ahead of competitors. In fact, this is what makes business structures flexible and innovatively active, able to respond promptly to changes in market conditions. The decision support system, using the available information, presents projected revenue figures and expected market changes in the future;

– lower decision-making costs. Deployment of a decision support system significantly reduces the cost of collecting, sorting, processing and analyzing data. The cost of storing information, hardware, computing and internet technologies drops significantly. This means that the cost of extending decision-making technology of the hierarchy even to lower levels is reduced.

Based on the foregoing, a number of recommendations can be fromed for a company that creates products and services In order to ensure their high competitive potential in the markets.

Firstly, at the initial stage, it is necessary to assess the current state of a company and create banks and libraries of data containing information about the products and services manufactured, the technologies used, and the existing competencies (including those that are not in demand, but which can potentially be used in their development). This will allow you to systematize the sources of creating competitive advantages and monitor the effectiveness of the use of certain competencies and technological solutions when shaping the image of products and services. In addition, it will assess the compliance of a company's technological and competence potential with the modern technology platform that is being formed in the global economy and determine the range of competence development areas that will ensure the transition to this platform at the optimal time.

Secondly, it is important to solve the problem of organizing effective management of business processes by describing them, detailing them, and fixing them at the company level. Solving this challenge will streamline the business processes and provide a foundation for using a digital approach in the development, production, marketing and management of products. In this case, the tasks of the company's divisions and their functions will be clearly defined, and redundant functions will be reduced, leading to additional costs and losses when creating unique products.

Thirdly, since the use of management decision support systems is becoming more and more widespread in the world practice, it is necessary to evaluate the possibilities of developing or acquiring such a system adapted to the specifics of a particular company. As part of this event, the potential effect of using such systems is assessed, which is expressed in reducing the cost of performing operations, reducing the time for decision-making (resulting in more opportunities to create a unique product and bring it to market in a short time, while receiving high market share and high profits), as well as in minimizing various kinds of risks, by predicting and considering them in the process of substantiating management decisions.

Fourthly, it is important for an industrial company not only to create unique products and services, but also to develop a unique production, since a number of competitive advantages and unique product characteristics are developed precisely through the use of unique tools and methods of its creation. At the same time, unique production is based primarily on radical competencies created by a company or in research centers and research institutes, the development of which is carried out within as part of promising areas identified at the state level.

Fifthly, the development of unique products using radical competencies should be focused primarily on meeting the needs of a given country, providing the population with high-quality goods and services of national production, which will create the potential for economic growth of domestic producers. Thus, a certain independence of a country from external supplies will be formed, foreign trade risks will be minimized, and a country's economic stability will increase. Further distribution of unique products to the world market will not only create an image of the country as a manufacturer of in-demand products, but also contribute to the economic and political influence on the world stage.

The potential for building competitive advantages of products and increasing the attractiveness of companies and countries in the international arena is created by global informatization and transformation processes in this area, arising from the enhancement of competences to the intersectoral level.

47

1.3. GLOBAL INFORMATIZATION AS A TOOL FOR TRANSFORMATION AND EXTENSION OF COMPETENCIES TO THE INTERSECTORAL LEVEL

The process of accumulation and distribution of competences, ensuring their transfer between economic actors and society, the rate of the creation and introduction of new radical competences in the implementation of economic activities largely depend on the pace of Informatization, the emergence of new tools and methods of interaction of economic entities and principles of their business models under the influence of transformation processes.

All transformational processes in a company and society and connected with the increase of the application of information technologies in the 21st century has led to the phenomenon of global informatization, which is a process of spreading information solutions (technological, economic, infrastructural, social, institutional, etc.), resulting in the integrated system of global digital communications – a product of the modern era of globalization, similar to the first global information network in the era of early globalization, developed by the use of telegraph[4].

The process of global informatization of all spheres of society offers constantly expanding opportunities for industrial companies to actively use information methods and tools, as well as to acquire information as a product or service in the process of implementing their economic activities in order to improve the effectiveness of management tools and control of all business processes. In particular, in the processes of creating unique products, the focus of using IT solutions is aimed at accelerating the achievement of radical key competencies, through which building radically new products is possible.

The rate of distribution and application of IT solutions in each specific business structure depends primarily on its readiness

[4] Nagirnaya, A.V. The global process of informatization of society: factors of territorial unevenness / A.V. Nagirnaya. – Text: direct, electronic // Young scientist. – 2014. – No. 11 (70). – S. 160-165. – URL:URL: https://moluch.ru/archive/70/12136/ (date of request: 15.04.2020)

to implement these processes, which are not feasible without at least two necessary components: resources (primarily material, technical and financial) and the competence of management and staff members in the use of information solutions in the business management process.

The basic elements of automation or their step-by-step implementation and adaptation to the specifics of business activities are the starting point in the process of informatization and the basis for the development of appropriate strategies and programs aimed at qualitatively changing the existing "ways" of management and production activities associated with digital transformation trends. All management decisions within development programs should be made reasonably with an assessment of the efficiency of existing organizational principles and business models, as well as predicting the impact of the most promising approaches and methods aimed at improving the quality of business processes due to their digitization increasing control of their implementation and optimization through the use of information solutions. When choosing information solutions, the main task is to find or create the solution that will be maximally adapted and interconnected with the competence component and the competence management system of a company. As a result, informatization becomes a part of the activities of every company, striving to comply with market trends as well as to work in the advanced development mode, demonstrating its leading positions in the world market, covers all spheres of society and becomes a global phenomenon, and at the same time a tool for stimulating economic development.

When considering the processes of economic development of a company in modern conditions, the most important information source for managing it is data from the global information space, advanced knowledge and prospects for the development of fundamental science, as well as the results of intellectual processing of this information by modern mathematical methods (neural networks, machine learning, discrete mathematics). As part of a company's digitalization process, a new organizational and economic environment integrated into the information space is being formed, in which many aspects of activities related to the organization of the manufacture of new products and services are evolving.

Currently, most researchers of the role of informatization in the development of the economy consider the global information space as a set of information resources and infrastructures that make up state and interstate computer networks, telecommunication systems and public networks, and other cross-border information transmission channels[5].

The active process of innovation and technological convergence which began in the XXI century in the world economy caused by the rapid evolution of the global information space, stimulated the development of mechanisms of mutual influence and convergence of competences, when the boundaries between the individual competences and technologies are erased, and the final results of the use of competencies are manifested in the interdisciplinary research and development at the intersection of various fields of science, resulting in radical competences, covering the cross-sectoral level. The synergistic effect caused by the development of convergent information solutions and the expansion of the global information space contributes to a significant economic and productive effect in the economy as a whole by generating synergistic innovations.

Convergent information solutions contribute to building a bank of key radical competencies, which, subject to the ability of other resources, make it possible to create a product that can potentially meet the needs of society and take a dominant position in the market. Such a product will be developed on the principle of "semi-finished product", when its final image is shaped taking into account the requirements of a particular consumer. Such a mechanism can be implemented within the framework of the new business model M2C (manufacturer to customer) and the reverse model C2M, in which personalized production is implemented, involving the production of goods that have the necessary (or desirable) original properties for a given consumer. The closer the manufacturer is to the consumer, the more opportunities he will have to generate income. In the context of global informatization, the "sprouting" of competencies in various branches of science and their

[5] Kozoriz N. L. Security issues and access to global information resources. / / Pravo i gosudarstvo, 2013, No. 6, pp. 103-107

integration, the accumulation of intellectual capital by both pro-duction companies and society, the distance between the producer and the consumer is reduced at all stages of the product life cycle, and especially at the stage of its operation, as a result of the increasing spread of service models of the economy.

The considered effects of the evolution of the global information space and the processes of convergence of competencies and technologies taking part in it lead to the following axiom describing the process of creating unique products in the context of the evolution of the global information space:

the global information space develops by expanding new knowledge that underlies building of key competencies and radical innovations. Moreover, the global information space stimulates the processes of innovative and technological convergence, in which the boundaries of various competencies and technologies disappear, and innovation is the result of interdisciplinary research, a "semi-finished product" that a manufacturer, given resource opportunities, can bring to the level of a radically new unique product.

The formulated axiom is proposed to be considered in this monograph as one of the bases for further theoretical studies of the processes of advanced satisfaction of long-term needs that occur under the influence of the information environment and digital technologies to ensure the economic growth of a company.

The active development of the information environment and infrastructure that provides a platform for the implementation of a company's production activities leads to a significant variety of products and services through the organization of personalized production, the development of new forms of marketing (for example, targeted marketing) and increased productivity through automation and robotics. The economic growth achieved by these and other factors is justified by modern models of economic growth, which explain it by the increasing variety of products and services and the active development of the service sector.

In terms of economic growth and the development of industrial business structures, a single global information space without taking into account the efficiency of its application and the level of key competencies of a company is not able to become a source of economic growth.

Therefore, an important issue in the context of managing the economic development of a company and the process of creating unique products that satisfy current and future needs is the implementation of targeted entry into the global information space for a company interested in developing the necessary key competencies. **In this case, the global information space is considered as a set of services (information is provided in the form of a service for a certain fee), where the consumer purchases them specifically, based on their interests in solving specific production and economic problems.**

It is necessary to assess and compare the costs of obtaining and processing information from the global space with the costs related to obtaining information from other sources, for acquiring the necessary competencies of developers and their remuneration create products. The use of global space is reasonable, in the case if the cost of global space information and the efficiency of its use are justified.

From the point of view of a manufacturer striving for stable economic development (with the prospect of reaching advanced development and market dominance), the key direction of its investment and innovation activities is both the intensive development of scientific and technological capacity and radical competencies, including through the integration of the resources of the global information space and the use of modern digital technologies in the planning, management and control of all business processes and the development of new mechanisms for bringing products to markets.

In this context, given the constant competition of manufacturers in the markets, they are adopting new business models based on the sale of services that will stabilize and increase profits, as well as build stronger long-term relationships with consumers. Thus, a manufacturer acquires new key competencies related to the skills to effectively adapt a product to personalized needs; the cost of production is of paramount importance. When designing and manufacturing products, the manufacturer has to focus on the need to maintain the cost within the specified limits, ensuring its economic competitiveness with the established technical specifications. In addition to the design methods, a manufacturer improves the pre-production system and production, increasing their flexibility and efficiency. All this brings to a powerful synergistic effect, expressed in increasing the level of key competencies that allow to effectively implement each stage of the product life cycle, as well as to increase the competitiveness of an enterprise as a whole.

The growth of product personalization is connected with an increase in the level and composition of the required key competencies of a manufacturer. Product design, production, and assembly must be synchronized with in-house inventory and supply, order processing and logistics, as well as marketing, customer relations, and field support.

As products become more intelligent and interconnected, it becomes increasingly difficult to separate a product from the powered technology, especially software. The convergence of hardware and software, as well as their respective competencies, links the continuous use of a product directly with the manufacturer. This allows manufacturers to build ongoing relationships with consumers throughout the product lifecycle, complementing it with service, providing support, and adding functionality to existing products through software updates over wireless networks.

The world information space in its current state began to actively form and develop with the advent of the Internet in 1982 as a response to the need of the scientific community to exchange information. We can assume that it was from this moment that the global space of digital information began to form; since then, it has been actively developing, complementing all the new components, such as forums, social networks, the Internet of things, etc. Each of these blocks is both a structural particle of the virtual world and a bridge connecting it with the real world. Obviously, these worlds are interconnected and interdependent, as, for example, a real person and his virtual image in a social network. Today we can identify each entity, classifying it as part of this or that world, but after a while for many objects we will not be able to apply such a division. A modern smartphone today stores a lot of data: phone numbers, birthdays, photos, passwords, etc. and we can say

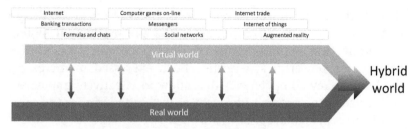

Figure 1.20. Merging the virtual and real worlds to form a hybrid world

that the process of merging the real and virtual worlds is aimed at forming a hybrid world (Figure 1.20).

Global digitalization is changing the structure of the national economy of countries. If previously the largest companies in terms of market capitalization were companies from various industries, including energy, industry (electronics), and the banking sector, now the giant companies in terms of market capitalization have become companies whose main activity is the development of information products and provision of information services.

The leading modern trend leading to a qualitatively new use of information as a valuable resource in predicting future needs is the development of cognitive technologies, which is viewed today by many scientists as an impending technological revolution. Cognitive technologies will penetrate, intervene, and cause significant changes at all stages of the lifecycle of goods and services, including in the process of consumption (Figure 1.21).

Cognitive science is able to bring, and in some industries it already does, a tremendous amount of the most important theoretical

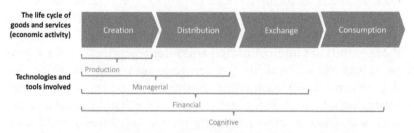

Figure 1.21 – Place of cognitive technologies in the value chain

and practical results aimed at understanding the processes of transformation of consumer expectations, market dynamics, etc. It gives knowledge of the internal and external environment to intelligent information systems, and the results obtained today affect not only the development and economic growth of their industry, but also act as a factor in the development of competencies in other areas of knowledge.

The interpenetration of competences in such areas as nanotechnology, biotechnology and cognitive science are of particular importance. This process is called NBIC convergence. The definition was introduced in 2002 by M. Roco and W. Bainbridge. It can be can generally stated that the currently emerging phenomenon of NBIC convergence is a radically new stage in scientific and technological progress and, in terms of its future possible consequences, it may become a new major factor in the formation of a new wave of innovation. The characteristics of NBIC convergence are:

– close complementarity between scientific fields;
– significant synergistic effect, observed quantitatively and qualitatively;
– the breadth of scientific knowledge – from the atom to intelligent systems;
– significant growth of opportunities for individual and social development.

The changes caused by convergence can be described as revolutionary in the range of phenomena under consideration and the scope of the upcoming transformations.

At the same time, it should be noted that scientific and technological development requires significant resources for research and development, as well as close cooperation with university and academic research centers and research laboratories. The most successful new economy is formed in the centers of concentration of scientific institutions and innovative industries, creating clusters of competencies. In these centers, the innovative potential of combining science and industry is of high importance. It is free from the constraints typical for large businesses, which instinctively try to reproduce exactly the business model that brought them success in completely different economic conditions.

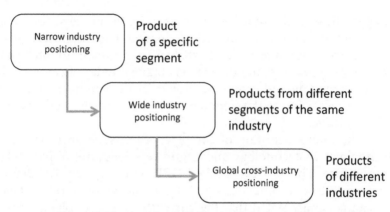

Figure 1.22 – Levels of positioning key competencies

Given clustering, the key competence can be represented at several levels of positioning – from narrow industry to global intersectoral positioning. The levels of positioning competencies are clearly shown in Fig. 1.22.

The level of key competence determines the development of technological sectors of three types:

- technologies for various purposes are created on the basis of the respective physical principle based on the corresponding key competence (for example, microelectronic technologies, etc.);
- to solve a single task, technologies based on different physical principles are used, which requires a set of key competencies (for example, data transfer technologies);
- technologies created based on interdisciplinary research, arising from cross-sectoral competencies (for example, NBIC technologies).

An example that demonstrates the result of scientific and technological convergence taking place in the information space is service industrial platforms (systems), where favorable conditions are already being created for the maximum integration of the physical and digital environment of a company.

As a tool for implementing this unifying concept, it is proposed to create geographically distributed platforms, where through the means of Internet communications, all the links of product creation – from ordering to development and production – are integrated in a single information space. This approach involves a gradual rejection of verbal communication between the customer, developer and manufacturer of certain products. Market actors are moving to interaction within a single electronic information space.

Such a model of interaction can significantly reduce the period from development to introduction of technology and will allow reformatting the market towards creating a fairer and more efficient model of mutually beneficial participation of the manufacturer and the consumer. In this system, small innovative companies or small enterprises that have perfectly mastered a certain technological process and received key competencies will be able to enter cooperation in the production of complex expensive equipment along with giant corporations without bureaucratic difficulties.

As a technological basis for combining competencies into an intersectoral cluster, it is proposed to consider a cloud-based software platform, due to which it is possible for all competence carriers to interact in a single space. This platform also involves «production units» that have their own set of equipment and competencies.

The considered processes of the evolution of the world information space, related to the emergence of its intellectual component, allow us to formulate a hypothesis about the formation of an intersectoral competence cluster:

Cognitive technologies contribute to the emergence of effective tools for learning the global information space, in which production units, representatives of fundamental and applied science, as well as consumers of goods and services are integrated. These tools make it possible to determine the future needs and requirements for the image of new products, as well as form a virtual cluster of key competencies necessary for creating a new product. The global information space with integrated production structures, the scientific community and consumers is a digital market that allows you to predict the behavior of products in real markets in order to create advanced design solutions.

An illustration of the proposed hypothesis is shown in Figure 1.23.

Global informatization and the development of information processing and transmission environments in an enterprise is based on the constant creation and implementation of innovative solutions.

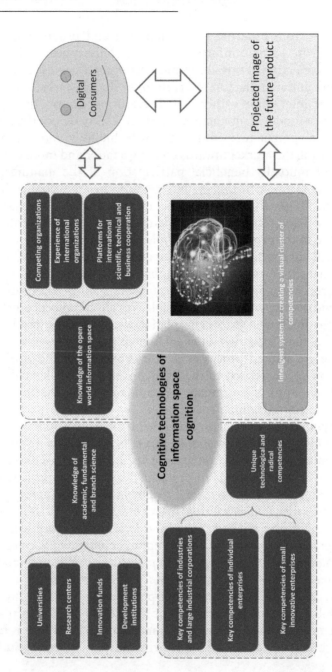

Figure 1.23. Digital market as a result of global informatization

Naturally, we consider informatization as a means of increasing competitiveness, and information as a kind of product or service, the acquisition and use of which will lead to an increase in the efficiency of an enterprise in terms of manufacture of new products to ensure development. A cyclical process takes place: the broad development of informatization promotes the search, development and implementation of innovative solutions, the formation of new radical competencies (including those reaching the intersectoral level), which makes it possible to create the techno-economic image of products in accordance with the promising needs of the market and, therefore, increase competitiveness, which will increase the volume of sales of products and services.

The functioning of the above-mentioned cyclical process requires, particularly by industrial business structures to use informatization tools as a mechanism for forming virtual intersectoral clusters of competencies to solve the problem of effective management and achieve competitive advantages throughout the entire cycle of design, manufacture, and sales of products, which is possible only with the development of the information infrastructure of large organizational and economic automated systems, operating in all areas of a company's activities contributing to the development of cross-industry competencies. Such infrastructure provides the process of creating popular products using digital production technologies focused on the need to achieve a given level of competitiveness in the market, taking into account the personification of needs, the increasing intellectual potential resulting from the accumulation and synthesis of competencies of companies and society.

The greatest effect from the synthesis of competencies and their extension to the intersectoral level will be obtained if the most promising competencies are involved in the process of such synthesis, the development of which can lead to economic growth or create conditions for building radical competencies. In this regard, companies need to form a pool of the most promising competencies based on their assessment and selection.

The process of formalizing the entire list of competencies for their evaluation and forming a pool of the most promising ones can be implemented through several successive stages.

The first stage. The assessment of the value for the consumer of certain properties of products and services – allows to identify the competitiveness of specific products. Next, product competencies or competencies providing a high consumer value are identified.

The second stage. An expert assessment (questionnaire, round table, etc.) can be used to identify a complete list of competencies (including corporate ones) and preliminary highlight key positions. Here, a list of all identified competencies related to certain business processes and indirectly related to the development of any product in demand by the market will be formed.

The third stage. Business processes, which were selected as the most important in the first two stages, are formalized in the IDEF business process description standard and are subjected to quantitative comparative assessment with reference samples (which are taken as the most promising competencies that can stimulate economic growth or create new radical competencies). Thus, the superiority will be objectively confirmed or rejected.

This sequence is graphically shown in Fig. 1.24.

The main goal for a manager in resolving the issue of assessing and identifying competencies, the development of which can lead

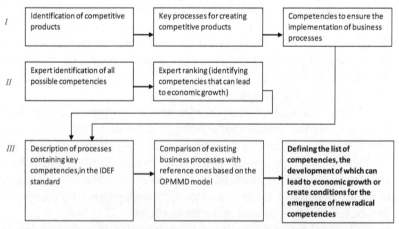

Figure 1.24. Scheme for identifying competencies, the development of which can lead to economic growth or create conditions for the emergence of radical competencies

to economic growth or create conditions for the emergence of radical competencies, is to strengthen the harmonization of the links between the implementation of a strategy or program of informatization and business process management through the management of related competencies; identify the processes required to implement strategies through business process management; determine the competencies and resources that a company must have to reliably turn strategy into projects and the results of their successful implementation using digitalization tools; to identify ways to increase the maturity of organizational management in the context of global informatization, which requires the transition of enterprises to new technology platforms as a result of the introduction of radical competencies.

The introduction of radical competencies in practice and their use in industrial turnover by companies that create and market highly demanded unique products is possible with the use of such tools inherent in global informatization, such as the creation of information databases that store information about competencies and their use in certain technological or managerial processes, as well as automated product lifecycle management systems, which reflect the relationship between the implemented business processes and all the company's competencies, including radical ones.

Radical competences and their active use in expanding the possibilities of global informatization allow further analysis of modern trends in considering information as a service and its application for the implementation of economic processes, taking into account the continuous accumulation of large databases containing, among other things, information on competencies. Such an analysis will enable forecasting the applicability of various targeted amounts of information and the development of cross-industry competencies for creating unique products. The processes of global informatization and the development of a modern information infrastructure can be considered within the framework of the economic development cycle according to the scheme "competencies → industry → personalized needs" using economic and mathematical models, in which information is viewed as the most important resource and product in the economy. Such models will allow to evaluate the effectiveness of activities to create new products and analyze their impact on the economic system.

CHAPTER 2.
MODELING ECONOMIC GROWTH

2.1. ECONOMIC GROWTH AS A RESULT OF BUILDING INTERSECTORAL RADICAL COMPETENCIES USING METHODS OF EXTRACTING "USEFUL" INFORMATION

It was ascertained that in the conditions of the development of the knowledge economy and the acceleration of the rate of their distribution due to the dynamic growth of funds and methods of their collection, processing, storage, analysis and transfer by inertia, the rates of formation and development of new (including radical) competencies increase, which are increasingly becoming interdisciplinary and cross-sectoral, covering activities within sectoral and cross-sectoral complexes.

As a result of the close interrelation of intersectoral complexes, on the one hand, there is a diffusion of knowledge and competencies accumulated within these complexes, and on the other hand, there are opportunities to develop a final product that will ensure the activities of each complex of a single interconnected structure (Figure 2.1), while forming a balanced intersectoral development.

There is a mutual penetration of knowledge and competencies created in various complexes, their synthesis, which ensures the operation of interconnected complexes, as well as the creation of radically new products and services with high competitive potential.

Here, the following axiom can be formed:

The interaction of intersectoral complexes due to the intensification of information flows and the synthesis of knowledge and competencies leads to the building radical intersectoral competencies of a higher level, creating a dynamically increasing synergistic effect, which consists in accelerating the pace of renewal and the creation of radically new products, expanding markets (by increasing the volume of supply and demand), increasing trade and cash turnover, which ultimately leads to economic growth.

There are a number of factors that determine how quickly and effectively the exchange, distribution and formation of cross-industry competencies will take place, creating opportunities for the development of highly competitive (including radically new) products and services. These factors include the following:

- the degree of interconnections between industry complexes that form the basis for information exchange and the possibility of synthesizing knowledge and competencies;
- the level of readiness of the industry complex to accept and ensure the synthesis of intersectoral competencies with the existing base;
- of employees of the industry complex to integrate new knowledge and competencies;
- sufficiency of the resource and technological base;
- the opportunity to invest in development by allocating funds for the acquisition and implementation of new competencies that go beyond the country intersectoral complexes abroad etc.

In this case, since the source of the formation of new intersectoral competencies is the convergence of information, we will consider it as a service with its own cost and quality (value of information) parameters. Like any service, information has its own

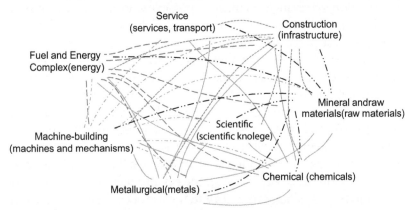

Figure 2.1. Structure of interrelations of intersectoral complexes

parameters of competitiveness, determined by its value for the consumer in terms of completeness and accuracy necessary to solve the problems of the consumer.

As soon as information becomes competitive, the demand for it as a service, sales volumes, as well as the volume of contribution to building a country's GDP grows. Thus, only valuable useful information, as a result of its sale as a service, becomes an additional source of economic growth at the present stage of development of the world economy by stimulating the processes of building radical competencies, leading to the development of radically new products created by intersectoral complexes.

In this case, the question arises of assessing the quality (value for the consumer) of information, which determines its value (including the cost of information involved in the formation of radically new competencies, creating bases for «nurturing» these competencies, etc.) and the ability to participate in the creation of a radically new product that provides new markets and ensures economic growth.

The processes of creating radical new products involve, first of all, techno-economic information, which today is defined as information used in the production, distribution and consumption of material goods, as well as in the planning and management of the economy of a State. Techno-economic information includes information about objects and processes in the economy. Combining techno-economic information into a single set makes it possible to form not only the technical competitiveness of products created by enterprises, but also to manage the processes of forming economic competitiveness.

Techno-economic information is a set of information that characterizes the technical or economic side of a certain object (for example, production, infrastructure, farmland, etc.) and is the object of storage, transmission and transformation. The objectivity of the reflection of economic and other processes is the main requirement that must be met by information, which is one of the key services in the modern world. Objective information about an object is the basis of the economy – economic activity in which the key production factor is digital data, processing of large volumes and the use of analysis results, which can significantly increase the efficiency of various types of production, technologies, equipment, storage, sale, delivery of goods and services compared with traditional forms of management.

At present, there is a tendency in the economy of developing countries when the tasks of achieving the technical competitiveness of products and their effective market launch are not solved as a single techno-economic task. The combined amount of techno-economic information can be effectively used for a comprehensive solution of techno-economic problems, such as design for a given cost and competitiveness[6]. Techno-economic information becomes the main resource of intelligent systems for managing the life cycle of new products[7]. Based on the processing of techno-economic data, intelligent systems form recommendations on the boundaries of the cost of a future product manufactured in accordance with a given techno-economic image, which should be set and further used when creating a product at a given cost. The analysis of the possibility of creating a product using the planned design and technological solutions is carried out, provided that price competitiveness is ensured. If a product turns out to be uncompetitive in price, the system, based on the processing of techno-economic data, provides recommendations for choosing the most effective design and technological solutions in order to bring the product price to a competitive one. Given account techno-economic data, intelligent systems form recommendations for the implementation of measures aimed at maintaining or increasing competitiveness, optimizing costs in the production cycle, recommendations for the choice of materials and technologies (their recombination), which will create a unique product, as well as for organizing pre-production in the most efficient way, taking into account its maximum automation and reducing the time period for the implementation of this stage of the life cycle.

---

[6] Boginsky, A.I., Chursin, A.A. Optimizing Product Cost // Russian Engineering Research, 2019, 39(11), p. 940-943.

[7] Boginskiy, A.I., Chursin, A.A., Nesterov, E.A., Tyulin, A.E. Assessing the competitiveness of production of a high-tech corporation to ensure its advanced development // Journal of Advanced Research in Dynamical and Control Systems, 2019, 11(11 Special Issue), p. 73-81.

Unlike simple knowledge, which is descriptive in nature, techno- conomic knowledge has a certain value that can be monetized. There is an urgent task of assessing the consumer value of information obtained as a result of the use of methods of its extraction, synthesis and analysis.

Such an assessment of the consumer value of information is based on the concept of quantitative measurement of information in information theory. The quantitative assessment of information allows to measure information flows in information systems, regardless of their nature and physical implementation.

We will consider the assessment of techno-economic information obtained as a result of data processing through the application of appropriate methods.

The general approach to estimating the amount of information is based on the following considerations. We will suppose that a recipient of information is interested in which of the N possible states the object is in. If the recipient does not have any information about the state of the object, then the amount of required information can be considered equal to reducing the uncertainty of the state of the object. This measure in information theory is called entropy by analogy with physics, where entropy characterizes the degree of disorder (chaos) of a physical system. Disorder can be interpreted in terms of how little the recipient of information knows about a given system. If a conditional observer (a person, an intelligent system) has identified something in the techno-economic system, its entropy for the observer has decreased. In our case, the maximum entropy corresponds to the absence of information about the state of the object. The minimum entropy (zero) corresponds to the complete information about the state of the object. According to Shannon's formula, the entropy of an object with N possible states is equal to

$$Hn = -\sum pi \cdot log2pi,$$

where the summation is carried out by from i from 0 from N, p is the probability with which the object is in a certain state.

In the case of a techno-economic system, its states can be defined as different degrees of specification of techno-economic information about an object. For a certain type of object, a scale for detailing the states of the object under study can be developed. The state of the object, determined with a certain probability, corresponds to a specific point on such a scale.

Using the information approach based on such a scale and the calculated values of probabilities, the value of information in solving a specific problem can be determined as the value of entropy. Depending on this value, the cost of the information received can be determined.

To obtain an estimate of the value of the information description of a certain object, we will consider the vector of its techno-economic characteristics, determined as a result of data processing by means of appropriate processing and analysis methods:

$$Q(t) = \begin{pmatrix} q_1(t) \\ q_2(t) \\ \vdots \\ q_N(t) \end{pmatrix}$$

To determine the integral indicator of the value of information for the consumer, characterizing the quality of information, we introduce a convolution of techno-economic parameters, which is a generalized indicator based on normalized values of technical characteristics of products.

To assess the value of information, it is necessary to use the normalized values of the obtained data on techno-economic characteristics. We will evaluate each product indicator using a finite number of points, for example, from zero to 5.

$qn0 \in \{0, 1, 2, 3, 5\}$.

If the initial parameter has a numerical value qn, then it can be normalized using the following formula (for a positive parameter):

$qn0 = [5 \cdot (qn - min) / (max - min)]$,

where min and max are the minimum and maximum values of the parameter obtained as a result of various data processing methods, and square brackets are rounding to the nearest integer.

For a negative parameter, use the following version of this formula:

$qn0 = 5 - [5 \cdot (qn - min) / (max - min)]$.

Suppose we have a certain set of objects of the same type, the data about which are obtained through the application of methods for extracting, summarizing and analyzing information. This set will contain the vectors normalized in points

$Qm = (qm1, qm2, ..., qmN)$, $m = 1, 2, ..., M$.

The set of these vectors can be represented as a matrix, where each row is the indicators of each object, and each column is the values of the indicators in the entire set of objects.

For each column numbered, we define the entropy by the following formula. Assuming that each value of this column is a realization of some random variable on, which accepts values

on $\in \{0, 1, 2, 3, 4, 5\}$,

we can estimate the probability for each value of this random variable using the following formulas:

$pi = Mi / M$,

where Mi is the number of times when the exponent n accepts the value $I \in$

$\{0,1,2,3,4,5\}$.

The entropy of a random variable is calculated using the following formula:

$Hn = H[on] = -\sum pi \cdot log2pi$,

where the summation is carried out by i from 0 to 5. As is customary in information theory, we assume that $0 \cdot log20 = 0$.

Thus, to convolve the normalized vector with the technical indicators of a product, we will use the following formula:

$Qm = \sum Hn \cdot qmn$,

where the summation is carried out by n from 1 to N.

Therefore, when convolving the indicators, we consider the information content of each techno-economic characteristic.

The more information each characteristic carries, the more weight this characteristic is considered in the convolution. It is possible to use this formula taking into account the weighting factors

$$Qm = \sum wi \cdot Hn \cdot qmn,$$

where wi is a weight index for the n-th techno-economic characteristics.

The widespread use of modern methods of extracting, summarizing and analyzing information leads to a qualitative transformation of many traditional economic technologies and, ultimately, to the growth of global or national economies by improving the management efficiency of individual, smaller economic systems, such as an industry or enterprise, as a result of extracting useful information from large amounts of available data, the use of which allows to solve target management problems.

It should be noted once again that the share of services in the GDP structure shows rapid growth. Speaking of the structure of the service sector, it should be noted that in the process of developing methods for extracting, summarizing, processing and analyzing information, the volume of the IT services market is growing, in which the segment of processed information and services aimed at obtaining economic or technical and technological knowledge from a large array of information is actively increasing.

In this regard, it is logical to assume that in the current conditions, the fundamental factor of economic growth should be an increase in labor productivity, which today can be ensured by using automated methods for extracting, summarizing and analyzing information, followed by the allocation of useful knowledge that can create radical competencies and radically new products in various areas of management. The economic growth that occurs under the influence of valuable knowledge obtained through processing large amounts of information, requires the harmonized development of the infrastructure for obtaining such knowledge, carrying value in terms of the possibility of creating radical competencies on their basis. The dynamics of development of individual markets observed today is ambiguous. In the developed countries there will be a more active increase in labor productivity in view of the fact that in technologically developed countries the degree of readiness for the implementation of technologies and methods of extracting utility from the entire dynamically growing volume of available data is higher than in developing countries.

The growth in the number of information services and companies developing them is largely due to the development of new intelligent data processing methods and machine learning technologies as until recently, the analysis of data sets was an expensive, time-consuming and mostly manual process, and due to intelligent algorithms, many data processing procedures have been automated, and new methods for forecasting the processes described by such data have been developed. Machine learning algorithms are rapidly becoming more productive, sometimes surpassing human capabilities. Figure 2.2 shows the progress of intelligent systems in solving the object detection problem in the Large-Scale Visual Recognition Competition (LSVRC), which evaluates object detection and image classification algorithms based on large-scale images and videos.

The task of assessing economic growth under the influence of the processes of extracting useful techno-economic information that can become the basis for the formation of radical competencies is multivariate in essence, i.e. requiring consideration of a large number of factors. This ambiguity is due to the fact that economic growth,

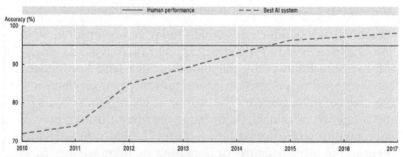

Figure 2.2 – Comparison of the capabilities of humans (solid line) and intelligent systems in detecting objects in large-scale images (LSVRC competition was organized by the Vision Lab of Stanford University from 2010 to 2017)
Source: Artificial Intelligence Index: 2017 Annual Report,
http://cdn.aiindex.org/2017-report.pdf

both based on traditional technological progress (capital-intensive and labor-intensive) and on the basis of progress displacing labor, will lead to an increase in production, but in the second case, the demand for labor and average wages will decrease. On the other hand, increased productivity and increased automation, demand for labor and wages can increase (employment is generated to solve new problems).

Based on the research, the following hypothesis can be formed: The rate of economic growth under the influence of the development of automated methods for extracting, processing and analyzing «useful» techno-economic information depends on how quickly new development methods begin to contribute to the creation of radical competencies and radically new products able to dominate the market.

The scheme of achieving (accelerating) economic growth may look as follows, shown in Fig. 2.3.

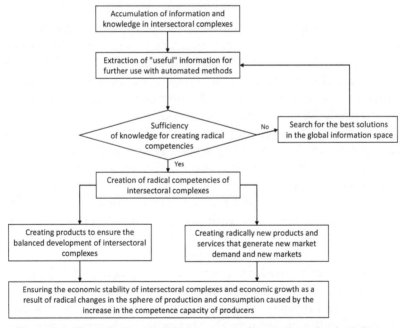

Figure 2.3. The scheme of achieving economic growth under the influence of the development of automated methods for extracting, processing and analyzing «useful» techno-economic information

The pattern of steps shown in Figure 2.3 is already confirmed today by the effects arising from the digitalization of many business processes, the processing of data from the global information space, the wide involvement of the intellectual potential of fundamental and applied science, as well as the transfer of knowledge accumulated in various industries to build new unique competencies, as well as as a result of the speed of introduction of innovative developments, i.e. effectively established mechanisms and methods for extracting, processing and analyzing useful techno-economic information, which becomes the basis for the creation of radical competencies and mechanisms for their implementation in the processes of economic development.

2.2. MODELING THE IMPACT OF KEY FACTORS ON ECONOMIC GROWTH

The development of the economy of different time periods occurs under the influence of various factors and growth drivers, which create the basis of world economic relations. First of all, these factors are closely related to the types of development of society, which are transformed with the development and structural transformation of the economies of the world.

During transformation periods, economic development and growth are determined by several groups of factors and drivers that belong to the previous economic stage and new emerging trends. For example, the world economy is currently undergoing a transformation of the post-industrial society that has already developed in most countries, which tends to develop a digital environment, as a result of which a post-industrial society with a developing digital economy is being formed.

Such transformations began with the active development of the knowledge economy, when knowledge became one of the key resources and driving forces for the development of innovations. In these conditions, not only the service sector is actively developing (its growth is undoubtedly much higher than in other segments of the economy), but also other spheres typical for previous social structures. This is due to the fact that the digital economic environment and its tools cover all sectors of the economy, from traditional to service sectors, while increasing efficiency and creating added value in each of them, but with different rates of growth.

These processes take place under the influence of a number of factors, and as it was noted, the key and most influential factors for economic growth and its development are the following factors listed in Table 2.1.

Table 2.1. Key factors influencing economic growth and development

At State level	At industry level	At company level
External investments	Cross-sectoral cooperation (within cross-sectoral complexes)	Development and application of new production technologies
Growth in demand for goods from national producers	Integration of small business into the economic system of the state	Investments in promising R&D
Infrastructure development	Stimulating the development of key strategically important industries	Accumulation of competencies (creation of competence centers)
Territory development		Energy saving technologies
Economic policy (including industrial) that stimulates growth	Development of sectoral and cross-industrial technology platforms for the accumulation of competencies and their transformation into radical innovations with the involvement of enterprises of several industries or directions within an industry	
The emergence of new tools that accelerate the development of economic systems of different levels linked with digital transformation, covering all areas of activity		

As noted, many of these factors are widely known and studied in the world economic literature, however, the issue of changes arising from the development of the digital economy is just beginning to be examined by all scientists of the world. Digitalization should be viewed as a means of developing economic systems, which has many positive effects, which come down to reducing costs and increasing efficiency. The key factors and features of the radical digital

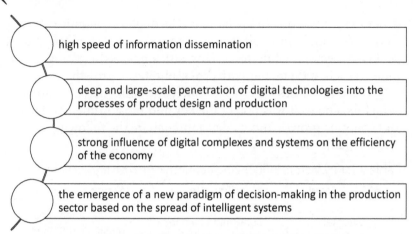

Figure 2.4. Factors of the digital economy

transformations that the world economic order is undergoing at the present stage are those shown in Fig. 2.4 factors.

The key drivers of economic growth shown in Figure 2.4 stimulating economic growth, including using the advantages of broad digital transformation and its penetration into industrial production and design, led to the creation of a digital production paradigm characterized by high ability to transform and adapt, resource efficiency and ergonomics, as well as the integration of all economic actors (consumers, investors, partners, etc.) into business processes and consumer value creation processes.

The digital industry focuses on the individual wishes of customers and relies on trends in scientific and technological development, which is achieved through the widespread use and intelligent and operational analysis of the available heterogeneous data obtained from many different sources.

In our works[8] an economic law was formulated and proved about the relationship of competencies with the emergence of new markets, which proclaims that the creation of unique competencies increases resources in high-tech companies, which lead

---

[8] Chursin, A.A., Shamin, R.V., Fedorova, L.A. The mathematical model of the law on the correlation of unique competencies with the emergence of new consumer markets // 2017, European Research Studies Journal 20(3), p. 39-56.

to an abrupt emergence of unique innovative technologies based on competencies that are used in the development of fundamentally new products. The emergence of these products leads to an increase in the demand for new goods and the economic growth stimulates further demand for unique technologies.

The development of key competencies in the use of modern methods of organizing digital production and design provides a significant synergistic effect in the economy, which is manifested in the fact that the creation and development of radical competencies and the emergence of new radical innovations generated by them offers conditions for the development of new consumer markets. Unlike traditional industry, competition in the development of radical competencies and radical innovations based on them has other mechanisms that respond much faster to changes in the activities of competitors, which significantly motivates companies to quickly and effectively change their behavior.

In the context of the introduction of modern digital methods and means of production and management in industry, there is a transition to a system of economic relations that functions in a dynamically expanding information space, which ensures optimal connections and interaction between subjects and objects of economic relations in the production, exchange and distribution of material goods. Based on the digital approach, an enterprise resource management system is formed, which is the basis for the development and implementation of new technical and technological solutions. An important issue in the context of digital transformation is the task of managing the technological platform and production system of an enterprise to release the products that dominate the market.

Methods for achieving a dominant position in the market, based on the digital transformation of an enterprise, can be systematized and broadly divided into 4 groups: institutional sphere, personnel management sphere, scientific and technical sphere and information and communication sphere. Combining the indicated methods allows to obtain a synergistic effect through the exchange of technologies and the attraction of key competencies from the market, allowing to build up scientific and technical capacity.

International practice has shown that the main efforts in the development of innovatively active industries should be focused on ensuring the right balance between market mechanisms of self-regulation and mechanisms of governmental incentives. Within large corporations, competencies are universalized, ensuring the effectiveness of all stages of product development and marketing.

This scheme seems to be significantly more effective than the scheme existing in developing countries, which organizationally «locks» all suppliers and contractors to the state customer and thus does not give them the opportunity to effectively build up competencies in the field of market use of the latest technological solutions.

An example of introducing digitalization elements in industry can be the so-called service industrial platform (system), where today conditions have been created for maximum integration of the physical and digital environment of business processes.

The tool for the implementation of this unifying concept is the creation of geographically distributed design and production sites, which, based on Internet communications and elements of the Industry 4.0 concept, integrate all stages of product manufacturing – from order to development and production. This approach implies a gradual rejection of direct communications between the customer, the developer and the manufacturer of certain products. Market participants are moving towards interaction within a single digital space.

This model of interaction significantly reduces the period from development to implementation of technology and will allow reformatting the market towards creating a fairer and more efficient order distribution model. In the same system, "production units" that have a set of equipment characteristics and employee competencies will operate. The term "production unit" refers to a specific function – from individual workstations to automated machining centers. Each of these units receives a technological digital passport – a program code that defines all its capabilities and technological tolerances.

For example, the machining center is faced with the task of making a hole in the part with certain parameters – diameter, speed, etc. In the digital passport, all this information is described as a comprehensible program of structured writing, where variables

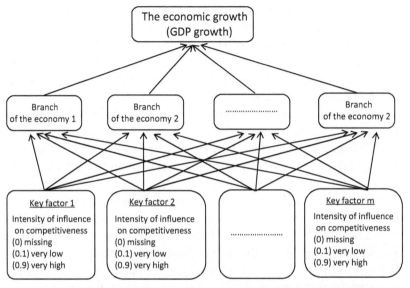

Figure 2.5 Generation of economic growth influenced by key factors

are parameters that can be used for programming in the algorithm. Thus, in an automated mode, guaranteed quality, terms of work and quick convenient access to all information without the need for verbal communication are achieved. All interaction takes place in a language comprehensible to digital systems. The system automatically regulates all actions in production in accordance with the documentation. It will be impossible to use materials of a different quality, set a different distance between parts, use other semiconductor products or a different case, etc.

The scale of the changes under the impact digital transformation can be analyzed based on the simulation model, using which various scenarios of such changes can be played.

Economic and mathematical modeling of the impact of digital transformation on the processes of economic growth is one of the most important components of the analysis of the digital economy. In accordance with the task of describing the process of achieving economic growth through digital transformation, it is necessary to determine the impact of new digital methods of production and management on the competitiveness of sectors of the economy that use these methods to their advantage, and, ultimately, economic growth, which will be expressed in the growth of a country's GDP. The process of forming economic growth as a result of increasing the competitiveness of products and services due to key factors can be conditionally represented in a hierarchical structure:

The top level of the hierarchy is the expected final level of economic growth. At the second level, sectors of the economy are distinguished, each of which contributes to GDP and is influenced by key factors on its competitiveness and potential for economic growth. For each consequence, we will assign numbers Contr1 Contr2, ...Contrk representing the contribution of each of the industries to the growth of the economy, i.e., to the increase in GDP.

The third level of the hierarchy consists of key factors $F_1, F_2, ..., F_m$ that affect the competitiveness of industries, for solving economic problems in which they are used and also take into account the growing needs of industries when managing their own level of competitiveness. In addition, it must be borne in mind that the overall growth of the economy also due to the industry that is the source of digital transformations. In this regard, the model should consider the assessment of the impact of key factors on the competitiveness of the industries they affect (σ).

The meaning of these values is as follows. As can be seen from Figure 2.5, the contribution of industries Contr1 Contr2, ...Contrk to overall economic growth can be influenced by a whole set of key factors from a common set $F_1, F_2, ..., F_m$.

It is natural to assume that for some services, the degree of this influence may be less than for others, or even not exist (if the service is not used in the interests of the industry). For this purpose it is necessary to determine for each industry the contribution Contr1, Contr2, ...Contrk and factors $F_1, F_2, ..., F_m$ of σ_{ij} $i = 1..m$, $j = 1..k$. The value σ_{ij} reflects the degree of influence of the key factor on the competitiveness of an industry Contrj.

After assessing the impact of key factors on the competitiveness of industries, it is necessary to assess the intensity of the competitiveness management process.

To assess the intensity of the influence of key factors, we will use the Harrington verbal-numerical scale, where the following values are used as reference points:

0.00 – no impact on the competitiveness of industries;

0.10 – very low intensity of impact on the competitiveness of industries;

0.29 – low intensity of impact on the competitiveness of economic sectors;

0.50 – average intensity of impact on the competitiveness of sectors of the economy;

0.72 – high intensity of impact on the competitiveness of economic sectors;

0.90 – very high intensity of impact on the competitiveness of economic sectors.

In general, the assessment depends on the impact on competitiveness of dynamically changing internal and external factors. In this case, the intensity of the influence of key factors on the competitiveness of industries $F_1, F_2, ..., F_m$ is random, i.e. the intensity can be considered as a random variable with a certain probability distribution:

Table 2.2. The law of distribution of the intensity of competitiveness management

$I(F_i)$	0.00	0.10	0.29	0.50	0.72	0.90
q_l^i	$q_{0.00}^i$	$q_{0.10}^i$	$q_{0.29}^i$	$q_{0.50}^i$	$q_{0.72}^i$	$q_{0.90}^i$

Under the general formula of the aggregated hierarchical assessment, the formula for assessing the level of risk is written as:

$$L = \sum_{j=1}^{k} \Delta_j \sum_{i=1}^{m} w_{ij} \sum_{l \in I} l \cdot q_l^i,$$

where

$$l \in I = \{0.00, 0.10, 0.29, 0.50, 0.72, 0.90\}$$

q_l^i is the probability of the influence of key factors F_i with an intensity value exactly equal l.

Let us represent the probability $q_{l_i}^{i}$ as a function of the of cost ξ aimed at increasing the competitiveness of the industry due to the influence of key factors.

We define the type of functional relationship that can be used to describe the function of the intensity of influence on the competitiveness of economic sectors. Let us introduce a support function

$$Q(\xi) = P(I(F_i) \geq l),$$

i.e. a function describing the intensity of the impact on the competitiveness of economic sectors with a value greater than or equal to l. We assume that this function is twice continuously differentiable on the set of positive real numbers. Thus, the intensity of competitiveness management will never be equal to one, which means an asymptotic approximation of the probability to one for large amounts of costs. Hence, the function $Q(\xi)$ increases, which means that $Q'(\xi) \geq 0$ for all $\xi \geq 0$.

Let ξ_1 and ξ_2 be the values of the volumes of efforts, and then the corresponding probabilities are of the form:

$$Q_1 = Q(\xi_1) < Q_2 = Q(\xi_2).$$

Let us make some additional efforts $\Delta\xi$. We will get

$$Q_1' = Q(\xi_1 + \Delta\xi) \qquad Q_2' = Q(\xi_2 + \Delta\xi).$$

and

We assume that the law of diminishing resource efficiency holds for function $Q(\xi)$. This means that the response of function $Q(\xi)$ to the additional costs of $\Delta\xi$ decreases with the growth of ξ Then the increments of the functions are related by the inequality:

$$Q_1 - Q_1' < Q_2 - Q_2'$$

We divide both parts of the last inequality by the amount of additional costs $\Delta\xi$:

$$-\frac{[Q(\xi_1 + \Delta\xi) - Q(\xi_1)]}{\Delta\xi} < -\frac{[Q(\xi_2 + \Delta\xi) - Q(\xi_2)]}{\Delta\xi}$$

or

$$\frac{\left[Q(\xi_1 + \Delta\xi) - Q(\xi_1)\right]}{\Delta\xi} > \frac{\left[Q(\xi_2 + \Delta\xi) - Q(\xi_2)\right]}{\Delta\xi}.$$

When moving to the limit in the last inequality with $\Delta\xi \to 0$, we obtain the relation for the derivatives:

$$Q'(\xi_1) \geq Q'(\xi_2).$$

From this inequality and the condition that $Q'(\xi) \geq 0$, follows that the second derivative is negative $Q''(\xi) \leq 0$. Hence, the function $Q(\xi)$ is convex upwards.

In accordance with the above reasoning, the desired probability function $Q(\xi)$ is conveniently approximated, for example, by the following function:

$$Q(\xi) = P(I(F_i) \geq l) = 1 - \frac{A}{A + x^2},$$

where A is some constant.

In our problem, when we consider M digital solutions in production and management, the following set of functions can be written:

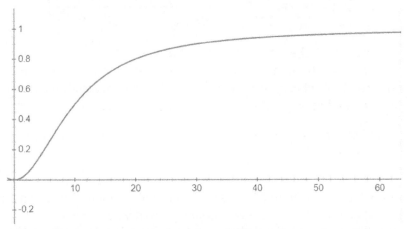

Figure 2.6 Graph of the intensity function $Q(\xi)$ depending on the volume of costs for the development of digital solutions in production and management

$$Q_l^i(\xi) = P(I(F_i) \geq l) = 1 - \frac{A_l^i}{A_l^i + \xi^2},$$

where $i = 1, 2, ..., M$.

The probability that the intensity of managing the competitiveness of the industry through digital solutions in production and management accepts value q_l^i, exactly equal to l, is expressed as follows:

$$q_l^i(\xi) = P(I(F_i) = l) =$$

$$= P(I(F_i) \geq l) - P(I(F_i) \geq l + 1) = Q_l^i(\xi) - Q_{l+1}^i(\xi),$$

Depending on the costs ξ spent on the development of digital solutions in production and management, the formula for assessing economic growth as a result of their implementation in economic sectors can be written as follows:

$$L(\xi) = \sum_{j=1}^{k} \Delta_j \sum_{i=1}^{m} \sigma_{ij} \sum_{l \in I} l(Q_l^i(\xi) - Q_{l+1}^i(\xi)) =$$

$$= \sum_{j=1}^{k} \Delta_j \sum_{i=1}^{m} \sigma_{ij} \sum_{l \in I} l\left(1 + \frac{A_l^i}{A_l^i + \xi^2} - 1 + \frac{A_{l+1}^i}{A_{l+1}^i + \xi^2}\right),$$

where l is the set of intensity values.

To assess the dynamics of changes in economic growth over time as a result of managing the development of digital solutions in production and management, the following functionality can be used:

$$Z(t_{i+1}) = L(t_i) - L(t_{i+1}),$$
$$i = 0, ..., T,$$

where the values of $L(t_i)$ correspond to the values of economic growth at points in time t_i, T is the value of the point in time to which the dynamics of changes in economic growth is considered.

The proposed simulation model for analyzing the impact of key factors (including digital transformation and the use of digital solutions in production and management) on economic growth allows us to formalize the relationship between the effectiveness of managing the digitalization of economic sectors and economic growth.

Thus, the key factors related to digital transformation and digital solutions, which are tools to increase efficiency in production and management, when implemented will entail changes that lead to the transformation of the economy as a whole, which will also affect the principles of activity of manufacturing enterprises. The development and implementation of digital solutions in the area of production and management will contribute to a qualitative increase in labor productivity and, as a result, to an increase in product output and its consumption, if it carries value for the consumer. As a result, both economic development and growth of the manufacturer of products are ensured, leading to an increase in the economic welfare of employees of a company, and an increase in GDP. Moreover, the higher the rate of economic development, the higher the level of welfare in the country. That is, an increase in labor productivity generates an increase in employees' wages, which in turn entails an increase in their ability to meet a wider range of needs.

Due to the growth of effective demand, the requirements for purchased goods and services, both in terms of quality and functional characteristics, are also increasing, that is, there is a transformation of needs, which necessitates the development and production of new goods and services in service industries, which will lead, according to our research, to a synergistic effect in the form of accelerated economic growth. Thus, digital transformation increases labor productivity in industries and the level of welfare of the population, primarily due to wage growth in these industries, which provides opportunities to meet growing and newly emerging needs by creating popular products and services in the service industries. This is consistent with our proven law of competitiveness management [9], which proclaims that the production and exchange of goods take place based on their competitive advantages, the set

---

[9] Chursin, A., Makarov, Y. Management of competitiveness: Theory and practice // 2015, Management of Competitiveness: Theory and Practice p. 1-378.

and quality of which is determined by the level of technological development, the efficiency of management processes that accelerate the development and implementation of radical competencies, the efficiency and intensity of the introduction of new technological solutions at an enterprise, in an industry, in a State as a whole.

If the competitive advantages of products are of a higher level than the average level of development of the productive forces in society, then the exceeding part of the competitive advantages cannot be completely absorbed and copied by the market, which enables using these competitive advantages in the long term.

The key competitive advantages and their maintenance is directly dependent on the presence and degree of development of radical competencies that provide conditions for the development of new products with high value to the consumer and thus are able to bring a company to the path of advanced development, creating economic growth potential of an industry and the economy as a whole.

As noted, radical competencies develop on the basis of technological platforms and cross-platform interaction, leading to the diffusion and synthesis of knowledge and innovative solutions accumulated within these platforms, becoming a source of radically new products. However, technological platforms should not be static; only their dynamic development will allow business to create breakthrough innovations that provide growth in demand and production, exerting a positive impact on GDP

The development of a company's technological platforms, as one of the key factors and sources of economic development, is carried out at several levels corresponding to the stages of the life cycle of production of radically new products. The development of the platform is not an instantaneous, but a continuous process, the course of which is determined by the flexibility of a company and the impact of external factors – trends in global technological development. The initial stages of the development of the technological platform a company (including the integrated structure) and the creation of competitive advantages that ensure its stable development are shown in Figure 2.7.

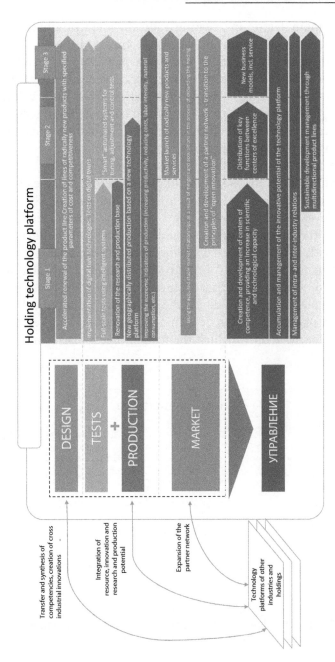

Figure 2.7. Expansion of an technological platform for increasing the competitive advantages of a company/holding

The main factor in creating radically new products aimed at long-term satisfaction of needs is the continuous growth of the innovative potential of the participants of the technology platform, connected with conducting a large amount of fundamental research, extracting valuable information from large volumes, mastering and developing a set of radical competencies, technologies and equipment based on this valuable information and studies, improving management methods.

The acceleration of the processes of accumulation of intellectual potential in the world, its implementation as radically new products and services that change markets and their needs, results in the development of technology platforms, their wider positioning at the intersectoral level, and, ultimately, to the formation of a network structure of a technology platform consisting of a core and independent (possibly related to each other) sub-platforms. The core of such a network structure is intersectoral cross-industrial competences that influence the generation of a radical product in sub-platforms, which determines the economic development of the entire industry to which the technological platform belongs (Fig. 2.8).

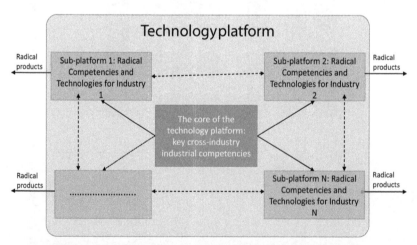

Figure 2.8. – Network organizational and industry structure of a technology platform

The synergistic effect of the factors

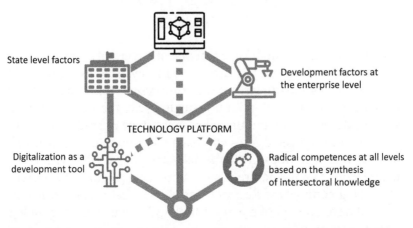

Figure 2.9. Impact of key factors on the development of a technology platform

Moreover, technological platforms are not developed in a confined space; they are influenced by all of the above factors that affect economic growth and development.

The positive impact of the factors shown in Figure 2.9 encourages the creation of radically new products within the technology platform. Acceleration of the development and deployment of new technologies results in a reduction in the life cycle of innovations that underlie the competitiveness of goods produced and sold on the market, leading to increased competition in the markets and forcing manufacturers to improve or generate new products through the development of radical innovations and use of the acquired and developed competencies.

Efficient use of «useful» information obtained from various sources, development of radical competencies within the technological platforms provides a product able to capture the market by creating a growing demand for it.

Growing demand in accordance with economic laws will increase production and sales, which together will provide economic growth within the technological platform forming the growth of a country's GDP.

2.3 THE MODEL OF THE ECONOMIC DEVELOPMENT CYCLE ACCORDING TO THE SCHEME "COMPETENCIES → INDUSTRY → PERSONALIZED NEEDS"

According to modern concepts of economic development, the corresponding models are generally cyclical in nature with a change of ups and downs, but with the preservation of a constantly increasing component. Within a single cycle, the initial intensive stage of development and the subsequent stage of gradual development are distinguished. This approach is common both in the field of investment activities and in the field of technical systems development. Moreover, the nature of such a process is realized for systems of varying complexity. Research has shown that there is a natural cycle of development of macrotechnology, on which the technological order is based:

- development of fundamental science, ideas that can be put into practice, training of personnel and development of radical competencies, organization of experimental development activities (10–15 years);
- creation of technologies, their rapid improvement, production and the beginning of the implementation of the new opportunities (10–15 years);
- diffusion of emerging radical innovations throughout the technosphere and the economic system (10–15 years).

The highlighted phases of the development cycle of macrotechnology can be described by the "competencies → industry → personalized needs" scheme, within which such processes can be interconnected as:

- forecasting the required technical level of the created products of the new technological order and the competencies necessary for their development, i.e. the technical level of the created sample or technological systems, intended for use in the production of the new technological order, which would ensure the necessary level of competitiveness of the created products for a long period;

– forecasting the amount of financing for industry, which includes the following factors: determining the amount of financing based on the optimal ratio: a set of characteristics of the products created, the amount of costs to achieve them at a given stage of development of the country's scientific and technical potential;
– determining the feasibility of the level of change in the technical characteristics of the system in a specific design, i.e., solving the problem of choosing between the development or modernization of previously designed products, which is closely related to ensuring the personalized properties of products.

As already noted, today the key direction of companies' activities, maintaining the existing market niche and having capacity to enter new markets, is to stimulate their innovative activity through the intensive development of innovative potential and the use of modern digital technologies and intelligent systems in the planning, management and control of all business processes, which requires companies to adapt to new methods of organizing the production process associated with the use of intelligent systems for processing and analyzing big data, industrial Internet technologies, artificial intelligence, expert analytical systems, etc., which in turn entails the need for continuous investment in innovative projects for the production of high technology products and increasing their investment attractiveness.

Today, intelligent systems in an automated mode can solve a wide range of design problems for new products, which include the following:

Multi-variant solution of problems of mathematical and digital modeling at all stages of creating a sample of a new product, optimization of the parameters of the product as a whole and its components, selection of the optimal layout and visual design. Solving these problems already at the early stages of design allows laying the best possible solutions, significantly improve the technical characteristics of products and reduce the volume of subsequent field tests.

Modeling and analysis of kinematic schemes of mechanisms, search for optimal solutions (structural and parametric optimization). This allows you to optimize not only the structure in terms of overall weight and reliability characteristics, but also its functioning.

Spatial modeling and improvement of the shape of structural elements using modern methods of strength, thermal, mass-inertial calculations, dimensional development of a structure, with the choice of rational tolerances for geometric dimensions. This allows to significantly reduce material consumption and overall dimensions of structures, to minimize errors in decision-making by developers. Provide high manufacturability of the structure, especially during its assembly.

Elaboration and release of design documentation using intelligent systems. This practically excludes subjective errors of the developer and, consequently, production defects.

Thus, among the positive effects of using intelligent systems in design, we can note an increase in labor productivity, an increase in the technical and price competitiveness of products, and an increase in the efficiency of management decision-making processes.

The development of intelligent control systems follows the path of increasing the complexity and nomenclature (component) of the elements of controlled systems. Today, intelligent systems are actively developing, capable of managing complex economic processes, in which many objects and counterparties are linked. The widespread digitalization of the modern economy is accompanied by a large information flow for any production or organizational activity, and most of this information is not available for direct analysis by decision makers. One of the reasons for this is the high dimension of information flows, in which any informational events are simultaneously described by a large number of different indicators. Moreover, these indicators constantly change over time. In addition, for a true assessment of the state of the system, instead of analyzing individual indicators, it is necessary to simultaneously analyze the entire set of multidimensional data. Thus, the actual task is to build intelligent systems for the operational analysis of multidimensional data flows describing the state of a complex economic or technical system. This system should have the ability to machine learn from the source data in order to automatically identify significant events in information flows. In addition, this system should be very clear when presenting a multidimensional information flow. Such intelligent systems are currently being developed for such objects as:

Economic condition of enterprises. The performance of any enterprise is related to a large number of economic and financial indicators that describe the state of the enterprise. Only a comprehensive analysis of all the data allows to assess the true condition of an enterprise, as well as to detect dangerous trends connected with the economic state of the enterprise. A complex technical system is also described by a large number of indicators, which in total can allow to detect a possible disorder in the system operation.

Multi-agent organizational and technical system. Many technical systems, such as satellite and ground infrastructure systems, are described by large data flows, which can include both telemetry and organizational and management information. Moreover, the success of the entire system is not limited to the successful operation of each component, but the correct coordination of the entire system is required.

Today, attempts are being made to create intelligent systems that manage entire industries or regions. They are based on the latest advances in the digital economy and big data technologies. However, the study of technical problems, as well as economic and mathematical problems, using supercomputing capacities and statistical data Big data, financial technologies, blockchain, etc. cannot solve the most important economic problem of crisis-free or proportional economic development on its own, since the main reason for the continuation of the global crisis is the disproportionality of economic development or the inconsistency of the development of economic sectors with the needs of its end consumers – households, the State, exporters. Disproportionality and chronic inflation are accompanied by the centralization of world capital, absorbing bankrupt states, small and medium-sized businesses, increasing poverty, environmental degradation, etc. The spontaneous introduction of various areas of the digital economy can be effective in terms of reducing the costs of individual subjects or processes at the micro level, but it cannot be effective in terms of social costs, and it cannot automatically help the world economy to recover from the protracted global crisis. The lack of scientifically grounded economic and mathematical models that allow developers of the digital economy to improve the efficiency of management decisions leads to the lobby of technocratic interests. In practice, this turns into additional steams of «big data», explicitly requested from enterprises. The information contained in them is repeatedly duplicated both in internal forms and in other forms filled out by enterprises for other authorities. In fact, the «manual», routine, labor-intensive work of enterprises repeatedly increases the unreliability of» big data», reduces labor productivity, which together contradicts the very idea of the digital economy about the effective use of the capabilities of modern information technologies.

In this regard, the task of developing a scientific methodology for creating a digital economy as a cyber-economic system that ensures interaction between a State, households and business to move the economy towards harmonious development is urgent. The construction of cyber-economy can be based on a dynamic model of the input-output balance, which reconciles the planned input-output calculations for the effective satisfaction of the needs of end consumers by manufacturers.

To change the vector of economic development towards growth, it is required to organize digital meso- and macroeconomics as a cyber-economic system that imitates the mechanism for coordinating planned input-output calculations of all levels of the economy to ensure its proportional and harmonious development. If the cyber-economic model organizing the digital economy imitates the operation of the law of value and the law of saving time in planned input-output calculations, then proportionality is achieved in the efficient distribution of the social resource of labor in accordance with social needs. Simulation in planning the operation of the law of value means the creation of conditions under which this law does not work as a spontaneous regulator, i.e. disproportionality is eliminated as the main cause of the crisis. The principal difference between the dynamic model of intersectoral balance and the kinematic (econometric) models is the description of the movement of the economy from its initial state in the direction set by end consumers (households, the State, exporters) in the form

Dynamic system wtith real-time feedback

Monitoring of the most important indicators of the input-output balance and the system of national accounts (coefficients of direct and total costs, intermediate links, the sectoral structure of the final consumer, etc.)

Identification of key structural constraints hindering sustainable development of the regional economy

Modeling Interregional Value Chains

Development of a complex of regional intersectoral balances

Support for management decision-making based on the structural analysis of production in economic sectors; the formation of goods and services; prices of buyers by type of goods and services; industry demand (including a breakdown of domestic and imported goods and services), etc.

Defining directions for increasing the number of redistributions in existing technological chains; calculation of the effects for economic agents (population, companies, government) from the proposed lengthening of value added chains

Optimization of production programs and plans, taking into account warehouse stocks and logistics, as well as signals of deviations

Optimization of daily, monthly, yearly and other plans, taking into account changing needs in real time

Plan-fact monitoring at all production facilities in the industry

Figure 2.10. Tasks of the dynamic model of the intersectoral balance

of a system of algorithms with live feed and feedback, specifying the needs of end consumers depending on the capabilities of producers, including their proposals for new technologies in real time.

The controlling parameter of the model is public production investment, which can be joint with business (public private partnership). Calculations based on this model determine the distribution of industrial investments by sectors of the economy, the maximum increase in the real solvency of the national currency by optimizing the structure of the final product for the consumer market. Thus, such a cyber-economic system acts as an economic regulator that harmonizes the development of industrial economies and is focused on cconsidering the dynamism of needs. Currently, there is a transformation of the consumption system itself, when the needs for personalized products that meet the specific requirements of a particular customer come to the fore.

The result of such changes is the creation of radically new products aimed at meeting personalized needs through the implementation of a continuous innovation process connected with the development and implementation of new technologies and equipment, improving management methods.

Emerging breakthrough technologies are embodied in the creation of unique products or services with high consumer value. The drive to commercialize such technologies compels high-tech companies to develop or facilitate the creation of new markets to promote their new products. A model of "competence – production – personalized needs" arises, which shows that building radical competencies contributes to the growth of consumer markets due to the development of new products that are focused on meeting future need. Market mechanisms also contribute to the growth of investments in breakthrough technologies that are used to create these products, which helps to shorten the cycle of their development and production.

This model will be built according to the following algorithm: in the first stage, a hypothesis is put forward about a model of economic development that links competencies, industrial production and satisfaction of personalized needs. Further, the issue of advanced forecasting of future needs that determine the vector of development of competencies and industrial potential is considered in detail, and an algorithm for determining the needs for personalized products is proposed. At the next stage, the influence of information resources on the processes of forming competencies and production potential for the manufacture of personalized promising products is analyzed. The principles of information management in the model of economic development are determined according to the scheme «competence – production – personalized needs». Finally, a dynamic mathematical model is built, which illustrates well the various modes of dynamics of the key variables in the process of economic development according to the scheme «competence – industry – personified needs».

Product personification is an important task, the solution of which is aimed at obtaining a reasonable method for identifying and predicting the full spectrum of society's needs for a particular product or service. Let us formulate a hypothesis about the model of economic development according to the scheme "competences → industry → personified needs". The hypothesis is that the model of economic development founded on personified production is based on the principle of advanced forecasting of future needs, for the timely satisfaction of which a company forms the appropriate competencies and research and production potential. The efficiency of these processes is enhanced by the use of modern information technologies for continuous monitoring of the external and internal environment in order to identify the actions of competitors to produce similar goods and make decisions on activities to increase the competitive advantages of the products being created. Moreover, such monitoring should be carried out taking into account the evolutionary trends of the global information space based on the use of modern intelligent technologies. Let us reveal the main provisions of this hypothesis.

According to the hypothesis stated, the personalized production is based on the principle of advanced forecasting of future needs. Identification of of needs for a certain type of product and assessment of the manufacturer's prospects for obtaining a share of this market is carried out in accordance with the following algorithm, presented in Figure 2.11.

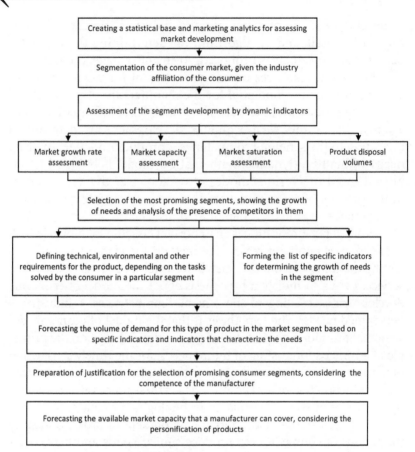

Figure 2.11. Algorithm for identifying the needs for personalized products

The effective implementation of the proposed algorithm is possible on the platform of a digital enterprise due to the operation of various information systems that, based on big data analytics, are able to build effective economic, technical and technological processes of the life cycle of a personified product.

Digital transformation of production contributes to the development of new strategic approaches to the implementation of technologies, building competencies and launching products. The advanced paradigm of digital design and modeling is based on the use of complex multidisciplinary mathematical models with a high level of adequacy to real materials, structures and physical and mechanical processes (including technological and production) described by equations of mathematical physics, primarily 3D non-stationary nonlinear differential equations in particular derivatives. Such mathematical or «smart» models aggregate big data that is used in the design and personalized production:

1) fundamental laws and sciences (mathematical physics, theory of vibrations, elasticity, plasticity, etc., fracture mechanics, mechanics of composite materials and composite structures, contact interaction, dynamics and strength of machines, computational mechanics, hydro-aerodynamics, heat and mass transfer, electromagnetism, acoustics, technological mechanics, etc.);

2) geometric and computational finite element full-scale models of real objects and physical and mechanical processes;

3) complete data on the materials from which the product is made, including data on the behavior of materials when exposed to thermal, electromagnetic and other fields;

4) information on operating modes (normal operating conditions, violations of normal operating conditions, emergency situations, etc.), including information that ensures the specified behavior of the structure in certain situations (the so-called programmed behavior);

5) data on the production and assembly technologies of both individual elements and structures as a whole;

6) other characteristics and parameters.

Trends in the development of the digital economy and high-tech industries make urgent the need to take into account personalized requirements when creating promising products through the convergent use of knowledge from the global information space and breakthrough academic and scientific developments. Over the years, large companies have accumulated and continue to accumulate information about user requests, on the basis of which they form consumer profiles. Knowing potential needs allows companies to form new consumer niches, create competitive products and services, and organize the effective implementation of both their services and those of their customers. In this way, the coherence of information about groups of potential consumers is achieved, which can be posted on various digital platforms.

Information becomes a new strategic resource, which can be obtained both through building new knowledge inside a company, and through receiving data from the external environment, including from the global information space. This resource becomes the main one in the process of identifying and personalizing the needs of the market or its individual segments.

In this regard, information resources, as well as all other resources, must be managed in order to obtain the maximum possible amount of data for the analysis and personalization of needs, as well as assess the scientific and technical potential of an enterprise and the industry from the standpoint of its sufficiency to meet emerging needs. The impact of information resources on production processes and the creation of consumer value is shown in Figure 2.12, which illustrates the chain of «competencies → industry → personalized needs».

Information management today will allow reaching a fundamentally new level of economic management. We are talking about

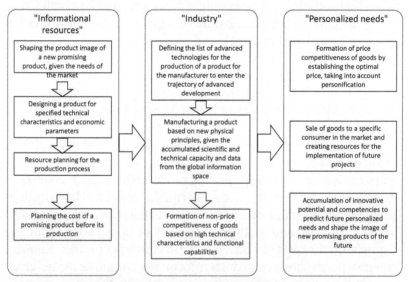

Figure 2.12. Economic development by the chain «competencies → industry → personalized needs»

creating not only new products and services for the needs of a particular consumer, but also conditions in society for a more complete self-fulfillment of a person. This thesis is confirmed by the fact that over the past two decades in developed and rapidly developing countries, there has been a significant modernization of the management infrastructure linked with favorable conditions for ensuring information development and the changing needs of the world economy in favor of cognitive management competencies and optimization of information and management relations between state, interstate structures and international companies.

Information technologies and the space are rapidly developing due to large investments in the development and application of digital technologies in all areas of activity. This contributes to the development of information and computing management services created through the application of strategic qualitatively new management competencies. It is necessary to emphasize the concept of «digital convergence», which refers to the process of interpenetration and fusion of digital technology and digital data transmission systems based on the primary digitization of heterogeneous information messages. Thanks to digital convergence, the costs of processing and delivering information are reduced, while increasing and improving the functionality of the complex of information and telecommunications systems and networks. Digital convergence contributes to the generation of new needs, a more complex interweaving of global networks and global production interactions.

According to our research, it is currently possible to predict future needs that will inevitably appear in the context of a rapid change in technological orders and global digitalization. Such needs are primarily related to the creation of information and analytical services that aggregate heterogeneous information and provide ready-made solutions to the consumer. Thus, information should not only be provided, it must be collected, systematized and structured in such a way as to bring value to its consumer at the moment.

However, it should be noted that through the evolution of the economic system and its transformation into a digital ecosystem, the volume of material production in physical terms does not decrease, but the characteristics of goods change significantly, which is linked with meeting the developing and emerging needs of society and organizations.

As a result of the ongoing transformation of the economic system, products acquire the properties of «smart» things that can be integrated into economic systems (smart homes, smart cities). The ongoing significant changes are observed at various levels of the world economy.

As a result of the cycle «growth of markets – contraction of markets» in the modern high-tech economy, a sufficient reserve of resources remains (accumulates) to providing preconditions for the emergence of a new cycle of market growth. High-quality development of innovative technologies provides rapid development of new consumer markets, while the development of consumer markets leads to a further increase in resource potential and the creation of innovative technologies. Thus, on the one hand, there is a spiraling mutual development of new technologies, the acquisition of new resources and stable economic development of the manufacturer, and on the other hand, new consumer markets and advanced development of the manufacturer are developed.

It is well known that new markets arise not only as a result of consumer demand for new types of goods, but also as a result of the supply of new products to consumers. In the industrial era, it took many years and decades from the emergence of new types of goods to the creation of sustainable consumer markets, and in the context of digital transformation, this period is very compressed – up to a few months.

Based on our research, we come to the conclusion that there is a pattern of the processes of creating personalized products, which determines their progressive and cyclical nature. Forward movement is related to the development of science, technology and technology. The cyclical movement is due to the fact that the dominance of products in the market provides a manufacturer with increasing resources and, improving their technical and technological capabilities, which is transformed into innovations and a new personalized product with high competitive properties that meet the new needs of society. In the next chapter, we will consider this issue in detail from the standpoint of proving the correctness of the deduced pattern.

CHAPTER 3.
THE LAW OF ADVANCED SATISFACTION OF PERSPECTIVE NEEDS

3.1. THE LAW OF ADVANCED SATISFACTION OF PROSPECTIVE NEEDS

It was determined above that the development of technologies and the creation of radical innovations is largely with cyclical fluctuations in the economy and their impact on innovative development; and periodically arising crises in some countries and the global economy fluctuate the effectiveness of scientific and technological progress as a deep and decisive reason.

These economic processes are due to the general principles formed in economic theory, in particular in the theory of managing competitiveness at various levels in the context of various macro- and microeconomic factors. Referring to the already formed aspects of this theory in the previously published books "Management of Competitiveness. Theory and Practice" and "The new Economy of the Product Life Cycle. Innovation and Design in the Digital Era"[10], given on the basis of the sequence of its development in Table 3.1, we will complete it with new stages that become relevant for study and further theoretical and methodological developments in view of modern transformations associated with the development of consumer society.

Table 3.1. Evolution of the theory of competitiveness management

Development of the basic provisions on competitiveness management:
– development of production and economic relations;
– the emergence of the concept of «competition»;
– development of world economic science in the field of competition;

---

[10] Chursin A. Makarov Yu. "Management of competitiveness. Theory and Practice" // Springer International Publishing.. – 2015. P378.; Tyulin A. Chursin A. "The new Economy of the Product Life Cycle. Innovation and Design in the Digital Era" / // Springer International Publishing. – 2020. P.400.

– the emergence of the theory of management of economic objects;
– the emergence of the concept of «competitiveness»;
– the emergence of the theory of competitiveness;
– formation of the main provisions for the management of competitiveness. General theoretical foundations of competitiveness management:
– economic laws;
– economic laws of market relations;
– theoretical laws of organization and management concerning the issues of competitiveness and the creation of competitive advantages, in statics and dynamics;
– laws and approaches to the management of competitiveness;
– theory of objects competitiveness management.
Conceptual foundations for the creation of the theory of the research direction « Competitiveness management»:
– the concept and definition of a competitiveness management system;
– goals and functions of competitiveness management;
– features of competitiveness management at the micro, meso and macro levels;
– assessment and ranking of factors of the external and internal environment from the standpoint of managing the competitiveness of the object;
– parameters, indicators of the competitiveness management system;
Methodological foundations of the theory of competitiveness management:
– methodology for the development and creation of systems for managing the competitiveness of products, organizations (business structures), industries;
– methods for assessing the competitiveness of products, organizations, industries;
– methods of creating competitive advantages;
– methodology for managing the factors influencing competitiveness and creating competitive advantages;
– methods of planning, organizing, receiving and processing information, protecting information, controlling and communicating in management;
– mutual influence and interfacing of various control systems.
Methodological foundations of the theory of competitiveness management:
– development of specific systems for managing the competitiveness of objects (algorithms, mathematical models, construction concepts);
– development of construction technology;
– development of technical tools used in the competitiveness management system;
– methodology and practice of using competitiveness management systems;

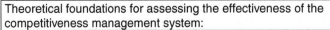

Theoretical foundations for assessing the effectiveness of the competitiveness management system:
– methodology for assessing the economic impact and application of competitiveness management systems;
– criteria for evaluating the effectiveness of the system;
– methods for analyzing the functioning of competitiveness management systems.
Development of the main provisions of the theory of advanced development management
– development of the theory of innovation management
– formation of the theory of competence management as a key resource of a company in the conditions of the knowledge economy functioning
– development and substantiation of an economic law on the relationship of competencies with the emergence of new markets
– development of the theory of life cycle management of an innovative project and finished innovative products on the market
– formation of the main provisions for the management of advanced development based on the economy of the product life cycle
– formation of the law of advanced development.
General theoretical foundations of advanced development management, given the characteristics of the economy of the product life cycle:
– the development of technologies and the needs of society in the context of a change in technological structures and deepening of informatization processes in all spheres of society
– development of fundamental science, ensuring the creation of products based on new physical and technical principles
– development of modern technologies of the digital economy
– formation of prerequisites for creating products of the future with high technical characteristics and high added value.
Methodological foundations of the theory of advanced development management:
– methodology for calculating the cost of the product life cycle
– methods of adaptive creation of promising products for the needs of the «future» based on big data analytics
– methods for assessing innovative capacity in the context of the rapid emergence of competing innovative solutions and the expansion of the global information space
– methods of creating competitive advantages
– methods for predicting the development of unique competencies to meet future needs and the organization of their transfer

– formation of models of resource support for the implementation of new promising projects of the future
– methods of digital design, modeling and product development. Mechanisms for managing the creation of a product of advanced development:
– mechanism for the formation of the idea of a product and its technical and economic image
– mechanism for the comprehensive assessment of resources required for product development
– mechanism for managing the development of the production and technological base
– cost optimization mechanism for product development, preproduction and production
– mechanism for assessing the economic efficiency of design and production processes
Fundamentals of advanced product Lifecycle management:
– production management system for the formed product image when designing for a given cost and competitiveness
– system of principles of preproduction based on new physical principles with high technical and economic characteristics
– intelligent automated control system for preproduction processes
– flexible automated production taking into account the advantages of digital technologies
– a digital platform for supporting the process of making effective management decisions in product lifecycle management.
Development of the main theoretical and methodological provisions of the management of advanced satisfaction of prospective needs:
– theoretical and practical foundations of a breakthrough scientific and technological development of a company and industry and intensive build-up of radical competencies within the framework of technological platforms and cross-industrial interaction
– methods of forming competitive advantages of unique products based on radical innovations
– law of anticipatory satisfaction of prospective needs
– the postulates of the theory of creating radically new products capable of creating new demand and leading to economic growth of the industry and the economy as a whole
– axiomatic foundations and postulates of the theory of advanced development and economic growth of a company

– strategic approaches and tools for managing the economic growth of a
company and industries based on the creation of radically new products

The evolution of the theoretical and methodological foundations of competitiveness management given in Table 3.1 is the basis
for the development of patterns and the wording of the law of advanced satisfaction of prospective needs given the rapid response
to dynamically changing consumer expectations in the long term.

The existing theoretical basis continues to develop amid
the emergence of new discoveries and transformations in technologies that change the idea of the laws of development of the world
economy, subject to globalization with elements of imperfect competition due to the hegemony of individual States.

Accelerating innovation processes in the economy is one
of the ways to overcome deep crises and transition to a new wave
of scientific and technological development. Production, management and other technologies, as well as the needs of society inevitably change in the context of dynamic processes of economic development, stimulating each other's development, i.e. new unique
technologies created in the process of innovative development
(sometimes being an accidental discovery) stimulate the emergence
of new needs, thereby generating demand, but at the same time,
the growing needs of society require the continuous development
of technologies and the creation of new products and services that
can satisfy them. A large number of works are devoted to the study
of the processes that determine the dominance of unique products
in the markets. The studies have shown[11],[12],[13],[14] that the creation
of highly competitive products is based on the processes of accumulation of innovative capacity by a manufacturer and building

[11] Batkovskiy, A. Regulation of the dynamics of creating high-tech products /
A. Batkovskiy, A. Leonov, A. Pronin, A. Chursin, E. Nesterov // International Journal
of Engineering & Technology. — 2018. — Vol. 7. — No 3.14. — P. 261–270. DOI:
10.14419/ijet.v7i3.14.16904
[12] Tyulin, A.E. Theory and Practice of Competence Management Determining the
Competitiveness of Integrated Structures / A.E. Tyulin. – M., 2015.
[13] Porter, M.E. On Competition: trasnl.. from English / M.E. Porter. – M., 2000 .– 331 p.
[14] Vyunova, R.R. Approaches to assessing the innovative potential of an enterprise /
R.R. Vyunova // Society: Politics, Economics, Law. – 2015. – No. 2. – P. 35–38.

key competencies that determine the creation of competitive advantages of products.. However, these works do not provide quantitative and qualitative estimates of the parameters of the complex process of creating unique products with radically high consumer properties. In order to establish the necessary conditions for creating unique products, we will conduct a study of the processes of achieving a dominant position in the market. We will investigate the processes of achieving a dominant position in the market by unique products, namely, the processes of creating competitive advantages for unique products, the processes of accumulating scientific and technological capacity and building key competencies of a manufacturer, as well as the processes of achieving dominance in the market under conditions of imperfect competition.

The first step towards achieving a dominant position in the market for products is the creation of radical innovations based on the accumulated scientific and technological capacity and key competencies of a manufacturer. Further, radical innovations are transformed into the competitive advantages of unique products through the use of various economic instruments, technical and technological solutions, which are the result of the scientific and technological development of a manufacturer. In order to quantify the parameters of scientific and technological development, let us consider in detail the process of breakthrough scientific and technological development of a company and the intensive build-up of its key competencies.

The scientific and technological capacity of a company is a combination of various types of resources and factors, including production and technological, financial and economic, intellectual, research and other resources necessary for the implementation of innovative activities. Each component of the scientific and technological capacity is based on a certain set of knowledge, which is transformed into the competence of a company and its teams. In practice, some components of the scientific and technological capacity may reach a high level, while others may remain at a lower level. Areas with insufficient scientific and technological capacity require the formation and development of new competencies.

The assessment of scientific and technological capacity can be built on the basis of the following system of criteria (see Table 3.2).

The integral assessment (index) of scientific and technological capacity is a weighted sum of evaluation criteria:

$$IP_{R\&D} = \sum_{i=1}^{N} w_i y_i,$$

$$\sum_{i=1}^{N} w_i = 1.$$

where N is the number of considered components of scientific and technological capacity, w is the coefficient of importance of each of the components.

Similar estimates can also be obtained for other components of the scientific and technological capacity. In accordance with the calculated indices, each component of the scientific and technological capacity is given a category:

- «High» level of the component of the innovative capacity, indicating the presence of radical innovations, with the value of the corresponding integral index (0.75; 1];
- "Average" level of the innovation capacity component with the value of the corresponding integral index (0.45; 0.75];
- «Low» level of the innovation capacity component with the value of the corresponding integral index [0; 0.45].

The high level of scientific and technological capacity demonstrates to a company's ability to create unique products.

The management of each component of the innovation capacity is related to the development of relevant competencies due to the resource costs directed at this process. A company seeking to dominate the market must launch a self-replicating process of improving competencies and increasing resource efficiency. If such a competence is difficult to reproduce for competitors, it can be recognized as a radical key one.

The process of forming key competencies and the development of radical innovative technologies on their basis requires significant

Table 3.2. Criteria for assessing the scientific and technological capacity of a company

№	Criterion		Criterion value
1	Intellectual property management	y_1	the ratio of registered in a company IPO (object of intellectual property) to the total number
		$y_2 = \dfrac{J'}{J}$	J' the number of IPOs introduced in the production and technological process; J – the total number of IPOs in a company
		$y_3 = \dfrac{\sum_{i=1}^{N} C_i + \sum_{j=1}^{K} C_j}{\sum_{r=1}^{R} C_r - \sum_{q=1}^{Q} C_q}$	N – the number of innovative solutions developed without the involvement of third-party organizations; K – the number of acquired innovative solutions; R – $N + K$; Q – the number of innovative solutions not implemented in the company's activities, but implemented outside of it; C_j – the cost of acquiring the j-th innovative solution; C_r – Development and acquisition costs of the total number of innovative solutions; C_q – income from the implementation of the q-th innovative solution.
2	Intellectual property security ratio	$y_4 = C_t/A_{na}$	C_t – IPO total funds; A_{na} – Other noncurrent assets
3	Scientific research	y_5	share of contracts of an industrial company with organizations of the scientific and technical complex from their total number
		y_6	share of experimental productions in the company related to innovations
4	R&D costs	$y_7 = N_{R\&D}/N$	The ratio of the income of the staff engaged in $R\&D$ to the income of the other employees of the company
		$y_8 = N_{R\&D}/Q$	$R\&D$ cost to total sales ratio

5	Cost on innovations not included in R&D	$y_9 = N_{nonR\&D}/Q$	The ratio of innovation costs to total company sales
6	R&D personnel ratio	$y_{10} = S_{R\&D}/N_e$	$S_{R\&D}$ – amount of staff engaged in $R\&D$, people; N_e – average number of company employees, people.
7	Ratio of property intended for R&D	$y_{11} = O_{om}/O_{nh}$ $y_{11} = C_{EQ}/C_E$	C_{EQ} – cost of experimental equipment, rub; C_E – cost of equipment
8	The level of development of new science-intensive technologies	y_{12}	The share of new industrial technologies developed in a company of the total number of implemented technologies
9	Innovative business development programs	y_{13}	= 0.25, if only short-term plans are developed in accordance with current market opportunities, the company does not have a consistent innovation program; = 0.5 if the company is developing an annual plan in accordance with the current situation; but the company does not have enough resources to develop innovative programs; = 0.75, if the company develops plans for 2-3 years, innovative programs are adopted if the company is forced to do so due to market competition; = 1, if the business plan is based on the implementation of innovations as inseparable conditions for achieving the company's goals.

№	Criterion	Criterion value
10	The emergence of innovation	y_{14}	= 0, if the monitoring of new ideas is not carried out, since the company does not need it; = 0.5 if the company does not block employee initiatives in this area; innovation is introduced if it is potentially beneficial for the company; = 0.75, if the company regularly collects and evaluates new ideas, they serve as a source of product and / or process innovations; in parallel, an analysis of the costs and risks associated with innovation is carried out; = 1 if company leaders are constantly working towards identifying opportunities for using new ideas, both from their own employees and from external sources; systems of motivation and assessment of a creative approach to work have been created; when introducing new ideas, a feasibility study is carried out

resource costs. In conditions of high financial costs for radical innovations, special attention is given to the issue of efficient use of all types of resources.

The effectiveness of the competencies formed and the radical innovations developed on their basis should be assessed in terms of the technical and cost characteristics of products achieved through their use. At the early stages of shaping the technical and economic image of promising products, the most effective way to build such an assessment is to use the methods of economic and mathematical modeling.

The formula for calculating the assessment of the EK key competence index is as follows:

$$EK = \sum_{i=1}^{N} \left(w_i \cdot M_i \cdot l_i \right),$$

where N is the number of characteristics that describe the key competence (for example, the availability of a professional competent team with a powerful research and development sector and a modern production base; functional environment in which a team conducts research and production activities; the degree of maturity of technologies developed through the competence in question; ability to spread key competence to other industries; availability of competing entities – carriers of similar key competencies; subject to availability of competitors – advantages or disadvantages compared to them; availability of a scientific school leading research related to key competencies; availability of licenses, certificates, awards (primarily those with international recognition); the prospect of maintaining key competencies in the medium and long term);

w_i are weight coefficients satisfying the ratio $\sum_{i=1}^{N} w_i = 1$, the values of the weight coefficients characterize the relative contribution made by the corresponding parameters of key competencies to the overall assessment of the EK;

l_i is the estimate of the corresponding attribute on the scale l: $0 \leq l_i \leq 1$;

Mi is the ratio of stability of a feature and expresses the degree of threat of elimination for a given feature of the considered competence from a set of key competencies: $0 \leq Mi \leq 1$, in this sense, the stability ratio depends on the level of risk connected with a possible decrease in the assessment of a feature.

The EK estimate of the key competence level accepts values from the interval [0; one]. If this indicator accepts a value close to one, then we can talk about having a unique scientific and technological solution. This solution becomes the most promising when creating unique products.

The process of forming competitive advantages of unique products based on radical innovations

An enterprise-developer of unique products faces an important challenge – to determine the consumer properties of unique products at the stage of forming of its technical and economic image, the competitive characteristics of which will provide it with a dominant position in the market, that is, to create such a techno-economic image of the product, which will acquire all the competitive advantages laid at the stage of forming the image.

The complexity of creating a technical and economic image with high competitive advantages is that it takes a long period of time from the moment of its formation to the moment of production of finished goods and their launch on the market, during which the market has new product with new characteristics, new competitors, new scientific discoveries are made, technologies are developing and the needs of society and the State are increasing. All this reduces the competitiveness of a product's image over time, if it is not constantly improved by refining it given the advanced achievements of science and technology, newly acquired or developed competencies.

An important task in this context is the conduct of the initial study and further continuous monitoring of the situation in the development of science, technology, market conditions through available data from the global information space using modern information methods and technologies for collecting, processing and analyzing heterogeneous data for the timely adoption of operational solutions to improve the techno-economic image of a product to ensure the demand for future products on the market.

In order to create high competitive advantages, techno-economic image of the product is changed and refined during all stages of the project life cycle. Both technical and economic parameters are improved, so that the product created in accordance with the developed image could have superiority compared to analogues and could take a dominant position in the market in the future.

Thus, the main difficulty in achieving competitive advantages in forming the techno-economic image of a product is to predict the technical and economic characteristics, so that it is able to generate significant competitive advantages that can ensure a dominant position in the market.

When designing unique products, it is necessary to focus not only and not quite on the existing requirements for the products, but on the requirements that will be in demand in the future.

The above conclusions, as well as the results of other studies[15,16,17,18,19] of the theoretical foundations of creating highly competitive products, allowed us to formulate the economic law of advanced satisfaction of promising needs and prove it. Consider the process of market formation for unique products (Fig. 3.1).

The pie chart (Figure 3.1) shows that the creation of unique products and ensuring their dominance in the market leads to accumulation of significant resources due to large sales volumes of such products, which should be aimed at maintaining the competitive advantages of unique products to increase their presence time on the market. On the other hand, given the dynamics of society's

---

[15] Tyulin, A., Chursin, A.: Fundamentals of management of innovation processes in knowledge intensive industries (practice), Moscow (2016)

[16] Tyulin, A.: Theory and practice of creating and managing competences to enhance the competitiveness of integrated structures, 312 p. Moscow (2015)

[17] Chursin, A., Tyulin A.: Competence Management and Competitive Product Development (2018)

[18] Tyulin, A., Chursin, A., Yudin, A., Grosheva P. Theoretical foundations of the law of managing for advanced development of the organization // Mikroeconomika. 2019. № 1. p. 5-12.

[19] Tyulin, A., Chursin, A., Yudin, A. Production capacity optimization in cases of a new business line launching in a company //Espacios, 2017.

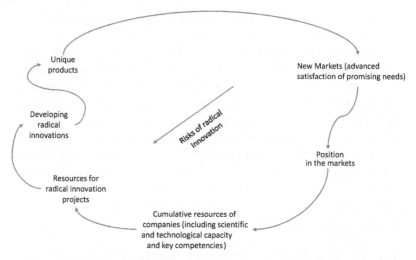

Figure 3.1. Creating unique products as a result of meeting future needs

needs as a result of the impact of new competencies and transformations in technology, it is necessary to direct resources to the process of creating new unique products.

This model can be represented as a general law of advanced satisfaction of prospective needs:

Radical innovations are created as a result of a breakthrough scientific and technological development of a manufacturer and an intensive build-up of its key competencies. The acceleration of the development and sale cycles of unique products is ensured, stimulating the emergence of needs and creating a market in which a manufacturer becomes a temporary monopolist and moves into a state of advanced development, ensuring its global competitiveness due to the permanent (constant, continuing in time) spiral process of "need – competence – resources – products – new markets – needs".

To describe these processes, it is necessary to use various mathematical approaches in dynamical systems. To do this, consider the formalization of the proposed scheme.

Our proposed economic model can be described using several dynamic parameters that will change over time. The most important condition for the development of these parameters is their constant mutual dependence. Let us describe the main economic parameters that will be considered in the model of linking the level of key competencies and the creation of consumer markets, while it should be noted that each subsequent parameter is closely interconnected with the previous one. We will consider the following parameters:

- the level of key competencies (describes the achieved level of technological, organizational, managerial and other competencies that can be used by knowledge-based industries to develop unique products);
- the level of scientific and technological capacity (describes the various components of the innovation capacity);
- consumer utility of unique products (reflects the degree of compliance with prospective needs and the possibility of market dominance);
- the level of development of markets (describes the creation and development of markets as a result of the proposal for unique products or their new consumer qualities).

To build a mathematical model, it is necessary to formalize the basic concepts. It should be noted that we will consider constant processes with continuous time $t \in [0,T], 0 < T < \infty$.

The dynamic model of the proposed law is based on the following variables:

EK(t) – quantitative assessment of the level of key competencies;

IP(t) – quantitative index of scientific and technological capacity;

$\gamma(t)$ – quantitative index of consumer utility of unique products;

q(t) – the share of products in the market (reflects the relationship between the innovation potential and the possibility of producing goods that dominate the market). EK(t), IP(t), $\gamma(t)$ and q(t).

Consider the following formal system of differential equations:

$$
\begin{cases}
\dot{EK}(t) = F_1(EK(t), IP(t), \gamma(t), q(t)), \\
\dot{IP}(t) = F_2(EK(t), IP(t), \gamma(t), q(t)), \\
\dot{\gamma}(t) = F_3(EK(t), IP(t), \gamma(t), q(t)), \\
\dot{q}(t) = F_4(EK(t), IP(t), \gamma(t), q(t))
\end{cases}
$$

The numerical values of the functions EK(t), IP(t), and q(t) represent the values of integral indicators to describe the level of key competencies, the state of scientific and technological capacity, the consumer utility of unique products and their market share. The dynamics of the indices we are considering can be described using a linear model:

$$
\begin{cases}
\dot{EK}(t) = A_{EK}EK(t) + A_{q,EK}q(t), \\
\dot{IP}(t) = A_{IP}IP(t) + A_{EK,IP}EK(t), \\
\dot{\gamma}(t) = A_{\gamma}\gamma(t) + A_{IP,\gamma}IP(t), \\
\dot{q}(t) = A_{q}q(t) + A_{\gamma,q}\gamma(t),
\end{cases}
$$

where A are some coefficients to be determined based on the statistics of the described process.

Here we consider a system of linear differential equations in which each dynamic variable has a certain diffusion coefficient, which reflects an objective decrease in all indicators over time in the absence of additional control.

However, in the proposed model, we use a cyclical relationship between these indices, which consists in the fact that each subsequent index increases under the influence of the previous index, and the last index is the share of products on the market, which affects the initial index of the level of competence through the resources allocated to increase the level of competence.

The proposed linear dynamic system for describing the relationship between the level of scientific and technological capacity and key competencies with the creation of unique products and a new market formation for unique products by a manufacturer and the transition to a state of advanced development can describe only the period of increasing these values, so to reflect the cyclical phenomena in the development of the level of competencies and consumer markets, it is necessary to consider nonlinear dynamic models.

Cyclical phenomena, which have two distinct stages: the growth stage and the decline stage, can be described by the following hysteresis-type function:

$$H[Y(t)] = \begin{cases} H_{min}, & Y(t) > T_{max} \\ H_{max}, & Y(t) > T_{min} \end{cases}.$$

To describe the interdependence of the level of competence and the consumer market, we will use the following dynamic model:

$$\begin{cases} \dot{EK}(t) = A_{EK}EK(t) + H_{EK}[EK(t)]A_{q,EK}q(t), \\ \dot{IP}(t) = A_{IP}IP(t) + H_{IP}[IP(t)]A_{EK,IP}EK(t), \\ \dot{\gamma}(t) = A_{\gamma}\gamma(t) + H_{\gamma}[\gamma(t)]A_{IP,\gamma}IP(t), \\ \dot{q}(t) = A_{q}q(t) + H_{q}[q(t)]A_{\gamma,q}\gamma(t). \end{cases}$$

The proposed model describes only the qualitative dynamics of values about the relationship between the level of scientific and technological capacity and key competencies with the development of new needs and product markets that satisfy them. For the quantitative analysis of specific situations, it is necessary to use accurate statistical data, through which it is possible to estimate the indices included in the dynamic equations. The proposed wording reflects the progressive-cyclical nature of achieving market dominance in the form of a spiral pattern, each turn of which is described by a circular process (Fig. 1). Progressive movement in a spiral is connected with the development of science and technology, and the cyclical movement is due to the fact that the dominance of products in the market provides a manufacturer with an increase in resources and, consequently, an increase in their technical and technological capabilities. The transition time from one phase of the circular cycle to another depends on the intensity of the processes of creating unique products and their launch on the market. That is, this time is proportional to the parameters obtained above, describing quantitative assessments of scientific and technological capacity (IPR&D), the level of competencies (EK), as well as the competitiveness of the created unique products (Q). The higher the value of these parameters, the faster the cyclic process of creating unique products moves from one phase to another.

Thus, the organizational and economic challenge of creating unique products is to build a management system for creating unique products in such a way as to ensure the design and development of products considering the concept of advanced development of a company, expressed in its long-term dominance in certain markets. The problem solution should be should be underpinned on the following postulate, which will provide a theoretical basis for creating unique products.

Postulate 1.

Forecasting the dynamics of technological and economic needs based on monitoring the global information space provides acceleration of the processes of creating unique products that occupy a certain market niche, replacing previously presented products.

Postulate 2.

Flexible planning of the trajectory of advanced development of a manufacturer, based on unique achievements in technology and technology, allows to make effective decisions to shape the image of unique products at the pre-investment stage focused on meeting future needs.

Postulate 3.

Long-term competitiveness and domination of products in the future is ensured by the timely modernization of the image of unique products based on continuous monitoring of the global information space, which allows making the necessary decisions in a timely manner to match the technical and economic characteristics of products to current consumer demand, enabling a manufacturer to maintain a state of advanced development.

Postulate 4.

Development of unique products is carried out under conditions of risk of loss of economic stability of a company and the position already occupied in the market, which is related to an insufficient preliminary analysis of the feasibility of innovative projects and the high cost of resources for investment and innovation activities.

The practical implementation of the above-formulated law of advanced satisfaction of prospective needs and the above postulates in relation to the problem of developing unique products that ensure the dominance of the developer in the market will be described below within the confines of the description of the axiomatic foundations of the theory of advanced development and economic growth of a company, as well as the development of strategic approaches and tools for managing economic growth through the creation of radically new products.

3.2 AXIOMATIC FOUNDATIONS OF THE THEORY OF ADVANCED DEVELOPMENT AND ECONOMIC GROWTH OF A COMPANY

To meet the challenge of building strategic approaches and tools for managing a company's economic growth, we will use the axiomatic method, which is one of the main directions of development of modern economic science. The algorithm for the formation of axioms (postulates) is as follows: first, a number of objects are selected that are considered basic and conventionally understandable. After selecting the main objects, the system of axioms is established. Their definitions are not provided, but the rest of the objects of the theory are built on their basis, i.e. the initial and accepted assumptions without proof, through which it is possible to build the theoretical and methodological foundations of the scientific theory under consideration.

Thus, the introduction of the axiomatic method into economic theory is based on such fundamental properties as: validity, scientific nature, objectivity, the impossibility of replacing it with any other method, universality. This latter quality implies that it has such characteristics that allow it to be applied in a number of sciences, both natural and humanitarian. The universality of this method is based on the fact that its development reflects the establishment of human cognition in general. The axiomatic method is an essential part of the general scientific methodology of cognition. This reveals the need for its use in economic theory. The need for its application in this science is also justified its reliability and approbation, by its high efficiency when applied in mathematics and other sciences.

We will describe the process of advanced development of the company on the based on the axiomatic approach. This approach makes it possible to formulate the main provisions (postulates) of the theory of a company's economic growth based on the creation of unique products focused on meeting future needs and ensuring the economic growth of a manufacturer.

The postulates formulated below are based on our research showing that radical innovations usually do not originate independently, but this process is associated with global scientific and technological development, and also depends on certain economic and political conditions. The speed of market entry of unique products created through breakthrough solutions is determined by the efficiency of management of the development and implementation of the results of innovative activities in production. This management efficiency depends on the methods and tools used by a company or a State, depending on the current economic situation and the selected development priorities. It should be emphasized that the management of the creation and implementation of innovations that provide competitive advantages involves the attracting a significant number of different resources, and therefore it is necessary to assess in what conditions and for what purposes and with what efficiency these resources will be attracted. In our opinion, the attraction of significant resources for the development of breakthrough solutions to create new products, a significant increase in the competitiveness of goods in the markets and the provision of economic growth of a company should be carried out upon receipt of the first signals from the global information space, as well as from various competitiveness management systems about the emergence of any kind of risks related to the loss of markets or financial and economic instability of the company, industries, countries and the world economy as a whole. Such signals begin to appear amid the emergence of new competitors in the markets, signs of an impending crisis, or other negative phenomena arising in the economy. Timely addressing of such weak signals allows adjusting the image of a unique product or the planned trajectory of its market launch.

A distinctive feature of the proposed approach to the formulation of postulates is the use of mathematical models that describe the processes of creating unique products in dynamics and the impact of management on the development indicators of a company that creates a unique product.

Postulate 1. Forecasting the dynamics of technological and economic needs based on monitoring the global information space provides acceleration of the processes of creating unique products that occupy a certain market niche, replacing previously presented products.

Society and its needs are undergoing a continuous transformation. Today, such a transformation is associated with the increasing presence of digital technologies in various spheres of society and human life. This is due to the progress in the areas of microelectronics, information technology and telecommunications. The forecast of a promising technological and economic outline for the product under consideration in the consumer market is a fundamental point to successfully develop products of the future. That is, at each stage of the product life cycle, it is necessary to make forecasts based on existing information. In modern conditions, the development of unique products is based on a digital twin of a product, which is developed based on multivariate modeling. Therefore, the analysis of the digital twin of a product is the most important source of information for predicting the position of a unique product in consumer markets. On the other hand, when developing products of the future, it is also necessary to use external information, with which it is possible to get a vision of the compliance of the developed product with the realities of the market and consumer expectations.

The mathematical description of this postulate is as follows. The competitiveness index of the created unique products is the numerical function of time, the value of which reflects the competitiveness in a certain area. Vector indicators of competitiveness are traditionally used to describe the competitiveness of products.

Thus, a separate index of competitiveness is expressed by the following positive function $q_i : R \to R_+$. Therefore, when assessing the competitiveness of the created unique products, we will base on a comprehensive assessment of the competitiveness of products. Thus, the competitiveness of the products under consideration is expressed by the vector of competitiveness indicators:

$$Q(t) = \begin{pmatrix} q_1(t) \\ q_2(t) \\ \vdots \\ q_N(t) \end{pmatrix}$$

When addressing the competitiveness of unique products, it is always necessary to consider the dynamic indicators of competitiveness, since products generally tend to become out of date due to constant scientific and technological development and competition. According to the general principles of managing the competitiveness of knowledge-based industries, the decline in competitiveness indicators is proportional to the current value of the competitiveness indicator. Consequently, the dynamics of competitiveness indicators without regard to external factors can be represented as a system of linear differential equations:

$$\frac{dQ}{dt}(t) = A(t)Q(t)$$

This dynamic system describes the process of natural decline of competitiveness in the absence of control actions, the decision about which is related to the analysis of data from the global information space. These external factors can affect the indicators of competitiveness both positively and negatively. Let us denote these factors arising from the analysis of the information space by the following vector:

$$F(t) = \begin{pmatrix} f_1(t) \\ f_2(t) \\ \vdots \\ f_M(t) \end{pmatrix}$$

Here we are considering M different factors. Here the number of factors and indicators of competitiveness can be different, since each factor can affect many indicators of competitiveness. To do this, we will consider the matrix of the relationship of the impact of factors. This matrix will be denoted by:

$$B(t) = \begin{pmatrix} b_{11}(t) & \cdots & b_{1M}(t) \\ \vdots & \ddots & \vdots \\ b_{N1}(t) & \cdots & b_{NM}(t) \end{pmatrix}$$

Taking into account environmental factors affecting the dynamics of competitiveness indicators, the dynamic equation is as follows:

$$\frac{dQ}{dt}(t) = A(t)Q(t) + B(t)F(t)$$

This equation can have different qualitative behavior, while the values of the indicators of competitiveness are not required to approach zero.

Environmental factors, which can be taken into account based on the results of the analysis of the global information space, can have a significant impact on the competitiveness of the unique products created.

Let us consider the characteristic features of the factors affecting the competitiveness of the created unique products. Within the framework of the economic and mathematical model, these factors will be represented in two ways.

Firstly, these factors can be considered as terms that are functions of time. These are short-term factors that directly affect competitiveness indicators. Examples of such factors can be information about the actions of competitors to create similar products. At the same time, there is a big competition, which naturally affects the competitiveness of the products created. Based on the information received, timely management decisions can be made that increase the competitiveness of unique products at the time of their introduction to the market.

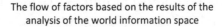

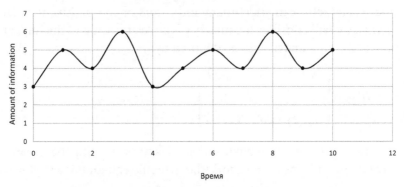

Figure 3.2. Information flow on forecasting technological and economic needs

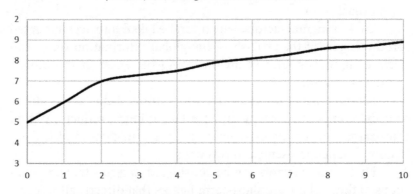

Figure 3.3. The possibility of achieving a high level of competitiveness considering the global information space factors

Secondly, the factors that influence the competitiveness of the unique products created as a result of the analysis of the global information space will be taken into account in the economic and mathematical model in the form of structural changes in this model. We are speaking of such results of the analysis of the world information space that will affect the scientific and production system of an enterprise. An illustration of the proposed dynamic approach is shown in Figure 3.2 and Figure 3.3.

Forecasting future technological and economic needs in the market is a difficult task, but the proposed concept assumes that the mechanisms of digital modeling should be fully used not only for the products of the future, but also for the construction of an analogue of a digital twin for the markets under consideration.

The digital market model is an imitation model of the behavior of consumers and other product developers, which is formed around the considered digital twin of a unique product.

Based on the digital market model, you can analyze various options for digital twins of unique products in order to predict the behavior of products in the markets aimed at the creation of proactive solutions in the field of product design for future needs.

For economic and mathematical modeling of the market, various approaches can be used for simulation modeling. Another method for implementing the digital twin of the product market is a game-theoretic approach for playing out possible scenarios of the behavior of the digital twin of the market.

Postulate 2. Flexible planning of the trajectory of advanced development of a manufacturer, based on unique achievements in technology and technology, allows to make effective decisions to shape the image of unique products at the pre-investment stage focused on meeting future needs

According to postulate 1, the fundamental point in creating unique products is to predict the development of the scientific and technological capacity of competitors and their products, as well as the possible scientific and technological capacity based on the achievements of fundamental science. As a rule, when forecasting, the so-called planning horizon is established, which reflects the possible depth of the forecast. The use of information technologies for creating digital twins and analytics of large amounts of information in predicting the outline of unique products can significantly expand the capabilities of this forecast. To do this, it is necessary to use a flexible planning horizon, which will be determined by the capacity of information technologies to describe the digital twins of markets, as well as the amount of information in the global information space associated with the actions of competitors to develop their own unique products.

To implement a flexible planning horizon, it is proposed to use a cascade-based forecasting method using digital twins. The cascade-based forecasting method allows expanding the planning horizons based on existing forecasts. With this approach, the original techno-economic image of a unique product is only the initial stage for predicting the outline of a product with high consumer properties. After receiving the first forecasts of the dynamics of consumer expectations, the techno-economic image of a unique product is built, a new version of its digital twin appears and changes, given the forecasted factors affecting the appearance of the product, then the new version of the digital twin can be reused to build a new forecast of the dynamics of consumer expectations. The result is an advanced projection of the outline of unique products, which can be supplemented by taking into account market factors and risks (see postulate 4).

Postulate 3. Long-term competitiveness and domination of products in the future is ensured by the timely modernization of the image of unique products based on continuous monitoring of the global information space, which allows making the necessary decisions in a timely manner to match the technical and economic characteristics of products to current consumer demand, enabling a manufacturer to maintain a state of advanced development.

To ensure the advanced development of a company, it is necessary not only to design and create unique products, but also to constantly manage its competitiveness. To do this, a developer must constantly upgrade their own products according to changes in consumer desires and market conditions. When forecasting, the digital model of a product and its techno-economic image are improved in order to better match the consumer characteristics of products to future market demands. In some cases, predictive values about market parameters can be used to create next generations of products, which should better meet the forecasted market demands. Such recommendations and requirements for new versions of products can be generated automatically using intelligent control systems for creating unique products. For this purpose, it can be suggested to use automatic expert systems that will be based on the knowledge bases obtained from the digital counterparts of the products of digital market models.

Postulate 4. Development of unique products is carried out under conditions of risk of loss of economic stability of a company and the position already occupied in the market, which is related to an insufficient preliminary analysis of the feasibility of innovative projects and the high cost of resources for investment and innovation activities.

There are many examples of high-tech companies (Motorola, Ericsson, etc.) that have invested heavily in the development of new unique products which have failed to achieve market dominance. Moreover, traditional markets for these companies have been lost. The developed unique products can be presented on the market only after their production, therefore, it is necessary to create fundamentally new production facilities to develop new products or modernize existing ones. The head of a company should determine which direction to follow based on the company's competence, financial resources, delivery terms of products or market entry, given the possible risks, including the risk that competitors may be ahead of schedule and bring to the market similar products with higher technical characteristics.

Let us further consider mathematical models that are a qualitative illustration of the proposed axioms (postulates) of management of advanced satisfaction of prospective needs, designed to demonstrate the proposed ideas. On the other hand, mathematical models provide a more rigorous approach to managing advanced satisfaction of long-term needs.

To describe the process of advanced satisfaction of prospective needs due to unique products dominating the market, we will consider the conditions of imperfect competition that are relevant to the conditions of real markets. The main characteristic of the proposed model is the use of forecasting prospective consumer expectations, sales volumes and market efficiency of promising products, which will largely outstrip the sufficiency of a company's existing scientific and technological capacity.

Products with high consumer properties are characterized by the emergence of oligopolistic product markets. In such markets, the products of several (usually no more than 10) manufacturers are sold. The barriers to entering such a market are high, since the products have strong technical and economic characteristics, which are formed due to the significant scientific and technological capacity of the company developing such products. Every company operating in such a market follows its chosen strategy of competitive behavior.

The market of imperfect competition, where unique products can be presented, will be described by the following parameters at a fixed point in time:

A_n – demand for unique products;

C_n – market capacity of unique products;

P_n – growth potential of the market for unique products.

The units of measure for A_n are financial units. The product market capacity C_n describes the maximum possible expansion of the market in the future, units of measurement describe financial units. The growth potential of the market volume for product P_n describes a possible increase in the market volume depending on the current market size. Strictly mathematically this parameter is a random variable and percentages are used as units of measurement.

The dynamics of demand for unique products can be described using the following model. At the initial moment, for each buyer/consumer, the model parameters will be considered as set. At the subsequent point in time, these parameters are recalculated taking into account changes in external parameters, which primarily include the weighted average price of the products sold, which we will denote as follows:

$$R_t, t = 1, 2...$$

where t is the symbol of the time interval in which the customer parameters change.

So, at each moment of time, there is a change in the parameters of buyers of products according to the following rule:

$$A^{t+1} = A^t + f(C^t, R^t),$$
$$C^{t+1} = C^t - g(A^{t+1}) + C^t P^t,$$
$$P^{t+1} = h(P^t, R^t),$$

where f, g, h are some functions. The specific type of these functions can be selected taking into account the specifics of the group of potential consumers and the emerging conjuncture of market segments. In general, these functions may be as follows:

$$f(C^t, R^t) = k_1 \cdot \sqrt{C^t} \cdot \frac{k_2}{1 + k_3 R^t},$$

$$g(A^{t+1}) = k_4 \cdot \sqrt{A^{t+1}},$$

$$h(P^t, R^t) = P^t - k_5 \sqrt{R^t}$$

where k_1, k_2, k_3, k_4, k_5 are some positive coefficients.

To perform calculations based on this mathematical model, it is necessary to perform sequential calculations taking into account the forecast of the cost of unique products.

The proposed model allows us to quantify and predict the volume of new markets for unique products with high competitive advantages and popular consumer specifications.

The criterion for determining market dominance may differ in markets in different countries. For example, in Japan (one of the world leaders in the high-tech products market), the dominance threshold is legally set at 50% of the market volume.

The need to achieve a dominant position in the market created by unique products requires proactive forecasting of the compliance of its technical and economic characteristics with promising consumer expectations. We will describe this process taking into account the above postulates of creating a unique product to ensure its dominance in the market, as well as the well-known method of dynamic calculations, called «predictor-corrector». We will describe this process taking into account the above postulates of creating a unique product to ensure its dominance in the market, as well as the well-known method of dynamic calculations, called «predictor-corrector».

Forecasting the compliance of the technical and economic characteristics of unique products with promising consumer expectations will be carried out in dynamics at various successive points in time:

$t0 < t1 < ... < tT,$

where T is the total number of time steps. At each time step, we will consider the state of competitive advantages of a unique product, which we will describe by a vector:

$Q(t) = (q1(t), q2(t),..., qN(t)),$

where N is the number of components of the vector Q(t). For simplicity, we will assume that qn(t) $\geq$ 0, n = 1, 2, ..., N.

Besides the real object – a projected unique product, according to postulate 1, we will consider consumer expectations regarding the created unique product:

$S(t) = (s1(t), s2(t),..., sN(t)).$

Unlike the vector Q (t), which we know only at the current moment of time, the vectors S (t) dynamically change over time.

At each moment of time tk we make a forecast step:

$[Q](tk) = P(Q(tk-1), S(tk), S(tk+1), ..., S(tT)).$

Here, [Q](tk) denotes the forecast value of the vector Q(tk) at time tk, and P is the forecast operator («predictor»), which makes a forecast based on the value of the vector Q at the previous step and on the basis of the techno-economic image at all subsequent steps.

However, the real value of the vector Q(tk) is determined by the following formula

$Q(tk) = K(Q(tk-1), [Q](tk)).$

Here, K stands for the operator («corrector») who performs the next step to build a unique product, but taking into account the obtained forecast of the dynamics of consumer expectations.

The proposed equations are recurrent relations that allow us to simulate the trajectory of updating the competitive advantages of unique products:

$\Gamma(Q) = \{Q(tk): k = 0, 1, \ldots, T\}$.

In addition to the trajectory of updating the competitive advantages of unique products, we have a trajectory for the evolution of consumer expectations:

$\Gamma(S) = \{S(tk): k = 0, 1, \ldots, T\}$,

with which it is possible to assess the accuracy of compliance of unique products with consumer expectations in dynamics:

$\Delta = \Sigma \,|Q(tk) - S(tk)|$,

where the summation is carried out for all $k = 0, 1, \ldots, T$.

Using this value, we can get a quantitative assessment of how close the developed unique product is to the prospective consumer expectations in the market.

In solving the task of creating unique products, the following factors should be taken into account:

Compliance with world trends in technology development and advanced achievements of fundamental science in shaping the image of unique products.

Scientific progress and technological development contribute to building new radical innovations, on the basis of which unique products are created.

Shaping the image of unique products should pursue the goal of gaining leading positions in the market and meeting the existing trends in the development of society.

In this case, the image of the product should be shaped in such a way that it surpasses the products that dominate the market today in terms of their technical and economic characteristics. Thus, even at the stage of planning and shaping a product's image, promising market requirements and developed technology should be considered to create products with a significant competitive advantage.

Shaping the image of the products of the future takes into account changes in the technical and economic parameters of products in the target markets in the future.

In this case, we are speaking of predicting changes of the needs of society and the technological capacities of a manufacturer in 3–5 years, when a unique product will be introduced to the market. Shaping a product image that outperforms the products currently dominating the market will not ensure the advanced development of the manufacturer. It is possible only when the image of unique products will surpass the characteristics of the future products of competitors, and unique products will be able to meet the future needs of society and individual consumers.

In its content, the process of managing the development of unique products is a complex phenomenon that combines a set of relatively independent, but still inextricably linked mechanisms that ensure the creation, application and maintenance of competitive advantages.

The formulated postulates of the processes of advanced satisfaction of long-term needs enables further formulation of strategic approaches, mechanisms and tools for managing a company's economic growth and describe them mathematically based on the economic and mathematical approach. This approach allows us to formulate some provisions through which it is possible to present the basic principles of managing the creation of unique products. A distinctive feature of the proposed approach is the use of mathematical models that describe the dynamics of the process of meeting future needs, given dynamically changing factors and risks.

The proposed axiomatic method for constructing the theory of advanced development and economic growth of a company will allow to describe the economic mechanisms and tools for creating unique products on a qualitatively new basis that can be developed in the form of an applied software solution that has high practical significance for industrial companies.

3.3 Strategic approaches and tools for managing a company's economic growth through the creation of radically new products

In the context of overcoming global economic crises, outdated economic mechanisms and technological solutions are being rehabilitated, and only the most innovative organizational and economic structures, due to the previously created competitive advantages and resource provision, are able to find new economic and technological niches, offer conditions for the creation and development of markets for unique goods. The strategy and tactics of increasing competitiveness are the basis for creating a sustainable strategy for a company's economic growth and should be supported by economic tools, with which estimates of the effectiveness of managing the processes of creating unique products are formed.

A company's economic growth strategy, focused on increasing competitiveness to a level that allows it to dominate the markets, is understood as a management influence aimed at balancing the external and internal factors of the development of the managed system, which ensures consistent growth and improving the quality level of its development, along with identifying and preventing negative consequences of economic activity in the foreseeable future. The ultimate goal of a company's economic growth is the creation of new markets or a significant expansion of its presence in existing markets. Thus, the strategic economic development of a company should be guided by the trends in the development of economic relations, emerging under the influence of global economic processes and crises, and based on the constant implementation of breakthrough solutions at key stages of creating unique products. This thesis is confirmed by our proposed law of meeting future needs, showing that the creation of unique products and ensuring its dominance in the market leads to significant resources of a company due to large volumes of sales of such products, which it should direct to preserve the competitive advantages of unique products to extend its stay on the market. Investing resources in the process of creating new unique products, taking into account the dynamics of society's needs as a result of the impact of new competencies and changes in technology is a strategic necessity.

The postulates of the law of advanced satisfaction of promising needs formulated above allows to determine the necessary conditions that a company should meet to be able to satisfy promising needs at a high level by creating radically new products. Let us consider these conditions in detail.

In industrialized countries global trends in scientific and technological development warrant the need to combine national and global scientific and technological, as well as innovation strategies. Although globalization is driving a a significant part of innovation abroad, its base is still home-based. The main reason is the close dependence of the innovation process on the conditions of each country, the established relations with the scientific community and consumers, resource opportunities and human capacity. In every industrially developed country all this leads to the development and implementation of state innovation policy aimed at creating a favorable climate for the implementation of innovation processes.

The analysis of the main instruments of state regulation of innovation activity shows that the environment formed by the State is aimed at establishing the following conditions necessary for both public and private companies to carry out activities to create unique products:

- ensuring the conditions for achieving the economic sustainability of a company;
- ensuring the conditions for achieving the competitiveness of manufacturers and their products;
- providing acceptable conditions for access to key resources (including personnel and competencies) necessary to create unique products.

The balanced work of public instruments for regulating innovation activity contributes to generating sustainable economic growth of both companies and the economy as a whole. The role of resource provision in the strategic management of balanced economic growth is extremely important, moreover, the sufficiency of resource provision is essential for maintaining competitiveness and sustainability of development based on the production of high-quality products with unique characteristics that could meet emerging market needs or stimulate the emergence of needs met by these products. The lack of resources will definitely have a negative impact on the final result, while also negatively affecting the other parameters, by regulating which it is possible to achieve effective management of a company's competitiveness.

The sustainability of manufacturers' development with changes in various economic indicators of its activities also has an important impact on the competitiveness of the economy and its ability to move to the advanced development through the development of products capable of creating new markets or significantly expanding the boundaries of existing ones on the basis of ensuring product competitiveness in quality and price.

Let us illustrate these provisions by using a mathematical model for constructing a contour of the minimum permissible values of a company's performance parameters that characterize its economic stability, competitiveness and the level of resource provision. Without loss of generality, we will assume that the better value of the indicator corresponds to the larger value of the quantitative indicator.

The dynamics of each indicator of the company's activity can be reflected by a ray representing the totality of the values of the corresponding financial, economic or any other indicator of the company's activity in relation to a particular moment in time τ. The number of such indicators is generally not regulated ($i = \overline{1,I}$).

The model for constructing the contour of the minimum permissible values of a company's activity parameters can be represented in fragments as follows:

$$Z = \sum_{n=1}^{N} Z_n$$

$$Z_n = \sum_{j=1}^{J} Z_{nj}$$

$$Z = \sum_{n=1}^{N} \sum_{j=1}^{J} Z_{nj} \times X_{nj},$$

where X_{nj} is the boolean variable and $X_{nj} = \{1$, if there is a change in the value of the n-th indicator; 0 – otherwise$\}$.

At different moments in time ($\tau = \overline{1,T}$), a company's performance indicators accept the corresponding values ($\Pi_{i\tau}$). Thus, the entire set of indicators in relation to time ($\Pi_{i\tau}$; $i = \overline{1,I}$; $\tau = \overline{1,T}$) can be represented by a «bundle» of multidirectional rays emerging from the same point of the plane. The number of these rays should be equal to the number of the tracked indicators.

Each of the rays contains specific values of the monitored indicators in relation to a specific point in time, presented in various measures: natural, conditional, labor, cost, etc. The use of various planning and accounting units (pieces, rubles, percent, standard hours, etc.) to characterize the indicators that form the contour is justified. However, since in each time demention the measure of the value of the indicator does not change, the ratios between them at each moment of time remain equally reliable, objectively characterizing the real ratio of costs and benefits, that is, the information value of the results obtained does not decrease, but the assessment procedure is simplified, since there is no need in scaling units. Thus, the use of different units of measurement will not distort the picture of the actual relations of these indicators.

If then the values of the indicators related to a particular moment in time τ, – points on the rays ($\Pi_{i\tau}$), – are sequentially connected, we get a polyline that characterizes the «section» of the monitored indicators at the moment , which is a polygon.

There can be any number of such «sections» depending on the number of developers working with themThe set of these polygons forms an n-dimensional space, and their vertices are a cloud of points, including those that characterize the optimal, permissible or not permissible flow of economic processes in a company (Figure 3.4).

If we connect all the points of the minimum and maximum permissible values of indicators, we will get an area outside of which, the indicators will undoubtedly correspond to the state of readiness of the company for advanced development through the creation of unique products.

In the case when the monitored indicator is located the contour, it is necessary to find out the reasons that led to the current situation, and, depending on the estimate obtained, make the necessary management decisions. Through the reallocation of resources or other measures (for example, the creation of a risk fund), it is possible to neutralize the negative impact of uncertainty factors on a company's performance. If the boundaries of the permissible values of the indicators determined by the contour are exceeded, then it is necessary to review the planning documents, including the strategy. At the same time, the market opportunities of an economic entity are determined by the quantitative and qualitative characteristics of its resources and the efficiency of their distribution,

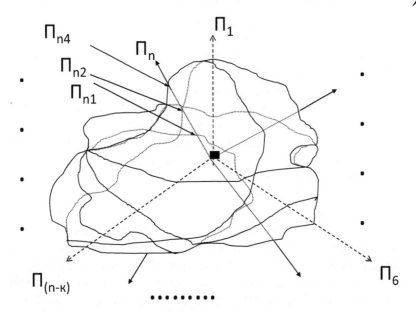

Figure 3.4. Conceptual representation of the contour of the minimum
permissible values of a company's performance indicators

the ability to additionally attract them on favorable terms, the ability to achieve sustabable economic development based on the use of innovative technologies, taking into account the actions of competitors to increase their competitive advantages. A company can establish strategic guidelines of development by reallocating resources.

For example, it can be:
– creating competitive advantages that will allow to strengthen position in a certain market segment or enter new ones;
– organization of new types of activities that can generate significant income;
– creating new markets based on the development of a product previously unavailable on the market.

Let us identify the requirements that must be met by a company's economic growth strategy in order to increase its competitiveness in the world market:

A rational strategy for economic growth and business development should be based primarily on the effective implementation of breakthrough technological innovations at the main stages of design and large-scale production of a unique good.

A company's economic growth strategy, aimed at increasing its competitiveness, should be closely linked to the local and global legal and regulatory framework and include measures to promptly respond to possible changes in the legal area, as well as with the state policy in the country in the innovation support and should not contradict the set of legally approved programs.

The main reference point of a company's economic growth strategy should be to increase the efficiency and speed of introduction of innovative solutions, and periodic qualitative and quantitative assessment of this efficiency in the framework of the strategy implementation should be mandatory at all management levels.

Since the main indicator of efficiency is the ratio of the result to the resources spent, it is possible to increase efficiency and achieve economic growth both by increasing efficiency and reducing the level of resources used while maintaining the necessary results, as well as combining these processes. In doing so, different methods can be used and various functional areas can be application objects.

A rational strategy for the company's economic growth, especially in the case of product sales in foreign markets, should be developed taking into account not only global trends, such as changes in the structure of the direction of financial flows, the development of industrial outsourcing, the introduction of remote forms of employment, etc., but also considering unforeseen risks, and thus should contain a carefully crafted element of strategic management of economic growth in the context of rapid economic crisis, instability, inflation, etc., that is, have a full-fledged subsystem for the implementation of strategic alternatives.

The most effective mechanisms for managing a company's economic growth, in our opinion, can be proactive mechanisms of preventive and proactive impact on factors that can negatively affect the economic development. In the context of ensuring strategic sustainability, the main purpose of proactive mechanisms is to develop spheres and sectors of activity that increase the overall sustainability of a company, as well as prevent the negative impact of various manifestations of globalization on the economy (the modern world financial and economic crises is a striking example). The solution of these tasks can be achieved by using proactive mechanisms of two main types – strategic and operational. Strategic mechanisms should be aimed primarily at diversification and modernization, reducing a company's dependence on a narrow product category, which results in increasing the sustainability of economic development.

Operational mechanisms are primarily economic rather than organizational in nature. At the present stage of the development of the global economy, with its specifics due to the high level of development of the financial infrastructure, financial mechanisms come to the fore. Financial mechanisms can be viewed as a priority, also because in the context of globalization the main threat to stability are the financial markets with their unstable market conditions and high volatility, so operational mechanisms of a proactive nature should be focused on preventing these threats.

A company's achievement of economic growth is related to the efficiency of resource allocation for the development of new unique products throughout its entire life cycle. The developed product should be focused on the needs of the market or its individual segments and considers the increasing intellectual potential and capacities of society. As we have stated, the creation of unique products requires solving a number of problems related to ensuring the economic sustainability of an enterprise, planning its resource provision, building up competitive advantages, developing unique competence through the use of accumulated innovative capacity and effective management of investment projects for its development.

Solving the problem of achieving sustainable economic growth of a company requires a systematic approach and the implementation of a complex of various management impacts on business processes. Consequently, there is a need to develop an integral system for the creation of unique products, which is a set of economic mechanisms aimed at ensuring an effective management of the development of products that meet promising consumer needs.

The economic mechanisms of such a system and the tools and methods that ensure their operation are based on obtaining and using information from two sources: internal information and data from the global information space. The use of analytics obtained through processing information from various sources enables increasing the validity of decisions made when managing the process of creating unique products with high competitive advantages.

The first mechanism in the management system of a company's economic growth based on the development of unique products is the mechanism for shaping the idea of a unique product and its techno-economic image. This mechanism makes it possible to forecast a company's product line, able to bring it to the advanced development mode and ensure market dominance. Under this mechanism, it is necessary to have methodological forecasting tools that can be used to determine the future needs of organizations and society, based on their growing intellectual potential and developing competencies. Such a forecast should be based on the intelligent analysis of big data in the global information space, taking into account the development of the current wave of innovation and the forecast characteristics of the next wave order.

At the same time, a company that seeks to dominate the markets must take the initiative to create new or expand existing markets. To do this, with the appropriate resource support, an enterprise must direct its development towards creating new unique competencies and technologies, which will create new unique products that meet market trends, consumer expectations and technologies of the next technological wave. Such companies have the opportunity to develop at an accelerated pace and make a technological breakthrough that provides them with a competitive leadership in the market (Figure 3.5).

Based on the characteristics of the developing and promising wave of innovation, a company can forecast the techno-economic image of new products and plan the development of the necessary competencies using appropriate methodological tools. These processes should be sensetive to the advanced achievements of fundamental science in the development of new technologies (biosystems, 3D technologies of the neurosystem, etc.) and chart the development directions of a company's new key competencies.

Market
dominance

Achieving global
competitiveness

Creation of new
product markets

Shaping the image of the
products of the
future, developing new
competencies

Figure 3.5. A company's path
to market dominance

Methodological forecasting tools should identify the main technologies that will be incorporated into a product, as well as determine the techno-economic parameters of a product's image. Already at this stage, it is necessary to obtain reasonable forecast estimates of the future cost of products on the market.

Product cost management must be carried out at all stages of the life cycle, especially at the stage of the techno-economic image formation. This is due to the fact that the production cost (especially industrial) is one of the key factors (along with innovation and product quality) that determine competitiveness in the global market, and should also determine the future product's image.

The second important economic mechanism included in the integral system of managing a company's economic growth based on the development of unique products is the mechanism for the comprehensive assessment and management of resources required to develop unique products. In addition to material resources, it is necessary to consider the key resources of the digital economy – information and unique competencies. The corresponding economic mechanism should include a set of tools that allow to assess the level of existing capacities and technologies, determine competencies that need to be additionally attracted or developed, assess the sufficiency of financial, labor and material resources to create unique products.

The processes of various stages of the life cycle of unique products involve the integrated use of a company's resource capacity, and therefore it is necessary to manage all types of resources, taking into account the peculiarities of its economic activity. In the practice of resource planning, the use of ERP systems is widespread, implying complex automation of planning processes. In the digital economy, the most optimal schemes for using the available resource base can be obtained through systems with methods for constructing neural networks and machine learning, which can build automated expert conclusion using big data processing and knowledge bases.

The third economic mechanism necessary in managing the economic growth of a company by regulating the cost of the product life cycle is the mechanism for managing the development of the production and technological base necessary to create unique products, in which it is important to form management tools for its modernization in order to achieve advanced development. In the digital economy, the modernization of the production and technological base should be aimed at:

– development of a modern infrastructure for the implementation of R&D and the accelerated creation of products with high competitive advantages;
– development and introduction of new technologies that improve the efficiency of the production process;
– development of the innovation infrastructure in a company and at the industry level;
– ensuring the improvement of energy efficiency, environmental friendliness of production, compliance with international standards;
– creation of an intelligent infrastructure that determines the increase in the efficiency of business processes while reducing the cost and complexity of work (digital organization, digital design office, widespread use of automated control systems).

Thus, the development of the production and technological base can be carried out, for example, through the transition to the widespread use of digital economy technologies, which make it possible to increase the level of organization of economic processes for creating high-tech products. This is due to completely new digital production technologies that form the basis of the Industry 4.0 concept.

The technological basis for the functioning of such a "smart plant" is cyber-physical systems (CPS), in which software components are connected to mechanical and electronic parts through the data infrastructure, as well as the Internet of things, in which physical objects – such as devices, sensors and systems-can send and receive data over the Internet without human intervention. The use of IoT technologies creates a number of positive effects in production:

– ensuring production flexibility as a result of the rejection of rigid "conveyor" solutions, the ability to fulfill individual orders to meet the needs of specific customers;

– the functioning of a single technological platform of production, which ensures the "customizability" of production;

– increasing production efficiency by reducing costs caused by the human factor (errors, downtime, high cost of human labor, etc.).

The fourth economic mechanism of the proposed system for managing the company's economic growth is a mechanism for optimizing the costs of developing unique products, pre-production and production. This mechanism should have such basic economic instruments as:

– a tool that allows you to analyze the impact of design changes on the cost of products at any stage of its life cycle. With such a tool, "bottlenecks" can be identified, components that have a significant impact on cost (which is especially important in the early stages of the development process). In this situation, in the work of the mechanism, ways to reduce the production cost should be proposed. An objective analysis of the cost of manufacturing products will allow to reproduce various scenarios of its production;

– a tool for analyzing the cost of purchased components to calculate the cost of parts and raw materials purchased on the market. An automated analysis of the feasibility of implementing such costs should be carried out, and it is also necessary to assess the possibility and feasibility of producing the necessary components by the company itself (how appropriate it is to purchase new equipment/tools/rigs for production of piece or small-scale parts.).

The fifth economic mechanism as part of an integrated management system for a company's economic growth based on the creation of unique products is represented by a mechanism for managing the cost of unique products and the complexity of their manufacture, which must be carried out in parallel with the process of product design and preparation of the production and technological base. At each development stage, it is necessary to supplement, concretize and correct the input data and information used to assess the cost and labor intensity. The more specific the project becomes in all its parameters (technical, risk, and others), the more accurate and specific the assessment of its cost and labor intensity is.. Design and economic analysis should be related processes, and the results of economic analysis should influence the work of a developer up to the definition of tolerances, fits and other parameters of the product design.

Since it is necessary to have estimates of the cost and forecast price at the earliest stages of the product life cycle, it is advisable to have an economic mechanism and an information system for decision support that allows to:

– fairly accurately estimate the production cost, taking into account the use of certain materials (provided that the target technical characteristics are achieved) and the appointment of acceptable processing accuracy, assembly complexity, etc.;

– simulate the cost and labor intensity of manufacturing products with varying processing accuracy, materials used, etc. taking into account the need to achieve the specified technical characteristics and determine the most optimal design;

– identify the complete structure of the cost of products and their modifications by components based on specifications and technological routes;

– identify and clarify the direct costs and production costs related to the use of various technological operations and processes, the use of certain materials and the achievement of parameters (for example, processing accuracy).

Finally, the sixth mechanism in the system of managing a company's economic growth based on the creation of unique products is the mechanism for assessing the economic efficiency of the development and production of unique goods. With methodological tools, it is necessary to assess how effectively the resource capacities were used (personnel competencies, financial resources, production and technological base, etc.). Such use of resource capacities that has led to the creation of new competitive products that can bring a company to the advanced development mode can be considered effective.

As we have noted, the functioning of each mechanism is ensured by the use of a set of economic instruments presented in Table 3.3.

Table 3.3. Economic instruments that ensure the operation of the mechanisms of a company's economic growth management system through the creation of unique products

№	Mechanism	Toolkit
	The mechanism of shaping the idea of a unique product and its techno-economic image	A tool for forecasting the future needs of organizations and society based on their growing intellectual potential and developing competencies A tool for assessing the competitiveness of a future unique product at the stage of shaping its techno-economic image A tool for predictive assessment of the competitive value of unique products on the market
	Mechanism for the comprehensive assessment and management of resources required to develop unique products	A tool for assessing the level of competencies and the level of technology development A tool for assessing the sufficiency of financial, labor and material resources Resource potential assessment tool
	Mechanism for managing the development of the production and technological base required to create unique products	Management tools for the modernization of the production and technological base in order to create a unique product and achieve advanced development
	Mechanism of cost optimization for the development of unique products, preproduction and production	A tool for analyzing the impact of design changes on the cost of products at any stage of its life cycle A tool for analyzing the cost of purchased components for calculating the cost of parts and raw materials purchased from the market

Mechanism for managing the cost of unique products and the complexity of their manufacture	A tool for estimating the cost of products, taking into account the use of certain materials and the purpose of acceptable processing accuracy, assembly complexity, etc.
Mechanism for evaluating the economic efficiency of the development and production of unique goods	A tool for planning costs associated with the use of various technological operations and processes, the use of certain materials and the achievement of parameters

Most of these tools are described in our works [20].

All of the above mechanisms in the system for creating unique products should be adaptive, since for promising high-tech products it is advisable to use an adaptive life cycle, suggesting the possibility of adjusting resource provision, deadlines and other parameters (while maintaining the same requirements of the technical specification) at various stages of the life cycle. The emerging new technologies of the digital economy make it possible to effectively adapt the life cycle management system of new products to constantly changing internal and external conditions.

[20] Chursin A., Tyulin A. Competence Management and Competitive Product Development: Concept and Implications for Practice. – Heidelberg, Germany: Springer International Publishing, 2018. – 234 p.

Chursin A., Makarov Y. Management of Competitiveness: Theory and Practice. Heidelberg, 2015. 378 p.

Chursin A., Vlasov Y., Makarov Y. Innovation as a basis for competitiveness: theory and practice. Heidelberg, 2016.

Artyakov V.V., Chursin A.A. Innovation management. methodological tools: textbook / Moscow, 2019. Ser. Higher education: Master

Boginsky A.I., Chursin A.A. Design solutions for optimizing the cost of production // Vestnik mashinostroeniya. 2019.No. 8.P. 74-78.

Boginsky A.I., Uchenov A.A., Chursin A.A. Assessment of the needs of companies in support systems for effective management decisions // Microeconomics. 2019. No. 6 (89). p. 22-30.

Chursin A.A. An integral indicator of the economic efficiency of a complex organizational and economic system // Bulletin of the Moscow University. Series 26: Government audit. 2019.No. 2.P. 114-126.

Tyulin A.E., Chursin A.A. Fundamentals of managing innovation processes in knowledge-intensive industries (practice). Moscow, 2017.

Vlasov Yu.V., Chursin A.A. Assessment of the technical level of production for placing a government order // Microeconomics. 2016. No. 2. p. 17-25.

The practical application of the economic mechanisms of the system for creating unique products involves the use of information and analytical systems. They are built on the principle of an automated expert system, which should be based on a knowledge base with information on the costs connected with the development of high-tech products.

Our research has shown that as a result of the simultaneous action of the described economic mechanisms and tools, there is a synergistic effect at each stage of the life cycle of unique products, which consists in increasing the effectiveness of management actions that lead to a reduction in the time of design and launch of unique products with high value for the consumer, as well as to optimal cost management for its development at all stages of the life cycle. The resulting synergistic effect is expressed in the achievement of economic growth by a company.

The development of the company's economic growth strategy also requires laying the methodological foundations of such necessary elements as:

- development of indicators of a company's economic growth. Here it is advisable to systematize the specialized indicators of a company's economic development, taking into account modern economic development, the dynamics of world markets and the frequency of emergence of innovative products and solutions.

- development of fundamentally new scientific approaches, with which it is possible to effectively evaluate quantitative and qualitative indicators characterizing the management decisions taken at all levels as part of the implementation of the company's economic growth strategy.

- development of quality indicators of management and increasing competitiveness, including the ranking of innovative projects, highlighting their priorities and long-term price determination of promising unique products.

These issues will be discussed in detail in the course of the further presentation.

CHAPTER 4.
BASES FOR TRANSFORMATION OF SCIENTIFIC AND TECHNOLOGICAL CAPACITY AND UNIQUE TECHNOLOGICAL COMPETENCE INTO A RADICALLY NEW PRODUCT

4.1. THE CHAIN OF TRANSFORMATION OF SCIENTIFIC AND TECHNOLOGICAL CAPACITY INTO COMPETITIVE ADVANTAGES OF RADICALLY NEW PRODUCTS TO ENSURE A COMPANY'S SUSTAINABILITY

The process of creating radically new products and their competitive advantages is based on a number of foundations, without which unique value for the consumer cannot be formed.

The unique value for the consumer determines the position of a product in the market, and the higher the unique properties, the more radical they are, the higher the market share of a company in the market, the higher the volumes of products manufactured and sold, and the higher the consumer's loyalty to the brand and the manufacturer's image, etc.

The increase in product sales creates opportunities for a company to accumulate various types of resources necessary for the further development of the product line, which ultimately creates conditions a company's sustainability. The availability of these resources allows to develop new business areas, as well as implement new, more profitable business models (for example, company's service models).

Based on these assumptions, which form the main provisions of a company's sustainability and its development at a high pace with a long-term entry into the trajectory of advanced development, as well as the research conducted above, we systematize the foundations of creating a unique product value for the consumer and identify those that require additional study due to their importance and the significance of the impact on the creating competitive advantages.

As noted, the following components are involved in the process of creating competitive advantages of product value for the consumer:

Radical competencies created on the basis of developing technology platforms, reaching the intersectoral level and allowing creating breakthrough innovations.

"Useful" information that forms a manufacturer's idea of market trends, prospective (including personalized) needs, the dynamics of the development of equipment and technologies within intersectoral technology platforms, etc., which ensures a high competitive potential for the product being created.

Strategic thinking aimed at achieving advanced development and advanced satisfaction of future needs in accordance with the relevant economic law; at the same time, the basis of the law of advanced satisfaction of prospective needs is the achievement of a dominant position in the market by promising products through the creation of radical innovations based on the accumulated scientific and technological capacity and key radical competencies of the manufacturer.

Scientific and technological capacity accumulated and developed in a company, as well as industry and cross-industry technology platforms.

The importance of the first three components has already been substantiated in detail, but the creation of competitive advantages is not possible without the fourth component – scientific and technological capacity, which ensures obtaining the maximum efficiency of the first three components. In this regard, describing and assessing the impact of scientific and technological capacity on the created competitive advantages of radically new products becomes an important challenge.

Methodically, the solution of this problem is carried out in four stages, shown in Figure 4.1.

Stage 1. The economic essence of the transformation of scientific and technological capacity into competitive advantages of radically new products

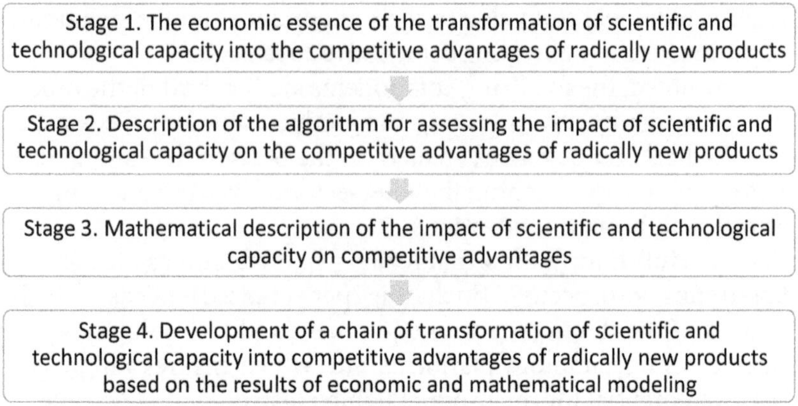

Stage 1. The economic essence of the transformation of scientific and technological capacity into the competitive advantages of radically new products

Stage 2. Description of the algorithm for assessing the impact of scientific and technological capacity on the competitive advantages of radically new products

Stage 3. Mathematical description of the impact of scientific and technological capacity on competitive advantages

Stage 4. Development of a chain of transformation of scientific and technological capacity into competitive advantages of radically new products based on the results of economic and mathematical modeling

Figure 4.1. Stages of assessing the impact of scientific and technological capacity on the created competitive advantages of radically new products

Previously, the issue of forming the scientific and technological capacity of a company was considered, its components were identified (various types of resources and factors, including production and technological, financial and economic, intellectual, research and other resources necessary for the implementation of innovative activities), as well as for each component, criteria and methods of their quantitative assessment are defined. On this basis, we will research the processes of transformation of scientific and technological capacity and unique technological competencies into a radically new product (the impact of a company's potential on the creating competitive advantages of products).

The potential of a company in the general sense is the totality of available resources, which determine its capabilities and borders of functioning in certain conditions. To describe various aspects of business activity (for example, innovation and investment, commercial, etc. activities), various types of capabilities are considered:

– innovative, which determines the measure of the company's readiness to perform tasks that ensure the achievement of innovation[21];

---

[21] Clayton M. Christinsen, Assessing Your Organization's Innovation Capabilities // Leader to Leader. -2001. -№ 21.

– commercial, reflecting a company's ability to adapt to market changes, calculated on the basis of commercial costs and various indicators of market performance[22];

– cientific, determined by the totality of resources and conditions for the implementation of scientific fundamental research[23];

– technical, reflecting the ability of an enterprise to generate new scientific and technical ideas, carry out their scientific, design and technological development and implement them in production[24] etc.

These concepts are related to the scientific and technological capacity of an enterprise as a set of accumulated knowledge, available scientific and technical personnel, material and technical, information, financial resources and organizational structure that ensure the actual development of new technical means, technologies, materials, new products, new forms and methods. organization of production and labor, as well as new methods of promoting goods to the market and the creation of new markets aimed at increasing competitiveness and production efficiency.

Scientific and technological capacity is inherently closest to innovation capacity, which is characterized by a combination of all types of resources and conditions for ensuring the research and practical development results that increase production efficiency, methods and tools for the development of new technologies and the implementation of specific technological processes for the development of new materials and new products. That is, the main difference between the scientific and technological capacity is the organiza-

[22] Falco C.G. Controlling: modern challenges // Modern enterprise and the future of Russia: collection of articles. scientific. Proceedings of the International Forum dedicated to the 85th anniversary of the Department of Economics and Organization of Production of the Moscow State Technical University H.E. Bauman, Moscow, December 5-6, 2014 / Ed. Dr. econ. Sciences, prof. C.G. Falco. M .: NP "Union of controllers". 2014.p. 4–7.

[23] Lifshits A.S. Development of industrial enterprises through the prism of the resource-targeted approach and the theory of limitations // Entrepreneurship. 2014. No. 4. P. 50–59.

[24] Plotnikov A. N., Litoninsky S. N. Analysis of methods for assessing the innovative potential of an enterprise and directions for their improvement // Problems of the modern economy. -2012. -№ 7. -p. 248–263.

tional and management component, which ensures the flexibility of a company's technology platform and the ability to quickly address research and production and technological challenges to ensure the competitive advantages of the products being created.

Scientific and technological capacity is a dynamic category that develops inseparably with the entire economic system of a company and under the influence of the external environment (global trends in economic development, the emergence of new scientific discoveries, the development of technology at the intersectoral level, the accumulation of competencies within technology platforms, etc.).

Scientific and technological capacity ensures the creation and maintenance of high competitive advantages of products, which are reduced even at the initial stages of the life cycle due to the risks of losing competitiveness due to the dynamic development of competitors and the development of new similar or more advanced technologies and products offered by them. In this regard, it is necessary to carry out control actions aimed at ensuring constant increase through the development of all components, and first of all those that are required to create such advantages that will significantly bypass competing solutions in the market.

Scientific and technological capacity-building occurs in parallel with the stages of the production cycle, and as it accumulates, it transforms into competitive advantages of products at the stage of the cycle corresponding to the moment when it is possible to increase such advantages.

To manage scientific and technological capacity and its impact on the competitive advantages of radically new products in dynamics, it is recommended to develop an appropriate algorithm.

Stage 2. Description of the algorithm for assessing the impact of scientific and technological capacity on the competitive advantages of radically new products

The modern economy is developing more rapidly as a result of the simplification and automation of many production and management processes that occur due to the high rate of technological development of countries in the direction of applying digital solutions that increase efficiency in various areas of activity (on the one hand, the time for developing radical innovations is reduced, on the other hand, the efficiency of resource management is increased).

As noted, there is a trend of rapid growth of competencies in industry and society. The generayion of intellectual resources, knowledge in various industries occurs at an ever faster pace, and upon reaching a critical point theres is "intellectual explosion" occurs, in which new scientific directions and discoveries allow solving pressing and relevant, but not yet solved problems using radically new methods. This, in turn, also contributes to the expansion of the scientific and technological capacity of intersectoral technology platforms and individual manufacturers, provided that the level of investment in scientific and technological development is constantly maintained, which subsequently allows to form unique competitive advantages of manufactured products with consumer utility and value.

The process of forming competitive advantages of products covers all stages of its life cycle, the implementation of which is accompanied by the generation of its own information flow:

– product development;
– production planning;
– preproduction and engineering;
– production;
– maintenance and repair.

Scientific and technological capacity is involved at all stages of product development and is crucial for ensuring its competitive advantages. Forming the techno-economic image of a product is one of the most important stages of the product life cycle, where its main parameters are laid and competitive advantages are formed. At this stage, the selection of competencies and elements of scientific and technological capacity created both in a company and in industry and cross-industry technology platforms play a decisive role in the process of developing competitive advantages and endowing products with radical novelty, uniqueness that create value for the consumer.

When creating the image of a product, the features to ensure the longest service life and maintain leading position on the market should be laid down. This is achieved largely due to the fact that the developers of the image of products, as a rule, acquire high-quality individual components, units, and machines in specialized organizations (competence centers), and also use the fundamental achievements of science in practice.

However, the high rates of development of equipment and technology, the emergence of new competencies create the risk of reducing competitive advantages in passing the product life cycle from the moment of shaping the image to the moment of market entry. In this regard, it is necessary to make managerial decisions on changing the design and production technologies already in the process of creating a product according to the designed image, which will increase competitive advantages and thereby "postpone" the point of maximum saturation of the market.

Building competencies and scientific and technological capacity of competitors forces the dynamic development of a product line to maintain competitive (leading) positions in the market by ensuring the growth of its scientific and technological capacity and its transformation into value characteristics (competitive advantages) of the product at all stages of the life cycle, which is shown in the diagram (Fig. 4.2).

Dynamic scientific and technological capacity-building (due to the development of its components (intellectual, resource, efficient, organizational, marketing), forming an integral assessment, discussed in detail in Chapter 3), when used in production and management processes, results in the creation of competitive advantages of a radically new product at different stages of the life cycle. Here are some examples.

For the stage of product design: building up intellectual, personnel, marketing, resource, effective components, for example, in terms of developing competencies and generating know-how, new scientific discoveries, in terms of creating a system for operational monitoring of changing consumer expectations, proposals and actions of other market players, in terms of the use of digital design, etc., will allow improving the technical characteristics and form high competitive advantages of a product that have value

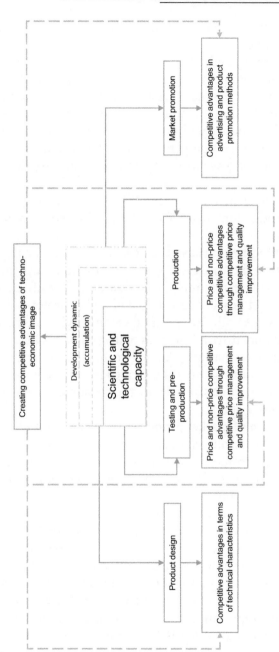

Figure: 4.2 Areas of creating competitive advantages of products based on scientific and technological capacity

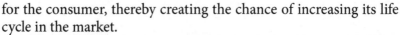

for the consumer, thereby creating the chance of increasing its life cycle in the market.

For the testing and pre-production stage (especially technological): the development of intellectual, organizational, resource, and performance components results in the creation and application of new production methods and technologies, while reducing the cost of the product and ensuring productivity growth. This, in turn, creates price competitive advantages and can geberate new, more efficient ways to meet needs and increase demand for the product.

As a result of increasing scientific and technological capacity, the preproduction stage of can be minimized by automating the processes.

For the production stage: the development of all components of the capacity will create the opportunity to modernize and build a system that will ensure the production of a radically new product in the shortest possible time based of digital prototypes created at the design stage with the specified technical characteristics that underlie the competitive advantages of the product. Thus, the competitive advantages that are planned to be created at the design and pre-production stage are transformed into real competitive advantages that play a decisive role for the consumer when choosing among competing offers.

For the stage of market promotion: development of predominantly marketing, resource, organizational components will ensure effective market promotion of a product with attractive advertising support (which can also be assessed as a competitive advantage when launching the product).

To assess the impact of scientific and technological capacity on the competitive advantages of radically new products, a corresponding algorithm has been developed and is shown in Fig. 4.3.

The algorithm shown in Figure 4.3 reflects the enlarged form of the process of creating competitive advantages of products as a result of the development of scientific and technological capacity.

One of the important activities is the scientific and technological capacity-building, which is further involved at various stages

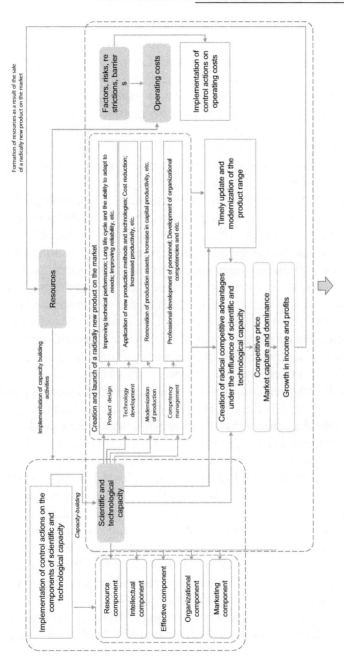

Figure 4.3 A dynamic model for transforming the scientific and technological capacity of an organization into the competitive advantages of a radically new product

of the life cycle of creating a radically new product and its lauche. Capacity building is carried out by implementing control actions on its components with the appropriate resourcing. The development of each component inevitably entails the development of other components involved in the creation of value, and their balance, which ensures the sufficiency of not only an individual component, but also their entire set, taking into account the links between them.

The description of this process will be presented below as an appropriate mathematical model for describing the dynamics of scientific and technological capacity.

The totality of manifestations of scientific and technological capacity at each stage of the life cycle ultimately results in the generation of competitive advantages of a product, as shown in Fig. 4.3, while having an attractive competitive price, which creates conditions for capturing a high market share and achieving market supremacy.

As a result, a manufacturer receives an economic effect in the form of additional profit, which in the future should be directed to the dynamic development and renewal of the product line, further continuous development of scientific and technological capacity, as well as the implementation of operational activities, accompanied by the emergence of various factors and risks.

The description of this process will be presented below as a relevant dynamic model of transformation of scientific and technological capacity into the competitive advantages of radically new products.

Mathematical description of the impact of scientific and technological capacity on competitive advantages.

Let us consider the last task in more detail. From a certain number of indicators characterizing the scientific and technological capacity of a company, it is possible to construct mathematical models describing the dynamics of indicators of scientific and technological capacity, taking into consideration various factors and allowing to assess the impact of the formed scientific and technological capacity for achieving the competitive level of the product features to ensure its radical properties.

The proposed model for transforming scientific and technological capacity into the competitive advantages of radically new products is a combination of two mathematical models for describing the dynamics of competitiveness indicators of radically new products being created. The first model describes the dynamics of indicators characterizing the scientific and technological capacity of a company depending on various factors affecting these indicators, and the second model based on the finite-automaton formalism, describes the impact of the scientific and technological capacity of a capacity on the competitive advantages and competitiveness of products created. Let us look at these models in more detail.

Assessment of the competitiveness of radically new products in shaping their techno-economic image is closely related to the indicators of scientific and technological capacity and the level of key competencies (including fundamental science) underpinning its creation.

As noted above, the scientific and technological capacity of a company consists of several components, which can be grouped as follows:

- the organizational component (Q1), which characterizes the level of organization of a company's innovation management, including innovative development directions in a company's strategy, etc;
- the intellectual component (Q2), which includes an assessment of the R&D performance, the presence of intellectual property objects at an enterprise (patents, know-how, etc.);
- the resource component (Q3), characterizing the volume of resourcing of an enterprise, as well as indicators of its financial stability, pointing to the possibility of attracting additional resources for the implementation of innovative projects, etc.;
- marketing component (Q4), which characterizes the effectiveness of marketing activities, conducting market research, involvement in network structures, cooperation and interaction within technology platforms;
- the effective component (Q5), which characterizes the results of the commercialization of the innovative potential of an enterprise and reflects the degree of implementation of the resources and capabilities available to the enterprise, etc.

Many researchers[25] identify a significant number of factors that, depending on the specifics of an enterprise, affect various components of the scientific and technological capacity: the proportion of highly qualified employees (doctors and candidates of science), the proportion of employees involved in R&D, the amount of a company's own funds that can potentially be invested in R&D, the development of prototypes, etc., the technical support (capital-labor ratio) of the release of innovative products and R&D, capital productivity of equipment involved in the innovation process, the share of exports of innovative products in the total export volume, the ratio of commercialization of intellectual property objects, the share of completed R&D that have entered the stage of commercialization, market research for innovative products, strategy for promoting innovative products to the market.

Let us describe the dynamics of an enterprise's scientific and technological capacity-building, depending on the level of various factors, using an economic and mathematical model. On a given time interval, we introduce the vector $Q = Q(t)$, that is responsible for the level of an enterprise's scientific and technological capacity:

$$Q(t) = \begin{pmatrix} Q_1(t) \\ Q_2(t) \\ ... \\ Q_n(t) \end{pmatrix}, n \geq 2$$

where $Q_i(t) > 0$ determines the level of the i-th component of an enterprise's scientific and technological capacity.

[25] Clayton M. Christinsen, Assessing Your Organization's Innovation Capabilities // Leader to Leader. – 2001. – № 21.
Falco C.G. Controlling: modern challenges // Modern enterprise and the future of Russia: collection of articles. scientific. Proceedings of the International Forum dedicated to the 85th anniversary of the Department of Economics and Organization of Production of the Moscow State Technical University afrer H.E. Bauman, Moscow, December 5-6, 2014 / Ed. Dr. econ. Sciences, prof. C.G. Falco. M .: NP "Association of controllers". 2014.P. 4–7.
Lifshits A.S. Development of industrial enterprises through the prism of the resource-targeted approach and the theory of limitations // Entrepreneurship. 2014. No. 4. P. 50–9.
Plotnikov A.N., Litoninsky S.N. Analysis of methods for assessing the innovative potential of an enterprise and directions for their improvement // Problems of modern economics. -2012. -No. 7. – P. 248–263.

We will assume that at the initial moment of time, the level of scientific and technological capacity is given:

$$Q(0) = \begin{pmatrix} Q_1(0) \\ Q_2(0) \\ \vdots \\ Q_n(0) \end{pmatrix}$$

This vector meets the system of ordinary differential equations:

$$\dot{Q}(t) = A(t)Q(t),$$

where A is a diffusion matrix, which expresses the relationship between the various components of the scientific and technological capacity.

Our research shows that an enterprise seeking to dominate the market is able to form radical innovations by using the accumulated scientific and technological capacity, which ensures the creation of radically new products that can form a new market. To describe the influence of various factors on the dynamics of indicators characterizing the components of scientific and technological capacity, consider the following equation:

$$\dot{Q}(t) = A(t)Q(t) + C(t)Q(t-h).$$

where C(t) is the coefficient matrix:

$$C(t) = \begin{pmatrix} c_{11}(t) \ldots c_{1n}(t) \\ \vdots \quad \ddots \quad \vdots \\ c_{n1}(t) \ldots c_{nn}(t) \end{pmatrix}.$$

The functions $c_{ij}(t)$ determine the degree of influence of various factors (expressed in the availability of competencies, technologies, etc.) on the level of scientific and technological capacity. The functions $c_{ij}(t)$ condition is fullfiled:

$$c_{ij}(t) = \text{for } t < h.$$

The parameter h > 0 is the time interval from the beginning of the effect of various factors on the result, expressed as scientific and technological capacity building.

The management of the scientific and technological capacity of the enterprise can be taken into account using the functions of the stimulating effect, which are included in the equation describing the dynamics of the scientific and technological capacity, as follows:

$$\dot{Q}(t) = A(t)Q(t) + C(t)Q(t-h) + B(t,Q(t)) \qquad (1)$$

As part of the proposed approach, it is possible to consider different types of incentive functions corresponding to different economic situations. For example, the following incentive measures can be applied related to the introduction of new technological solutions, professional development and the level of competence of personnel, increasing resouring, etc. However, these phenomena are periodic in nature, since a certain period of time is required to take a measure. During this time, the current level of scientific and technological capacity may decline, and the adoption of incentive measures leads to its increase. Thus, the process is cyclical. This property can be considered if the management of scientific and technological capacity is represented by the following function:

$$b_i(t,Q(t)) = b_i(t) = \xi_i \cdot \sin(\eta_i t + \mu_i) + \varphi_i Q_i(t) + \phi_i \qquad (2)$$

where $\xi_i > 0$ is the value characterizing the measure of an increase or decrease in the rate of change of scientific and technological capacity, depending on the implementation of various measures, $\eta_i > 0$ is the value that characterizes the frequency of changes in the scientific and technological capacity, μ_i is the time shift, $\varphi_i > 0$ and $\phi_i > 0$ are two sets of numbers that will determine the weighting factors that regulate the current level of scientific and technological capacity.

Figure 4.4 shows a graph of the solution of equation (1) with the functions of stimulating effects presented in the form (2).

The proposed model shows the need for continuous implementation of measures (management actions) for the development of scientific and technological capacity in order to form the image of products with high consumer properties.

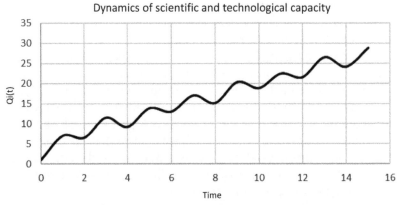

Figure 4.4 Example of solving the equation describing the dynamics
of the development of the scientific and technological capacity of a company

The dynamic model of the transformation of the scientific and technological capacity of an enterprise into the competitive advantages of radically new products can be described using a finite-automaton formalism. The finite-automaton formalism allows to build dynamic mathematical models taking into account various components and factors that can affect economic processes. As such components, we can consider the previously defined main components of creating competitive advantages and values: radical competencies, «useful information», strategic thinking aimed at achieving advanced development, scientific and technological capacity. The terms internal and external environment for the development of radically new products are economic barriers, sanctions, dynamically changing factors and risks of the external environment, as well as the level of characteristics of the created product and its competitive price connected with the labor intensity of production.

A finite state machine is a mathematical abstraction when we consider a system that can have a certain internal state able to change depending on incoming signals. As input signals, we will consider the influence of a company's scientific and technological capacity and its individual components, which in turn will determine the competitiveness indicators and competitive advantages of the radically new product being created.

By a (k) we denote the volumes of resources spent for the release of radically new products. We will assume that these resources are completely spent on creating products.

At each moment of time, we will also assume that the scientific and technological capacity of an enterprise is in a certain state, which we will evaluate using a number and denote Q (k), k = 1, 2,…

As a result of activities to create a radically new product, we will consider an enterprise's income, which will be denoted by b (k).

In the finite-automaton model, we believe that the level of scientific and technological capacity is a dynamic indicator that also changes at every step. Consider the following recurrent equations describing the dynamics of our model:

b(k+1) = f(a(k), Q(k)),

Q(k+1) = g(a(k), Q(k)).

In the simplest case, linear functions can be used:

b(k+1) = M ·a(k) · Q(k),

Q(k+1) = α ·Q(k),

where M> 0 is the scale factor, and the constant α > 0 expresses the dynamics of the internal state. Without control actions on the level of scientific and technological capacity α ≤ 1 takes place. If α <1, then the condition of the considered enterprise is worsening at each step, which represents a decrease in competitiveness because in the absence of investment.

Let us now consider a mathematical model that considers resource expenditure for the implementation of both current operating activities and innovation and investment activities. That is, the expended resources are a vector:

a(k) = (a0(k), a1(k)), k = 1, 2, …,

where a0(k) expresses an enterprise's resource expenditure for operating activities at time k, and a1(k) denotes the amount of funding for generating innovations in the enterprise at time k.

In this case, the reaction of an enterprise to the input vector a (k) will be described by a finite automaton, which is determined by the following recurrent equations

$b(k+1) = M \cdot a0(k) \cdot x(k),$

$x(k+1) = \alpha \cdot x(k),$ if $a1(k) = 0,$

$x(k+1) = \beta(a1(k)) \cdot x(k),$ if $a1(k) > 0.$

Here $\beta > 1$ is the function describing the dynamics of scientific and technological capacity.

Consider an example of modeling based on this automation. Let $x(0) = 1, \alpha = 0.98, M = 1, \beta(u) = 1 + 0.1 \cdot u.$ We will use the following sequences as funding:

$a0(k) = 10, k = 1, 2, \ldots, 20,$

$a1(k) = 0, k = 1, 2, 3, 4, 6, 7, 8, 9, 11, 12, 13, 14, 16, 17, 18, 19,$

$a1(k) = 1, k = 5, 10, 15.$

The result of numerical simulation of this automaton is shown in Figure 4.5.

We see that of an enterprise's performance increases significantly after the introduction of innovations in the creation of radically new

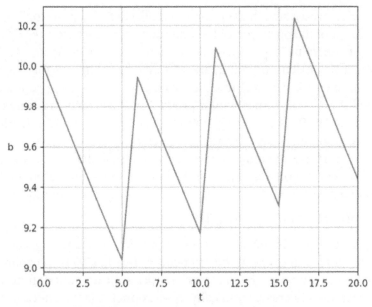

Figure 4.5 Dynamics of a company's income

products. When modeling of processes for research and technological development it is necessary to consider not only the income of an enterprise, but the expenditure, which includes costs for the implementation of measures for development of scientific-technological capacity. To do this, we will introduce the profit function of an enterprise:

$$T = (b(1) - a_0(1) - a_1(1)) + (b(2) - a_0(2) - a_1(2)) + \ldots + (b(K) - a_0(K) - a_1(K)),$$

where K is the number of countdowns in which we consider the activities of an enterprise.

To assess the effectiveness of costs for scientific and technological capacity-building and the creation of new products, consider the value

$$\Delta = T - T_0,$$

where T0 is calculated using the following formula:

$$T0 = (b(1) - a_0(1)) + (b(2) - a_0(2)) + \ldots + (b(K) - a_0(K)).$$

Here we assume that the quantities b(k) in the formula for T0 are the result of the operation of the finite automaton, where $a_1(k) = 0$.

If the value $\Delta > 0$, then the measures for scientific and technological capacity-building are effective, and the formed level of the scientific and technological capacity of an enterprise is sufficient to create a radically new product in the considered time interval. If $\Delta \leq 0$, then the expenditure of activities to build scientific and technological capacity are not effective.

Consider a dynamic model of the internal states of a knowledge-based enterprise, which are used in the finite-automaton model discussed above. Suppose we have the following recurrent sequence

$$q(k+\tau) = G(q(k), a(k), u(k)),$$

where q(k) is the state of the scientific and technological capacity of an enterprise at the moment of time k, a(k) is the volume of resource support for an enterprise, u(k) is the amount of funding for measures to create a radically new product, τ is the effective response time to innovation.

Assuming that all the coefficients are numerical, we can introduce an indicator of the competitiveness of a knowledge-intensive enterprise in terms of the ability to create radical innovations as follows.

$$Q(k) = \frac{q(k+\tau) - q(k)}{\alpha\tau + \beta u(k)}$$

where the coefficients α and β meet the conditions

$$\alpha \geq 0, \beta > 0$$

and have the meaning of the scale factors, as well as the significance of the innovation response time and the cost of innovation in the indicator of the competitiveness of an enterprise.

Since the introduced indicator of the competitiveness of a high-tech enterprise in response to radical innovations depends on time, when building a picture of information support for innovative processes, one can use the dynamics of the competitiveness indicator.

To further characterizing an enterprise by means of competitiveness in response to the development of radically new products, we can also use the finite differences of the competitiveness indicator, which will characterize not only the «instant» competitiveness of an enterprise, but also the trends of an enterprise competitiveness with constant financing of scientific and technological capacity-building. For this, we will also consider the following indicator of the trend of enterprise competitiveness:

$$DQ(k) = \frac{Q(k) - Q(k-\tau)}{\tau}$$

This indicator, together with the indicator of the level of scientific and technological capacity, is an important quantitative characteristic of innovative processes and can characterize the efficiency of transformation of the scientific and technological capacity of an enterprise into the competitive advantages of radically new products.

Stage 3. Development of a chain of transformation of scientific and technological capacity into competitive advantages of radically new products based on the results of economic and mathematical modeling.

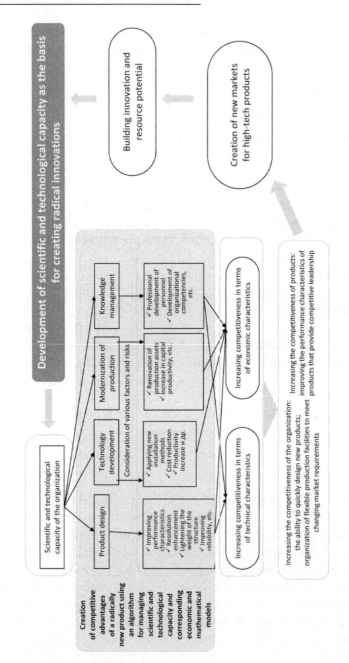

Figure 4.6. The chain of transformation of scientific and technological capacity into competitive advantages of radically new products

The developed economic and mathematical models make it possible to build a chain of transformation of scientific and technological capacity into the competitive advantages of the products being created (Fig. 4.6).

The chain takes into account the factors of uncertainty and risks at various stages of creating a radically new product.

The ability to effectively develop and use scientific and technological capacity is one of the most important organizational competencies of any company. These competencies are not directly related to products and technologies, but form the basis for their building. Understanding how scientific and technological capacity affects the level of competitiveness of an enterprise and its products, allows to concentrate resources for strategic planning of their activities and solving specific economic and production problems. The theoretical and practical assessment of the importance of scientific and technological capacity for increasing competitiveness is also related to how scientific and technological capacity operates in combination with other factors, how new competencies are formed on its basis, how radical innovations are formed using competencies, due to which highly competitive products can form new markets, resulting in the development of the company and providing prerequisites for its advanced development.

4.2. ESTABLISHING CHARACTERISTICS OF RADICALLY NEW PRODUCTS INFLUENCED BY SCIENTIFIC AND TECHNOLOGICAL CAPACITY AND UNIQUE COMPETENCIES

The establishment of the characteristics of a radically new product is based on the solution of the main task – to ensure high competitive advantages of this product due to certain parameters that create its value for the consumer.

Such value for the consumer, in addition to high competitive advantages in quality, is linked to such parameters as competitive price and costs of creating products, which payback should be ensured on the basis of an optimal competitive price that is acceptable for the buyer and the most profitable for a manufacturer. In doing so, a company will have economic growth and conditions will be created for its development due to the high competitive advantages of the products.

Having studied the issue of creating competitive advantages based on the effective use of scientific and technological capacity, we can conclude that the establishment and maintenance of competitive advantages occurs throughout the entire product life cycle. At each stage, a company's existing potential is aimed at solving various tasks in order to achieve the target result, which is manifested in the high price and non-price competitiveness of products.

It should be noted that radically new products are present in various spheres of economic activity (instrument engineering, mechanical engineering, etc.), and therefore the establishment of its techno-economic characteristics is based on the competencies and innovative technologies that the corresponding sphere of economic activity currently has. The basis for determining the economic feasibility of developing and producing radically new products is the study of prospective market needs, since the competitiveness of products is primarily the possibility of its sale on domestic and foreign markets given the actions of competitors Understanding the process of creating competitive advantages at the pre-project stage is the basis on which the entire process of product development, production and marketing will be built in the future. In this regard, we can conclude that when identifying the techno-economic characteristics of a radically new product, it is necessary to study similar products present in this market segment, as well as get reliable information about products developed by competitors. At the same time, it is necessary to study the issue of existing and emerging needs that have not yet been met, as well as to analyze consumer expectations and consumer behavior. To analyze the collected information, the weak signal control method can be used, which is discussed in detail in this work[26]. This method implies the ability of an enterprise to detect negative situations in advance and anticipate possible changes in the consumer market, so that

---

[26] Tyulin A., Chursin A. The New Economy of the Product Life Cycle. Switzerland: Springer Nature Switzerland AG, 2020. – 400 p.

the enterprise has the opportunity to make modern management decisions to adapt to possible changes and avoid the risk of reducing its own competitiveness.

In the pre-project period, the analysis of innovative technologies underlying the development and production of competitive products is of particular importance. An enterprise can make such an analysis only on the basis of certain knowledge about the techno-economic characteristics of the product designed and using methods for determining the basic indicators of competitiveness, set by technical specifications and allowing predicting the labor, material expenditure and costs of manufacturing a product already in the early stages of design.

To develop a product with competitiveness indicators that meet the technical requirements, it is necessary to monitor these indicators at all stages of product development pilot project, draft design, prototype, etc.).

Using special optimization economic and mathematical models and methods built on their basis for determining the amount of resourcing necessary for designing products for a given cost and competitiveness, the future production costs of the developed version of radically new products can be determined for each stage of design with a high degree of precision. If the achieved values of competitiveness indicators deviate from the set ones, it is necessary at the next design stage to use tools that allow improving the product characteristics and thereby increasing the competitiveness indicators to an acceptable level. The technical indicators of a product are the source of its competitiveness. They require concrete definition depending on the specifics of its purpose and conditions of consumption and operation.

Economic models for assessing the competitiveness of radically new products should be built on the basis of a minimum necessary, but sufficiently representative group of techno-economic characteristics of products that ensure their sale on the market. In these conditions, it is possible to achieve competitive techno-economic indicators in the market through the use of innovative technologies in the development, production and marketing of products.

171

When designing radically new products, the need to determine the components of this product as electronic component base, various analysis or control systems and devices included in the final multicomponent product is a significant difficulty, since these elements (components) of radically new products must be competitive in the long term, thereby ensuring the long-term competitiveness of the developed products. When designing radically new products, developers do not always have the opportunity to select components that are competitive in the long term in the considered area of economic activity, and therefore a developer may be forced to find appropriate components in related sectors of the economy or look for opportunities to design and produce the required component of radically new products based on the achievements of fundamental science.

However, the production of a designed product, its introduction into a finished product is equally challenging. The solution of this problem is closely related to the need to find or develop appropriate technological solutions, as well as production equipment. This task is extremely important in the manufacture of radically new products.

The issue of resource (including financial and personnel) support of the production process is equally important. Product design for a given cost, described in the work, is an effective solution to the issue of resourcing in the current economic conditions[27].

Based on the above-mentioned features of the development of radically new products, we propose an algorithm for establishing of techno-economic characteristics of such products (Fig. 4.7).

Explaining the algorithm for establishing of techno-economic characteristics of radically new products, presented in Figure 4.7, we note that as a result of testing a prototype of radically new products conducted in a virtual environment on its digital twin, a decision can be made to change the techno-economic characteristics of the developed products. In this case, you can return to the third stage of the described algorithm. This cycle can be repeated an unlimited number of times until a company achieves the development of a competitive radical new product.

---

[27] Tyulin A., Chursin A. The New Economy of the Product Life Cycle. Switzerland: Springer Nature Switzerland AG, 2020. – 400 p.

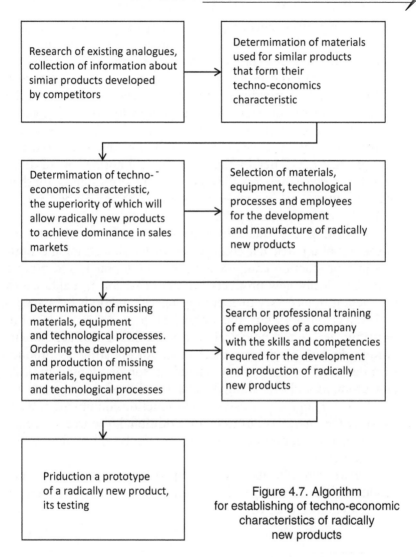

Figure 4.7. Algorithm
for establishing of techno-economic
characteristics of radically
new products

It should be noted that the long development period of a radically new product can have a significant impact on its competitiveness. Herewith, it should be noted that the long development period
for a radically new product can have a significant impact on its competitiveness. The dynamic development of the market and the high

173

level of competition encourage a company to continuously explore the market on the possibility of developing and producing more competitive products. For this reason, an excessively long development cycle for a radically new product can negatively affect its competitiveness if a competing organization introduces a product that is not inferior or superior in characteristics to the market earlier or simultaneously with a radically new product being developed by the company. In this case, it is highly probable that a radically new product developed by the company will not be able to dominate the markets; therefore the company will lose a significant share of the profit that could have been obtained if the developed product had achieved a dominant position.

Regarding the qualitative assessment of the effectiveness of the use of a particular component, material, technological process and production equipment in the development and production of radically new products, we note that for a qualitative assessment it is necessary to apply appropriate methods for assessing their effectiveness. Thus, the authors propose [28],[29],[30] an algorithm to minimize the technological cost of production of components of radically new products, a mechanism for updating the products manufactured by a company, including for developing radically new products and evaluating the effectiveness of components, materials, technological processes and production equipment, and also consider the nuances of introducing additional resources of a company when developing radically new products with higher quality characteristics.

So we can talk about the competitiveness of radically new products if the following techno-economic conditions are adhered, which guarantee their demand in the markets:

$$Tc \geq Td; Pn \leq Pdn.,$$

[28] Tyulin A., Chursin A. The New Economy of the Product Life Cycle. Switzerland: Springer Nature Switzerland AG, 2020. – 400 p.
[29] Boginsky A.I., Chursin A.A. The mechanism for updating the manufactured products // Economics and Management. 2019. No. 3 (147). Pp. 72-81.
[30] Tyulin, A. E. Corporate governance. Methodological tools. Moscow: LLC "SIC INFRA-M", 2019. 216 p.

where Tc – product characteristics;

Td – discrepancy in the technical and performance characteristics of the existing level of consumer needs for a certain period of time;

Pn – price of radically new products;

Pdn – financial capabilities of the consumer, the level of the price set by the market.

As noted earlier, when designing products and selecting their techno-economic characteristics, there is an extremely important task of maintaining the competitive cost of radically new products, in which the products will be in demand in the markets. A fairly common situation is when a developer, trying to develop products with the most highly competitive technical characteristics, ignores the fact that such characteristics require high costs when creating and reproducing them and significantly increase the cost of radically new products. For this reason, the most important process in creating radically new products is designing them for a given cost, which ensures a competitive price in the market and the necessary profitability for the continuous dynamic development of a company.

It should be noted that the implementation of the above processes is impossible without assessing and developing the scientific and technological capacity of an enterprise. In this regard, there is the question about the sufficiency of scientific and technological capacity for its use in the process of generating competitive advantages. The sufficiency of scientific and technological capacity is determined by the resources that comprise it. In this case, the key role will be played by intellectual resources and by competencies as a special category, since they are the basis for forming radical properties and characteristics of products that generate their competitive advantages. At the same time, intellectual resources and competencies are involved in production and management processes at each stage of the product life cycle and are manifested in various forms. For example, at the stage of shaping an idea (the techno-economic image of a new product), the unique knowledge and radical competencies accumulated within a company's technology platform are of particular value, allowing to develop a fundamentally new product that can solve the problems of consumers at a higher level or solve those problems that previously had no solution. At the design stage, scientific and technological capacity manifests itself not only in competencies (although they are the main element) basic), but also, for example, in sufficient equipment of a company with modern information methods and technologies that automate the design process and allow testing digital samples of a future radically new product.

Moving on to the stages of pre-production and directly to production, it should be noted that at these stages both the scientific and technological capacity of an enterprise (the implementation of unique technological processes, methods and technologies of production created at an enterprise, etc.), and scientific and the technological capacity of cross-industry technology platforms (the latest materials that create competitive advantages for radically new products, related competencies and technologies that can be involved in the process of its development and production, etc.) are actively involved.

At the stage of launching and selling radically new products, the part of the scientific and technological capacity is involved, which is responsible for marketing activities and PR.

Thus, we are speaking of marketing potential, which covers the task of promoting a radically new product to the market, as well as monitoring its competitiveness at all stages of the life cycle. At the same time, the marketing potential should be sufficient for timely identification of changing consumer preferences and market trends, so that a manufacturer has time to implement the necessary product updates or launch fundamentally new projects based on the acquisition and accumulation of radical competencies and the scientific and technological capacity-building of an enterprise. As a result, the main criterion for the sufficiency of scientific and technological capacity will be the ability of an enterprise to create a radically new product with high competitive advantages.

In accordance with the previously described in detail the process of quantitative assessment of scientific and technological capacity, it is determined by a formula representing the weighted sum of performance indicators characterizing its components.

Depending on the results of determining the sufficiency of scientific and technological capacity, two scenarios for the development of further activities are possible. The first scenario – scientific and technical capacity is sufficient, which means that a company, using certain economic tools and mechanisms, can ensure its involvement in the production and management processes to create radical properties and characteristics of new products. The second scenario – the scientific and technological capacity is insufficient, at which the challenge of increasing the scientific and technological capacity of an enterprise arises. It is necessary to determine the economic feasibility of capacity-building of an enterprise, assessing the prospective competitiveness of a new product. This challenge is also met with the use of a wide range of economic tools that allow to evaluate and analyze the activities for the development of an enterprise's capacity. All activities carried out under the second scenario should be aimed at increasing the indicators characterizing the components of scientific and technological capacity listed above.

Many economic tools were developed by us earlier in the series of books «Management of competitiveness «, «Innovation as a basis for competitiveness», « Competence Management and Competitive Product Development «, «The new Economy of the product life cycle». The diagram below shows the use of economic tools as part of the process of managing the scientific and technological capacity of an company in the formation of radical properties and competitive characteristics of new products that can create new markets.

As noted earlier, the creation and production of radically new products is not possible without using the scientific and technological capacity of an enterprise and its unique technological competencies, which are formed and developed in accordance with the trends in the transformation of industry technological platforms. Influenced by the accumulated scientific, technological and capacity of a company, the characteristics of radically new products are shaped, creating their value and consumer utility.

Let us return to the concept of a radically new product, defined as a product that has previously unknown or significantly improved functional properties or techno-economic parameters, capable of creating a new market, forming a new segment of consumers, and in some

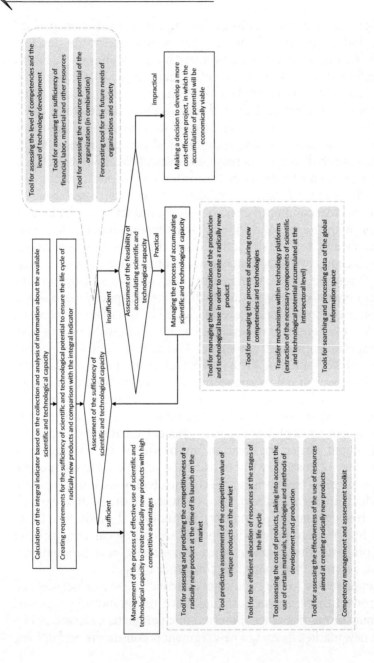

Figure 4.8 The use of economic tools as part of the process of managing the scientific and technological capacity of a company

cases even new needs. Based on this definition, the main properties and features of radically new products can be formed, which include:

- technical characteristics that significantly exceed the available market offers of competitors;
- the product is used for the first time for more efficient solution of certain tasks;
- the product is based on new advances in science and technology (including new physical principles);
- compliance of price characteristics with the capabilities of the buyer;
- the ability to satisfy the current and future needs of buyers, while occupying a high market share (market dominance).

These characteristics can be considered the key properties of a radically new product created as a result of the use of unique technological competencies and accumulated scientific and technological capacity. In this case, the scientific and technological capacity of an enterprise realized at all stages of the life cycle of a unique product, along with radical technological competencies, becomes a source of creating product value for the consumer. Scientific and technological capacity should continuously and dynamically develop and be able to flexibly reorient in accordance with long-term consumer expectations, since only flexible reorientation will allow timely development, creation and market launch of products with radically new properties.

Many radical properties and characteristics of new products are created through advanced newest methods and technologies of design and production, created on the basis of accumulated and new technological competencies within industry and cross-industry technological platforms. If we consider the radical nature of innovation, provided in the process of its creation, the main features are:

- radically new production methods and technologies;
- the use of the latest materials, their combinations and processing methods;
- new approaches in the organization of the production process, allowing to reduce the cost of the product being created, which will make it possible to approach the balance "product price – customer's capabilities".

However, the scientific and technological capacity of an enterprise should be used not only in the creation of a radically new product, but also in the process of its promotion to the market. In this regard, there is also the task of adapting sales methods and policies to the changing features of consumer behavior, which in turn increases the requirements for the development of organizational competencies.

According to research by the consulting company PricewaterhouseCoopers, there are similar behavioral trends among consumers at different levels. These include:

The growth of online shopping is a long-established trend. Currently, companies operating in market conditions use various means of digital communication and promotion of their products, since a large proportion of consumers search and select a online.

Priority for online support that can provide online clarification and product information.

Services, including in the case of territorial remoteness of the manufacturer and the buyer.

Increasing attention to the requirements of environmental friendliness and safety of products for health.

Growing demand for personalized offers: for companies – considering the specifics of their activities, for individuals – considering personal priorities and values.

In this regard, the properties of radically new products can be supplemented by a number of related properties that are more relevant to the organizational competencies of an enterprise, developing under the influence of external factors of the market environment. These include:

- new methods of forming a sales policy and pricing policy for a radically new product;
- new ways of promoting a product to the market using the advantages of online solutions;
- use of service business models;
- attractiveness for the consumer from the standpoint of environmental friendliness of products and convenience of purchase.

We cannot say that the above properties are typical only for radically new products, but they accompany the products in the process of their placing on the market. Without proper attention, radical new developments, embodied in a finished product with unique consumer properties, will not be able to create a new market due to insufficient or inefficient use of scientific, technological and competence capacity aimed at solving the problem of capturing and dominating the market.

Based on the described features of radically new products, we will form a three-stage list of features of radically new products created through the effective use by a company of its own scientific and technological capacity and unique competencies accumulated in a technological platform (Fig.4.9).

When talking about the features of radically new products that bring value to the consumer, one of the important issues is to achieve a balance of these features in their ratio with an acceptable price for the buyer. For example, if we talk about the durability of a product, at least two groups of products can be distinguished, for one of which durability is a key characteristic, despite the ongoing cost increase (for example, a reentry stage of a rocket or products with a long period of operation and renovation/modernization), and for the second group of frequently updated and modernized products, this characteristic will not be as relevant, while the price reduction will be more important. The second group may include, for example, some household appliances, digital technology, cell phones, etc., which are undergoing constant updates, thereby generating buyer's interest in purchasing new models. The profit of an enterprise when selling products of the second group is formed as a result of economies of scale.

In different cases, different features of a radically new product bring value to the consumer, as a result of which the buyer is willing to pay only for certain radical properties of the product, while ignoring the rest. Under these conditions, mechanisms for customizing products are launched, given the preferences of various consumer groups.

All mechanisms are in some way connected with the implementation of various combinations of scientific and technological

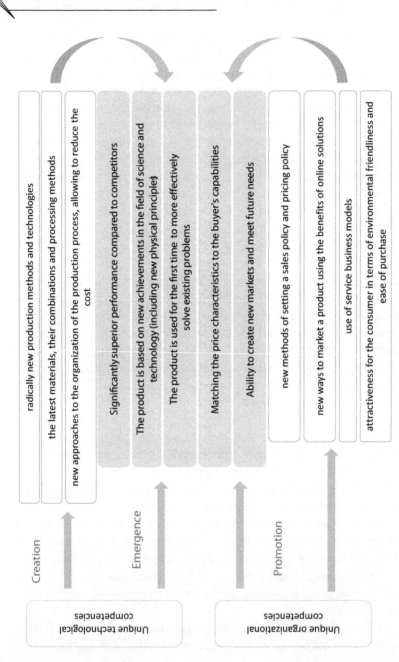

Figure 4.9. Features of radically new products

capacity and competencies of an enterprise in creating radically new products (their features and properties) and the so-called value innovations. The success of a radical new product in the market depends on whether it is a value innovation.

The concept of value innovation was put forward by the members of the INSEAD International business School Jang Kim and Renee Mauborgne. These researchers believe that value innovation implies a transition from participating in a competitive struggle to creating completely new markets or revaluing existing ones[31]. According to Jang Kim and Mauborn, value-driven companies challenge traditional competitive thinking on the five points presented in Table 4.1.

Table 4.1. Features of companies implementing value innovations

Criterion	Features of creating value innovation
Industry view	Go beyond the «rules of the game» in the industry
Strategic focus	Avoiding competition as such. The main goal is to create new markets where competitors will not be able to penetrate immediately
Consumers	Lack of segmentation, identification of common features that will allow the formation of a new market
Assets and abilities	Continuous development of new competencies and scientific and technological capacity- building that meet market requirements in terms of meeting consumer expectations
Offer of products and services	Creation of truly valuable products for consumers, even if it requires moving beyond the traditional boundaries of their enterprise

Thus, we can formulate the following axiom: the economic efficiency obtained as a result of the development of radically new products, created using various combinations of scientific and technological capacity and unique competencies, depends on the level of value innovations (the degree of value to the consumer), manifested in terms of quality, price, availability and awareness.

In these conditions, the consumers make their choice in the market taking into account the value effects that they will

---

[31] Kim W.C., Mauborgne R. Value Innovation: The Strategic Logic of High Growth // Harvard Business Review. 1997. Vol. 75 (1). P. 102-112..

receive from the purchase and use of radically new products that have a certain value, which may be due to its radical properties. It is assumed that not only the objective (formed due to radical properties), but also the subjective (perceived) value of a product, formed under the marketing information, may be significant at the time of purchase. The mechanism of consumer perception of value, as noted in the works[32],[33], functions through the perception of quality, price, availability of products (taking into account the timing of its creation and market launch) and consumer awareness. This complex perception of the total value of a radically new product forms an integral assessment of value innovation. Each value block included in the total value has a certain value for the consumer. Striving for the optimal choice, the consumer wants to purchase a product which value is determined by consumer value effects. Among the many offers of similar products, the consumer first evaluates the values of an innovative product and then compares it with the value of another product based on an integral assessment of value innovation. From this perspective, the following model for evaluating value innovation is proposed, taking into account the significance of each value block:

$$V = a1 \cdot Kqual + a2 \cdot Kp + a3 \cdot Kavai + a3 \cdot Kinf$$

where Kqual – quality significance coefficient;
Kp – price significance coefficient;
Kavail – availability significance coefficient;
Kinf – information significance coefficient
The proposed model describes the consumer choice of an innovative product based on value consumer effects that determine the consumer total value of an innovative product, the assessment of which, in turn, determines the consumer choice of a new product among other products on the market.

The potential profit on investment and scientific and technological capacity and unique competencies in value innovation turns are higher compared to the profit obtained in the case of investment

---

[32] Kotler F., Trias de Bez F. Lateral marketing. – St. Petersburg, 2009.
[33] Tyan E.G. Investigation of the features of the value of an innovative product in consumer perception // Marketing and marketing research. – 2011. – No. 5 (95).

in innovation that does not create radically new product features. In the second case, competitors may copy innovations or even develop better solutions much faster, which will lead to a loss of market share.

The above allows us to propose the following algorithm for obtaining high economic efficiency from the creation of value innovations (Fig. 4.10).

Analysis of the range of products manufactured by the organization. Determination of newly created competitive advantages, due to which it is possible to form a new market or new needs

Research and identification of ways to improve existing technological and production processes

Ranking of innovations depending on the amount of investments required for their development and implementation. Risk analysis and accounting for the expected economic effect from implementation

Defining investment volumes to create value innovations and radical product properties that ensure market dominance

Selection of an innovative solution that brings the greatest value to the consumer and provides the greatest economic effect from implementation for the organization

Ensuring the transfer of radical competencies and scientific and technological capacity into a ready-made radically new product

Development of measures to promote a radically new product that brings value to the consumer to sales markets

Figure 4.10. Algorithm for obtaining high economic efficiency from the creation of value innovations

185

Experience shows that high results from innovation activities can be achieved mainly through the use of strategic methods of managing value innovations. In this regard, the strategic management of value innovations must address the planning and implementation of innovative projects designed for a significant qualitative leap in ensuring high performance of radically new products.

We present the main goals of strategic planning of value innovations

- efficient allocation and use of resources – the so-called internal strategy. It is planned to effectively use the scientific and technological capacity and unique technological and organizational competencies in the process of forming the value characteristics of a radically new product;
- adaptation to the external environment. The task is to effectively adapt to changing consumer expectations and preferences, as well as the development of cross-industry technology platforms that integrate radical competencies forming the basis for the creation of radical value innovations.

Strategic planning for value innovation requires research and is based on data collection and analysis. This allows to constantly monitor the market with rapidly changing situation.

The examination of their potential plays an important role for value innovations. The task of the expertise is to assess the real value of a radically new product for the market and its compliance with consumer expectations, as well as the real possibility of its creation with the radical characteristics and economic efficiency laid in the techno-economic image.

The world's leading enterprises, in an effort to achieve technological advantage set the goal of not only forming a new market segment, but also providing the foundations for their long-term economic development. The driving force of economic growth in this case is the effective transfer of accumulated and dynamically developing scientific and technological capacity and unique competencies into a radically new product with high competitive advantages and high value for the consumer.

4.3. METHODS FOR MANAGING THE TRANSFORMATION OF SCIENTIFIC AND TECHNOLOGICAL CAPACITY AND UNIQUE TECHNOLOGICAL COMPETENCIES INTO A RADICALLY NEW PRODUCT TO ENSURE THE COMPANY'S SUSTAINABILITY

In economic science, there are a variety of methods for managing economic processes, which are the basis of tools and mechanisms for solving economic, production, and other tasks and together form a methodology for managing a certain process.

Such tools and mechanisms are used by a company in practice, which ensures its continuous dynamic development on the basis of technological platforms and the use of modern methods of managing economic processes, providing a company's efficiency and creating conditions for maintaining and improving market positions.

The choice of a particular management method depends on the nature of the implementation of the management function and on the management tools, resources and competencies available at that time. The essence of economic management methods is to organize effective management of various business areas by influencing economic processes with economic levers and tools.

In this case, the process of transformation of scientific and technological capacity and unique technological competencies into a radically new product is considered. An important task is to determine the most effective tools and methods of transformation to achieve the final goals at each stage of the product life cycle. In this case, the main goals at the stages of the life cycle are the following:

– when shaping the techno-economic image of a product and developing a draft design – creating the image of a product with the maximum involvement of scientific and technological capacity, which allows to create high competitive advantages of the product and maintain them for a long time period;

– in preproduction – the creation of the most efficient production with a high technical level, ensuring high labor productivity, resource saving with maximum resource efficiency;

– in production – ensuring the manufacture of a radically new product with set techno-economic characteristics at a competitive price, using the created production with a high technical level;

– in operation – ensuring the extension of a product's service life through its modernization and the generation of new competitive advantages that increase the product life cycle on the market.

Schematically, these processes look as follows, shown in Fig. 4.11. As previously determined, a high level of the indicator of scientific and technological capacity, sufficient to create a radically new product, is in the range of 75-100%. We will assume that a company that has started to create radically new product has a sufficient level of scientific and technological capacity and a sufficient level of unique technological competencies to create value-based innovations.

It is necessary to determine which consistently implemented measures and methods, depending on the stages of the life cycle, the scientific and technological capacity can be transformed into a radically new product.

Consider the sequence of such activities for the enlarged stages of the life cycle: shaping the techno-economic image of a product and design, preproduction and production. The algorithm for the implementation of activities will be different for each stage of the life cycle, but the first stage will be the same for all stages – determining (assessing) the level of scientific and technological capacity of a particular unit $IP^{II}_{R\&D}$ in which a particular stage of the life cycle is carried out.

Such an assessment is carried out by analogy with the assessment of the scientific and technological capacity of the entire enterprise $IP_{R\&D}$, except that there are changes in the distribution of weights of individual generalized indicators that form the integral indicator of scientific and technological capacity. As noted earlier, for the stage of shaping the image and design of the product, the intellectual, personnel, marketing, resource, and effective components have the greatest weight; at the stage of testing and preproduction (especially technological), the intellectual, organizational, resource,

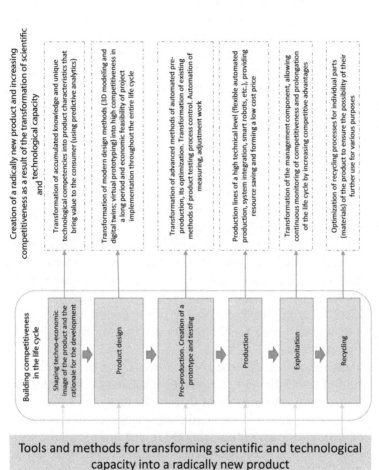

Figure 4.11. Transformation of scientific and technological capacity into a radically new product with high competitive advantages

effective components have the greatest weight; at the production stage, all components are involved, each of which has a fairly high weight; at the stage of promotion to the market, the most important are the marketing, resource, organizational components.

We will describe the process of transformation of scientific and technological capacity at the stage of shaping the image and design of a radically new product. This process is primarily associated with an assessment of the current level of scientific and technological capacity of the developing departments. If the level is high $(0.75 < IP_{R\&D}^{\Pi} \leq 1)$, the transformation of an enterprise's capacity and its transfer to the development division is not required; if the level is medium or low $(0 < IP_{R\&D}^{\Pi} \leq 0.75)$, it is necessary to carry out measures to transform the scientific and technological capacity of an enterprise for its most effective use in the design of a radically new product. These activities include:

- assessment O_1^1 of personnel competencies and training of employees (hiring new specialists) on the use of modern design methods (computer modeling, supercomputer engineering, etc.);
- identifying the technical level O_2^1 of the design, technological and software base for the implementation of the digital design process;
- identifying the sufficiency of resources O_3^1 for the transformation of scientific and technological capacity into a radically new product at the stage of shaping its image and design;
- elaboration of regulations and company standards (regulation of structure and functions) for the transition to digital design;
- based on the accumulated scientific and technological capacity of a company, the development of a platform for managing the digital profile of a product, providing full traceability throughout the entire life cycle: from the design of individual parts and components, including control at the production stage, to the operation of the finished product;
- enabling the transition to digital certification, which provides expert support for the development and application of simulation models and virtual test benches;

– development of platform solutions (as a method of systematizing the constantly increasing scientific and technological capacity) «Base of accumulated competencies», «Base of accumulated technologies», «Base of available capacities», «Base of developed innovations» used in the process of designing a radically new product.

As a result of the above measures at the stage of shaping the image and designing a radically new product, the scientific and technological capacity is transformed into high competitive advantages of the product, ensuring its long presence in the market.

At the pre-production stage, if the level of scientific and technological capacity of the division responsible for pre-production is medium or low $(0 < IP_{R\&D}^{\Pi} \le 0.75)$, the following measures should be taken to transform the scientific and technological capacity:

– identifying the level O_1^2 of material, technical, instrumental and technological base and its sufficiency for creating a radically new product according to the techno-economic image and digital twin (if the level is insufficient, it is necessary to improve it by modernization or updating in order to increase automation);

– assessment of the competencies of personnel O_2^2, involved in the pre-production and training of employees (hiring new specialists) to ensure the required level of competence;

– identifying the sufficiency of resources O_3^2 for the transformation of scientific and technological capacity into a radically new product at the pre-production stage;

– elaboration of digital regulations and company standards (regulation of structure and functions), given the use of new approaches to organizing pre-production;

– optimization of operating modes and equipment loading.

The implementation of these measures ensures the creation of the most efficient products (including virtually distributed) with a high technical level, ensuring high labor productivity, resource saving with maximum resource efficiency, while influencing the cost reduction.

At the production stage, if the level of scientific and technological capacity of the production unit is medium or low $(0 < IP_{R\&D}^{\Pi} \le 0.75)$, it is necessary to carry out the following measures to transform the scientific and technological capacity:

- identifying the sufficiency and increasing the level of «digital equipment» of production; O_1^3
- assessment of the competencies of production personnel O_2^3 and training of employees (hiring new specialists) to ensure the required level of competencies;
- identifying the sufficiency of resources O_3^3 for the transformation of scientific and technological capacity into a radically new product at the production stage;
- elaboration of regulations and standards, given the modernization and increased flexibility of product lines.

As a result of the implementation of the above measures in production, the transformation of scientific and technological capacity into a radically new product with set techno-economic characteristics with a competitive price is ensured, using the created products with a high technical level.

All the above-described measures aimed at solving the problem of transforming the scientific and technological capacity at the stages of the life cycle are designed to provide the created radical new product with a high consumer value and a competitive price, allowing the product to remain on the market for a long period of time due to its maximum use.

Let us describe the management processes for the development of radically new products using the formed scientific and technological capacity and competencies based on the economic and mathematical model.

The process of creating radically new products will be considered in the light of management at all stages of the life cycle. The management is aimed at achieving a high level of scientific and technological capacity of each division involved in a certain stage of the product life cycle. The effectiveness of creating new products is assessed on the basis of a set of indicators of the competitiveness of these products.

The main goal achieved as a result of the transformation of scientific and technological capacity and competencies into radical properties of new products is to ensure a high level of competitiveness, influenced by the effectiveness of processes at each stage of the life cycle. The transformation of scientific and technological capacity at a certain stage of the life cycle is considered effective if the competitiveness at the current stage corresponds to the level that allows a product to be classified as radically new.

However, if the competitiveness does not meet the specified level, it is necessary to take the following control actions both on the scientific and technological capacity, and on the processes of its transformation into radically new product characteristics, depending on the conditions at a particular stage of the life cycle:

- if the level of competitiveness of the techno-economic image is insufficient, it is recommended to make adjustments in order to increase competitiveness and create a new image with more promising characteristics that allow the products to be classified as radically new;
- if the lack of competitiveness in the design of a product (its digital twin) is identified, it is recommended to make changes to the designed digital twin that will increase the competitive advantage;
- if during the tests it is revealed that the sample is uncompetitive, there is a return to the design stage and adjustments are made to achieve compliance with the specified level of competitiveness;
- if it is determined that at the pre-production stage, quality decreases, labor intensity increases and the risk of defects increases, which leads to a decrease in competitiveness relative to a given level due to the use of, for example, outdated equipment, it is recommended to make comprehensive decisions throughout the production activity to improve the pre-production, use more modern equipment and other more effective solutions;
- if the loss of competitiveness occurs at the production stage, it is recommended to address the issue of its optimization and modernization (including the introduction of elements of lean production, which allows maintaining price competitiveness, etc.);

– if competitiveness decreases during the operation stage, it is recommended to make decisions either on the qualitative modernization of existing products, which will increase its competitive advantages, or on the development of new samples.

Let $x(t) \in RN$ be indicators of the competitiveness of products formed at various stages of the life cycle, allowing it to be classified as a radically newIn the resulting economic and mathematical model, we will consider continuous time, since the processes of creating new products are considered at large time intervals.

The control effects on the scientific and technological capacity and the efficiency of the processes defined by it at various stages of the life cycle are described by the vector-valued function $u(t) \in RM$, which also depends on time. The economic meaning of the management (control) function lies in the possibility of effective use of scientific and technological capacity and competencies in forming competitive advantages of products, as well as in the implementation of design, production and other processes at various stages of the life cycle. In this case, the dynamics of processes at different stages of the life cycle of a new product can be described by the following differential equation:

$$x'(t) = F(t, x(t), u(t)), \, t \in [0, T], \qquad (1)$$

where $T > 0$ is the time of the entire life cycle of development and market launch of a radically new product.

Equation (1) generally is rather complicated for economic and mathematical analysis, therefore, we can consider a linear approximation of this equation as follows,

$$x'(t) = A(t) \cdot x(t) + B(t) \cdot u(t), \qquad (2)$$

where $A(t)$ is an $N \times N$ matrix; $B(t)$ is an $N \times M$ matrix.

When creating a radically new product the goal of control is to minimize the target functionality:

$$J(u) = |xu(t) - x^*(t)| + \alpha \cdot \int a(t) \cdot |u(t)| dt, \qquad (3)$$

where $xu(t)$ is the solution of the problem for equation (1) or (2) in the case when control $u(t)$ is selected; $x^*(t)$ is the planned parameters of the process of creating new products; $a(t) \geq 0$ is the function of the cost of management decisions (resource costs for creating products); α > 0 is the dimension coefficient.

Moving on to the individual stages of the life cycle, namely, image shaping and design, pre-preparation, and production, the functional (3) can be presented as follows:

$$J(u) = |x_u(t) - x*(t)| + \alpha \sum_i a_i(t) \cdot |u_i(t)|$$

where specific values of i correspond to a specific stage of the life cycle. Control at various stages of the life cycle provides a high level of scientific and technological capacity due to the growth of parameters O_i^j.

The economic meaning of the functional J is that the first term shows how much the results of our control diverge from the planned values, i.e. to what extent the achieved level of indicators of the competitiveness of products differs from the planned level of indicators of competitiveness, which allows to classify the products as a radically new. The closer this difference is to zero, the higher the efficiency of the transformation of the scientific and technological capacity of an enterprise, given the costs of generating competitive advantages of the manufactured products, and the second term shows the resource expenditures related to increasing the scientific and technological capacity of the enterprise.

We will minimize the functional J on the set of admissible controls, which is defined as follows:

U = {v(t) ∈ U(t): t ∈ [0, T]}.

Thus, the optimization task of managing (controlling) the processes of creating products at all stages of the life cycle based on the presented economic and mathematical model of products is to find such a control u* ∈ U, so that

$$\begin{cases} J(u^*) = \min\{J(u) : u \in U\}, \\ IP^i_{R\&D}(u_i) \to \max \end{cases} \tag{4}$$

Problem (4) relates to the classical optimal control problem, and therefore it is possible to use well-known methods of calculus of variations and optimal principles to solve it.

The proposed model of optimal control allows to form a method of decision support in the management of scientific and technological capacity of divisions. According to the informational principle of decision-making in conditions of uncertainty, the key issue is the probabilistic assessment of the growth of indicators characterizing the scientific and technological capacity of a division, as a result of the implementation of certain measures in conditions of resource expenditure. Consider an intelligent method for obtaining such a probabilistic estimate.

Let, on the basis of the method described above, some control action $u \in U$ is recommended at a certain stage of the life cycle of a radically new product being created. Suppose that $R(u)$ (the set of possible reactions to u) is finite, i.e. $R(u) = \{ r1, r2, ..., rN \}$. By pn, n = 1, 2, ..., N we denote the probabilities of the reaction rn. Of course, the following condition must be met:

$$pn \geq 0, p1 + p2 + ... + pN = 1.$$

In the absence of any additional information, we will assume that the a priori probabilities of the reaction to the decision are given. In the case when we have certain information that can clarify the a priori probability of a reaction, we will denote this information as D. In this case, the probabilities of reactions can be expressed using the conditional probability:

$$pn = P(r = rn|D), n = 1, 2, ..., N.$$

Here, $P(r = rn|D)$ denotes the probability of the reaction rn, provided that there is data (information) D.

To actually calculate the conditional probability $P(r = rn|D)$ the Bayesian approach can be used, which is based on the same name formula. Using the Bayes formula, we can calculate the conditional probability as follows:

$$P(r = rn|D) = (P(D \mid r = rn) \cdot P(r = rn)) / P(D).$$

The process of constructing these conditional probabilities is also called Bayesian machine learning.

As a rule, the existing information is a set of some facts that, in our case, characterize the growth of various components

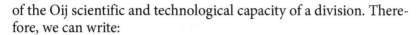
of the Oij scientific and technological capacity of a division. Therefore, we can write:

D = (D1, D2, ..., DM),

where Dm is the growth of the Oij components of the scientific and technological capacity of a division at all stages of the life cycle of unique products.

Different facts are usually mutually dependent, so calculating the probability P(D) may require knowledge of the correlation between different facts, which is a serious technical problem. To solve this problem, it is recommended to use a naive Bayesian approach when it is assumed that different facts are independent. In this case, the probability P (D) can be easily calculated using the following formula:

$$P(D) = P(D1) \cdot P(D2) \cdot ... \cdot P(DM).$$

This approach leads mainly to correct reliable results, which, according to research, provides sufficient efficiency of decisions made automatically by decision support methods. Such efficiency makes it possible to implement and operate the proposed control methods for the development of radically new products based on the built scientific and technological capacity at the established and already functioning digital enterprises. On the basis of the proposed method, the probability is established with which various variants of control actions on the scientific and technological capacity will lead to its growth and provide the possibility of its effective transformation into radical properties of new products due to the growth of private indicators of their evaluation.

To solve the problem of transforming scientific and technological capacity into a radically new product, it is proposed to use the following tools and methods:
- a method for assessing the readiness of enterprise divisions for build scientific and technological capacity-building;
- tools for capacity transformation ("transfer" to the applied plane) related to the regulatory and methodological regulation of this process at various stages of the product life cycle;
- a model for assessing the impact of control actions on the components of scientific and technological capacity, as well

as the impact on the growth of capacity and the process of its transformation into radical properties of new products.

These tools and methods can be used comprehensively in the process of creating and manufacturing different products. In real economic conditions, radically new products are created in companies that are already participants in the commodity markets and release products created on the basis of the established technology platform. When it comes to creating radically new products, this process is related to the continuous development of a technology platform through the constant of scientific and technical capacity-building and its transformation into highly competitive products that ensure a company's stability in the market.

Since the market is dynamic and rapidly changing influenced by consumer expectations, for a company in order to maintain competitiveness it is extremely important to have flexible production and management processes, created due to the flexibility of the technology platform.

One of the most effective tools of flexibility is a flexible technology platform that creates conditions for scientific and technical capacity-building with its subsequent transformation into radical properties of a new product at all stages of its life cycle, increasing the sustainability (economic efficiency) of a company, achieved by:

- ensuring flexibility, versatility and adaptability of production based on reducing possible losses per area of activity, as well as specialization of the production of components at an enterprise based on the most advanced technologies at a given cost;
- developing new competitive advantages of existing products and extending the period of their active sales by upgrading the basic samples;
- improving the effectiveness of marketing activities by identifying and predicting future needs in various market segments;
- design and manufacture of promising products for a given cost and competitiveness using methods of functional and cost analysis and optimization of design and technological solutions according to the cost criterion, given the introduction of digital technologies, as well as the processing and analysis of big data;

– ensuring the optimal level of its self- processing in the total volume of parts and components used in the manufacture of products;

– introduction of an automated enterprise resource management system based on digital technologies.

The scientific and technological capacity-building and use of the technology platform significantly affects the activities of an enterprise in various fields. This increases labor productivity, reduces the cost of manufactured products and the timing of their creation and production, given the reduction of certain stages of the life cycle (for example, pre-production, prototype testing, which is carried out in smaller quantities by creating a digital twin of new promising products of the future, etc.), frees up a significant amount of outdated low-performance equipment, replaced by new intelligent systems that can interact each and ultimately ensure the technological superiority of an enterprise. The flexibility of a technology platform and its ability to adapt to the emergence of new, more advanced technologies can be achieved by applying the concept of digital twins of products and production processes. Flexible product development and project implementation means that the current project plan is constantly updated according to incoming information about the current state of the project. For knowledge-based and high-tech products, changes in the course of project implementation are usually associated with serious financial and time costs, and often such changes are impossible. Therefore, the most important tool that allows the flexible development of science-intensive projects is the use of digital twins of products and production processes and parallel engineering, which involves development and design simultaneously with the modeling of manufacturing and operation. A digital twin is a digital copy of a physical object; changes to the digital model can be made easily. Moreover, when designing products of the future, it is necessary to use multi-variant design, when several technical solutions are considered simultaneously. The use of digital models allows not only to concurrently develop a product, but also to predict its technical characteristics. It is the digital product model that will allow us to create radically new products that will be able to meet the challenges of consumers and the condition of the market in the future. In this case, automatic project management systems play an essential role. Information support of the product lifecycle management system at an enterprise allows you to receive operational information for making management decisions in order to flexibly adjust the progress of the project. Automatic decision-making systems based on operational information cannot always be implemented in real production for various reasons, but they can be effectively applied on a digital twin of the product and a digital twin of production. After analyzing the results of applying automatic decisions in a digital environment, it becomes possible to make these decisions in real production.

The flexibility of a technology platform can be viewed as the optimization problem of resourcing of the various subsystems of the organizational-economic system, thereby creating a balance between operational activities related to the manufacturing and sales of already developed products and innovative-investment activity related to the strengthening scientific and technological capacity and development of new products on its basis. Let us consider the methods by which it will be possible to manage the scientific and technological capacity-building and use at the enterprise to create a radically new product based on a technology platform.

The most significant indicators that characterize the basis of scientific and technological development of an enterprise and determine its balanced economic development are indicators that characterize both its competitiveness and the ability to adapt to the task of creating radically new products, for which an enterprise must have sufficient resources and economic stability.

The process of balancing operational and innovation activities can be described on the basis of the concept of a Distribution center (DC), which is an element of an enterprise technology platform and is responsible for the distribution of resources between subsystems within the technology platform.

From this perspective, the resources distributed by the DC can be classified into two categories:

- resources required for the implementation of an enterprise's operational activities related to the release of already mastered products;
- resources directed by an enterprise to build scientific and technological capacity and create radically new products.

DC resources can consist of many separate components, but there always should be one manager. If there are several managers in a technology platform in one DC, then this is the result of a poorly constructed management system, since each manager can make a decision that is inconsistent with the rest of the managers.

To manage the scientific and technological development of an enterprise, balanced in terms of economic sustainability and the level of resourcing that enables the development of radically new products, the following methods are proposed, represented by management tools:

- a tool for assessing the level of scientific and technological capacity and competencies of an enterprise (discussed earlier in Chapter 3);
- a tool for assessing the competitiveness of an enterprise, given its economic stability and the level of resourcing as a measure of the ability to create new competitive products that are in demand in the market;
- a model of optimal management of the processes of creating new products based on the scientific and technological capacity and competencies of an enterprise and a method of decision-making for optimal management.

Using economic and mathematical modeling of the dynamics of enterprise competitiveness, we will describe the process of its sustainable development, which consists in a balanced use of enterprise resource support to create radically new products based on the built scientific and technological capacity, while maintaining high competitive advantages of already manufactured products. The issue of ensuring the economic sustainability of an enterprise is closely related to the management of the competitiveness of the enterprise and its resourcing.

The listed indicators form a vector U, the components of which determine the level of enterprise competitiveness:

$$U = \begin{pmatrix} IQ \\ \lambda \\ \mu \\ P \end{pmatrix}.$$

The proposed economic and mathematical model should describe the management of the balanced development of an enterprise through the implementation of management measures on its operational activities and development program.

The formula for calculating the integral indicator of enterprise competitiveness (Q) is as follows:

$$Q = w1 \times IQ \times \lambda + w2 \times P \times \mu, \tag{1}$$

where $w1 + w2 = 1$.

This method of forming an integral indicator of competitiveness makes it possible to link the competitiveness of products, the sustainability of operating and innovative activities and the sufficiency of a company's resources.

By regulating (control actions) all the described indicators IQ, λ, μ, P, using the proposed economic and mathematical model, it is possible to ensure the effectiveness of the mechanism for managing the balanced development of a company by implementing control actions on individual components that form its competitiveness.

The simulation will allow us to determine how the integral indicator of a company's competitiveness Q will change when changing the defining parameters. Thus, with the growth of the competitiveness of manufactured products, the income received from the sale of such products will increase. It will create new sources of resources both for the modernization of the production and technological system of a company's structure, and for the creation of new types of products. Improving the efficiency of the technological platform will improve the values of the parameters that determine the overall competitiveness of a company and, thus, will increase its economic sustainability. Thus, a synergistic effect is achieved from the joint use of management tools, which ultimately leads to an increase in a company's competitiveness as a whole.

The company's overall balanced development management (control) model should describe the impact of management actions on operational and innovation activities. The mathematical management model is described by the formula:

$$U(t) = D(t)U(t) + M(t,U(t)),\qquad(2)$$

where U(t) is the previously introduced four-component vector;

D(t) is a matrix describing the mutual influence of the components of the vector U:

$$D = \begin{pmatrix} 1 & \xi_{\widetilde{IQ},\lambda} & \xi_{\widetilde{IQ},\mu} & \xi_{\widetilde{IQ},[x]} \\ \xi_{\lambda,\widetilde{IQ}} & 1 & \xi_{\lambda,\mu} & \xi_{\lambda,[x]} \\ \xi_{\mu,\widetilde{IQ}} & \xi_{\mu,\lambda} & 1 & \xi_{\mu,[x]} \\ \xi_{[x],\widetilde{IQ}} & \xi_{[x],\lambda} & \xi_{[x],\mu} & 1 \end{pmatrix}.$$

At each moment of time t, the elements of the matrix take on new values. The economic meaning of the matrix element $\xi_{i,j}$ is to describe the tendency for the component j of the vector U to change under the influence of the component i.

M(t,U(t)) are control effects on operational and innovative activities for the management of scientific and technological capacity and the creation of radically new products.

The model mathematically describes the economic processes of the impact of all these parameters on the final result – the integral competitiveness of a company (calculated by formula (1)) and the company's launch of radically new products.

The most important element of the model is the matrix D(t) of the relationship of the elements of the vector U. As a result of the management of operational and innovative activities, the matrix should change according to the following economic principles. Thus, the growth of the competitiveness of products will increase the growth of a company's competitiveness as a whole, since the highly demanded radically new products create competitive advantages in the market. This ensures the growth and profitability of a company, which increases its economic performance and sustainability, while creating a resource reserve that can be directed to the development of the product line, the technological base, the competence component, and also increases the competitiveness of the company as a whole.

The role of resourcing in the mechanism for managing the scientific and technological development of a company is extremely large, moreover, the sufficiency of resourcing is essential for maintaining competitiveness and sustainability of development based on the production of high-quality products and with unique characteristics that could respond emerging market needs or stimulate the emergence of needs met by this product. Lack of resources will definitely negatively affect the final result, while also negatively affecting other parameters that can be regulated to effectively manage a company's competitiveness.

By regulating all the described indicators, using the proposed economic and mathematical model, it is possible to ensure the effectiveness of the mechanism for managing the scientific and technological development of a company by controlling the individual components forming its competitiveness. With effective management of scientific and technological development, a company's development trajectory should remain in a certain outline (see Figure 4.12). Exceeding the border of this corridor means the loss of sustainable economic growth related to overheating of a company's economy and the risks of losing its competitiveness due to refinancing of innovative activities, which is explained by the fact that unique products are developed in the conditions of the risk of loss of economic stability of a company and the already occupied position in the market, which is associated with insufficient preliminary analysis of the feasibility of innovative projects and large expenditures of resources for the implementation of investment and innovative activities. The descent of the trajectory beyond the lower limit means the lack of scientific and technological development and ineffective use of available resources.

We define the permissible boundaries for the advanced development corridor of a high-tech company as follows. At each moment of time, after the implementation of the control actions on the operational and innovative activities, new four elements of IQ, λ, μ, P will be obtained, which will determine the new value

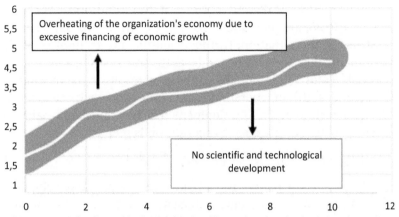

Figure 4.12 Outline of balanced scientific and technological development

of the competitiveness of company Q.

The balanced development of a company in the conditions of the proposed mathematical management model will correspond to a situation in which not only the company's competitiveness indicator Q will increase, but also the Pareto optimality condition of the resulting vector U will be met. Let the vector U have the following state at the initial moment of time:

$$U_0 = \begin{pmatrix} IQ_0 \\ \lambda_0 \\ \mu_0 \\ P_0 \end{pmatrix}.$$

As a result of the control actions on the operational and innovative activities, the vector accepted the following meaning:

$$U_1 = \begin{pmatrix} IQ_1 \\ \lambda_1 \\ \mu_1 \\ P_1 \end{pmatrix}.$$

The control is Pareto optimal if the conditions, $IQ_1 \geq IQ_0$, $\lambda_1 \geq \lambda_0$, P1>P0, are met, and at least one of these inequalities must be strict. In this situation, further scientific and technological development (expressed in the model as the transition to a new Pareto optimal vector U) is possible only as a result of major changes (structural shift) in operational and innovative activities. Scientific and technological development will be considered balanced and sustainable over time if the condition is met

$$\left(IQ_1 \cdot \mu_1 - IQ_0 \cdot \mu_0\right) \approx \left(P_1 \cdot \lambda_1 - P_0 \cdot \lambda_0\right) \tag{3}$$

It means that innovative activities related to the development of scientific and technological capacity and the creation of radically new products, subject to availability resources, are harmonized (corresponding in pace and intensity) with the development of the production system and business processes, accompanied by the economic stability of an organization. The boundaries of the sustainable development corridor will be defined by a set of control actions M (t, U (t)) M(t, U(t)) of equation (2), which will ensure the fulfillment of condition (3):

$$\overline{Q(t)} = \max_{M(t,U(t))} (w_1 \cdot IQ_{M(t,U(t))} \cdot \lambda_{M(t,U(t))} + w_2 \cdot P_{M(t,U(t))} \cdot \mu_{M(t,U(t))}),$$

$$\underline{Q(t)} = \min_{M(t,U(t))} (w_1 \cdot IQ_{M(t,U(t))} \cdot \lambda_{M(t,U(t))} + w_2 \cdot P_{M(t,U(t))} \cdot \mu_{M(t,U(t))}),$$

where $\overline{Q(t)}$, $\underline{Q(t)}$ are respectively the upper and lower boundaries of the contour of balanced scientific and technological development at time t.

The proposed model demonstrates that the process of developing scientific and technological capacity and radical competencies at high-tech enterprises forms a system of internal resources, the use of which provides an abrupt trajectory for the development of innovative technologies to create radically new products, the release of which involves the creation of new consumer markets. This creates a demand for new competitive products. All this contributes to the development of fundamental science, generates applied developments that form the basis of innovative technologies, which are subsequently translated into new products or services. The desire for economic and scientific and technological development encourages manufacturers of high-tech products to create or contribute to the creation of new markets for the promotion of their radically new products, since in the process of scientific and technological development, the scientific and technological capacity is transformed into the competitive advantages of products. Moreover, their growth should be ensured by obtaining the effect of using the scientific and technological capacity at different stages of the life cycle.

Thus, the developed model allows optimal planning of control actions associated with scientific and technological capacity-building and ensuring high efficiency of the processes of creating new products based on it, given resource costs at various stages of the life cycle, creating competitive advantages as radical properties of these products, capable of creating new markets and ensuring economic stability and advanced development of an enterprise through effective management decisions to manage scientific and technological capacity and radical technological competencies.

CHAPTER 5.
PRACTICAL METHODS OF CREATING AND SELLING PRODUCTS WITH HIGH CONSUMER UTILITY

5.1. METHODS FOR ASSESSING AND MONITORING MARKETS FOR PRODUCTS WITH HIGH CONSUMER UTILITY

Studies[34],[35],[36] indicate, that the creation of highly competitive products is based on the accumulation of scientific and technological capacity by the manufacturer and building key competencies, which determine the creation of competitive advantages of products and allow the successful implementation of appropriate measures at each stage of the life cycle of the products created. The process of creating products with high consumer utility begins with the shaping its idea and techno-economic image, accompanied by the use of various tools for evaluating and monitoring the target market, under which two important issues can be addressed. On the one hand, it is a market assessment consisting in the analysis of market trends and the development of society's needs, identifying the key features, technical and functional characteristics of products presented in this market segment. On the other hand, the company must determine its own vector for the development of innovative technical solutions and competencies that enable creating and manufacturing a product that will have significant advantages over similar products from other market players that will be introduced to the market by that time.

---

[34] Batkovskiy, A. Regulation of the dynamics of creating high-tech products / A. Batkovskiy, A. Leonov, A. Pronin, A. Chursin, E. Nesterov // International Journal of Engineering & Technology. — 2018. — Vol. 7. — No 3.14. — P. 261–270. DOI: 10.14419/ijet.v7i3.14.16904
[35] Tyulin, A.E. Theory and practice of management of competencies that determine competitiveness integrated structures / A.E. Tyulin. — M., 2015.
[36] Porter, M.E. On competition: trans. from English / M.E. Porter. – M., 2000 . – 331 p.

Let us consider the most promising methods of market monitoring in relation to the creation of new products with high consumer utility.

Traditional methods of assessing and monitoring the market involve the calculation of various quantitative indicators characterizing the needs of the segment, including:
- market growth rate;
- market capacity (available, actual, potential);
- market saturation level;
- volumes and rates of utilization of the segment's products (physical deterioration, obsolescence; natural breakdown, etc.).

These parameters represent important characteristics of the market, which can give an idea of the potential sales volume of products, their economic and financial efficiency. However, these parameters do not allow assessing many of the dynamic characteristics of the market and consider various changing environmental factors. In this regard, it is necessary to develop traditional methods of marketing analysis based on the use of modern mathematical methods.

The main methods of monitoring the markets of high-tech products with the assessment of their consumer value.

The existing classical approaches to the analysis and assessment of the market for a certain type of product give a general idea of the target market environment by assessing a certain set of indicators:

1) Market growth rates

The indicator is used to assess two main components:
- dynamics of market growth for the manufacturer;
- dynamics of economic growth in the sectors of consumption of products.

Market growth rate is calculated using the formula:

$$T = \frac{V_1}{V_0},$$

where V_1 is the total sales volume in the market in the current year;

V_0 is total market sales for the previous year.

At the same time, the volume of sales can be expressed both in currency units and in the number of units of goods sold.

The market growth rate is calculated annually or quarterly on cumulatively within a year.

It identifies common trends in the market; however, traditional simplified analysis of market growth does not address emerging dynamically changing factors and risks and the current trends of scientific and technological development of the market.

2) Market capacity

This indicator characterizes the possible volume of demand in the market and is determined by the formula:

$$C_{ap} = \sum_{i}^{n}(S_i \cdot k \cdot E_c) - (S_{at} - P_d - O_b) - A - C$$

C_{ap} is the market capacity;

S_i is the number of the i-th consumer group;

k is the level (coefficient) of consumption in the base period or consumption standard;

E_c is the coefficient of elasticity of demand depending on prices and incomes;;

S_{at} is market saturation;

P_d is the physical deterioration of goods;

O_b is the obsolescence of goods;

A are alternative forms of satisfaction of needs (substitute products);

C is the the the share of competitors.

In global practice, there are 3 types of market capacity: actual, potential and available (see Fig. 5.1). Each type of market capacity can be calculated in different units of measurement: in physical terms (in units), in value terms (in rubles), in the volume of goods (in liters, kilograms, etc.).

The potential market capacity refers to the size of the market based on the maximum level of development of demand for a product or service among consumers. The maximum level of demand means that the culture of using the product has reached its maximum: the product is consumed as often as possible. The potential market

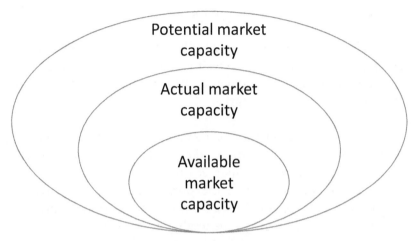

Figure 5.1. Market capacity

capacity is the maximum possible market size, based on the assumption that all potential consumers know and use the product category.

Actual or real market capacity – the size of the market based on the current level of development of demand for a product or service among the population. The actual market capacity is determined based on the current level of knowledge, consumption and use of the product among consumers.

Available market capacity – the size of the market that a company with its existing product and its characteristics (distribution, price, audience) can enter, or the level of demand that a company with its available resources can meet. In other words, when calculating the available market capacity, a company narrows the actual market size, considering as potential buyers not all consumers of the market, but only those who meet its criteria of the target audience.

In order to calculate the capacity of the target market, it is necessary to collect the necessary information through market research, as well as define the principles of calculating the capacity.

There are 3 basic methods for determining the capacity of a target market: the "low to high" capacity method, the "high to low"

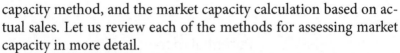

capacity method, and the market capacity calculation based on actual sales. Let us review each of the methods for assessing market capacity in more detail.

Each method has a universal rule: if the market is divided into several segments or submarkets, it is sometimes easier to calculate the capacity of each submarket and then add them up to obtain the capacity of the entire market.

"Low to high" method

The low to high method is the most common way to calculate market volume. It defines the market capacity in terms of the current level of demand. The market capacity according to the "low to high" method is equal to the sum of all expected purchases of goods by the target audience for the billing period (in practice, the annual market capacity is generally calculated).

Table 5.1. Formulas for calculating market capacity

Market capacity type	Calculation formula
Market size in quantitative terms (thousand units)	Market capacity for period N (thousand units) = Number of target audience of the market (in thousand people) * rate of consumption of goods for period N (in units)
Market size in currency terms (in thousand rubles)	Market capacity for period N (thousand rubles) = Number of target audience of the market (in thousand people) * rate of consumption of goods for period N (in units) * average cost of 1 unit of product on the market (in rubles)

"High to low" method

The method involves identifying the size of the market based on the internal sales data of all market players for the billing period (if it is impossible to cover all players, it is enough to consider only the large ones that make up 80-90 % of market sales).

The formula for calculating market capacity with the high to low approach is as follows:

Market capacity = The sum of the sales of all companies in the market, expressed in selling prices to the buyer (i.e. not shipping prices, but retail prices).

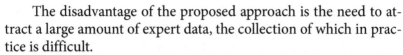

The disadvantage of the proposed approach is the need to attract a large amount of expert data, the collection of which in practice is difficult.

Method from actual sales

This assessment is currently used by many research companies, such as ACNielsen. The essence of the method is to track sales of certain categories of goods using actual customer receipts, which represent real purchases of the audience.

This method uses only large chain stores that have agreements to provide data. These stores are used as a representative sample and the data obtained can be extrapolated to the entire country.

With this method of determining the market volume, it is impossible to define a separate audience and estimate the amount of products that can be sold on the market at a certain price. Besides, this methodology does not cover market indicators and indicators characterizing the needs in the market segment under consideration.

3) Market saturation

Market saturation is the degree of availability of goods for consumer. For durable goods the formula is used:

$$Ae = Ab + S - D$$

Ae is the availability of goods at the end of the period;
Ab is the availability of goods at the beginning of the period;
S is the sales for the period;
D is the disposal for the period (based on the average service life of a product).

In contrast to the market capacity, which reflects the availability of goods in a certain geographic area, saturation reflects the upper limit of this capacity, above which it is impractical to increase the production of goods or supply them to the market. Thus, the market saturation parameter is very important in identifying the limits of the possibilities of various industry markets.

However, the proposed indicators do not take into account the macro-level parameters that characterize the general economic state in the world and in individual countries where the product is expected to be sold. These indicators include the index of industrial production, inflation, the level of technology development, the index of innovative development, etc.). In addition, they consider the effectiveness of launching products primarily in terms of the cost recovery of creating and promoting products by selling a sufficient volume to reach the break-even point.

In our opinion, the approach based on the classical concepts of the theory of competitiveness is more advanced. According to the provisions of the theory of competitiveness, the assessment of the consumer utility of created products is based on the fact that competitiveness as a measure of the consumer utility of products is of triune nature: comparative (competitiveness as a phenomenon arises in the case of competition), value (products must have some value that distinguishes them from similar products in order to meet consumers' needs) and economic (products must be sold and generate a company certain revenue).

We will reveal this provision based on the concept of the market triangle, reflecting the economic relations of three main market entities: the consumer, the company and its competitors, which will allow us to address the factors that determine the needs of all market entities and the trends in changes in these factors when elaborating modern methods for evaluating and monitoring markets for products with high consumer utility.

The review of the triune nature of the competitiveness of the products created (Fig. 5.2) allows to objectively assess the competitive advantages and consumer utility of the designed product, taking into account the characteristics of competitors' products, the customer needs, the developer (manufacturer) benefits based on market assessment and monitoring.

With regard to industrial products, the triune nature of competitiveness includes:
- value competitiveness – the composition of product characteristics that determines its value to the consumer;
- comparative competitiveness – a set of characteristics of the designed product that are important when comparing it with similar products of competitors;

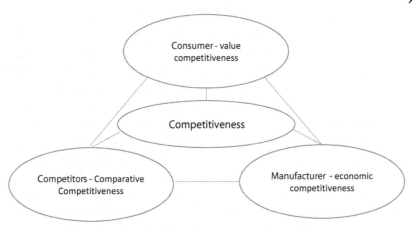

Figure 5.2. The triune nature of competitiveness

– economic competitiveness – a set of product properties that make its development and production profitable for a company (the necessary profitability is provided, the costs are covered). Cost efficiency is an important component of the consumer value. The price of a product must meet the expectations of consumers and be beneficial for its developer (manufacturer), provide cost recovery and increase its profitability. The concept of limit pricing is useful to determine the market price when designing new products in conditions of incomplete and uncertain information. According to this concept, the price is set in the interval between the upper maximum permissible limit (upper limit) and the lower objectively necessary limit (lower limit) of the price of the designed products. This price defines the limit of a product's cost, above which it is unprofitable for the consumer to purchase. Determining the upper limit of the price is based on the processing of statistical data on prices and sales volumes of products that are similar in characteristics to the newly created product. The price of the lower limit is determined based on the condition of profitability for the developer (manufacturer) of the new product. This price level is dictated by the costs that are required to develop (manufacture) products. To determine the prices of the lower limit, full-cost methods are used necessary for the development and manufacture of the product.

215

Thus, the ability to conduct in-depth analysis, assessment and monitoring of the market at a high quality level is the most important competence of the company at the stage of creating techno-economic image of products with high consumer utility. This is of particular relevance when creating knowledge-based products, since it takes a long period of time from the moment the idea and image of a product is shaped to the moment the finished product is manufactured and launched on the market (3 years or more depending on the complexity of a knowledge-based product). During this time, new products with new characteristics and new competitors appear on the market, new scientific discoveries are made, equipment and technologies are developing, as well as needs of society and the country emerge. All these dynamically changing internal factors should be monitored. Over time they can reduce the consumer utility of a product, if it is not constantly refined given the advanced achievements of science and technology, as well as newly acquired or developed competencies. such market factors can be monitored using modern methods of mathematics and fundamental computer science, which we will review later.

Development of modern methodological tools for assessing and monitoring the market for products with high consumer utility

The analysis of the existing tools for assessing and analyzing the market for products with high consumer utility revealed the need to develop existing approaches by paying greater attention to consumer expectations based on a system of market indicators, which can be implemented using modern methods of economic and mathematical modeling.

The complexity of covering factors that affect the needs of different market segments is that consumers usually formulate their wishes in an abstract form. A manufacturer's task is to transform abstract requirements of the consumer, representing a list of his wishes, into the integral value of the product with specific techno-economic characteristics. That is, the requirements of the consumer must be directly linked to the general characteristics of the product, in other words, this requires an economic tool for quantitative assessment of the conformity of the created product with a certain techno-economic image to consumer expectations, taking into account forecasting the development of the needs of companies and society (i.e., main consumers) in products of the type under consideration.

Based on the research carried out, the following algorithm can be proposed for addressing the needs of a certain market segment in shaping techno-economic image of products (Fig. 5.3):

To implement this algorithm, it is proposed to form methodological tools with which you can define future needs of companies and society based on the analysis of the dynamics of changes in traditional market factors that we have examined and specific factors affecting the dynamics of the market and its needs based on analysis of available market information (Table. 5.2). The proposed tools will be based on the use of modern methods of economic and mathematical modeling, which allow to obtain fairly accurate estimates of the parameters that characterize the needs in the market, without using a large number of expert assessments. Computational procedures, which are the core of the proposed tools, can be implemented in a subsystem for determining

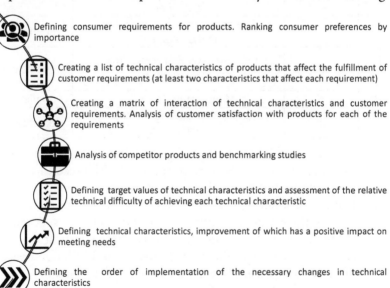

Figure 5.3. Algorithm for addressing the needs of a certain market segment in shaping techno-economic image of products

needs within the marketing information system of a company, which is part of the overall information system for supporting decision-making when creating products with high consumer utility.

Table 5.2. Baseline indicators for the analysis of the volume of supply of new products to the market

№	Notation in the formula	Indicator name	Unit of measurement
	T	The time interval at which the delivery of a particular product is predicted	year
	j	Consumer segments of a specific product	list
	i	List of competing products in the segment under consideration	list
	ΔGDP_w	GDP growth	trillion USD
	V_w	The volume of supply of certain types of products to the world market	pcs.
	V_i^j	Distribution of specific i i-th types of products in the j -th consumption segment	pcs.
	a	The entrys of new competitors in the segment	coefficient
	b	The emergence of replacement technologies	coefficient
	cj	Manufacturer's image	coefficient
	dj	Economic (including sanctions) restrictions	coefficient

The first set of data consists of general indicators that can affect the dynamics of market demand for products. The second set of indicators includes indicators that characterize the segments in which a particular product will be presented. The list of these indicators depends on the selected product type and the selected segment.

At the output of the subsystem, quantitative indicators of potential deliveries of a specific type of product in the planned period, as well as certain consumption segments, are determined.

We describe the stages of a subsystem for determining the needs for new products based on economic and mathematical modeling taking into account market factors.

Stage 1. At the first stage, the value T of the length of the time interval (in years), on which the forecast is based, is set. Typically T ranges from 1 to 10.

Stage 2. The consumer segment for the sale of a given type of product is selected.

Stage 3. A list of i types of competing products included in the selected segment is formed.

Stage 4. The ΔGDP_w growth for the entire time interval of the forecast T is projected. For projection, this algorithm for predicting the values of a time series is used. This algorithm is also used to forecast specific factors that affect the demand indicators in the segment. Let us consider in more detail the mathematical procedures underlying the construction of the forecast of market parameters.

To analyze the dynamics of market factors, it is advisable to apply the double exponential smoothing procedure, which is applied to the analysis of time series, when there is a trend in the time series, and the seasonal component is not decisive. This procedure is:

$$L_t = \alpha\, w_t + (1 - \alpha)(L_{t-1} + b_{t-1}), \text{ where}$$

Lt is the level of the time series, and the bt values that represent the trend are calculated using the following formula:

$$b_t = \gamma(L_t - L_{t-1}) + (1 - \gamma)\, b_{t-1}$$

Here the coefficients α and γ are the parameters of the method and accept values from the set [0,1]. The initial values for Lt and bt are selected according to the following formulas

$$L_0 = w_0 \text{ and } b_0 = w_1 - w_0$$

The forecasted value is calculated using the formula:

$$S_t = L_t + b_t$$

The method of double exponential smoothing allows to highlight the main trends in the dynamics of the considered market indicator, as well as to exclude various random fluctuations of this trajectory. In addition, this method is one of the main practical ways for forecasting the values of market indicators.

219

If there is a certain list of specific indicators P_1, P_2, ... P_n, a forecast is built for a given time period also using the above algorithm, and then a time series R(t) is projected based on the forecasts according to the following rule (for example, for two indicators):

$$R(t) = 0.5 \cdot \left(\frac{P_1(t)}{\max\limits_{t\in[t_1;t_2+T]} P_1(t)} + ... + \frac{P_n(t)}{\max\limits_{t\in[t_1;t_2+T]} P_n(t)} \right).$$

Stage 5. A number of indicators are assessed depending on the selected segment for each point in time of the forecast period T. The indicators evaluated on the basis of the expert method are "The entry of new competitors in the segment", "The emergence of replacement technologies", "Manufacturer's image", "Economic constraints". These indicators can be used to determine the volume of deliveries to both the Russian and foreign markets, which is provided by the scale of their assessment.

These assessments are carried out as follows (Table 5.3). For each type of product presented in the analyzed market segment, an expert assessment is entered in accordance with the scale.

Decision support when assessing the indicators «The entry of new competitors in the segment» and «The emergence of replacement technologies» is carried out by analyzing the information space: Internet, media, conferences, exhibitions, etc.

For each pair «segment j – a certain type of product i», an integral assessment of the action of factors is calculated taking into account their weight coefficients by the formula:

$$F_{ij} = 0.25 \cdot (w_a \cdot F_a + w_b \cdot F_b + w_c \cdot F_c + w_d \cdot F_d)$$

Stage 6. A forecast calculation of the volume of supplies of a certain type of product $V_w(t)$ of the selected segment to the world market is made based on the forecast of the world GDP growth, calculated time series of specific indicators, and statistical data on the supply of a certain type of product.

Forecasted values of supply volumes can be determined by the formula:

Table 5.3. Results of expert evaluation of indicators

№	Indicator	Optimistic scenario (1 point)	Neutral scenario (0 points)	Pessimistic scenario (-1 point)
1.	The entry of new competitors in the segment A	The national manufacturer is a «pioneer» in the manufacture of a new unique product in a segment which has no analogues	New players enter the market, ready to offer similar but less competitive products	New players appear on the market with new generation products that are fundamentally different from those already presented on the market
2.	The emergence of replacement technologies B	The national manufacturer uses the latest technologies and materials, which reduces the production time and product cost which allows creating new types of products that are in demand on the market	All market players use new technologies in production and expand their product line by creating new products with new consumer properties	The national manufacturer lags far behind competitors in the use of new technologies and does not create new products that replace standard products
3.	Manufacturer's image C	The company has a positive image, high investment attractiveness and reputation, and has a positive experience in the region. Low percentage of participation in court cases for completed transactions	The manufacturer's image is on a par with competing suppliers of similar products	The manufacturer has a low reputation and negative relationships with partners / customers or has never worked in a given region. High percentage of participation in court cases for completed transactions
4.	Economic constraints d	Sanctions are not applied, the state provides support to the national producer by stimulating its activities and restricting the activities of competitors in the domestic market	Sanctions do not limit the volume of supplies of products abroad and do not regulate the purchase of foreign components that are part of a certain type of product	Sanctions restrict access to foreign markets and the supply of foreign components necessary for the production of a certain type of product, the State does not carry out special regulation of the industry

$$V_w(t) = b_0 + b_1 GDP(t) + b_2 R(t)$$

Determine the shares q_{ij} of a certain type of product i in each of the market segments j. To do this, calculate the non-standardized values of the shares $q_i^j(t)$.

$$q_i^j(t) = \max\left(\frac{V_i^j}{\sum_i V_i^j}\right)\left(\frac{\sum_i V_i^j}{\sum_j \sum_i V_i^j}\right) \cdot (1 + F_{ij})$$

For each pair "a certain type of product i – a segment of the world market j" we obtain the values $q_i^j(t)$ that need to be normalized according to the following rule:

$$q_{ij} = \frac{q_i^j}{\sum_i q_i^j}$$

The potential number W_{ij} of units of a certain type of product that can be supplied to market segment j is calculated using the formula:

$$W_{ij} = q_{ij} \cdot \left(\frac{\sum_i V_i^j}{\sum_j \sum_i V_i^j}\right) \cdot V_w(t)$$

where V_i^j is the number of units of the i-th type of product in the j -th consumption segment,

$V_w(t)$ is the projected volume of supplies of a certain type of product to the market.

The potential volume W_i of supply of a certain type of product type i is calculated according to the following rule:

$$W_i = \sum_j W_{ij}$$

Thus, according to the results of the algorithm, the manufacturer receives information about the potential supply of a certain type of product [37].

---

[37] If necessary, a model calculation can be presented.

The developed method can be called the method of dynamic economic and mathematical modeling of the supply of new products to the market, taking into account various factors. The proposed tools for assessing and analyzing the market, which underlie the work of the subsystem for assessing market needs, differ from the considered classical approaches by economic and mathematical modeling of the volume of product deliveries to the market, taking into account various factors, which are analyzed by modern methods of data analysis using available information. Moreover, computational procedures allow to determine quantitative indicators that describe the current market situation, as well as determine the needs for a product in future periods.

This is especially true for manufacturers whose products have a long production cycle. Economic and mathematical modeling provides more accurate and correct results about the potential volume of product deliveries to the market in the future, since this approach eliminates the need to use a large amount of expert assessments, which are often difficult to obtain in practice. The proposed tools based on economic and mathematical modeling can be the core of the subsystem for determining prospective needs as an element of an information marketing system for evaluating and monitoring product sales markets, the elements of which we will discuss later.

Development of elements of a system for assessing and monitoring sales markets for products with high consumer utility

Taking into account the previously identified need for continuous monitoring of market factors that affect the creation and sale of products with high consumer utility, it is fair to say that it can be implemented mainly based on available sources of information and its processing by modern mathematical methods. Such a monitoring system includes subsystems for managing the processes of creating promising products of an enterprise that can secure its leading position in the market, as well as analytical tools based on methods of economic and mathematical modeling. Using these tools, it is possible to assess the state of promising markets, product sales segments, changes in consumer preferences in them, assess the competitiveness of products sold in the markets in the current and forecast situation, assess the competitive value of the products created, and form competitive advantages of products that will ensure its dominance in the market.

We propose a method for continuous monitoring of the market based on available information sources and their analysis by modern mathematical methods, the block diagram of which is shown in Figure 5.4.

Let us consider in detail the stages of organizing continuous monitoring of available information sources using the example of identifying the actions of competing companies within the proposed flowchart.

Identifying the main key topics

Depending on the task of identifying the actions of competing companies to create promising products, it is necessary to determine the range of main topics that should be in sight when monitoring

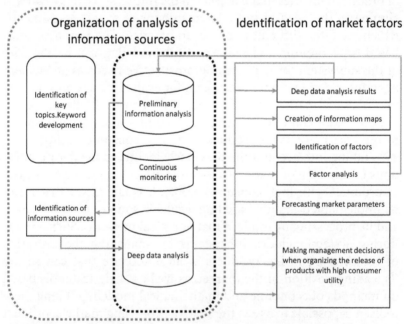

Figure 5.4. Flowchart of the functioning of the system for continuous assessment and monitoring of market factors

the global information space. To define these topics, it is suggested to use the following sequence of actions:

Step 1. Determine the main topic related to the product in question. This topic is filled in in the «Main topic» column.

Step 2. For the main topic, several related topics are selected, which are filled in in the "Related topic" column.

Step 3. When analyzing the main topic, subtopics of the main topic are highlighted. The highlighted subtopics are filled in in the «Subtopics of the main topic» column.

Step 4. If from the selected related topics and subtopics it is possible to formulate a new main topic that is related to the identification of the actions of competing companies, then proceed to step 1.

In the considered algorithm for determining key topics for monitoring available information sources, it is assumed that such an analysis should go through either the manufactured equipment, or within the framework of the technology used in the development of new products.

Development of keywords for the topics under consideration

After identifying the key topics that should be at the center of monitoring the global information space in terms of identifying the actions of competing companies to create products with new techno-economic characteristics, it is necessary to determine a set of key information in order to use modern mathematical methods for data analysis.

Defining the range of information sources

For continuous monitoring of the global information space in terms of identifying the actions of competing companies, it is necessary to define the main range of information sources that will be used in monitoring information flows.

A large amount of data is widely available on the Internet, with the exception of information that is a commercial secret.

Organization of continuous monitoring of information sources

After identifying information sources and key topics for continuous monitoring based on modern mathematical methods of data analysis in terms of identifying the actions of competing companies to create products with new techno-economic characteristics, it is necessary to develop a scheme for this monitoring.

For an express analysis of available information sources, it is proposed to apply various methods of data analysis, which are based on the following technologies:
- Data Mining methods for the analysis of text information,
- methods of fuzzy logic and fuzzy sets,
- use of linguistic variables,
- decision trees,
- methods of information classification based on neural networks.

Preliminary analysis of information flows

As a result of continuous monitoring of the global information space, an operational database is formed containing information about various market factors, in particular, about possible actions of competing companies to create products with new techno-economic characteristics. For further use of this information in terms of identifying the actions of competing companies, it is necessary to use a preliminary analysis of information flows.

This analysis should filter out duplicate information, since information flows are formed from information occasion, each of which can generate different information flows that relate to the same news topic. In this case, these information flows must be filtered or combined.

In addition to duplicate information, continuous monitoring of the global information space raises the problem of filtering incorrect or unreliable information. To solve this problem, artificial intelligence methods should be used:
- automatic classification of multidimensional data;
- assessment of the likelihood of information reliability.

Bayesian learning methods can be used to assess the likelihood of information reliability. As a result of a preliminary analysis of information flows, a knowledge base is formed from the operational database, on the basis of which a thorough analysis of information materials will be made.

Thorough analysis of information materials

Using the formed knowledge base through continuous monitoring of available information sources, it is necessary to conduct

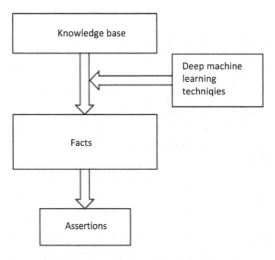

Figure 5.5. In-depth information analysis scheme

a thorough analysis of the information received in order to use it to generate information maps.

When analyzing multidimensional and unstructured data thorough analysis of information materials is carried out on the basis of in-depth data analysis methods (for example, machine learning).

Thorough analysis of information from the generated knowledge base transforms the information into statements regarding possible actions of competing companies to create products with new techno-economic characteristics. These statements may have a certain degree of credibility because they are based on information that is not always 100% accurate.

The scheme of in-depth analysis of information is shown in Figure 5.5.

Statements, unlike facts, are clearly formalized data structures that can already be used to identify the actions of competing companies to create products with high consumer value.

Creation of information maps

The continuous monitoring of available information sources results in information maps that consolidate statements. Such an information map is a report on the identification of the actions

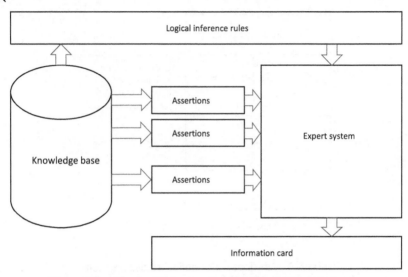

Figure 5.6 – General scheme of generating information maps

of competing companies to create products with high consumer utility. In fact, the information map represents answers to questions about possible actions of competing companies.

Information charts should be based on information statements, which are computed from continuous monitoring of available information sources. To form information maps, it is proposed to use analytical subsystems, the block diagram of which is shown in Figure 5.6.

The generated information maps are the result of continuous monitoring of the information space based on modern data processing methods in terms of identifying the actions of competing companies to create promising products with new techno-economic characteristics.

Identification of market factors based on information maps

Using the generated information maps, market factors are identified as a result of continuous monitoring of the information space. This information should be used to develop control decisions in order to respond to the information received aimed at achieving high consumer utility of the products created[38].

---

[38] If necessary, a model example can be proposed

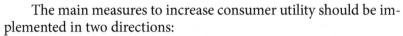

The main measures to increase consumer utility should be implemented in two directions:
– product price reduction,
– improving the technical characteristics of a product.

To solve this problem, it is necessary to focus on the information obtained as a result of continuous monitoring of the information space.

Such monitoring should be aimed at analyzing the achievement of conditions under which each of the created types of products will be in demand on the market due to its unique consumer properties and competitive advantages in terms of technical characteristics and cost.

In this regard, it is necessary to predict the development of each type of product, determine the boundaries of its life cycle and reach the break-even point, the level of marginal utility and market saturation, after which a decline in its sales will begin due to the rapid development and appearance of new technical solutions on the market.

Monitoring of the stages of product development across the entire range should be carried out from the moment a product is developed until the moment when the income from its sale still ensures the stable development of the company. The competitive advantages of a product ultimately increase the demand for it and, therefore, increase revenues and shorten the payback period for the launch of this product into production.

The proposed methods for assessing and monitoring sales markets for products with high consumer utility, based on modern methods of data processing and analysis allow forming information schemes and organizing business processes for monitoring and elaborating tools for processing the collected information. Methods for assessing various dynamically changing factors and risks arising from the creation of high-tech products and assessing their impact on changes in consumer utility and cost can act as such tools. The proposed approaches to the organization of a system of continuous assessment and monitoring of market factors allow to define the acceptable level of risks of loss of competitiveness and consumer utility of products using weak signals, which will allow to evaluate market factors based on weak signals given their mutual influence.

The competitive advantages of products should be implemented most intensively at the beginning of the design and the pre-production stages and until the break-even point of production is reached, or more precisely, until a company begins to profit from sales.

Next, we will discuss the issue of assessing the cost of a radically new product, given economic factors changing over time.

5.2. FORMING THE COST OF RADICALLY NEW PRODUCTS, TAKING INTO ACCOUNT TIME-CHANGING ECONOMIC FACTORS

Creating radically new products with unique characteristics is a complex task. As part of solving this problem, an important issue is to establish the sale price of products to the end consumer, which to a greater extent depends on the consumer properties of the product, defining its advantage over similar products on the market, as well as its competitive cost.

Cost management of radically new products must be carried out at all stages of its life cycle. This is because cost, along with innovation and product quality, is a key factor in successful market competition.

The cost of products is formed at the stage of development of the preliminary project. In the future, it should be achieved by technological solutions that will be proposed for its production. These technological solutions are determined by the quality of pre-production, the technical level of production, the competence and qualifications of employees, etc. However, the cost of production depends on many factors. Firstly, it is the level of competence of design and technological services and their equipment with software and other means that allow digital design and modeling, given the optimal choice of materials, units, systems, technologies that determine high consumer properties of radically new products. Secondly, it is the cost of competitors' products, which can change over time depending on various economic factors, risks, etc.

A radically new product is usually a complex product consisting of many modules, systems, assemblies, etc. In the scientific literature, the issue of determining the cost of multicomponent products is examined in considerable detail, for example, in [39],[40],[41]. Particular attention in this topic is paid to the issues of optimization of manufacturing costs and optimization of labor intensity of production and technological processes. However, a radically new product is diversified and can significantly differ from traditional types of products, since it has previously unknown or significantly improved properties or techno-economic parameters. Due to such products, a new market is created, a new segment of consumers and in some cases even new needs are formed. Such products with high consumer properties can be cost-effective if at the optimal price level for the consumer, the break-even point is reached within a reasonable time for a manufacturer.

The price of a radically new product determines the available consumer niches in which the consumer is willing to pay for high technical characteristics of the product. Otherwise, the consumer can choose products with a lower price.

This implies the task of managing the cost of radically new products, which consists in the fact that the cost characteristics of these products should be optimized at the stage of pre-design, pre-production and production. Product cost optimization is achieved through the use of well-known design methods for a given cost, lean production, through the modernization of production, increasing labor productivity, etc.

Based on the above provisions, we will determine the main factors that form its cost.

First of all, it is necessary to take into account production costs, that is, the cost estimate of the expenditure of creating and manufacturing products. It is necessary to determine the optimal way to shift fixed and variable costs to the price of radically new products. The concept of marginal costs (the increase in total costs in response to an increase

[39] Borodin, R. A. Features of accounting for production costs and calculating the cost of production of auxiliary production / R. A. Borodin. – Moscow: Laboratory of Books, 2011. – 141p.
[40] Aldaniyazov K.N. Analysis of actual production self-cost: factors and reserves of its decrease Problems of Economics and Management of Oil and Gas Complex. – 2014. – No. 7. – S. 8- 12.
[41] Vasin L. Directions of reducing the cost of production / L. Vasin. // Economic and Legal Sciences. – 2013. – No. 5. – p. 3-6.

in output per unit) is of particular importance. The determination of marginal costs makes it possible to establish the minimum price at which a specific volume of products can be sold on the market.

Another important pricing factor is the value of a radically new product as a product, which is defined as "the price of the best alternative product available to the buyer (the price of indifference) plus the value of those properties of the given product that distinguish it from this better alternative."[42]. Thus the pricing of indifference is based not only on the analysis of existing analogues, but also the examination of the products to the consumer with similar value properties.

The third pricing factor is demand, that is, consumers' ability to purchase a radically new product at a certain price. Demand depends on a number of factors (consumer income, their tastes and preferences, prices for substitute and complementary goods, etc.) and greatly affects a manufacturer's policy in setting prices. The sensitivity of demand in response to price changes is determined by the price elasticity of demand. The degree of elasticity of demand will determine the company's decision to revise prices: in the case of highly elastic demand for price, a slight increase in price can lead to a significant drop in sales and a decrease in revenue. However, the opposite is also true – a discount will mean an increase in the number of goods sold and an increase in the company's income.

In addition, when setting prices, it is necessary to understand the measure of the reaction of sales volume to the prices of interchangeable and complementary goods, for which in practice the cross-elasticity indicator can be used. Thus, information about consumer demand, as well as the degree of its elasticity (including cross- elasticity), is necessary for a company for competent pricing and successful competition.

The activity of any company (with rare exceptions of monopolies producing a completely exclusive product with no analogues) is associated with competition; therefore competition is the fourth price-determining factor.

In the conditions of price competition (competition through price changes), a company tries to set the price of its products

---

[42] G.A. Gorina, Pricing: a tutorial, M .: UNITI-DANA. P. 12

at a lower level than its competitors in order to increase sales. Such price competition will be successful in the case of constantly improving production and reducing costs. Otherwise, it will mean a significant drop in a company's profit margin and a loss of profitability. Non-price competition means improving products, improving their consumer qualities, ease of use, and related services. Such improvements will increase customer loyalty and, all other things being equal, will contribute to the success of the competition.

Based on the above, the following axiom is formulated:

The efficiency of the processes of conquering and creating new markets for radically new products is determined by optimizing the technical characteristics and cost of products based on the consumer capabilities of buyers and the economic effect achieved in a short time.

This axiom is based on the most important economic laws: the law of value, the law of the rise of economic needs and the law of decreasing marginal utility. Thus, the law of the rise of economic needs proves that the creation and production of goods based on new discoveries and transformations in technique and technology will ensure the emergence of new needs and values in society, as well as new markets in which the manufacturer will be a pioneer. The identified features of pricing for radically new products allow us to form an approach to determining the price of such products, which will be based on the synthesis of cost and value approaches to pricing for products and services.

When setting the price of a product, the manufacturer must be sure that all costs associated with its production and sale will be reimbursed in a reasonable time, and the profit from the sale should be received. At the same time, without an objective assessment of the market situation and studying the demand and preferences of consumers, the product may not be in demand. The the demand depends both on technical characteristics and on cost. In turn, the characteristics of the products form the market price and their cost. Based on these provisions, we propose a model for determining the market price of a radically new product.

The synthetic approach to determining the competitive price of radically new products on the market involves analyzing market prices for competitors' products, both for already launched and promising products, taking into account the possibility of competitors reaching a certain level of technical characteristics. This approach will allow to analyze the products presented on the market, depending on their techno-economic characteristics, and to determine the place of the radically new products created, depending on the value of their integral performance indicator.

Determining the market price involves an examination of the techno-economic parameters of both the radically new product being created and the products of competitors. In addition to the specific technical characteristics of the created products, it is necessary to consider integral indicators, such as performance, consumer utility, etc., since they reflect the ability of a product to meet consumer expectations. Therefore, it is initially proposed to select the main parameters of the products of the considered type and form their list $A = (a_1, a_2 \dots a_n)$, where n is the number of parameters under consideration.

Note that in addition to quantitative estimates of product parameters, qualitative parameters can also be considered.

Suppose that when determining the competitive price of a radically new product being created, the techno-economic characteristics of N different analogues are analyzed, for which their purchase cost is known. For the same characteristics of products from different manufacturers that have a quantitative measurement, they are normalized so that the total is one. Mathematically, this means the following.

Let us assume that the value of the parameter is known for the product under consideration, including the one being created a_i, $i = 1, 2, \dots, n$. The normalized value a_i' for each type of product is determined by the formula:

$$a_{ij}' = \frac{a_{ij}}{\sum\limits_{j=1}^{N} a_{ij}}.$$

To determine the normalized estimates of parameters represented by qualitative variables, as well as quantitative parameters about which there is no accurate information, the method of constructing matrices of paired comparisons can be used,[43] which compares different products based on the best value of the comparison parameter. The priority vector calculated using such a matrix represents the normalized estimates of a specific product parameter.

The next step is to build a matrix of global priorities, in which all the normalized values of the parameters of each of the products are synthesized. The average value of the standardized parameters of a product is the desired value of the global priority.

Table 5.4 – Calculation of global priority

Product Name	a1	a2	...	an	Global Priority
Product 1	a'11	a'21	...	a'n1	a1,gl= (a'11+ a'21+ a'n1)/n
Product 2	a'12	a'22	...	a'n2	a2,gl =(a'12+ a'22+ a'n2)/n
...	...	...	...	...	...
Product N	a'1N	a'2N	...	a'nN	aN,gl =(a'1N+ a'2N+ a'nN)/n

To objectively determine the competitive price, it is necessary to calculate the cost of 1 point of global priority. To do this, it is necessary to divide the prices for products already on the market by the obtained value of the global priority (Table 5.5).

Table 5.5 – Analysis of the ratio of techno-economic characteristics and market prices of M products on the market

Product Name	The value of global priority	Market price of products, standard unit	The cost of 1 point of the techno-economic characteristics of the product, standard unit (quantity 3 / quantity 2)
1	2	3	4
Product 1	a1,gl	S1	S1/ a1,gl
Product 2	a2,gl	S2	S2/ a2,gl
...	...	...	...
Product M	aM,gl	SM	SM/ aM,gl

---

[43] Saati T.L.Decision-making. Hierarchy analysis method. – M .: Radio and communication, 1989 .– 316 p.

Let be the value of the global priority of the products being created, and $a_{\tau-1,gl}$ and $a_{\tau+1,gl}$ be the nearest lower and higher global priorities of the other two products in relation to the considered. Then the competitive market price S_τ of the radically new products being created will be in the range of

$$S_\tau \in \left(a_{\tau,gl} \cdot \frac{S_{\tau-1}}{a_{\tau-1,gl}}; a_{\tau,gl} \cdot \frac{S_{\tau+1}}{a_{\tau+1,gl}} \right).$$

A point estimate of the competitive price of the created products can be obtained taking into account the quantitative assessment of the effectiveness of its application $(\Delta S_k)_\tau$ according to the Hurwitz formula:

$$S_\tau = \lambda \cdot \left(a_{\tau,gl} \cdot \frac{S_{\tau+1}}{a_{\tau+1,gl}} \right) + (1-\lambda) \cdot \left(a_{\tau,gl} \cdot \frac{S_{\tau-1}}{a_{\tau-1,gl}} \right) \qquad (*)$$

where the indicator of optimism λ can be found as follows:

$$\lambda = \frac{(\Delta S_k)_\tau}{\max\{(\Delta S_k)_{\tau-1},(\Delta S_k)_\tau,(\Delta S_k)_{\tau+1}\}}.$$

The point estimate of the competitive price of products, determined by the formula (*), corresponds to the conditions under which such products exceed the characteristics of existing analogues on the markets (k>1), and the cost meets the restrictions associated with the purchasing power of potential consumers.

If the value of the global priority of the products being created is less than the values of the global priorities of other products, then the competitive market price does not exceed the price of the products with the lowest global priority of those considered on the market. If the value of the global priority of the products being created is greater than the values of the global priorities of other products, then the competitive market price may correspond to the price of the products with the highest global priority on the market. However, in order to gain a market segment, decisions may be made to reduce this price.

Thus, when determining the competitive price of a radically new product being created, its main characteristics that form consumer utility are considered.

In practice, a developer of radically new products supplies several types of products to the market (each of which may have versions for different consumer niches), and the cost of S0 product development and pre-production is transferred to the cost of the final product as special costs as part of direct costs. However, the operation of each product may be accompanied by costs S1,S2,...,SN, connected with the operation of specific modules for each product. Each type of product is characterized by the price Zi, i=1,...,N on the market, which is determined by the technical characteristics of a product and the purchasing power of consumers. Such approach allows to analyze the cost recovery of creating radically new products, depending on the demand for it, provided that the revenue from sales on the market is maximized, and that the economic efficiency of radically new products is ensured.

Mathematically, this problem is described as follows:

$$\sum_{j=1}^{M}\sum_{i=1}^{N} n_i \cdot (Z_i - S_i - a_i \cdot \frac{S_0}{M}) \to \max,$$

where ai are the coefficients that determine the distribution of special costs as part of direct costs for the cost of each product, n_i is the number of consumers of each product, M is the number of years of the forecast.

The proposed approach allows to model the conditions for the transition of radically new products to market dominance over a given period of time and calculate financial efficiency as an operating profit from the sale of a portfolio of products on the market. Market dominance criteria may vary for different markets. For example, in Japan (one of the world leaders in the high-tech products market), the dominance threshold is legally set at 50% of the market volume.

Consider a model example that demonstrates the work of the proposed model. Let a company offer N =10 types of products on the market, one of which has radical characteristics and achieves market dominance in M =7 years, the graph of increasing financial efficiency

(cumulative operating profit) obtained in the course of solving the proposed optimization problem by the Monte Carlo method is shown
in Fig. 2. The initial data for the calculation are presented in Table 5.6.

Table 5.6. Initial data for calculating the financial efficiency
of radically new products

Year I	Competitive cost of a radically new product, c.u.	The number of consumers of a radically new product	Average competitive price of non-radical products, c.u.	Average number of non-radical products	Cumulative operating profit, c.u.
1	20	10	10	40	– 65000
2	22	30	10	40	– 62135
3	23	80	10	40	– 55476
4	25	150	11	45	– 48174
5	27	300	11	45	– 30025
6	30	600	12	50	– 15132
7	30	1000	12	50	2145

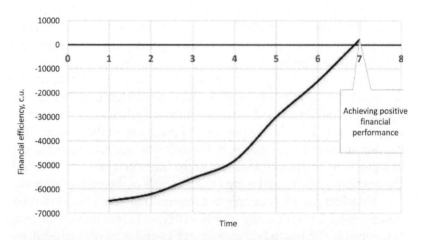

Figure 5.7 Forecasting the financial performance of a product portfolio

The conducted modeling of the financial efficiency of the port-folio of products allows us to determine the necessary sales volumes of products, taking into account their competitive price for the cost recovery for the creation and preparation of production. In the context of the given example, the cost recovery of creating products is achieved in the 7th year after the launch of a radically new product on the market.

The proposed methodological approach can be used as the basis for the management mechanism for the creation and sale of radically new products, taking into account dynamically changing factors and risks, which is associated with the use of special economic and mathematical models and algorithms within the mechanism. Also, when building a mechanism, the following provisions must be taken into account:

- the mechanism should reflect the scientific, technical and technological component of the process of developing radically new products;
- tthe mechanism should take into account the costs (and their recovery) for the design, preparation of production and, if necessary, the creation of the infrastructure required for the operation of the products;
- tthe methodological apparatus of the mechanism should provide opportunities for simulation of the process of managing the competitive characteristics of products in order to maintain a competitive price in the market.

5.3 FUNDAMENTALS OF THE MECHANISM FOR CREATING AND SELLING PRODUCTS WITH HIGH CONSUMER UTILITY

The issue of consumer utility of products has been reviewed by many economists [44]. As a rule, they either considered utility to be some initial property of the product, or, like marginalists and their followers [45], considered it to be a property of the consumer basket[46].

---

[44] Veblen T.The Limitations of Marginal Utility/ Voprosy Economici, 2007, no. – Pp. 86-98.
[45] Veblen T. Theory of the leisure class. – M .: Progress, 1984 .–244 p.
[46] Veblen T.The Limitations of Marginal Utility/ Voprosy Economici, 2007, no. – Pp. 86-98.

In the classical sense[47] consumer utility is expressed in the choice of a specific product from the list of analogues, the conditions of which can be its price, quality characteristics, etc. The consumer utility of a product is determined by the ratio of the benefits that the buyer receives when purchasing a certain product, and the costs of purchasing it. Customer satisfaction with a product depends on how well it matches the consumer's perception of its characteristics. If the product features are at a high level of quality, but they do not meet the expectations of the consumer, the perceived utility of the product may be low. In order to ensure sales of products with high perceived value, a manufacturer or seller must fulfill the consumer's expectations regarding the properties of the promoted product. Moreover, the manufacture of products with high consumer properties requires the improvement of production technologies, the use of high-quality materials, compliance with quality requirements at every stage of production, and the sale of products at a competitive price is possible with an effective organization of the sales system, supply chain management, inventory, etc.

The modern world market for products with high consumer utility is characterized, as a rule, by keen competition of their manufacturers, which determines the variety of forms and methods aimed at attracting consumers and ensuring the advantages of the created products over competitors' products. That is why developers of products with high consumer utility should pay great attention to the formation of their cost and competitive price – one of the key objects of management throughout all stages of the life cycle.

Competitiveness management (both price and non-price) involves the implementation of actions in certain directions, ensuring the creation of competitive advantages. A competitive price in the market can be achieved under the condition of high technical and consumer characteristics of products due to a well-thought-out pricing policy of the enterprise and the flexibility of the price strategy for selling the service, depending on the conditions and various factors. Competitive actions applied within the selected areas have

---

[47] Selishchev A.S. Microeconomics. – SPb .: Peter, 2003 .– 448 p.

their own mechanisms and methods of implementation. We will focus on the methods and issues related to the formation and evaluation of the cost parameters of a radically new product that has consumer value and utility, and we will form a mechanism for managing the creation and sale of products with high consumer utility and ensuring its economic efficiency.

In scientific literature, an economic mechanism is understood as a set of methods and means of influencing and regulating economic processes[48]. The need to manage the directed development of economic processes determines the high importance of various mechanisms for economic science. There are many examples of economic mechanisms working at both the macro and micro levels. The quality of the results of the mechanism is measured by quantitative and qualitative indicators that characterize both the degree and pace of development of an object, and the quality of the result as a whole.

The conditions or factors that promote or hinder the operation of the mechanism can be systematized into external (political, economic, legal, social, scientific and technical, etc.) and internal, characterizing the resource base of an object (material, labor, human, intellectual, information, etc.).

According to the definition of the economic mechanism and the goals of its creation based on the above developments, we will form a mechanism for managing the creation and sale of products with high consumer utility. The mechanism is based on the interaction of individual instruments aimed at managing a certain value – in our case, the economic efficiency of the products being created.

The mechanism for managing the creation and sale of products with high consumer utility includes a set of the following economic instruments (Figure 5.8):

To achieve economic efficiency of the created products with high consumer utility, the mechanism regulates the value of the set of parameters determined by the tools that form the mechanism. So, the tool for determining the future needs and criteria for radically new

---

48 Raizberg B.A., Lozovsky L.Sh., Starodubtseva E.B. Modern economic dictionary. 6th ed., Rev. and add. M .: INFRA-M, 2011.

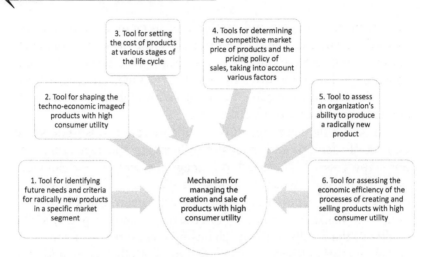

Figure 5.8. The economic mechanism for managing the creation
and sale of products with high consumer utility

products in a certain market segment allows to determine the available market capacity for a certain type of product and consider it when determining the sales strategy, as well as predicting the expected volume Nt of product sales for period t. The tool for forming the techno-economic image of products with high consumer utility allows you to create a set of techno-economic parameters of such products that meet the criteria of radically new products. On the basis of information on the techno-economic parameters of the created products and the products of competitors, using the appropriate tool, the competitive price of the created products Pnew is determined in relation to the prices of competitors Pcomp. The competitive price Pnew, together with the cost of the created products S0, calculated using the cost formation tool at different stages of the life cycle, are taken into account on the basis of the price policy of selling the created products on the market. Here the ability of an enterprise to manufacture a developed product is assessed and, if necessary, the costs of developing production assets and building up the competencies of production personnel are assessed as well, which ultimately is shifted to the cost of production. The set of parameters calculated using the listed tools determines the economic efficiency E of the processes of creating and selling products with high consumer utility.

The following methods and the corresponding economic and mathematical evaluation apparatus were discussed in detail earlier:

Methods for determining prospective needs and forming criteria for radically new products in a certain market segment, allowing to build a forecast of needs for a certain type of product, provided that price and non-price competitiveness is achieved by the time the product is launched on the market;

Methods of shaping the techno-economic image of products with high consumer utility, allowing to determine a set of techno-economic indicators of products, which by the time they are launched on the market will provide them with superiority over the products available on the market both in terms of technical characteristics and price;

Methods of forming the cost of products at various stages of the life cycle and determining its competitive market price, allowing to form the price of products, taking into account the costs transferred to the cost price, and reaching the break-even point in a reasonable time for the manufacturer.

The economic tools and methods discussed above make it impossible to form an effective mechanism for managing the creation and sale of products with high consumer utility. To complete the functioning of this mechanism, we will develop methods to assess the ability of an enterprise to produce a radically new product.

Assessment of an enterprise's ability to produce a radically new product.

As already noted, scientific and technological capacity is the basis that determines the ability of an enterprise to produce a product based on competencies and available resources. To solve the problem of assessing the ability of an enterprise to manufacture a radically new product, it is necessary to have tools that allow, on the basis of integral assessments of various components of scientific and technological capacity, to draw a conclusion about the ability of an enterprise to create, produce and effectively sell radically new products on the market.

To create radically new products, the characteristics of which meet the criteria defined above, it is necessary to build scientific and technological capacity to a level that makes it possible to achieve these technical characteristics, while ensuring a price acceptable to the consumer.

The economic efficiency of the processes of creating and manufacturing radically new products (taking into account measures to form a sufficient level of scientific and technological capacity) can be assessed on the basis of the ratio of the effect obtained from the sale of radically new products to resource costs (labor, financial, material and technical, information etc.) to create radically new products, and increase the scientific and technological capacity and competencies. The method proposed below for assessing the cost effectiveness of creating radically new products makes it possible to calculate and assess the degree of influence of each component of scientific and technological capacity on the change in the overall efficiency of its use, which makes it possible to make timely decisions on the management of various components of scientific and technological capacity. To build a factor model for determining the efficiency of resource use when creating a radically new product, the indicator E(P) is used, which characterizes the amount of necessary resources spent on obtaining each 1 ruble of profit from the sale of products on the market.

This indicator can be obtained as follows:

$$E(P) = \left(\frac{E_{R\&D}}{I} + \frac{E_{prod}}{I} + \frac{E_{sale}}{I} \right) \cdot \frac{I}{P};$$

where $E_{R\&D}$ is R&D and development costs (expenditure), E_{prod} is preparation and production costs (expenditure), E_{sale} – marketing and sales costs (expenditure), I is expected income from the sale of radically new products on the market, P is the expected net profit.

The resulting factor model for determining the cost effectiveness of creating and launching radically new products on the market allows to evaluate the effectiveness of using each of the components of the scientific and technological capacity using factor analysis methods. The proposed model allows to determine the «ideal» value of the cost-effectiveness indicator, which corresponds to the sales forecast of radically new products with specified characteristics and the price that the consumer is willing to pay for such products, as well as the timing of reaching the break-even point.

The ability of the enterprise to create and produce a radically new product will be evaluated both in terms of the achieved scientific and technological level for the implementation of research and development, the implementation of pre-production and production, as well as the development of marketing and sales, and in terms of the required volumes of resource support and projected revenue from the sale of radically new products.

The above problem can be solved on the basis of the approach consisting in the assessment of the specific indicators of the scientific and technological capacity for each of its components. We define quantitative indices as integral indicators that characterize the level of each of them. Integral indicators of the level of scientific and technical potential in the implementation of research and development, pre-production and production, marketing and sales can be determined on the basis of a system of partial indicators. The assessment r_i of each of the particular indicators of scientific and technological potential is subject to normalization in the range $[0; 1]$,

$$\bar{r}_i = \frac{r_i}{\max r_i},$$

where the value $\max r_i$ corresponds to the maximum attainable level of the particular indicator.

An integral indicator of the level of scientific and technological capacity for the implementation of each of the stages of creating a radically new product can be obtained on the basis of a system of private indicators as follows:

$$P = \sum_{i=1}^{N} w_i \cdot \bar{r}_i$$

where $\bar{r}_i$ are the values of particular indicators of scientific and technological capacity, w_i are the weight coefficients that sum to one.

This scheme allows to get three integral coefficients: PR&D is the level of scientific and technological capacity for the implementation of research and development work to create radically new products;

Pprod is the level of scientific and technological capacity for pre-production of radically new products;

Psale is the level of scientific and technological capacity for the implementation of marketing and sales of radically new products.

The above system of integrated indicators PR&D, Pprod, Psale, E(P) reflects, on the one hand, a company's ability to implement each of the steps of creating a radically new products (R&D, pre-production, marketing and distribution), and on the other hand, effectiveness of the expenditure for the implementation of these steps and, if necessary, increasing the level of scientific and technological capacity and competencies to a sufficient level.

Based on the proposed system of integral indicators, a single assessment Q of an enterprise's ability to create a radically new product can be obtained, the price of which will be acceptable to the consumer.

The calculation of the aggregate indicator Q of a company's ability to create a radically new product involves the comparison and assessment of integral indicators of a different nature. In this regard, to solve this problem, it is advisable to use a geometric method providing a joint integral assessment for several indicators.

With this method, each of the integral indicators PR&D, Pprod, Psale, E(P) can have its own measuring scale with its own dimension and range of variation. The joint graph for the model under consideration for assessing the Q ability of an enterprise to create a radically new product is a polygon, the number of sides of which corresponds to the number of integral indicators under consideration. Each side of the polygon (in the model under consideration – a square) is a scale for the integral indicators PR&D, Pprod, Psale, E(P). For the first three integral indicators, the limit values of the scale are 0 and 1. For the Integral indicator E (P), the upper limit is the calculated ideal value of the indicator, at which the price of a radically new product is acceptable to the consumer, and the break-even point is reached within the time acceptable for the manufacturer. The price of the products created can be adjusted by optimizing the cost in the design process for a given cost, introducing elements of lean production, etc. (see Figure 5.9).

Based on a schematic illustration (Figure 5.9) of an example of the method used by an enterprise, the algorithm for identifying the Q indicator of a company's ability to create a radically new product can be described as follows. The corresponding measurement scales (sides of the square) fix the values of the integral indicators

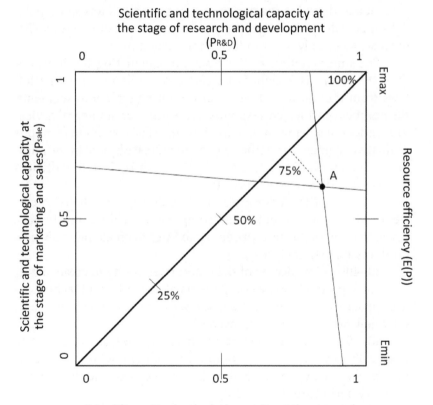

Figure 5.9 – An example of a graph for identifying the indicator Q of an enterprise's ability to create a radically new product based on the geometric method

247

at a certain point in time. Fixed values on opposite sides of the square are connected by straight lines, the intersection point of which (A) characterizes the total ability of an enterprise to create a radically new product. If the values of all integral indicators reach their maximum values, then the intersection point is in the upper right corner. This means the maximum value of the aggregate sufficiency of integral indicators and the a priori ability of an enterprise to create a radically new product. By plotting a diagonal with a gradation from 0 to 100 percent and dropping the perpendicular from the intersection point A to this scale, you can get the percentage of an enterprise's ability to create a radically new product at the current time.

The interpretation of the results of calculating the indicator Q of the enterprise's ability to create a radically new product follows from the uniform division of the rating scale into segments, the number of which corresponds to the number of integral indicators under consideration increased by one. The transition from one evaluative segment to another means an increase by one in the number of integral indicators, the level of which is close to sufficient to create a radically new product:

0–20% – critically low degree of an enterprise's ability to create a radically new product (all components of the capacity have a negative trend, the enterprise's capabilities to create radically new products are extremely low);

20–40% – low degree of the enterprise's ability to create a radically new product (some components of scientific and technological capacity have a negative tendency, the costs of creating a radically new product are not recovered);

40–60% – average degree of an enterprise's ability to create a radically new product (all components of the scientific and technological capacity are stable, the competitive price and the product recovery period are insufficient);

60–80% – moderate degree an the enterprise's ability to create a radically new product (the components of scientific and technological capacity have a positive trend, the achievement of a competitive price and cost recovery is possible subject to additional management decisions related to innovative capacity-building);

80–100% – high degree of an enterprise's ability to create a radically new product (all components of the scientific and technological capacity have a positive trend, an enterprise is highly likely to achieve the target indicators of a competitive price and cost recovery with the existing level of resourcing).

The growth of an enterprise's ability to create a radically new product is related to increasing its scientific and technological capacity and competencies, in particular, with the improvement and optimization of production, the creation of new technologies, an increase in labor productivity as a result of digitalization and automation, the introduction of intelligent enterprise management systems as a large organizational and technical system.

The stage following the development and manufacture of products is their marketing, the effectiveness of which is related to building a competent pricing strategy for a manufacturer of products with high consumer utility and establishing economically justified prices for products, taking into account pricing factors that affect the level, dynamics and ratio of prices. In this regard, we will consider the approaches to the formation of the price policy of sales of the created radically new products.

Approaches to the formation of the pricing policy of sales of created radically new products

The formation of a pricing policy for the sale of products with high consumer properties is based on the principle of continuous improvement, updating and expansion of the manufacturer's product line in accordance with market trends and needs, taking into account the time frame for reaching the break-even point for each of the products. As soon as the expenditure of creating and operating the created product exceed the income received from its sale, new products with unique competitive advantages should be launched on the market.

Forecasting the time frame for reaching the break-even point is carried out on the basis of continuous research of current and future market needs, especially the target segments, as well as new segments where the product developer has sufficient competencies and resource capabilities to create new unique products.

Various pricing strategies are well described in the scientific literature. Table 5.7 shows a sample of enterprise pricing strategies[49], applicable to the operating conditions of a manufacturer of products with high consumer utility.

Table 5.7 List of possible pricing strategies and their applicability to the satellite services market

Pricing strategies	Substance	Market applicability for radically new products
Market segmentation strategy, geographic strategy	Setting different prices in different market segments or for different buyers (the costs of creating and operating a radically new product are the same)	Setting prices depending on which region (poor or rich) the consumer is from and what offers exist in the market of his region
Market penetration strategy	It is usually used in the sale of consumer goods and consists in the initial establishment of relatively low prices for manufactured products. As a rule, this strategy is used when new products are introduced to the market or for a company to reinforce its presence.	In the marketplace, a manufacturer of radically new products can conduct price rallies to conquer the consumer. The effect of reducing average costs in terms of selling services as digital services is clearly expressed – the costs of selling an additional unit of service are minimal, and the value of average costs, in which constant ones prevail, will decrease.
«Set» Strategy	Setting prices for a set of several goods at a lower level than the sum of the prices of each individual good included in this set	One of the typical strategies in the digital services market. Consumers of such products can be offered a set of services the cost of which is lower than the sum of the prices of each of the services separately

49 J.J. Tellis, P. N. Golder, Will and Vision. Saint Petersburg: Stockholm School of Economics in Saint Petersburg, 2005.

«Above par» strategy	If there are two groups of consumers on the market (the first group is interested in a better quality product and is ready to pay a higher price for it, and the second group prefers to save money), then a company can release two versions of the product – premium and simple. The price for the premium model will be set at the highest possible level, but the simple version may even sell at a loss.	This versioning is widely used for products with a number of configurable options. Consumers with a high willingness to pay purchase a version of the product with full functionality, less affluent – a version with limitations. The manufacturer can provide some options free of charge
Periodic discount strategy	The basis is the characteristics of demand and its changes over a period of time. The same product can be sold at different prices at different times	May apply to products with seasonal demand fluctuations

The price strategy for the sale of a specific product with high consumer properties on the market can be determined already at the initial stage of its creation, when its idea and techno-economic image are shaped, which determines the ability of products to meet consumer expectations. The shaped image of such a product should correspond to the promising needs of companies and society based on their growing intellectual potential and developing competencies. This forecast is based on the intellectual analysis of the global information space, taking into account the development of the current wave of innovation and the forecast characteristics of the next wave.

A company's choice of a specific pricing strategy for the sale of radically new products on the market is determined by its pricing policy, which regulates the price management processes taking into account various factors. Depending on the type, universal pricing policies can be classified as follows [50] (see table 5.8):

The choice of a specific type of pricing policy of a manufacturer of radically new products is determined by traditional price-forming factors (the need to take into account production costs; the level of demand for a particular type of product; the consumer value of the product; the level of competition). For a developer of radically new products, an active pricing policy is preferable, which implies flexible price regulation depending on internal and external factors; rigid pricing policy towards competitors as rivals in gaining a dominant position in the market, with price differentiation (and, accordingly, product options) for buyers with different resource capabilities, i.e. affordable price policy; loyal pricing policy to key consumers of such products; long-term pricing policy, since several update cycles occur during the product life cycle. Such a pricing policy of a manufacturer of radically new products is well compatible with the proactive strategy of its competitive behavior aimed at achieving a dominant position in the market.

Table 5.8. Classification of universal types of pricing policy of a company

Classification attribute	Pricing policy type	Substance
Depending on the nature	Active	The company's management independently sets prices for the goods sold and can change them depending on the market situation and their goals, using various price techniques to attract buyers. Such a policy is usually carried out by enterprises that have advantages over competitors
	Passive	The company's management sets prices based on its own costs or prices of the market (prices of market leaders or competitors)

[50] Batraeva E.A. Pricing policy of the company. Methods of pricing in a market economy [Electronic resource] / E.A. Batraeva. – Electron. Dan. – Krasnoyarsk: Sib. Feder. un-t, 2013 – 75 p.

By degree of flexibility	Constant	Pricing approaches remain unchanged over a long period of time
	Flexible	The company varies prices depending on changes in external and internal environmental factors
Relative to competitors	Strict	The company competes in price with other companies, trying to occupy a dominant position in the market and exclude competitors and to gain a large market share
	Compromise	The company interacts with competitors, enters into pricing agreements with them, concludes contracts both on the price level and on the division of the market
Relative to the price level (to buyers)	Affordable price policy	The range of products sold by the company is represented by both expensive and cheaper products designed for consumers with different income levels
	Low price policy	The range of products sold is targeted at buyers with middle and low income. Using a policy of low prices, the company seeks to increase turnover and thereby reduce the level of distribution costs; increase the number of buyers
	High price policy	When setting prices for products sold, the company focuses on buyers with a high level of income, providing them with expensive goods and a high level of service
Relative to the State	Independent	The company does not take into account the government's pricing policy. It does not violate the legislation, but follows her own course
	Loyal	It is applied when the company participates in the implementation of the state pricing policy and follows the main recommendations
By implementation time	Long-term	Pricing approaches are determined for a long period and do not change during this period
	Short-term	Is valid for a short period of time

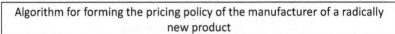

Algorithm for forming the pricing policy of the manufacturer of a radically new product

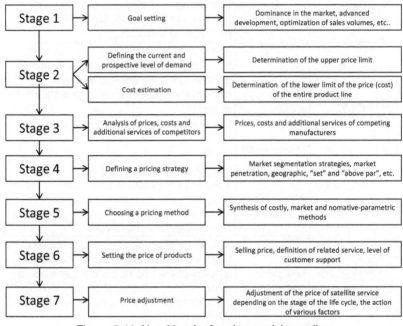

Figure 5.10 Algorithm for forming a pricing policy

Given the identified features, the algorithm for shaping a pricing policy for sales of products with high consumer properties in the market is as follows:

The effective use and interaction of the complex of the considered tools enables high economic efficiency of the created products with high consumer utility, which can be estimated as follows

$$E = \sum_{t=0}^{T} (N_t (k \cdot P_{trad} - P_{new}) S_t) - S_0,$$

where $t = 0,1,...,T$ are discrete time intervals (for example, a calendar year),

P_{trad} is the cost of the closest analogue existing on the market,

P_{new} is cost of developed products with high consumer properties,

N_t are expected sales of products for period t (predicted on the basis of a tool for determining the future needs of companies and society),

S_0 is the cost of development and operation of the designed product (calculated on the basis of a tool for determining the cost of a service at various stages of its life cycle),

S_t is the cost for periodic updating and modernization,

k is the correction factor of the consumer value of the created products. Its economic meaning is to increase the value due to the consumer properties of the products created.

Figure 5.11 shows a conditional example of the formation of the effectiveness of the created products over time. In this conditional example S0 = 1000, Ptrad=100, Pnew=60 (solid line), Pnew=70 (dotted line), St = 300 for t=2 and t=5, and St = 100 in all other cases, k=0,9, N0=5, N1=6, N2=N3=7, at other times, N accepts the value 8.

In the case of Pnew=70 (dashed line), the positive effect is achieved at time t=7, and in the case of Pnew=60 60 (solid line),

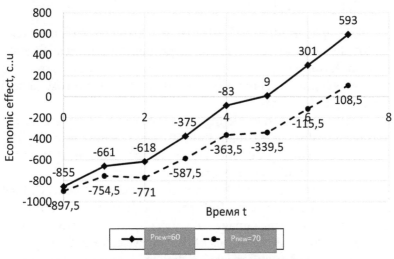

Figure 5.11 Illustration of the growth of the economic effect over time
as a result of the action of the mechanism for managing the development
and sale of products with high consumer utility

the positive effect is achieved already at t=5. By adjusting various parameters of the model, it is possible to determine the optimal ratio between the cost parameters included in the mechanism for managing the development and sale of products with high consumer properties. To solve the problem of optimal regulation of cost parameters, an optimization problem can be considered, in which the maximum value of the economic effect is determined, given the constraints on cost parameters:

$$E = \sum_{t=0}^{T} \left(N_t (k \cdot P_{new} - P_{trad}) - S_t \right) - S_{dev} \to \max,$$

$$\underline{S_{dev}} \leq S_{dev} \leq \overline{S_{dev}},$$

$$\underline{S_t} \leq S_t \leq \overline{S_t},$$

$$\underline{P_{new}} \leq P_{new} \leq \overline{P_{new}},$$

$$S_t = f_1(S_{dev}),$$

$$P_{new} = f_2(S_{dev}).$$

The optimization task allows to consider different scenarios for the development and sale of products at different financial costs in the development process, which affect its competitive price through generating competitive advantages, and the costs associated with updating products.

Using simulation modeling upon the proposed model, the contour of the values of the main indicators can be determined, which are defined using tools and regulated mechanisms that ensure the achievement of a given economic efficiency.

The proposed model for evaluating the effectiveness of satellite services allows us to link the developed tools for forming the techno-economic image of radically new products, form the cost price at various stages of the life cycle, form a competitive price in the market and pricing policy for its sale, as well as evaluate the economic efficiency of the created products. The model allows to regulate the elements of the mechanism for managing

the development and sale of products with high consumer properties and find a balance between the price of products and the volume of their sales on the market, which will give the manufacturer
the opportunity to build a pricing policy in the short, medium
and long term.

Further improvement in the economic efficiency of radically
new products is possible on the basis of service models of their distribution. Such penetration is especially noticeable in the high-tech
industry, whose products are of high value. At its core, the service
model assumes the transfer of the ability to use the product function to the consumer, and the manufacturer assumes all obligations
related to service, updating or support of the product. Next, we will
consider the tools that allow us to determine the limits of the applicability of service models for the products of a particular enterprise
and the effectiveness of its implementation at the stage of shaping
the idea and the techno-economic image of a product.

CHAPTER 6.
FORMING METHODOLOGICAL TOOLS FOR MANAGING SUSTAINABLE DEVELOPMENT OF AN ENTERPRISE BASED ON SERVICE MODELS

6.1. SERVICE MODEL OF ECONOMIC DEVELOPMENT OF THE COMPANY: SUBSTANCE AND MATHEMATICAL MODELING

Studies show that the use of service models can significantly increase the economic efficiency of a company by reducing the number of intermediaries between the manufacturer and the consumer, optimizing the manufacturer's costs, generating new revenue from services during the operation of the product, etc.

In scientific literature, these issues are covered in general terms without determining quantitative indicators for assessing the effectiveness of the transition from the traditional model of a company's functioning to the service model. In order to obtain such estimates, we will conduct the following studies, which allow us to assess the economic effect of the transition to the service model on the basis of a company's traditional indicators describing its operating activities.

Basically, industrial enterprises operating today focus their activities on the creation of production assets (machine tools, vehicles, turbines, etc.) and their supply to the market. As the market began to value service, consumers began to expect from manufacturers not only products, but also services related to them. Over time, manufacturers striving to ensure a high level of their own competitiveness began to form complex offers for products and services that involve the supply of complete turnkey solutions, including maintenance and repair of manufactured products, as well as business models that do not involve the sale of products, but only services.

Today, manufacturers see services not only as an addition to product value, but also as a separate value proposition and an independent source of income. At the turn of the 20th and 21st centuries, among the new business models that can increase the competitiveness of manufacturers, the so-called service model was formed.

For example, Rolls-Royce, which uses a service business model, does not sell aircraft engines to customers. It offers them the TotalCare service, which bills only the operating hours of each engine. The main services of TotalCare include technical condition monitoring, engine overhaul, work to improve engine reliability; the value-added package includes technical data management, engine transport, spare engine maintenance and a support line.

The demand for such services among consumers is due to the fact that the consumer, as a rule, is not interested in the products themselves, but in the target effect, the utility that the product provides.

Service business models are often viewed as a key factor in shaping the economic sustainability of an enterprise due to the ability to develop products with new competitive advantages at lower costs.

The scientific literature analyzes in detail the service models of many companies. Accenture (2014) examines the Michelin business model of selling "tires as a service" where customers pay for the distance traveled. ING (2018) analyzes the leases of household appliances for the home. Whisnant (2014) examines various service business models, such as subscription models (such as a monthly fee) and "pay for success", as in the case of Johnson and Johnson, receiving payment for an anti-cancer drug only if it is effective for the patient.

There are a number of options for the application of the service model in mechanical engineering, which are being considered by global manufacturers today. For example, machine tool manufacturers offer their customers an hourly or pay-per-output model. The new responsibility of the manufacturer in this model of cooperation is to monitor equipment performance and timely maintenance and repairs.

A monitoring and service model similar to that used by Rolls-Royce can also be introduced by manufacturers of other types of engines and pumps. So, manufacturers of engines for quarry

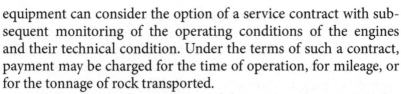

equipment can consider the option of a service contract with subsequent monitoring of the operating conditions of the engines and their technical condition. Under the terms of such a contract, payment may be charged for the time of operation, for mileage, or for the tonnage of rock transported.

All the proposed options are of the same nature — a similar model of interaction between the producer and the consumer. This model can bring new markets to producers, and new economic benefits both to producers and buyers.

The issue of forming an effective service business model for a specific type of product is quite complex and requires a separate study in each specific case. It focuses on sustainable consumption, which is defined as "the use of services and related products that meet basic needs and improve the quality of life with a minimum use of resources".

In order to encourage sustainable consumption of a particular product, it is important to take into account consumer behavior in the purchase, operation and disposal of products. Based on this analysis, it is possible to develop new innovative solutions and products with new competitive advantages focused on optimizing the operation of products.

At the present stage of development of existing approaches to enterprise management and taking into account the development of technology for analyzing and monitoring data from the global information space, forecasting and constant study of needs and consumer expectations is one of the most effective mechanisms for increasing the competitiveness of a manufactured high-tech product operating within the service business model. To ensure the competitiveness of high-tech products in the global market, it is necessary to improve the quality of strategic marketing of a company within the general concept of sustainable development management in the context of developing products with new competitive advantages, updating the product range and developing fundamentally new innovative products. Ensuring the competitiveness of any high-tech product in the global and domestic markets is carried out through its constant modernization and management based on the introduction of innovative solutions not only in the production process, but also in the sale and operation of products and management of these processes, provided that it is formed on the basis of complete and objective source information in the current market environment.

The effectiveness of the implementation of innovative solutions and the possibility of their generation, the effectiveness of the company as a whole in the transition from the traditional sales model to service sales is determined by the effectiveness of the service business model. The key elements of the business model that determine the content of the model are:

- the value and value to customers that a company offers in the form of its products and services;
- mechanisms for creating this value, including target customers and the supplier system, as well as value chains;
- the assets that a company uses to create value;
- the financial model of a company's activities, which determines both the structure of its costs and the methods of producing a profit.

Study of the practice of developing and implementing business models shows that business models can be created for the following purposes:

- for a specific product or service (group of similar products / services);
- for a company as a whole;
- for groups of companies, holdings, corporations.

Currently, amid the crisis and financial uncertainty, as well as in connection with the control of the markets of many types of products by strong players who use various mechanisms of imperfect competition to maintain their positions, allowing them to control entire market segments, many traditional business models have lost their effectiveness and competitiveness. , which leads to losses of new market players and companies traditional for the market, loss of market positions, bankruptcy. Service business models can be more effective in a crisis than in a period of economic stability and provide companies that use them with new growth opportunities. Continued use of inefficient business models and slowness in defining and moving to new business models can lead to significant financial losses and loss of the ability to stay in business.

For mathematical modeling of the effectiveness of product sales through a service business model, it is necessary to determine the structure of business expenses and incomes both in traditional production and sales and with services.

The above studies of the practice of applying service business models by various companies indicate that such an approach to product sales is one of the ways to increase the economic sustainability of an enterprise. The effect consists, firstly, in obtaining a greater profit for the enterprise and ensuring its smooth and break-even operation, and, secondly, in reducing possible losses in terms of one direction of activity, that is, in minimizing the average values of losses for all types of activities by diversifying consumption. The mechanism of obtaining an economic effect can be explained by the following rather simple formulation: since the financial and economic activities of an enterprise are always associated with the risk of losses, then by offering potential consumers various schemes for purchasing and using products, it is possible to minimize losses per type and increase the economic stability of the enterprise.

Let us describe the economic effect of the transition to a service business model using economic indicators.

As a quantitative indicator characterizing the change, consider the economic indicator $EBIT_\%$ of the operating profit of an enterprise, expressed as a percentage.

This figure for traditional business models is calculated as follows:

$$EBIT_\% = \frac{\sum_{i=1}^{N}(p_i - v_i)Q_i - FC}{\sum_{i=1}^{N} p_i Q_i}$$

where p_i is the cost of a unit of product of the type i, v_i is the variable production cost per unit of a product of the type i, FC is the fixed cost of production, Q_i is the volume of a product of the type i, N is the number of types of products.

As for fixed costs, they can increase in the case of a transition to a service business model due to the need to acquire additional competencies of an enterprise related to marketing of manufactured products, closer work with consumers, etc. That is, fixed costs increase due to the complexity of the functions of the top management of an enterprise and the need for new activities.

The variable costs of traditional production do not change per unit of output, but change to total output in proportion to the volume of output. At the same time, variable costs during the transition to a service business model can increase due to the cost of providing additional services.

In the service business model, the cost of a unit of production is replaced by a set of cost indicators corresponding to the consumer's expenses for obtaining a product and its operation. The disposal cost of the product can also be taken into account, and the products to be disposed of can be transferred both back to the manufacturer and remain with the consumer.

That is, as a result of the transition to service models, the structure of the cash flow changes.

Let us now consider an example of a manufacturing enterprise that produces several types of products at a certain cost. Consider how the indicator $EBIT_\%$ changes due to the transition to a service business model for existing or for newly introduced products. According to the example, before the introduction of the service business model, the enterprise produced 6 types of products. Let us assume that the fixed costs were $FC=3700$ in the manufacture of 6 types of products in the traditional business model. The volume of output of each type of product, the cost of a unit of each type of product, variable production costs per unit of product and the calculated values of the indicator $EBIT_\%$ are shown in Table 6.1. Then it was decided to sell 4 types of products through a service business model, and fixed costs were $FC= 4600$ in the case of manufacture of 10 types of products.

Variable costs for products sold through the service business model are also higher. A company receives more income through the provision of services, which is reflected in the value of the indicator of the cost per unit of production. The graph of the indicator value $EBIT_\%$ hange is shown in Figure 6.1.

Table 6.1 – Calculation of operating profit during the transition to the service model

Product type	Unit cost of product p_i	Variable costs v_i	Output volume Q_i	Operating profit $EBIT_\%$
1	20	10	50	
2	30	10	45	
3	27	12	30	11.68 %
4	26	10	55	
5	35	13	45	
6	30	9	40	
7	30	16	50	18.16 %
8	25	12	45	22.87 %
9	20	15	30	24.13 %
10	35	17	45	28.4 %

* The last 4 types of products are sold on the basis of a service business model. In this case, the cost refers to a time-distributed cash flow from the sale of services on the market.

The growth of operating profit, expressed as a percentage, indicates an increase in the economic stability of an enterprise. In this

Changes in the operating profit of an enterprise in the process of diversification

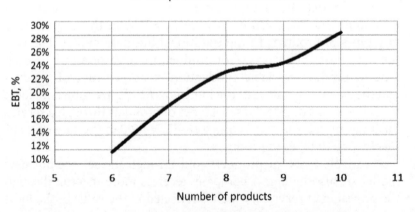

Figure 6.1. Change in operating profit $EBIT_\%$ during the transition of a number of products to the service business model

Change in operating profit as a result of a decrease in the cost of production

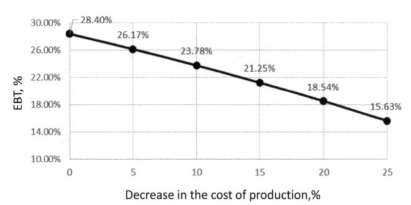

Figure 6.2. Change in operating profit $EBIT_{\%}$ with a decrease in product cost after the introduction of service business models

case, the application of the service business model can be considered effective.

In a market economy, one of the competitive advantages of an enterprise is the lower cost of its products while creating high consumer utility in comparison with the products of competing enterprises. In this regard, the urgent task is to reduce consumer costs for the purchase and operation of products as a result of the application of service business models. In the conditions of the previous example (production of 10 types of products, 4 of them are sold through service business models), we will consider the possibility of reducing the consumer value of the first 6 types of products by switching to the provision of services and also calculate the values of operating profit $EBIT_{\%}$. The calculation results are shown in Fig. 6.2

Thus, when the cost of each unit of products of the first six types is reduced by 25%, the operating profit $EBIT_{\%} = 15,63\%$ exceeds the value of this indicator (11.68 %) before switching to service business models, which again indicates their effectiveness.

Operating profit when sales volumes change

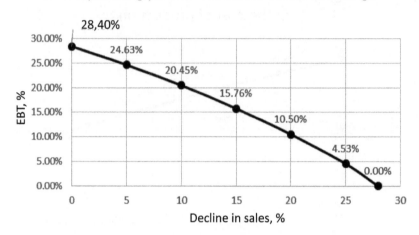

Figure 6.3. Changes in operating profit with a decrease
in the volume of services.

Another characteristic of the economic sustainability of an enterprise is its ability to remain profitable with some fluctuations in sales. For example, sales may decline as a result of some macroeconomic factors. Let us consider how the operating profit of an enterprise will change with a decrease in sales and the volume of services provided for each type of product by a given number of percentage points. It should be noted that the volume of production will not change, i.e. only the volume of service provision will decrease. Figure 6.3 shows the results of calculating operating profit $EBIT_{\%}$.

According to the results shown in Fig. 6.3, we can conclude that the marginal decrease in sales volumes, at which a company remains at break-even or does not reduce the profitability from the sale of other products, is 28%, and the level of decline in sales, in which a company receives the same profit as before the transition to service models, is approximately 20 %. Thus, with a decline in sales, an enterprise that has switched to a service business model also demonstrates its economic stability with a constant supply volume within the traditional business model.

To quantify the change in the volume of profit depending on the change in the volume of sales of services allows the degree of impact of the operational leverage DOL, which is calculated as follows:

$$DOL = \frac{\sum_{i=1}^{N}(p_i - v_i)Q_i}{\sum_{i=1}^{N}(p_i - v_i)Q_i - FC}.$$

DOL shows how the operating profit of an enterprise will change when the volume of sales changes by 1%. Let us compare this change both in the conditions of the traditional model of product sales and in the transition to the implementation of services for some types of enterprise products.

In terms of the structure of costs and incomes of the enterprise, presented in table. 6.1, consider the change in the impact of DOL during the transition to a service business model. We calculate the impact of DOL before switching to a new business model (production of types 1–6) and when adding to the traditional service model (7–10). The results of the calculations are presented in Table 6.2.

Table 6.2. DOL calculation

Types of products	1-6	1-7	1-8	1-9	1-10
DOL	5.3	3.3	2.62	2.45	2.07

The DOL calculated for each stage indicates an increase in operating profit for a 1% change in sales volume. For example, at the last stage, DOL = 2.07. This means that a change in sales volume (both traditional and service) at this stage, for example, by 10% leads to a change in operating profit by 10% * 2.07 = 20.07%. As noted above, DOL is also directly related to the level of operating risk: the greater the level of exposure to operating leverage, the greater the risk. In this regard, the decrease in the operating leverage from stage to stage also indicates an increase in the economic stability of an enterprise (Figure 6.4).

So, we have illustrated the increase in the efficiency of an enterprise and, consequently, the increase in its economic stability

Reducing operational risk in the diversification process

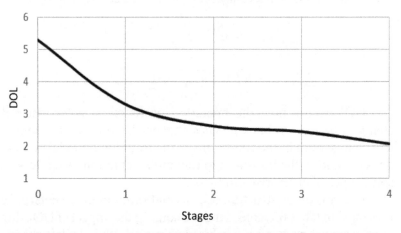

Figure 6.4. The decrease in the DOL indicator as a result of the transition to the service business model indicates an increase in the economic stability of an enterprise

as a result of the transition to the service model using economic indicators.

The obtained results of the analysis of the processes of transition to service business models allow us to formulate the following axiom: service business models are effective if they bring income to an enterprise higher than in the traditional sales model, and allow to improve innovative performance of this enterprise using additional income, focused on the release of new competitive products that exceed the existing performance characteristics.

Reducing fixed costs arising from the transition to service business models is possible due to the transfer of part of the management functions to intelligent control systems that have multifunctional capabilities that allow assessing the economic parameters of products and production at different stages of the life cycle. In addition, this allows, under various influencing factors and risks, to offer decision-makers recommendations for improving both product parameters and sales models in the market in order to maintain a given competitiveness or create new competitive advantages through the development of technical, economic and operational characteristics.

So, at the stages of product marketing and operation through the use of intelligent methods to create product advertising, interact with consumers, build optimal logistics schemes, assess malfunctions using intelligent product testing systems, such systems offer a multivariate choice or the most optimal option for service sales of products, their repair and service. The multivariate choice is made based on the analysis of operating costs, residual value, inflation rate, resale value, and other indicators by the intelligent system.

Another function of such an intelligent system is to manage the update of both the product itself and the range of services provided, taking into account the evolution of needs based on initial data on changing needs over time and recommendations for improving the product at all stages of its life cycle to maintain and create competitive advantages in the future.

Such an intelligent system can be described as a network of a finite automaton (state machine), which are a mathematical model for information transformation, described by the five ordered finite sets K=<A,B,Q,q0,F>, where A is a finite set that describes the input information; B is a finite set that describes the output information; Q is a finite set that describes the internal states of a state machine; q0 is an element of the set Q, denoting the initial state of the state machine; F this is a transition function that sets the evolution of the finite state machine according to the input information, i.e. $F : A \times Q \rightarrow B \times Q$.

The functioning of a finite state machine is defined as follows. The state machine operates at discrete points in time t=0,1,2,... In this case, at each cycle, the finite state machine receives elements from the set A at the input, while the finite state machine changes its internal state and outputs an element of the set B. This can be represented as follows: $b_n = F_b(a_n, q_{n-1})$, $q_n = F_q(a_n, q_{n-1})$.

The use of finite automata in the implementation of fragments of the decision support system is to describe not only the reflection on the input information, but also the mechanisms of assimilation of previously received information. In a certain sense, the use of a network of finite state machines is analogous to artificial neural networks. At the same time, finite state machines have a number of advantages in knowledge engineering.

In the functioning of an intelligent system, it is assumed that the representation of knowledge about changes in consumer preferences, new products of competitors, popular services, etc. as a network of finite state machines can change over time, depending on enhancing and/or updating of knowledge about the dynamics of consumer expectations.

Fragments of the decision support system for commercialization and launching products to the market must have the ability to machine learning from the source data in order to automatically highlight significant events in information flows.

The key features of the system are:

A decision support system based on the proposed network of finite state machines, which allows obtaining automatic estimates of economic parameters, starting from any stage of the product life cycle, incl. operational phase. There is no need to run the previous stages of the life cycle through the expert system, and automatic expert conclusion can be obtained starting from any stage of the life cycle if the source data necessary for the corresponding fragment of the network of state machines are available.

Continuous processing of information and its updating and adding data of the world information space.

The expert nature of the automatic system, i.e. the ability of the system to make management decisions without human intervention, to independently navigate in changing conditions, to choose specific management decisions taking into account advanced modeling and forecasting of the situation, which together allows you to replace the decision-maker.

The versatility of the system in processing any data arrays, which is achieved due to the ability of the system to learn and its connections with various databases and the world information space.

Thus, the proposed decision support system meets all the features of a classical system for processing large data arrays: a large amount of data, the requirement of an acceptable data processing speed, the ability to work with various data, the reliability of data processing results, the value of data processing results, the ability to respond to data changes. A distinctive feature of the system is to automatically develop multivariate recommendations for improving both product parameters and associated services in order to maintain a given competitiveness or create new competitive advantages.

Such systems form the basis for forecasting, managing the long-term development of enterprises through the design and manufacture of new products, their sales through the optimal model for this type of product (service, traditional, etc.), while they allow to effectively solve the problems of economic analysis and management at various stages of the product life cycle, taking into account the features and obligations imposed by service sales models. Thus, a company acquires new knowledge about consumer expectations in the market and the actions of competitors and thereby determines the development vector of its own competencies, which allow increasing the competitive advantages of products both through improving technical characteristics and through new operational properties.

6.2. SERVICE MODELS AS A TOOL FOR THE TRANSFER OF KNOWLEDGE AND COMPETENCIES TO ENSURE THE ECONOMIC EFFICIENCY OF A COMPANY

Having considered the nature and general approaches to the assessment of economic efficiency of the service business models will also examine the relationship between the obtained value and the level of competences that determine the effectiveness of the implementation of the various stages of creating and applying service models.

Solving the problems of obtaining high profits, a company seeks to determine the most effective ways of its implementation for specific types of products: classic sales to the consumer, granting the right to use the functionality under certain conditions, etc.

Not all companies today widely use service sales models due to the lack of competencies in various areas. On the one hand, a company must have the competence to create and manufacture goods with high consumer properties. On the other hand, it is necessary to organize the process of product development and production in such a way that it has high technical characteristics at the lowest possible cost. At the same time, the products created given these conditions should not be considered as the final product, which becomes the consumer's property after payment, but as a tool that although does not belong to the consumer, helps him to solve his own problems. Therefore, if we talk about the transfer to a service model of selling one or two products from the entire product line, then it can be argued that many companies are not following the path due to the emerging risks regarding the introduction and operation of the service model. On the other hand, the positive side of the transition to a service model is that it avoids intermediaries (one or more) who buy the final product and then resell it to the final consumer. Intermediaries take over a significant part of the services related to the maintenance of products, ensuring their operation, etc. Due to the presence of intermediaries in the chain of bringing the product to the end user, the price paid by the end user for the product may differ from the manufacturer's price by 100-200 %.

In search of high consumer properties of the created products, companies strive to identify their own opportunities and untapped abilities, around which an effective business model can be built. The tasks of identifying and developing internal resources and capabilities become the basis for creating new business competencies that increase the efficiency not only of design and production, but also the commercialization and operation of products. In these conditions, the expansion and use of competencies in conjunction with new, including service business models, makes economic sense, since this increases the competitiveness of a company.

It is important to bear in mind that the efficiency and value of acquiring and developing business competence are not universal categories: they are determined and self-growing only in the context of a specific strategy for the development of a company and the adaptation of its business model to new economic conditions. A company's competencies are developing most successfully in line with purposeful activities to create new products and services that were not previously provided, that is, a company's competencies are accumulated in order to capture new market segments or create new markets. This situation leads to the inability of a company to adapt to the service business model of sales, or to underestimation of the possibility of organizing sales through service models, which can bring the company revenues that exceed those in the classic sales model. But in order to switch to service models, a company must have a high level of competence in non-traditional areas of activity, that is, a company must not sell its product to an intermediary who already independently brings it to the end user, but must go directly to the end user, who will use this product and pay the manufacturer for it. In this case, the manufacturer must calculate the period for repayment of his costs through service sales and establish an acceptable cost for the consumer (operator) for services, taking into account that the manufacturer remains the owner of the product.

The formation of a set of methods for developing a company's key competencies in creating a competitive product is possible after analyzing the scope of activity, production and marketing processes, personnel support and the existing information infrastructure.

All large companies have organizational controls designed to regulate the flow of competencies and knowledge. These elements are necessary to encourage the sharing of innovative resources and the transfer of knowledge both within and outside a company. In other words, companies can manage the creation of new competencies and knowledge by acquiring already existing knowledge. This applies to all forms of knowledge: individual objects of intellectual property, technologies, non-formalized skills, experience, competencies.

In this regard, the problem of information exchange in high-tech companies should be considered in three aspects:

1) transfer of knowledge between individual structures of the intra-industry technological platform in order to intensify work to form radical consumer properties of products. Considering that high technology activities carried out on a cross-platform level involve enterprises that are technologically related to different industries (instrument making, electronics, radio

engineering, etc.), we can talk about an internal cross-industry transfer of knowledge, which becomes possible only under conditions of the formation and effective functioning of a cross-industry information space;

2) using the scientific capacity of companies in the industry for external technology transfer from related commercial activities. In this case, all structural elements of the sectoral technological platform, their research and production capabilities should be considered as a catalyst for innovation in other sectors of the economy;

3) the use of the international information space for the purpose of analyzing the existing sales technologies in the world based on service business models, selecting the most promising ones and attracting to the industry those technologies that can contribute to improving the consumer properties of the created products and achieving a leading competitive position in the market by providing products with new consumer properties.

In this regard, the following algorithm is proposed to achieve a high level of competence of the manufacturer in the application of service business models through transfer mechanisms (Fig. 6.5).

Let us consider in detail the stages of new services based on the transfer of knowledge and competencies.

Forming information bases and organization of the transfer of technologies and competencies in services at the enterprise level.

At the first stage, it is necessary to solve the issue of creating information bases that allow for the transfer of technologies and competencies within corporate and holding structures. This stage is fundamental in the overall system of achieving leading positions, as it is the basis for the further formation of competence centers for the provision of services at the level of technological platforms in the industry. It is important that in relation to the enterprise at the current management level, the transfer of technologies and competencies can be: internal – between various business areas of enterprises – participants in the technological platform; quasi-internal – the movement of technologies within the technological platform, including between

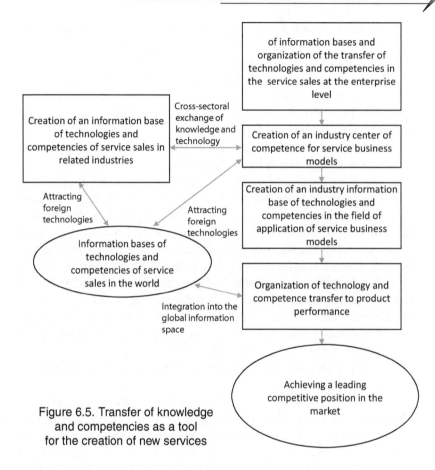

Figure 6.5. Transfer of knowledge
and competencies as a tool
for the creation of new services

enterprises with wide product lines; external – in relation to the enterprises of the technological platform.

The formation of an information base that will allow for the systematization, ranking and search of popular technologies and competencies for use in a particular division of an enterprise is of great importance for the successful transfer of technologies and competencies.

Competencies go through several stages of development before they turn from basic to key competencies. Registration of a key competence is possible only after the creation of the technology, the release of finished products and its successful sale on the market or the implementation of services, provided that there is no direct transfer of ownership from the manufacturer to the consumer. To stimulate innovative development, the transfer of competencies should be proactive. Such a mechanism will contribute to the development of competence transfer and scientific and technical cooperation between all enterprises within the technological platform and at the cross-platform level.

Forming an information base of technologies and competencies in providing services by related industries.

The long-term goal of knowledge transfer is to support economic growth for the foreseeable future through the development and commercialization of new technologies. For this reason, the problem of knowledge transfer cannot be limited to sectoral boundaries, but the transfer includes an external component in order to achieve a leading competitive position in the market. In this regard, it is necessary to create information bases of technologies and competencies in all high-tech industries in order to organize an intersectoral transfer of technologies and competencies, ensuring a reduction in the amount of resources required to form a pool of services for the sale of high-tech products on the market.

Forming an industry center of competence in the implementation of service business models.

Formal permission to transfer knowledge allows to optimize the process of knowledge transfer, choose a convenient form (outsourcing, training of customer personnel, development of a business process for the specifics of the customer, etc.), taking into account all the associated costs. At this stage, the acquirer decides the question of the advantage of obtaining knowledge from the outside over intensifying his own efforts.

In the commercial world, knowledge transfer involves intermediaries, i.e. specialized structures (venture capital firms, innovation incubators, technology parks, engineering and consulting firms, etc.) that specialize in the final stage of industrial adaptation of intellectual products to a specific production. With regard to competencies, such functions can be combined within the framework of the above-mentioned structures or be carried out by specialized centers of competence.

This infrastructure significantly saves the cost of preparatory work, because the competencies in most cases are related to technology, and those, in turn, with the pre- production, training of personnel, etc. In practice, this means that the need for knowledge transfer in organization service sales should be related to economic feasibility, and the transfer should be considered as a commercial project, in which all the participants (owner of competence, its consumer, technological mediation center of competence) will benefit.

Thus, it is best to identify competencies in advance, before they turn into key ones. This can only be done on the basis of continuous monitoring. Since there are no objective criteria for the significance of competence in the form of a ready-made competitive product, the enterprise cannot establish the level of its competence according to market criteria. It remains to use the procedures for comparing the effectiveness of the implementation of individual components of the activities of enterprises at the level of business processes, and this requires a single industry Competence Center, which, based on interaction with enterprises and the use of data from the global information space, will coordinate the identification and transfer of competencies to manufacturers interested in increasing the profitability of their own activities.

The task of a manufacturer seeking to obtain more income through the transition to service models of sales is to determine the conditions for ensuring the economic feasibility and efficiency of using the service model, which is achieved due to a high level of business competence at all stages of the functioning of service models, incl. personnel, production, technological, marketing and other competencies. That is, it is necessary to determine the level of competence of an enterprise that can allow it to switch to the service model for most types of products, and the level of risks that can be leveled by capacity-building.

Let us consider the main components of the transition to service business models.

First, a company must have a level of competence that will allow it to create products, the operation of which on a commercial basis will interest the end user. Such a product should have high consumer properties in comparison with other products, and its operation should bring the target effect to the customer. Here it is necessary to understand that the manufacturer does not cover the cost of production at a time, and the cash flow generated by the service during the operation of the product is distributed over time. At the same time, the total cash flow received by the manufacturer from the implementation of services, as a result, may exceed the income that could have been obtained as a result of applying the classical sales scheme, and the income received in a larger amount can be used for the scientific and technological development of the company.

Secondly, a manufacturer that sells products through service models must have marketing competencies that allow it to search for product consumer on conditions when they do not become the property of the consumer. Moreover, the manufacturer must understand that at various stages of operation (delivery, installation of equipment, maintenance, repair), there are costs that must be covered by the consumer's payment for services. The manufacturer's ability to minimize these costs depends both on his competence and on the technical level of the product. A preliminary analysis of the economic efficiency of the transition to a service business model by modeling costs and income based on traditional economic indicators is required. Such a model, which takes into account all the costs and revenues from the sale of products through a service business model and allows to draw a conclusion about the economic feasibility and efficiency of the transition to a service model, was proposed in the previous paragraph.

Thirdly, the competence of a company must be analyzed at all stages of product development and production, for which we will consider the following enlarged stages of product development:
– the stage of design,
– the stage of creating a prototype and testing,
– the stage of preparation for production and production,
– the stage of sales and operation.

Each of the presented stages requires the use of financial resources, fixed assets of an industrial company, information resources and employee competencies.

Stage 1. Design stage

For the design stage, personnel competencies (K_1) are important – the ability to design unique product characteristics that ensure competitiveness with the unification of the applied standard technologies and components. The development and subsequent design of a high-tech product assumes that an enterprise has the appropriate personnel. At this stage, personnel competencies are fundamental-the qualifications of employees and their professionalism. The need for product design requires qualified engineers and technologists to ensure the development of a competitive product. Human resources are the main competence of the stage, regardless of the level of automation of design processes.

Stage 2. Stage of creating of a prototype and tests

At the stage of creating a prototype, it is necessary to provide virtual prototyping of the product – a digital twin – in order to assess the parameters of the product's functioning at the operational stage. This stage requires competencies to ensure the functioning of virtual and experimental laboratories. To create a prototype, it is necessary to ensure the availability of simulation modeling and computer prototyping tools that make it possible to clarify the required characteristics, identify the strengths and weaknesses of the product, and provide the necessary margin of safety through model experiments in a virtual environment. It is necessary to create a prototype, which can be either digital or full-scale. To create a full-scale prototype, it is necessary to have experimental laboratories – tools for testing a prototype.

Stage 3. Stage of pre-production and production

At this stage, the key competence of an enterprise is the ability to automate production using digital technologies. Digital automation makes it possible to improve the accuracy of the components produced, to reduce the defects associated with production, and to shorten the production time. This competence involves the use of information infrastructure at all stages of production. The availability and effective use of digital technologies is the key competence of an enterprise in modern conditions.

Stage 4. Operation stage

At the operational stage, the key competence of an enterprise, which provides a competitive advantage, is service and after-sales support of products. This competence includes: selling not the product itself, but its functions, the ability to produce the necessary components in the required volume, prompt product repair, development and delivery of software updates for the product to consumers.

Let us review a mathematical model for quantifying the effectiveness of management of various stages of the life cycle of products being created, taking into account the capacity-building. We will evaluate the efficiency of the enterprise using the vector of private efficiency indicators corresponding to various stages of the product life cycle. We will consider N numerical indicators of enterprise efficiency, which we will denote by Qi. We will combine these indicators into an efficiency vector:

$$Q(t) = \begin{pmatrix} Q_1(t) \\ Q_2(t) \\ \vdots \\ Q_N(t) \end{pmatrix}$$

Since we will examine evaluating efficiency taking into account the dynamic factors associated with the emergence of new competitive advantages and consumer properties that arise as a result of the acquisition of relevant competencies by the enterprise, we consider the performance indicators as time-dependent.

The basic dynamic equation can be written as follows:

$$\frac{dQ(t)}{dt} = F\big(t, Q(t), G(t, Q(t))\big)$$

This formula reflects the influence of external and internal factors on the dynamics of efficiency using the function G. In particular, the formalism of this function will take into account the impact of competencies and risks on a company's activities.

It is well known that dynamic models describing the behavior of economic performance indicators are subject to natural diffusion

This diffusion leads to the fact that in the absence of external factors, the numerical indicators have a constant downward trend. The mathematical interpretation of this phenomenon is expressed as follows:

$$\frac{dQ(t)}{dt} = A(t)Q(t) + G\big(t, Q(t)\big).$$

In this formula, A(t) is an N × N square matrix with variable elements. A diagonal matrix can be considered as a matrix A(t), where the eigenvalues of this matrix are on the main diagonal:

$$A(t) = \begin{pmatrix} \lambda_1(t) & 0 & \cdots & 0 \\ 0 & \lambda_2(t) & \cdots & 0 \\ \cdots & \cdots & \cdots & \cdots \\ 0 & 0 & \cdots & \lambda_N(t) \end{pmatrix}.$$

However, in more complex models, full matrices should be used. The non-diagonal elements of the matrix reflect the economic fact of the mutual dependence between various performance indicators.

To calculate the impact of an enterprise's competence on the dynamics of efficiency, let us consider in more detail the function G on the right side of the main equation:

$$\frac{dQ(t)}{dt} = A(t)Q(t) + \sum_{k=1}^{M} B_k(t)G_k(t).$$

Here we consider the use of M competitive advantages to manage the performance of an enterprise. These competitive advantages are described by vectors:

$$G_k(t) = \begin{pmatrix} g_1^k(t) \\ g_2^k(t) \\ \vdots \\ g_{N_k}^k(t) \end{pmatrix}.$$

In the considered mathematical model, dimensionless quantities are used to describe economic processes, which allow us to focus more on the functional description of the phenomena under consideration.

Bk denotes matrices that describe the quantitative impact of competitive advantages on the dynamics of enterprise efficiency.

$$B_k = \begin{pmatrix} b_{11}^k & b_{12}^k & \cdots & b_{1N_k}^k \\ b_{21}^k & b_{22}^k & \cdots & b_{2N_k}^k \\ \cdots & \cdots & \cdots & \cdots \\ b_{11}^k & b_{11}^k & \cdots & b_{NN_k}^k \end{pmatrix}.$$

Thus, we will consider a linear differential system that will describe the dynamics of enterprise performance indicators at various stages of the product life cycle. In this case, there is a controlled dynamic system. The goal of managing this system is to increase significant performance indicators. For the mathematical formalism, it is possible to form the target functional in the form of an integral performance indicator:

$$IQ = \alpha_1 Q_1(T) + \alpha_2 Q_2(T) + \ldots + \alpha_N Q_N(T).$$

As already mentioned, the main tool for performance management in this model is the transition to the sale of products through the service business model. The advantages of an enterprise are formed due to the development of key competencies, which are a scientific and technological groundwork that allows the development and implementation of services demanded by consumers.

Let us consider a mathematical model for the dependence of the efficiency of the processes of creating and operating products on the competencies of an enterprise in the provision of services.

The competencies of an enterprise that affect the consumer properties of products are complexes of various single competencies. To create meaningful competitive advantages, many different competencies need to be considered. The mathematical model for the formation of the competitive advantages of the enterprise through the acquisition of competencies will be based on the use of the formalism of finite state machines. The finite-automaton approach allows us to consider complex economic processes in which the dynamics are described not only by external influences, but also by the internal state of the system.

Let the consumer properties of products be described by the following finite set:

$$H = \{H_1, H_2, ..., H_K\}.$$

Although the basic dynamic equation is a differential equation with continuous time, in this equation we will consider individual consumer properties, which we will describe by a finite set, which corresponds to the economic model under consideration.

Consumer properties arise as a result of offering the consumer services. Consider a finite set describing services that determine the consumer properties of products. Let us denote this set as follows:

$$I = \{I_1, I_2, ..., I_L\}.$$

We will assume that at the initial moment of time the system is in the state I1, and this set changes as a result of the emergence of new competencies. In the considered model for assessing efficiency, taking into account the competence of the enterprise, we will consider the following set of possible competencies:

$$G = \{G_1, G_2, ..., G_M\}.$$

The dynamics of the system of consumer properties, depending on the competencies created, is as follows. Let the following sequence of competencies arise as a result of enterprise performance management:

$$G_{i_1}, G_{i_2}, ..., G_{i_p}, ...$$

Then we get a sequence of services:

$$I_{j_1}, I_{j_2}, ..., I_{j_p}, ...$$

In addition, as a result of innovative technologies, a chain of consumer properties arises:

$$H_{k_1}, H_{k_2}, ..., H_{k_p}, ...$$

According to the finite-automaton model, these sequences are interconnected by the following relationships:

$$I_{j_p+1} = A\left[I_{j_p}, G_{i_p}\right],$$

$$H_{k_p+1} = B\left[I_{j_p+1}\right].$$

In these relations, we use the transition functions:
$A : I \times G \to I$ and $B : I \to H$.

Using these relationships, it is possible to formally define an economic and mathematical model that describes the chain of «competence – services – consumer properties». This chain shows that the impact of competencies on consumer properties is non-linear. Moreover, this influence can include various types of time lag, since the economic implementation of competence in the form of services that can bring certain competitive advantages in knowledge-based companies takes a long time.

Consider a controlled dynamic system described by a differential equation:

$$\frac{dQ(t)}{dt} = A(t)Q(t) + B_1(t)\left[H^1(t)\right] + B_2(t)\left[H^2(t)\right] + \ldots + B_M(t)\left[H^M(t)\right]$$

In this equation, impulse functions are indicated on the right side, which reflect the influence of consumer properties on the dynamics of business performance indicators, taking into account the emergence of new competencies. These functions are as follows:

$$H^k = \begin{cases} 0, & t < a_k \\ h^k(t), t \in [a_k, b_k] \\ 0, & t > b_k \end{cases}$$

Thus, the action of these functions has a finite time interval. For some competitive advantages, the time interval can be quite long.

Now we will consider the issue of the impact of the key competencies of the enterprise on obtaining consumer properties of products, which can significantly affect the dynamics of economic efficiency indicators. According to the proposed mathematical model for assessing the efficiency of an enterprise, depending on consumer properties, the dynamics of indicators is described by a differential

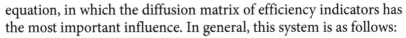

equation, in which the diffusion matrix of efficiency indicators has the most important influence. In general, this system is as follows:

$$\frac{dQ(t)}{dt} = A(t)Q(t) + G\big(t, Q(t)\big)$$

However, the impact of some key competencies can be taken into account not only in the equation, but also in the matrix A(t). Consider the key competencies that lead to obtaining the fundamental consumer properties of products through the provision of services. We denote this factor by U(t). Then, in general form, we obtain the following dynamic equation:

$$\frac{dQ(t)}{dt} = A^{U(t)}(t) + G\big(t, Q(t)\big)$$

We assume that the following relation is satisfied:

$$A^0(t) = A(t)$$

Here is an example of the influence of the function U(t) on the matrix A(t):

$$A^{U(t)} = \begin{pmatrix} a_{11}(t) + u_{11}(t) & a_{12}(t) + u_{12}(t) & \cdots & a_{1N}(t) + u_{1N}(t) \\ a_{21}(t) + u_{21}(t) & a_{22}(t) + u_{22}(t) & \cdots & a_{2N}(t) + u_{2N}(t) \\ \cdots & \cdots & \cdots & \cdots \\ a_{N1}(t) + u_{N1}(t) & a_{N2}(t) + u_{N2}(t) & \cdots & a_{NN}(t) + u_{NN}(t) \end{pmatrix}$$

The economic interpretation of these models is that the performance indicators of an enterprise are more inert, since the consumer properties of products that arise as a result of the use of the acquired competencies by the enterprise have an indirect effect on the performance indicators. In fact, there is a certain delay in efficiency, since the increase in the consumer properties of the products must be properly reflected in competitive markets, so that this leads to a significant economic effect for an enterprise. In this case, there are not only processes of time lag, but also processes when the previous values of an enterprise's performance indicators are defining in assessing its current efficiency.

The proposed mathematical formulation shows that if a manufacturer sells a small range of products through a service model, then a large increase in economic efficiency cannot be obtained. And the transition to service models as a whole can be quite effective if there is a clear transition algorithm that allows all conditions of economic efficiency to be met. The development of an enterprise through the transition to service business models will allow, on the basis of the accumulation of resources of various directions, to create a point of growth for the enterprise by generating radically new consumer and operational properties of the product. Next, we will consider these issues in more detail and propose models that allow forecasting economic growth and development at the enterprise and industry level as a result of the transition to service models.

6.3. FORECASTING THE ECONOMIC GROWTH OF A COMPANY AS A RESULT OF THE TRANSITION TO SERVICE MODELS

It was found above that the service business model allows an enterprise, with a high assessment of its economic efficiency, to receive more income from the sale of products and associated services than with the traditional sales model. At the same time, we have determined that an effective service model affects a company's revenue, depending on the share of products sold in the market through the service model. However, due to many circumstances, a company cannot replicate the service business model for the entire range of products. This raises the question of predicting a company's economic growth through the judicious application of service models to a wide range of products while ensuring high consumer performance across the entire product line.

In this sense, the service business model can become a new growth point for the company and the main driving force for the sale of highly competitive goods and services with high technical characteristics and operational properties, as well as an acceptable price for the consumer, which allows products to provide a high market share or create a new market with a high level of commercialization of product-related services.

However, at the same time, the economic growth resulting from the implementation of services is influenced by various factors that can restrain or increase the impact of cost-effective service business models on the economic growth of a company. Such factors, first of all, should include the level of competence for shaping services, the amount of resourcing for the provision of services and the level of scientific and technological capacity (primarily its marketing component), which allows to address changing consumer expectations when updating both the products and the services offered.

In order to solve the issue of forecasting the economic growth of a company as a result of the transition to service models, we will describe the impact of each of these factors on it.

Level of competence

Each component of a company's economic growth capacity is based on a certain set of knowledge, which is transformed into the competence of the company and its teams. In practice, some components can reach a high level, while others can be at a lower level. Those areas where the growth potential is not sufficient require the formation and development of new competencies.

Management of each component of a company's economic growth potential is related to the development of relevant competencies due to resource costs aimed at this process. A company seeking to dominate the market through active development and implementation of services must launch a self-replicating process of improving competencies in marketing products placed on the market. If such a competence is difficult to reproduce for competitors, it can be recognized as a radical key one.

In the context of digital transformation and the rapid emergence of new consumer expectations in the market, a company is required not only to possess certain knowledge, but also to have dynamic organizational skills to quickly adapt to emerging new needs through new schemes for bringing the consumer value of products to the end consumer through a service model. This will allow to constantly develop the organizational knowledge base and maintain it at a level not lower than the main competitors.

In the context of economic efficiency, the process of creating and transferring competencies is of particular importance when creating services offered to the end user, and centers of competence in certain areas of development of services, which combine marketing resources with available necessary competencies for their use.

The effectiveness of the formed competencies in the provision of services should be evaluated in terms of the cost characteristics of the products (associated services) achieved through their use.

Based on our research, the assessment can be carried out using an economic and mathematical model (discussed in detail by the authors in their work [51]), the result of which is an aggregated value (index) characterizing the value and importance of the competence based on a number of features identified in accordance with the developed format for describing the key competence.

The amount of resourcing

The process of forming new competencies and developing approaches to creating services based on them requires significant resource costs. In the context of high financial costs for the development of new competencies, the issue of effective use of all types of resources is of particular importance. Based on the methods of assessing key competencies and selecting effective technologies for forming services, it is possible to build a program of activities and determine the most relevant areas of financing the development of new competencies and marketing technologies. For this, the mechanisms for managing the development of competencies should include the need to replicate them to create services for a wide range of products. That is, the possession of technologies for the provision of services and their successful use for one of the types of products does not yet indicate the possibility of their rapid implementation in another direction.

In the issue of resourcing, it is important to optimally plan resources for the provision of services according to their availability. For example, some resources may be stored by the company, for others – a clear scheme of their supply may be established, some resources may require additional time to obtain them (for example,

---

[51] Tyulin A., Chursin A. Competence Management and Competitive Product Development: Concept and Implications for Practice // 2017, Springer.

if it is necessary to develop additional competencies of specialists engaged in marketing of manufactured products, it is necessary to send them to additional training, which will require additional time and material costs). Thus, an important task is to plan the timely availability of resources necessary to ensure the effective provision of the entire range of services.

The level of scientific and technological capacity

It should be noted that the implementation of the above processes is impossible without the assessment and development of the scientific and technological capacity of an enterprise. In this connection, a natural question arises about the sufficiency of scientific and technological capacity for its use in the process of creating the operational properties of products. The sufficiency of scientific and technological capacity is determined by the resources that comprise it. In this case, marketing resources and competencies will play a key role, since, first of all, they are the basis for forming the operational characteristics of products that create their competitive advantages. That is, when the stage of launching and operating new products is reached, the part of the scientific and technological capacity that is responsible for marketing activities and PR is involved. Thus, we can talk about marketing potential, which covers the task of promoting a new product to the market, as well as monitoring its competitiveness within the implementation of the service business model. The marketing potential should be sufficient for the timely identification of changing consumer preferences and market trends so that the manufacturer has time to update both the product itself and to the services associated with it.

Establishing the above-described conditions for ensuring, accelerated innovative growth and economic development of a high-tech enterprise through the implementation of service business models is impossible without the use of modern information technologies that allow us to qualitatively transform existing approaches to bringing products to market and its operation. The use of such technologies will provide a high-tech enterprise with new opportunities to meet demand at affordable prices for consumers, which will contribute to the achievement of competitive leadership in the markets.

289

Interest in studying patterns and predicting economic growth and development is associated with attempts to explain economic growth based on indicators of the stock of labor and capital, as well as the general variable of technological change, which was assumed to have a constant growth trend. Thus, the Nobel laureate P. Romer proposed a model of economic growth – the Learning-by-doing model, which is a model of endogenous economic growth, showing the possibility of sustainable economic growth due to the effects of increasing a company's resourcing and increasing the level of its competencies.. Economic growth and development are manifested primarily in increasing the variety and quality of existing and new goods and services created as a result of the development of design, production, marketing, etc. technologies. In our opinion, such a model is most suitable for describing economic growth through the development of service business models, since it allows to address the consumer's choice regarding the method of obtaining the consumer value of the product and its functions, as well as to link economic development with a company's competencies and resource provision aimed at developing a service business model.

To describe the economic growth of a producer, let us consider as a basis the model of P. Romer, which explains economic growth through a variety of types of products and services on the market. It claims that the speed with which on average, the demanded consumer properties of products spread depends on the level of a company's competence in developing and bringing these properties to consumers and how much the current level of satisfaction of needs is less than a certain "theoretical" level, achievable with instant consumer delivery of product value to the consumer.

A widely used basic model of a company's economic growth, expressed by the dynamics of the volume of its gross product, is some function Y:

$$Y(t) = Y(L(t), K(t), A(t)) \tag{1}$$

in time t from production factors: L(t) are a the company's resources allocated for the development and implementation of service models, which are usually accepted taking into account their quality, K(t) is the level of competence in creating service models, A(t) is the marketing component of scientific and technological capacity.

For convenience, we will consider the well-known function of the Cobb-Douglas type as the functions of the economic growth of organization Y(t):

$$Y(t) = A(t)K^{\alpha}(t)L^{1-\alpha}(t) \tag{2}$$

where α is the elasticity parameter, which shows the sensitivity of a company's development rate, arising from the transition to the service model, to changes in the defining parameters: the level of resourcing, scientific and technological capacity and the level of competencies. For the convenience of calculations, let us log the production function:

$$\ln Y(t) = \ln A(t) + \alpha \ln K(t) + (1-\alpha)\ln L(t) \tag{3}$$

Subtracting this equation from the same one for the moment of time t+1, we get the difference equation:

$$\Delta \ln Y(t) = \Delta \ln A + \alpha\Delta \ln K(t) + (1-\alpha)\Delta \ln L(t) \tag{4}$$

Taking into account the known approximation

$$\Delta \ln X = \frac{\dot{X}}{X} \approx G(X),$$

where G is the growth of the value of X (in percentage), it is possible to obtain a formula convenient for practical calculations (in percentage):

$$G(Y(t)) = G(A(t)) + \alpha G(K(t)) + (1-\alpha)G(L(t)) \tag{5}$$

General model (5), describing the change in the rate of economic development of an enterprise under the influence of service models.

Under these conditions, economic growth can be mathematically expressed by the following relation:

$$R(A(T)) = c(t)\left(\frac{T(t) - A(t)}{A(t)}\right),$$

where c(t) is a function that depends on the level of development of specialists' competencies in the use of information for managing economic processes, T(t) is the theoretically possible level of satisfaction of needs that would occur if all the necessary technologies were developed and brought to the consumer immediately (i.e., in the absence of a time lag between the industrial development of technology and its use by the consumer for their own purposes).

As noted, it is impossible to unequivocally assess the change in economic growth rates based on the mere fact of introducing a service business model. The economic growth and development of a company, which are influenced by the introduction of the service business model, are also associated with the level of development of the infrastructure that ensures the use of services. It is the level of development of the infrastructure for the service delivery that largely determines the convenience of their use for the consumer. The development of infrastructure for the provision of services in our model can considered using the indicator of infrastructure development $\gamma(t) \in [0, 1]$. The maximum single value indicates sufficient preparation of the infrastructure for the application of the service business model, and a zero value indicates the complete absence of infrastructure. Economic growth and development, given the indicator of infrastructure development, will be written as follows:

$$R(A(T)) = \gamma(t) \cdot c(t) \cdot \left(\frac{T(t) - A(t)}{A(t)} \right) \tag{*}$$

From the formula ($*$), it follows that the gap between the theoretical and real level of satisfaction of needs is smaller, the higher the level of competence in bringing a specific product functionality to the consumer through a service business model:

$$A(t) = \frac{\gamma(t)c(t)}{\gamma(t)c(t) + \lambda(H)} T_0 e^{\lambda(H)t}$$

The level of a company's competence in building a service business model ensures the growth of the economy in the short term, and in the long term it grows at a rate $\lambda(H)$ due to the growth in the diversity of supply in the market, which is also confirmed by the previously considered model of economic efficiency of the service business model.

The proposed model (5) makes it possible to assess the nature of economic growth and development of a company depending on the level of its marketing potential, resource provision for the processes of creating services and the level of competencies in creating services. The above studies of a company's economic growth show that the rate of economic growth depends linearly on changes in scientific and technological capacity, and the impact of resourcing and the level of competencies is adjusted for the elasticity coefficient, which is traditionally assumed to be 1/3 for high-tech industries[52]. The graph of a company's economic growth in the context of a uniform increase in the company's marketing potential, its resourcing and the level of competence in creating services is as follows:

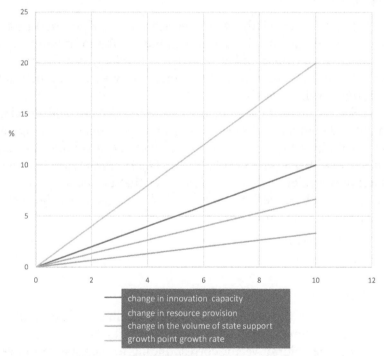

Figure 6.6. Modeling the rate of economic growth of a company

[52] Shackelton, R. Total Factor Productivity Growth in Historical Perspective // working Paper 2013-01. – 2013. – 21 p.

In the context of the proposed model of a company's economic growth under the influence of service models, let us consider a mathematical model describing the increase in the operating profit of a company as a result of the implementation of a service model. Let the products, the sale of which is possible through the service business model, constitute a set $Q_1, Q_2, ..., Q_N$. For each product, the known values are the unit cost p_i and the volume of variable costs per unit of each type of products vc_i, $i = 1, 2, ..., N$.

Thus, the difference between the values of the cost and variable costs is a known value β_i:

$$\beta_i = p_i - vc_i,$$

$$i = 1, 2, ..., N$$

The values a_{ij} (i is the type of service, j is type of product) are also given values and constitute a matrix, the number of rows of which corresponds to the number of types of services, and the number of columns corresponds to the number of types of products sold through service models.

So, the management of the economic growth and development of a company is based on maximizing the increase in operating profit by selling new types of products N in volumes through the service business model $Q_1, Q_2, ..., Q_N$. For each type of product, the known value is the cost of services that are paid by the consumer. The objective function of the task is to maximize the operating profit arising from the sale of services:

$$a'\beta Q \to \max,$$

$$\begin{cases} AQ = b, \\ Q \in Z_+ \end{cases}$$

where Q is the column vector corresponding to the desired values of the optimal output of each type of product,

a is the column vector corresponding to the total cost of services received by the consumer,

β is the column vector corresponding to the difference between the unit cost and the variable costs of manufacturing a unit of output,

b is the vector-column corresponding to the revenue from the sale of a service for the entire range of products.

The solution to the linear programming problem is a vector whose components correspond to the volume of production:

$$Q^* = (Q_1^*, Q_2^*, ..., Q_N^*).$$

The value of the optimization function is the operating profit resulting from the sale of products through the service business model in certain optimal volumes without taking into account fixed costs.

According to the definition of operating profit, fixed costs are the amount that contributes to its reduction. Thus, another aspect of the transition to non-service models is the possible reduction in fixed costs.

The management plan should determine the predicted trajectory of changes in profit arising from the implementation of various areas of service provision. We can also set an acceptable corridor (see Figure 6.7), in which the trajectory of changes in the amount of operating profit can be located. In this case, deviations from the ideal trajectory are considered insignificant if they occur within

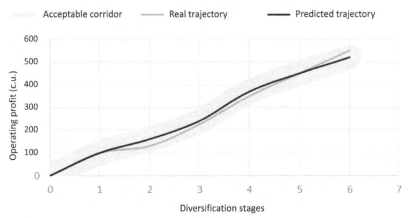

Figure 6.7. Forecast trajectory, real trajectory and admissible corridor of changes in operating profit arising from the transition to a service model (example)

the designated corridor (such changes occur as a result of the action of any random factors, which are difficult to predict).

The effect of moving to service models, which consists in increasing the company's operating profit, can be considered as a source of generating resources for its advanced development. Appropriate resourcing allows planning the development of the entire set of activities and optimizing the dynamics of changes in the operating profit of a company as a whole.

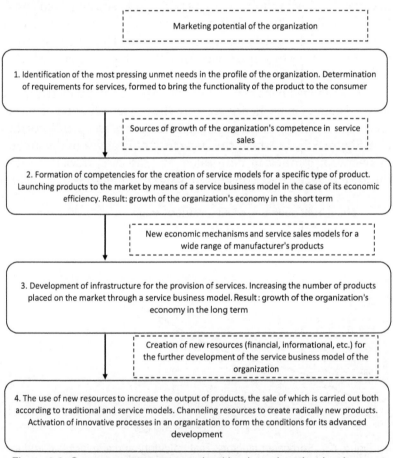

Figure 6.8. Company management algorithm based on the development of service models

Based on the analysis, we will propose a scheme for managing the economic growth of an organization as a result of using a service business model (Figure 6.8).

Thus, the following axiom can be formulated:

economic growth resulting from the introduction of cost-effective service business models leads to an increase in resourcing, which is the basis for maintaining the competitiveness and sustainable development of a company, moving into an advanced development through the production of high-quality goods with unique characteristics that could meet emerging market needs or stimulate the emergence of needs that are met by these products.

Long-term leadership and advanced development of a company is possible only in the case of continuous superiority over competitors, both through advanced and continuous innovative development, and innovative product marketing, which is possible by the active implementation of service business models. The development goal of a modern company is to form an economically stable, innovative, competitive, diversified company capable of solving strategic tasks of improving and developing not only technological innovations, but also marketing ones that qualitatively change promising markets through new mechanisms for bringing product functionality to the consumer.

Service business models are effective if they bring a company higher revenue than in the traditional sales model. This is achieved by forming a company's product line from products that can be sold to the consumer through service business models, as well as through the continuous development of competencies and the introduction of service business models and the development of effective services that increase the operational properties of products.

CHAPTER 7.
MECHANISMS FOR MANAGING
A COMPANY'S ADVANCED DEVELOPMENT
BASED ON TECHNOLOGY PLATFORMS

7.1. TECHNOLOGY PLATFORMS AS THE BASIS
FOR THE ADVANCED DEVELOPMENT
OF A COMPANY

The current state of the world economy is characterized by un-even trends in the scientific, technological and economic development of regions of the world that are in different waves of innovation. Due to this, there is an uneven distribution of technologies of various waves in the State and industry sections. Some countries or industries are adapting advanced breakthrough technologies that correspond to the promising wave faster, while others are slower Thus, several waves of innovation co-exist in different proportions in one country.

The intensity of these processes is influenced by the development of globalization, which creates corresponding trends in establishing national economies of the countries of the world. These trends are characterized by the fact that developing countries are turning into donors of resources for the largest transnational corporations (TNCs) concentrating their resource potential mainly in economically and technologically developed countries, as a result of which the pace of their technological development is high and these countries are currently dominated by the 5th and 6th waves of innovation. The high rates of their scientific, technological and innovative development make it possible to create products (value innovations) with high consumer properties and added value at an accelerated rate.

Moreover, countries with developing economies (which have mainly resource-oriented models of economic development) continue to actively use the technologies of the fifth wave and are moving to the sixth one.

These countries generally do not develop radically new products (or they do so slowly), and they continue to be resource donors, which reduces their national competitiveness compared to other countries.

As technological development has proven the importance of its place in economic development and growth processes, emerging economies are increasingly seeking to integrate advanced technologies and world discoveries in science and technology into their economic systems. Such integration will create opportunities for economic growth and development for the countries.

Thanks to globalization and inter-country cooperation, the resources accumulated in national economies are spreading to the global level. This is due to the creation and development of large multinational corporations (TNCs) involved in mergers and acquisitions, which leads to their constant increase and the growth of their economic and political influence in world markets. The influence of TNCs on global processes is determined by their scale.

As a result of the penetration of TNCs in various countries, the main assets around the globe are concentrated in the hands of several major corporate players. According to researchers at the Swiss Federal University of Technology, 90% of the corporate income of the global economy through various forms of ownership belongs to several hundred corporations, and 60% of the income of the real sector comes from financial corporations. Among these companies, there are several regional groupings, the largest of which can be called «western». It consists of a number of financial companies (Goldman Sachs, Morgan Stanley, JP Morgan Chase, Barclays, UBS, Deutsche Bank, Credit Suisse, etc.), which mutually own each other and control 40% of all other corporations.

In these conditions, the development of the processes of globalization and the increasing influence of large corporations leads to the fact that market competition per se ceases to exist. In this case, the processes described in Figure 7.1 arise.

A discriminatory monopsony hires more input than a non-discriminatory monopsony. Such price discrimination benefits those who offer the services of their factors of production in the markets of economic resources. Further, discriminatory monopsony is forced to incur more significant total cost (TC) as it hires more input. In addition, the "non-economic" income per unit of input service (TC/VF) is lower in terms of employment by a discriminatory monopsony compared to a non-discriminatory monopsony. As for "economic" incomes, the comparison shows that they are also higher with non-discriminatory monopsony than with discriminatory monopsony.

In modern conditions, the behavior model of large TNCs corresponds to a discriminatory monopoly, and competition is almost not-existent, and the market is divided into spheres of influence. TNCs are gradually taking over small and medium-sized companies, including state-owned enterprises in different countries, buying up their assets and property.

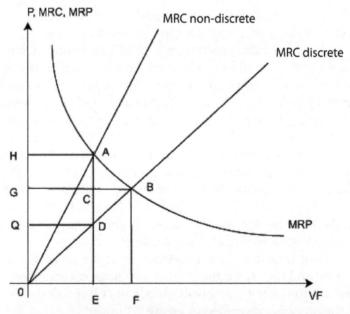

Figure 7.1. Equilibrium for discriminatory and non-discriminatory monopsony cases [53]

---

[53] Monopsony is a type of market in which only one buyer of a product, service or resource acts.

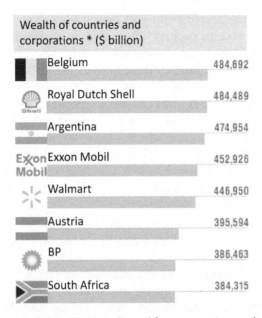

Wealth of countries and corporations * ($ billion)

Belgium	484,692
Royal Dutch Shell	484,489
Argentina	474,954
Exxon Mobil	452,926
Walmart	446,950
Austria	395,594
BP	386,463
South Africa	384,315

For states, GDP is indicated,for corporations, sales
are indicated.Source: company data; GDP at
current prices in dollars, according to the IMF.

Figure 7.2 Comparison of the sales volumes of some energy TNCs
with the GDP of large states

As a result of the mechanisms of mergers and acquisitions, a new paradigm of competition for markets is emerging, and smaller national companies (both private and public) are forced to look for new ways and tools to influence the market in order to maintain their niche and expand it to ensure a stable position in the market.

Turning to the question of comparing the size of the assets of large TNCs with the GDP of some countries of the world, their assets are comparable to GDP. For example, Figure 7.2 shows a comparison of the sales volumes of some energy TNCs that are comparable to the GDP of large states.

It is quite natural that such companies with such volumes of financial resources become unmanageable by the state due to the following circumstances:

Large TNCs receive monopoly power on a global scale, which allows them to receive superprofits, which is confirmed in Fig. 7.2.

Many multinational corporations use tax evasion mechanisms by opening branches in countries with a low income tax rate. They direct most of all their financial flows through countries with the lowest tax rates – for example, Bermuda, Ireland, Luxembourg. For example, in 2011, Google corporation's sales in the UK amounted to 2.5 billion pounds, but only 3.4 million pounds were paid in taxes. Thus, the tax rate was 0.1%, while the company's margin was 33%. This means that TNCs are getting out of state regulation in the field of tax legislation, implementing their financial transactions through other countries.

TNCs also move their cash reserves abroad, which is an irretrievable loss of investment for a country. For example, Apple holds 93% of its cash reserves abroad.

The loss of control over the activities of transnational corporations is typical for all countries. As a result, there is a mismatch in the economic activities of TNCs and the Sate, and the additional control and regulation of prices is complicated. Large TNCs may not always take into account country specificities and needs. The needs of the least economically developed countries remain unmet due to the lack of solvency and the lack of cheaper offers from national small companies, which are being squeezed out of the market.

Due to their global scale, TNCs act as «carriers» of economic recessions (crises) to other countries. This thesis is justified in the works of Markus Biermann (Belgium) and Kilian Huber (USA), who study the role of multinational corporations in the spread of the global recession, analyzing the wave effects of the struggle of a German bank during the financial crisis of 2008-2009.

Commerzbank was the second largest commercial credit bank in Germany after Deutsche Bank. Losses from foreign trade and investment hit the bank hard, especially after the collapse of Lehman Brothers in September 2008. Commerzbank's capital fell 68% in two years, causing the bank to reduce its gross credit base by 17%. The reduction in credits available to German parent companies has led to a decline in the economic activity of subsidiaries in other countries, thereby contributing to the economic downturn. Since the parent companies could not borrow from Commerzbank, they withdrew shares and borrowed money from their affiliates, limiting the operations of foreign branches.

Due to the high economic integration within transnational corporations and the inability to control their economic (often monopolistic) activities in different countries, there is an increasing globalization of business cycles.

Against the background of these processes, multinational companies are united in conglomerates, syndicates, unions, and other forms of cooperation that have different goals, such as establishing a unified policy in trade activities to expand spheres of influence, ensuring the redistribution of capital from less profitable to more profitable areas to maximize profits, etc.

Within the associations of large TNCs, there is a joint activity planning and a common strategy for achieving the goal is formed.

International organizations are being created, which also have some elements of economic and political planning to some extent. These include universal organizations such as the World Trade Organization (WTO), the North American Free Trade Area (NAFTA), the International Atomic Energy Agency (IAEA), the World Nuclear Association (WNA), the World Association of Nuclear Operators (WANO), the organization United Nations Industrial Development Organization (UNIDO). There are also regional and international organizations that implement a single planning policy in the association: the European Union (EU), the Organization of American States (OAS), the League of Arab States (LAS), the Association of Southeast Asian Nations (ASEAN), the Organization of African unity (OAU), interstate association BRICS, etc. The main goal of such international associations is to integrate the potential of countries to solve world-class problems. Within the regional organizations, joint activity planning is carried out on the basis of signing cooperation agreements (membership) and participation in programs developed at the association level.

In addition, as part of strengthening their national economic security, countries are pursuing their own policy of program-targeted planning to support their economies. These phenomena lead to the creation of a hybrid economy, which includes elements of planning within the associations of TNCs that cover the interests of the states on whose territory they operate, as well as state regulation implemented by these states to ensure their national security and mechanisms of market relations at the micro level with certain elements of protectionism.

The development of a hybrid economy requires a separate theoretical comprehension with the development of practical foundations for the application of such a theory in managerial decision-making both at the level of countries and individual economic entities.

In parallel, the growing role of TNCs, stimulating the emergence of a hybrid economy, their participation in the economic activities of the countries of the world and the ongoing competition not just for markets, but for spheres of influence in the world market, are growing into economic and political wars, provoking military conflicts with decrease in constraints. In this case, the critical situation leads to an economic downturn, when the growth rate of a country's GDP, trade turnover and financial flows decrease, which requires the introduction of new economic mechanisms.

In modern conditions of economic development, such a critical continues to grow due to the fact that the existing economic systems (planned and market economy) have almost exhausted themselves in their current form, and in this case there is a need to create a new economy based on theoretical research in this area[54].

The main mechanisms of this new economy must be in-depth, comprehensive forecasting of economic actors at all levels (from a company to the world economy), on the basis of which interorganizational and interstate economic relations are built. In our opinion, this can be achieved by forming a complex system of interaction between the subjects and objects of economic relations arising in the process of production, exchange and distribution of material goods, aimed at increasing the efficiency of economic processes through optimal management of links between the subsystems of subjects and objects of economic relations.

By the formation and practical application of such a system, new tools are created to support the process of managing economic

---

[54] https://link.springer.com/book/10.1007%2F978-3-030-37814-1#about

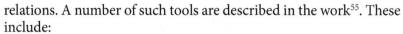
relations. A number of such tools are described in the work[55]. These include:

- tools for coordination and management of knowledge-intensive industries, taking into account the current stage of economic development;
- methodology for forecasting the competitiveness of knowledge-intensive industries and companies, etc.

The following tools are specified in the work[56]:

- a tool for assessing the competitiveness of a company based on the competitive advantages arising from new competencies;
- a tool for evaluating the effectiveness of the introduction of modern methods of competence management, taking into account the law of mutual influence of the level of financing of key competencies with the emergence of new consumer markets, etc.

The fundamentals of the functioning of these tools at the current pace of technological development come down to the development of global informatization and the penetration of information solutions into all spheres of society at all levels of economic relations between subjects. The increase in the rate of information dissemination makes information processes less manageable, and information flows are fragmented and unstructured, which does not allow a sufficient degree of objectivity to assess the economic situation in the world, the country and individual sectors of the economy.

The proposed system cannot work without appropriate tools for information and analytical support for the interaction of economic entities at various levels, which would allow a company, as well as a State (which still remains the legislator) to navigate and objectively assess the pace and direction of development of the world economy in the context of countries and areas of production and economic activity. Based on his information, companies can form their promising areas of activity that allow them to increase

---

[55] Chursin A.A., Diversification of issued goods as the basis for stable economic development under the conditions of the cyber economy/ Contributions to Economics. Part 2,2019, p. 39–49

[56] Tyulin, A.E. A strategy for implementing the technologies of industry 4.0 and the tools of competency management in the digital economy / Contributions to Economics, 2019, Part 2, p. 291–304

the volume of production of products with the necessary consumer properties that have value for the consumer.

It should be noted that reliable and valuable information is not always available. At the first stage of the development of the system, the process of accumulation and exchange of information between interested economic entities, as well as available information located in the information space (official statistics), should be established.

At the second stage, it will be possible to obtain not complete, but sufficient information to form reasonable analytical conclusions due to the accumulation and processing of information by intelligent systems (as the experience of large systems of Google, Yandex, and other information giants shows, technically this possibility exists. Depending on the behavior of individuals and legal entities, these systems can generate statistical reports). Otherwise, the management apparatus, which must analyze information flows and make decisions outside of such intelligent systems, will have to constantly grow, which is unproductive for the economy and reduces the objectivity of decisions made due to the presence of the human factor.

As a result, at the third stage, an integrated information system is created, which would make it possible to assess the economic condition of economic entities for their benefit, while not violating their economic security.

Such an information system operates on the basis of mechanisms for continuous monitoring of information at various levels in order to obtain economic knowledge about the processes under study and can look like this (Fig. 7.3).

The creation of such a comprehensive information system to obtain economic knowledge about the processes under study will allow us to solve the issue of collecting or analyzing economic information at different levels, thereby providing economic entities with the opportunity to make informed decisions on the choice of promising areas of development both within a country and on the world market.

The proposed information system is the base for supporting management decision-making in the planning and development of a company's activities in the development of products that are value innovations for the consumer, and is presented in the diagram (see Figure 7.4)

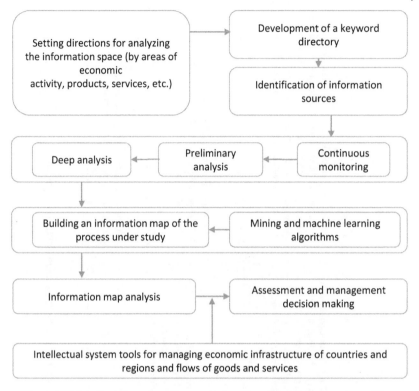

Figure 7.3 Intelligent system for assessing the state of economic entities.

The main elements of such a system, shown in Figure 7.4, are:

Block for collecting and monitoring heterogeneous data and extracting «useful» information from open sources;

Methodological block describing the basic principles and algorithms of the system aimed at solving the problem of analyzing promising areas of development, taking into account market trends;

Software represented by information and analytical computing systems that ensure the interaction of all other blocks with each other by means of appropriate algorithms;

Platform block (technology platform), which is the core of the entire system, setting the direction of its development to achieve maximum results.

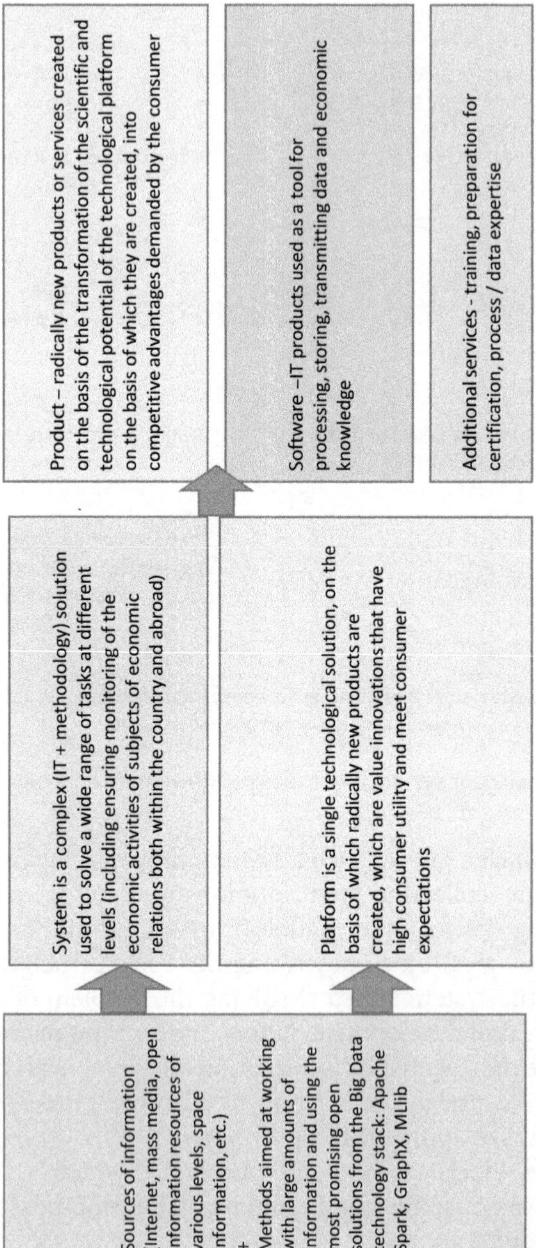

Figure 7.4 Structure of comprehensive intelligent system

Product – radically new products or services created on the basis of the transformation of the scientific and technological potential of the technological platform on the basis of which they are created, into competitive advantages demanded by the consumer

Software –IT products used as a tool for processing, storing, transmitting data and economic knowledge

Additional services - training, preparation for certification, process / data expertise

System is a complex (IT + methodology) solution used to solve a wide range of tasks at different levels (including ensuring monitoring of the economic activities of subjects of economic relations both within the country and abroad)

Platform is a single technological solution, on the basis of which radically new products are created, which are value innovations that have high consumer utility and meet consumer expectations

Sources of information (Internet, mass media, open information resources of various levels, space information, etc.)

+

Methods aimed at working with large amounts of information and using the most promising open solutions from the Big Data technology stack: Apache Spark, GraphX, MLlib

Our research has shown that the creation of technology plat-forms on a global scale is impossible without the development of technology platforms of a company that can accumulate scientific and technological capacity and distribute it in the process of forming radical properties of new products that ensure advanced develop-ment. Since the dynamic nature of the economic situation is rapidly changing due to various factors, a technology platform must have the properties of automatic adaptation (with elements of self-learn-ing) to changing economic conditions. Therefore, a company's tech-nology platform must be adaptive, flexible, intelligent, and responsive to changes in the external economic environment.

Thus, a company's technology platform must always dynami-cally develop, which ensures its flexibility.

In theoretical aspect, we will consider the general model for the development of a company's technology platform, taking into account the increase in its scientific and technological capacity and the development of competencies. As part of solving the is-sue of developing a company's technology platform, we will build on the existing development models of the company itself.

Models of economic development of a company are generally based on various scenarios for the use of resourcing, human capital and competencies, as well as innovative (or scientific and techno-logical) capacity[57]. A widely used basic model of a company's eco-nomic development is a certain function of Y:

$$E(t) = Y(L(t), K(t), A(t)) \tag{1}$$

in time t from production factors: L(t) is an assessment of hu-man capital and the level of competencies, K(t) is the total volume of various types of company resources, A(t) is the level of innova-tive (scientific and technological) capacity, in fact, this is the level of development of technology platform of a company.

For convenience, we will consider the following type of CES func-tion as the functions of economic development at the company level Y(t), which is the main tool in the analysis of production and its efficiency:

[57] Galaso, P., & Kovářík, J. (2018). Collaboration Networks and Innovation: How to Define Network Boundaries. Journal of Eurasian Economic Dialogue, 3(2), 1–17.

$$Y(t) = A(t)K^{\alpha}(t)L^{1-\alpha}(t) \qquad (2)$$

where α is the parameter of elasticity (traditionally in theoretical studies it is accepted equal to $\alpha = 1/3$). For the convenience of calculations, let us logarithm the function:

$$\ln BP\Pi(t) = \ln A(t) + \alpha \ln K(t) + (1-\alpha)\ln L(t) \qquad (3)$$

Subtracting this equation from the analogous one for the moment of time t+1, we obtain the difference equation:

$$\Delta \ln BP\Pi(t) = \Delta \ln A + \alpha \Delta \ln K(t) + (1-\alpha)\Delta \ln L(t) \qquad (4)$$

Taking into account the known approximation

$$\Delta \ln X = \frac{\dot{X}}{X} \approx G(X),$$

where G is the growth of the value of X (in percentage), it is possible to obtain a formula convenient for practical calculations (in percentage):

$$G(BP\Pi(t)) = G(A(t)) + \alpha G(K(t)) + (1-\alpha)G(L(t) \qquad (5)$$

The general model of a company's economic development is supplemented by a system of models for growth factors [58]. We are interested in the indicator of the development of the technology platform A(t), since the development and implementation of technologies of a new technological paradigm is part of scientific and technological progress, which pushes up A(t) in the model of a company's economic development[59].

According to statistics (Goldman Sachs), the rate of technology development currently for corporations that make the main contribution to the growth of global GDP is $\approx 1{,}3\%$, which leads to an increase in labor productivity by about 2% per year. For developing innovatively active enterprises, the rate of development of a technology platform A(t) depends on the speed of mastering borrowed

---

[58] Shackelton, R. Total Factor Productivity Growth in Historical Perspective // working Paper 2013-01. – 2013. – 21 p.
[59] Dominic Wilson, Roopa Purushothaman. Dreaming With BRICs: The Path to 2050. Goldman Sachs. 1st October 2003. Global Paper. No 99.

innovations within the investment process and transferring them to the development or creation of their own innovations[60].

The intellectual explosion resulting in the development and significant acceleration of the pace of development of a company's technology platforms occurs during the emergence and introduction of new technologies into the economy, which have significantly changed the production and other processes in the economy.

To describe the growth rate of development of the company's technology platform, consider the Nelson-Phelps model as a basis[61]. It claims that the speed of the average return on the development and implementation of new technologies depends on the level of competence of employees and on how much the current level of innovative (scientific and technological) capacity is less than the "theoretical" level, achievable with the instantaneous development and implementation of new wave technologies. Under these conditions, the development of a technology platform influenced by a new technological paradigm can be mathematically expressed by the following relationship:

$$R(A(T)) = c(t)\left(\frac{T(t) - A(t)}{A(t)} \right) \tag{6}$$

where c(t) is a function that depends on the level of competence development of specialists in the field of new – wave technologies, T(t) is the theoretically possible level of development of new – wave technologies, which would take place if all the necessary technologies accumulated within a company's technology platform were mastered and implemented immediately (i.e., in the absence of a time lag between the appearance of technology and the beginning of its industrial development).

The economic development of a company and its technology platform, influenced by new technologies, is related to the level of

---

[60] Wilson D., Trivedi K., Carlson S., Ursú J. The BRICs 10 Years On: Halfway. Through The Great Transformation Goldman Sachs // Global Economics Paper, № 208. December, 7 2011. Available at http://blogs.univ-poitiers.fr/o-boubaolga/files/2012/11/Goldman-Sachs-Global-Economics-Paper-208.pdf

[61] Nelson R.R., Phelps E.S. Investment in Humans, Technological Diffusion, and Economic Growth // American Economic Review. 1966. Vol. 56. № 1/2. P. 69–75.

development of the company's scientific and production infrastructure, which ensures the development, implementation and application of these technologies. Infrastructure development in the model can be calculated using the infrastructure development indicator $\gamma(t) \in [0, 1]$. The maximum single value indicates that the infrastructure is sufficiently prepared for the use of new technologies, and the zero value indicates the absence of the necessary infrastructure. The growth rate of a company's technology platform influenced by the new wave of innovation, taking into account the infrastructure development indicator, will be recorded as follows:

$$R(A(T)) = \gamma(t) \cdot c(t) \cdot \left(\frac{T(t) - A(t)}{A(t)} \right) \qquad (7)$$

The gap between the theoretical and actual level of development of the company's technology platform can be measured by the level of scientific and technological capacity H, which ensures a company's transition to the new wave of innovation.

From formula (7) it follows that the gap between the theoretical and real level of development of a company's technology platform is the smaller, the higher the level of competence in the development of technologies of a new paradigm and the higher the level of infrastructure for the development, use and implementation of technologies of the new wave:

$$A(t) = \frac{\gamma(t)c(t)}{\gamma(t)c(t) + \lambda(H)} T_0 e^{\lambda(H)t} \qquad (8)$$

It is the level of competence that ensures the economic development of a company in the short term, and in the long term, growth occurs at a pace $\lambda(H)$ due to the increase in the scientific and technological capacity of a company.

A high level of scientific and technological capacity (from 0.75 to 1) minimizes the gap between the theoretically achievable and the actually mastered level of new-wave technologies. This ensures the fulfillment of the necessary conditions for a company to create radical innovations, which, according to the law of advanced satisfaction of prospective needs, arise as a result of the breakthrough scientific and technological development of the manufacturer and the intensive build-up of its key competencies.

Based on the proposed model, we describe the process of managing advanced development in a market of imperfect competition. In fact, the considered CES-function of an enterprise connects the economic resources used in the production process and the volume of products manufactures by using them. The efficiency of production will mean the use by an enterprise of the available economic resources (factors), namely: labor (competencies)) $L(t)$; capital $K(t)$; innovative (scientific and technological) capacity $A(t)$, with the help of which it is possible to manufacture the optimal volume of products $Q(t) = f\left(L(t), K(t), A(t)\right)$ (the optimality conditions will depend on the optimization goals), where the moment in time $t \in T$ (T is a sufficiently long period of time during which the advanced development of the enterprise is analyzed). To analyze these processes in the economy, the concept of marginal output of products is used (MP). The output of products (MP) shows the change in the value of the productivity of any variable factor of production, provided that the value of at least one of the other factors of production remains constant.

In the management of advanced development, the scientific and technological capacity is the most important factor. The marginal output provided by the scientific and technological capacity, i.e. innovative technologies of a new wave of innovation used in the production process (MP_A), is possible in the case when the production process is «driven» by changes in technologies $(A = \text{var})$ with constant amounts of labor and physical capital $(L = \text{const}, K = \text{const})$.

The following mathematical expressions allow us to determine the value of the maximum output provided by the scientific and technological capacity:

$$MP_A = \frac{\partial Q}{\partial A} \text{ or } MP_A = \frac{\Delta Q}{\Delta A}.$$

The downward change in the performance of a variable resource is known as Law of diminishing marginal utility. In the case of marginal output by innovation potential, the law of decreasing utility is the Law of decreasing technology utility: $A \uparrow MP_A \downarrow$

(L = const, K = const). In other words, the longer the technologies used for ensuring the advanced development are used, the less their return in the form of product competitiveness in the market. It follows that the ability to advance development is a dynamically changing concept over time, and to maintain the state of advanced development, the company must manage it.

The described processes for achieving advanced development show that the most effective tool in solving this problem in the context of rapidly changing economic conditions and globalization is a technology platform capable of accumulating scientific, technological and resource capacity for their further transformation into radical properties of new products and directing resources to solving strategic tasks that determine the progressive development of a company in the long term and provide leadership in the competition in domestic and foreign markets.

The management of the advanced development of a company based on the creation of a technology platform as a whole must be carried out both by managing the introduction of additional resources (resources can be understood as competencies and innovative capacity), and by managing the process of selecting priority points for the application of these resources. The management process should be considered effective when the company takes a significant part of the existing market or creates a new market. The price of the product in these conditions will be determined by minimizing the introduction of resources with their efficient use.

At the same time, to determine the effectiveness of management of advanced development, it is necessary to review other estimated parameters. Such assessments can be based on the statement that innovation and the creation of unique products (or new markets), provided with resources, should be synchronized (in terms of pace and intensity) with the development of the production system and business processes, accompanied by the economic stability of a company. In practice, this means the following. With the growth of the competitiveness of the products, the income received from its sale will increase. It will create new sources of resources both for the modernization of the technology platform, and for the creation of radically new products that form new market niches. Increasing the efficiency of the functioning of scientific, design, production-technological and other organizational parameters will improve the values of the parameters that determine its overall competitiveness, and, therefore, will increase economic sustainability, which will allow in the long term to maintain its position on the trajectory of advanced development. All these processes can be implemented through an intelligent technology platform.

7.2. BASIS FOR THE CREATION OF KEY COMPONENTS OF A COMPANY'S ADVANCED DEVELOPMENT MECHANISM

The main function of the advanced development mechanism of a company is to control the processes occurring in the company and related to the development and production of radically new products, the growth of the volume of which creates conditions for the transition to advanced development.

The essence of a company's advanced development is to achieve global market superiority through the production and implementation of radically new goods and services, which is achieved through effective management of research, development, innovation, production, organizational and other processes, which determines the generation of its capacity sufficient to create a completely new product with radically new, high consumer properties, allowing to win a significant share of the existing market or create a new market.

To achieve the advanced economic development of a company, primarily, when developing its strategy and development program, it is necessary to take into account a number of economic laws, including the law of diminishing marginal utility, the law of rising economic needs, the law of advanced satisfaction of prospective needs, the law of advanced development of a company, etc.

Following these laws and the research carried out above, we will form a mechanism for the advanced development of a company.

Like any economic mechanism, the developed mechanism being developed, which is based on these laws, should consist of quantitative assessment tools and management actions that ensure the functioning of this mechanism to support management decisions in the process of the most effective management of production and economic processes when creating radically new products.

The concept of "economic instrument" refers an economic category that is consciously used in the interests of economic entities and a country to quantitatively and qualitatively influence economic processes.

The authors who give this definition consider an economic instrument in isolation from the economic mechanism under which it functions. Given that each economic mechanism has its own characteristics, the tools can be used if they are adapted when interacting with other tools of this mechanism. In this regard, in our opinion, it is necessary to introduce such a new concept as a mechanism component.

A mechanism component is an economic tool that is connected to other tools by means of input and output parameters received and transmitted during the operation of the mechanism.

The complex of all components is aimed at solving the target problem of the mechanism, and the economic mechanism itself in the classical sense is a set of methods and means of influencing economic processes and their regulation in order to ensure the achievement of the set goal.

With regard to the mechanism of advanced development, it must comply with the following basic principles of its formation, which are determined on the basis of previous studies. The mechanism being developed should:

- correspond to the previously proposed model of the cycle of economic development according to the scheme "competencies → industry → personalized needs";
- contribute to the implementation of the transformation of scientific and technological capacity and unique technological competencies into a radically new product;
- to provide management actions in solving the problem of creating and maintaining the competitive potential of products and services in the markets in the long term;

– contribute to the achievement of advanced satisfaction of promising needs.

In accordance with the target task of the advanced development mechanism and the basic principles to which it must comply, it is advisable to divide its components into two groups: tools for the quantitative assessment of economic processes and conditions and tools for managing economic processes.

The first group of components represents methods and techniques that can be used to quantitatively calculate various parameters that describe the process of advanced development or its individual parts.

The second group of components is the management methods, which are designed to ensure the relationship of quantitative assessment tools related to the first group of components, and form the basis of decision-making algorithms for the implementation of certain managerial influences on economic processes.

In Table 7.1, we present both groups of previously developed tools that encourage a company to achieve advanced development. These tools form the corresponding components in the mechanism. Considering the mechanism of advanced development of a company through the prism of the above-mentioned laws of advanced development and advanced satisfaction of long-term needs, we can conclude that these tools are sufficient to ensure the effectiveness of the created mechanism.

Based on the tools presented in the table, components will be formed that are key for creating a mechanism for the advanced development of a company. An important issue in ensuring the operation of this mechanism is the level and dynamics of the development of a company's technology platform and the indicator of its scientific and technological capacity, since these indicators launch the process of creating products with radical properties.

As a result, subject to availability of the above components (ensuring the efficient operation of the mechanism) and a sufficient level of scientific and technological capacity, the scheme of interaction of the components that ensure the functioning of the mechanism can be as shown in Fig. 7.5.

Table 7.1. Tools that encourage a company to achieve advanced development

Quantification tools	Management tools
Methodological tools of the law of advanced satisfaction of prospective needs	Algorithm for creating conditions to ensure advanced economic development and the development of a technology platform
A tool for assessing economic growth as a result of generating intersectoral radical competencies	Algorithm for decision support in the development and production of goods with high competitive potential
Method for assessing scientific and technological capacity	Tools for extending competencies to the intersectoral level
Model for outlining the minimum feasible values of the parameters of the company's activities	Methods for expanding the technology platform to increase a company's competitive advantages
Model for assessing the total consumer value of an innovative product	Methods for managing the transformation of scientific and technological capacity and unique technological competencies into a radically new product
	Service model of economic development
	Key competency management methods
	Tool for improving the efficiency of the company through using service models
	Tool for managing the development of the use of service models in direct interaction between suppliers and consumers
	Methods for managing the balance of resource opportunities, scientific and technological capacity and ideas for creating promising products and services with high consumer utility

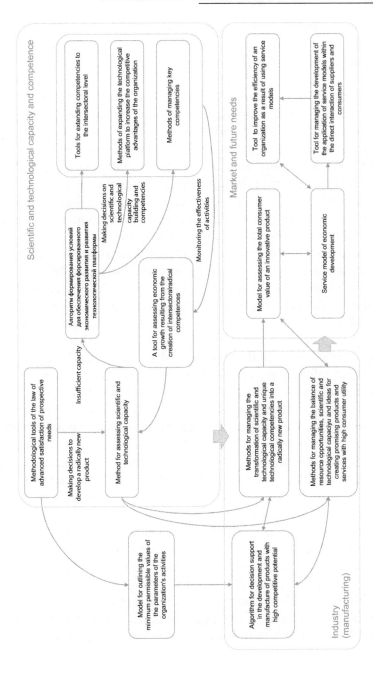

Figure 7.5 Diagram of interaction of the components of the mechanism for the advanced development of a company

Let us describe the algorithms for the operation of diagrams of interconnection of the components of the advanced development mechanism of a company shown in Fig. 7.5.

The input data for launching the mechanism is statistical and analytical data, primarily accumulated in a company based on the results of its activities and marketing research, which is used to monitor markets and competitors for timely determining the achievement of break-even points and the maximum market saturation and making decisions about launching new projects.

The output data of the advanced development mechanism are recommendations for organizing the process of development, production and market promotion of radically new products with high consumer properties and competitive potential.

As already noted, the components of the advanced development mechanism are interconnected by sequential and parallel connections by means of input and output data transmitted to each other for the implementation of analytical operations, based on the results of which recommendations are made on the use of certain management actions in creating radically new products to ensure a company's entry into the trajectory of advanced development.

Input information enters the component «Economic tools included in the analytical base of the law of advanced satisfaction of prospective needs», which implements quantitative assessments, which is based on monitoring the development of market trends (the level of market development) and internal state (the level of key competencies; the level of scientific and technological potential; consumer utility of unique products) determines the change in these indicators in dynamics, taking into account cyclical phenomena occurring at the macroeconomic level. Based on these evaluation indicators, prospective competencies and the most significant components of a company's scientific and technological capacity are identified, which are involved in the development of products that contribute to the emergence of new needs and the establishment of new market segments.

The information obtained allows us to support decision-making on establishing of a set of new projects for the development of products with radical properties and selecting the most promising ones.

Two parallel processes start: 1) assessment and analysis of the sufficiency of the scientific and technological capacity and its individual components for the implementation of the project; 2) contouring the minimum feasible values of a company's performance parameters. Let us review each process.

To analyze the sufficiency of scientific and technological capacity, the mechanism uses the Method for assessing scientific and technological capacity. After obtaining quantitative estimates, they are interpreted in terms of sufficiency to create radically new products. If the level of scientific and technological capacity is insufficient, a cycle of its building and accumulation of technological competencies is launched using the appropriate methods and algorithms as part of the mechanism.

First of all, information about the lack of scientific and technological capacity is transmitted to the Algorithm for creating conditions for ensuring accelerated economic development and the development of a technology platform, which implements management actions based on the structuring of possible directions for the development of the company and its scientific and technology platform, after which a signal is received about the planned directions for the input for the following three components of the mechanism, including the Tools for extending competencies to the intersectoral level, Methods of expanding the technology platform to increase a company's competitive advantages and Methods of managing key competencies.

Each of them, as part of the mechanism, is designed to solve its own task, united by a common goal – to organize effective management of the processes of scientific and technological capacity -building of a company for its re-evaluation for sufficiency to develop a product with radical properties.

Thus, the Tools for extending competencies to the intersectoral level manage the processes of building and developing competencies in technology platforms of different levels, especially cross-industrial ones. This ensures the transfer and fusion of competencies to achieve the radical properties of a new product. This tool creates conditions and recommendations for attracting unique competencies for development and production.

Methods of expanding the technology platform to increase a company's competitive advantages involve management actions aimed at increasing the scientific and technological capacity of a company's technology platform both from within and through cross-industrial interaction. Here, management actions for capacity development are carried out at all stages of the life cycle in which it will be involved. As a result, recommendations are formed for the implementation of measures that ensure the increment of the missing components of the scientific and technological capacity to a sufficient level for the development of radically new products that create new markets.

Methods of managing key competencies provide management of developed key competencies with modeling scenarios for their most effective involvement in production and management processes. As a result, recommendations are formed for the implementation of management actions that lead to the systematization of competencies and their transformation into radical properties of new products.

In this way, the management of economic processes is ensured to create conditions for the economic growth of a company. In this case, we are talking about the effect that is achieved through the creation of intersectoral radical competencies that ensure the expansion of the technology platform. This effect is evaluated using the Tool for Assessing Economic Growth with the establishment of intersectoral radical competencies If the effect is insufficient, the mechanism starts a repeated cycle of building competencies and expanding the technology platform. If the effect (growth) rate is low, the data is transmitted for re-evaluation of the sufficiency of the scientific and technological capacity.

As soon as the appropriate algorithms set in the mechanism determine that the scientific and technological capacity is sufficient to create a radically new product, Methods for managing the transformation of scientific and technological capacity and unique technological competencies into a radically new product and Methods of managing the balance of resource opportunities, scientific and technological potential and ideas for creating promising products and services with high consumer utility are applied.

Methods for managing the transformation of scientific and technological capacity and unique technological competencies into a radically new product provide support for decision-making to create radical properties of new products based on the rational and effective use of accumulated competencies and scientific and technological capacity. As a result, management actions are implemented on intellectual potential and on the process of using it to create value for the consumer.

Using the Methods of managing the balance of resource opportunities, scientific and technological potential and ideas for creating promising products and services with high consumer utility, all types of resources are evaluated and planned for the full life cycle of a product with radical characteristics. The determined balance of product characteristics that carry value for the consumer, and the resources required for their creation, becomes the starting point for launching the next algorithm, which is one of the most important in the mechanism of advanced development, since it has a direct impact on the processes of managing the creation of new market segments, Algorithm of decision support in the process of development and production of products with high competitive potential, forming recommendations for managing the product life cycle to ensure its competitive price and high competitive advantages, and the initial data for the Model of assessing the total consumer value of an innovative product, in which he level of consumer interest in purchasing a particular product is quantitatively assessed. This quantitative assessment acts as input data for the Service Model of Economic Development, which implements control actions in the mechanism, allowing to develop the most promising schemes for the launch of a radically new product on the market, stimulating a company's entry into the trajectory of advanced development.

Thus, the proposed mechanism of advanced development and its components allow us to solve the complex task of managing a company's transition to the path of advanced development.

Based on the above, we can emphasize that the proposed mechanism of advanced development and its components have controlling effects on the entire life cycle of a product, thereby ensuring its radical properties that lead a manufacturer to a leading position in the market or create new markets. With this mechanism, decision makers will be provided with informed analytics that increase the objectivity of these decisions.

However, objectivity will depend on the efficiency of the mechanism itself and the interaction of its components. To assess the effectiveness of the mechanism of advanced development, in our opinion, it is possible to use the contour of the effective interaction of all its components. The estimates defining the contour will be the outputs of the quantification components of the mechanism. They allow assessing the degree of effectiveness of the implemented control actions and the mechanism as a whole. These include the following indicators:

- indicator of economic growth as a result of the creation of intersectoral radical competences;
- indicator of scientific and technological capacity;
- company performance indicators (their minimum feasible values);
- indicator of the total consumer value of an innovative product.

We will build a contour effective interaction of all components of the mechanism of advanced development and present its mathematical implementation for practical solutions to the challenge of achieving global competitiveness and advanced development.

Let us consider a mathematical model for building a contour of the efficiency indicators of a company's advanced development mechanism, determined within the framework of the use of tools (methods, models) for assessing economic growth Q as a result of creating intersectoral radical competencies, evaluating the scientific and technological capacity of the company's IP, constructing a contour of the minimum feasible values of the company's performance parameters Π, evaluating the total consumer value of an innovative product V.

As our research shows, intensive management of global competitiveness and advanced development with the involvement of significant resources, ensuring the creation of competitive advantages for both products and companies, must be carried out continuously to ensure the growth of production and sales of innovative products.

We will proceed from the fact that the effectiveness of the mechanism for the advanced development of the company is associated with the use of the resources available to the enterprise that manufactures the products G_i $(i = 1,...,n(t))$, the resources necessary for this, as well as the level of scientific and technological potential, competencies and indicators that determine the main parameters of the company's activities.

Let the company, using the available resources, accumulated scientific and technological potential and competencies, have the opportunity to produce a certain volume of product $Q_i(t)$, sell it on the market at a price and make a profit $\pi_i(t) = p_i(t)Q_i(t) - TC_i(t)$, where the total cost of production is set by a random function $TC_i(t)$. We will assume that it is possible to set a production function $Q_i(t) = f_i(L_i(t), K_i(t), A_i(t))$, the dynamics of which determines the economic growth of the company. The components of the production function were described in detail earlier when we considered in detail the issue of achieving economic growth by creating cross-industrial innovations.

To further build the contour of the efficiency indicators of the advanced development mechanism, we will consider the competitive environment $\Sigma(L_i(t), K_i(t), A_i(t))(i = 1,...,n(t))$, in which the enterprise is located. The state of the enterprise in a competitive environment is determined by a set of probabilities $p_i(\pi_i(t), Q_i(t), IP_i(t), \Pi_i(t), V_i(t))$ $(i=1,...n(t))$, that describe the position of an enterprise in the market depending on the behavior of competitors, i.e., with a certain probability, the enterprise can occupy a dominant position and be a leader, with a certain probability the enterprise can follow the leader, and with some probability it can be an outsider. Since the sum of such probabilities is $\sum p_w = 1$, then as the state space of the enterprise we obtain the area $\overline{\Sigma}$:

$$\left\{ \overline{\Sigma}: \quad p_w \geq 0, \quad \sum_w p_w \leq 1 \right\}$$

We will denote the points of the area
$p_0(\pi_i(t_0), Q_i(t_0), IP_i(t_0), \Pi_i(t_0)), V_i(t_0)$ if they relate to the initial state of the advanced development process, $p_i(\pi_i(t), Q_i(t), IP_i(t), \Pi_i(t), V_i(t))$ if they denote the current state of the enterprise.

The trajectory of enterprise development in a competitive environment, starting at some point $p' = (p_1', p_2', \ldots) \in \Sigma$ at the moment t_0 (further lows, without loss of generality, we will assume that $t=0$), at the moment of time t can be in different areas of space with certain probabilities. Let $p_t(\pi_i(t), Q_i(t), IP_i(t), \Pi_i(t), V_i(t))$ denote the current state of an enterprise in a competitive environment Σ. The efficiency of advanced development is determined by the contour of indicators $IP_i(t), \Pi_i(t), V_i(t)$ that determine the efficiency of the advanced development mechanism. To determine the specific values of the indicators that confine the desired contour, let us consider the management of advanced development based on the model of evolutionary dynamics using stochastic models. Consider a model of the advanced development of a company based on its evolutionary dynamics in a competitive environment.

Let us define the evolutionary process

$$p_i(t) = x(\pi_i(t), Q_i(t), IP_i(t), \Pi_i(t), V_i(t)) \in \Sigma$$

by the formula

$$p_i(t+\delta) = p_i(t) + M\big[p_i(t)\big]\delta + \sigma\big[p_i(t)\big]\xi_\delta(t+\delta),$$

$$p_i(0) = p_w$$

Here δ is the time interval between successive changes in the state of an enterprise in a competitive environment Σ, $M(p)$, and – non – random functions of mathematical expectation and standard deviation for , $p_i(t) \in \Sigma$, $\xi_\delta(0), \xi_\delta(\delta), \xi_\delta(2\delta), \ldots$ – independent in the aggregate random variables for which, at any $\delta > 0$.

$$E\{\xi(t)\} = 0,$$

$$E\{\xi_\delta^2(t)\} = \delta,$$

$$E\{\xi_\delta^m(t)\} = o(\delta), \quad m > 2$$

Let's denote the difference by $\Delta_t p_i$ (change in the state of the enterprise). The process defined in this way will be markovian, and the coefficients M and $V = \sigma^2 \geq 0$ have a probabilistic meaning:

$$M\left[p_i(t)\right]\delta = E\left\{\Delta_t p_i \mid p_i(t)\right\},$$

$$V\left[p_i(t)\right]\delta = E\left\{\left(\Delta_t p_i - M\left[p_i(t)\right]\delta\right)^2 \mid p_i(t)\right\} = E\left\{\left(\Delta_t p_i\right)^2 \mid p_i(t)\right\} + o(\delta),$$

$$E\left\{\left(\Delta_t p_i\right)^m \mid p_i(t)\right\} = o(\delta).$$

Here we see that both $V=\sigma^2$ and M represent the variance and the average value of the process increment per unit time and are called the diffusion coefficients, respectively. Due to the fact that the described process of advanced development is markovian, the dynamics of further development of the company is determined by the current values of the indicators of economic growth Q, the assessment of the scientific and technological potential of the company IP, the values of the parameters of a company П, the assessment of the total consumer value of the innovative product V.

The contour of indicators that provides a positive increment of the value $\Delta_t p_i$, indicating the advanced development of a company, is considered acceptable

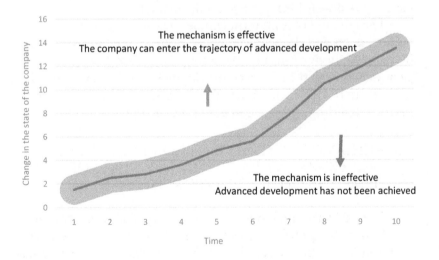

Figure 7.6 The trajectory of advanced development of a company

Thus, the presented model allows to control the parameters (properties) of products that determine their consumer value $V(v_1(t), v_2(t),...,v_m(t))$, which requires the involvement of resources both for research and development, ensuring the increase in consumer value, and for measures to increase the scientific and technological capacity of a company. Moreover, it ensures the growth of production and sales, which, together with the building of scientific and technological capacity, will lead to positive economic growth Q of a company, at least until the moment T when the costs of creating competitive advantages cease to provide an increase in revenue $\Delta TR=0$, and this will lead to the need to update products G_i $(i=1,...,n(t))$. In order to maintain the maximum value of profit from the sale of products $\pi \to \max$ in the long term, it is necessary to create competitive advantages that not only improve the basic characteristics of products $V(v_1(t), v_2(t),...,v_m(t))$, but also radically change them by applying the achievements of fundamental and applied science, which ensures the creation of not only new generations of a particular product ,but also a completely new type of products $(v_1(t), v_2(t),...,v_m(t)) \to (\overline{v}_1(t), \overline{v}_2(t),...,\overline{v}_r(t))$ that has not previously been present on the markets.

The creation of long-term competitive advantages of radically new products and the achievement of global market excellence can be ensured by dynamically increasing the parameters of the efficiency contour of the advanced development mechanism and managing them through scientific and technological capacity and competence- building within a company's technology platform.

7.3. ACHIEVING THE GLOBAL COMPETITIVENESS OF A COMPANY BASED ON THE DEVELOPMENT OF TECHNOLOGY PLATFORMS

Theoretical foundations of a company's global competitiveness

Under the global competitiveness of an industrial company, we mean its complex state, in which it is possible to create a fundamentally new technology (products), organize its manufacture on the basis of innovative technical and technological solutions, advanced achievements in engineering and technology, giving newly created products highly competitive advantages and consumer properties, the level of which allows to take a significant share of the existing market or create a new market.

According to the classical concepts of the theory of competitiveness, the achievement of global competitiveness of high-tech companies involves the creation of a set of conditions:

– company management as a special self-organizing system interacting with other systems based on corporate (industry) technology platforms and through macroeconomic mechanisms;

– long-term financial and economic stability of a company;

– development and production of fundamentally new goods focused on meeting future needs, with new properties, functions and consumer values;

– organization of a full life cycle (from the formation of a techno-economic image and the organization of mass production to operation and disposal) of radically new products created on the basis of the latest advances in engineering and technology;

– continuous and systematic development of scientific and technological capacity and competencies based on the accumulation of knowledge and unique experience in the creation and production of high-tech piece and small-scale products with unique technical characteristics and functions, as well as fundamental and applied research and development;

– formation of a high level of competitiveness (in the classical sense);

– active participation in the development of industry technology platforms and centers of competence for the generation of cross-industrial innovations and technological solutions at the global level;

– active development of mechanisms for intercorporate and cross-sectoral transfer of breakthrough innovative technologies to significantly reduce the time required to launch radically new products to the market.

Achieving the global competitiveness of a company is closely related to the effective management of research, development, innovation, production, organizational and other processes, which determines the creation of scientific and technological capacity sufficient to create a completely new (radically new) product with high consumer properties, allowing to win a significant share of the existing market or create a new market for high-tech products.

As can be seen from the wording, with such a complex of interrelated activities, a company should have a wide range of different competencies that are transformed into the creation of a new product. Practical development for the creation of complex high-tech products is carried out, as a rule, by several companies and various their design and technological divisions, which can be combined within a company (corporation) through a corporate (industry) technology platform, on the basis of which enterprises or organizations can interact. The overall result of the project of creating radically new products will depend on the degree of effectiveness of joint product development by these related organizations in terms of fulfilling their technical tasks and creating the final result with the necessary technical characteristics, materials, and components, thus providing the necessary techno-economic characteristics that allow to meet the needs of the customer and the market, or to ensure the establishment of a new market for sales of developed products due to their consumer properties.

The developed products can be presented on the market only after their production, which arises the issue of creating fundamentally new production facilities for its production or modernize existing ones. The direction of development of a company's technology platform should be determined based on the availability of the company's competencies, financial resources, and terms of market entry, taking into account possible risks, including the risk that competitors may be ahead of schedule and deliver similar products with higher characteristics to the market. It follows that when creating and developing corporate (industry) technology platforms, it is necessary to take into consideration mutual production and technical ties, the possibility of technology transfer and the exchange of unique competencies, and a company's measures to increase its scientific and technological capacity.

When improving a company's technology platform, it is necessary to address the issue of complex integration of the competencies that are part of the company, which can lead to a powerful synergistic effect. The synergistic effect of such integration will make it possible to actively introduce and use radical innovations that allow creating high added value of products, effectively compete in domestic and foreign markets, adapt a company's management strategy to rapidly changing customer needs and market conditions, ensure the company's economic growth, and achieve high productivity. Effective use and development of unique competencies can provide global competitive advantage and enable the establishment of a market for fundamentally new products and technologies, as well as create new market segments based on them.

Forming the main characteristics of a company, allowing to achieve global excellence

The most significant indicators that characterize the basis of a company's global competitiveness and determine its stable economic development are indicators that characterize the global competitiveness of the company, which implies an the company's opportunity to reformat to solve a fundamentally new task of creating radically new products, which is related to an assessment of the level of competence of the company and its scientific and technological capacity.

The assessment of the global competitiveness of a company consists not only of the characteristics of the company itself, but also of the analysis of the competitiveness of the products manufactured by the enterprise in the conditions of management of the system under consideration.

To analyze the global competitiveness of a company that manufactures radically new products, the method of analyzing the competitiveness of objects is used. This method considers the analysis of the aggregate competitiveness of individual objects, which are, firstly, products developed in the conditions of the existing technology platform, and, secondly, a set of technological and functional capabilities of a company's technology platform. The essence of the proposed method is to analyze the dynamics of changes in the global competitiveness of a company as a whole, depending on the dynamics of changes in the competitiveness of products, as well as the technological and functional capabilities of its technology platform.

The assessment of a company's global competitiveness consists of the values of the following indicators, each of which can be measured quantitatively:

1) Parameters that form the competitiveness of developed and manufactured products:

q – techno-economic indicators of products that form their competitiveness (vector of indicators);

u – techno-economic indicators of market leaders (or indicators achievable at the current level of scientific and technological development) (vector of indicators);

S0 – the cost of incurred resource costs for creating products and launching production for its release;

S1 – cost per unit of production;

SF – the price of similar products on the market (if there are no analogues, then SF = S1);

N – the estimated number of units that will be sold on the market;

R – internal factors that arise in the process of creating new products;

F – external factors that accompany the sale of products on the market.

2) Private indicators of enterprise competitiveness:

Indicator groups	Indicators	Designation
Production	Return on assets	O1
	Material efficiency	O2
	Turnover	O3
	Costs per ruble of products sold	O4
	Product line update rate	O5
Financial	Equity to borrowed funds ratio	O6
	Ratios of absolute and current liquidity	O7
	Financial stability ratio	O8
Marketing	Profitability of production activities	O9
	Profitability of products sold	O10
	Return on equity	O11

Innovative	Share of sold innovative products in the total volume of sold products	O12
	Competitiveness of high-tech products	O13
Organizational	Qualification factor and structure of employees	O14
	Number and level of key competencies	O15
	Labor productivity	O16
	Labor-capital ratio	O17
Resource	Resource efficiency ratio	O18
	Capacity utilization ratio	O19
	Depreciation of fixed assets	O20

As a rule, the private indicators of the competitiveness of an enterprise are determined according to the data of statistical reporting and management accounting.

3) Parameters that determine the technological and functional capabilities of the technological platform of an enterprise:

K1 – integral indicator of the effectiveness of managing the processes of shaping the techno-economic image of a product:

– the number of factors taken into account by the system to build a sales forecast $k11$;

– the value of the error in forecasting sales volumes $k12$;

– the value of the forecasting error of the competitive price $k13$;

– quality of the competitive pricing process $k14$;

– quality of the competitiveness management process $k15$;

– number of parameters considered when assessing competitiveness $k16$;

K2 – integral indicator of the effectiveness of product design process management:

– quality of the resource planning process $k21$;

– the value of the error of the planned estimated indicators of the resourcing of the project for the manufacture of products $k22$;

– share of cost-effective projects recommended by the system for implementation $k23$;

– share of completed projects with high economic results, recommended by the system for implementation $k24$;

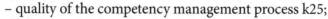

– quality of the competency management process k25;

– quality of the product design process for a given cost k26;

K3 – integral indicator of the effectiveness of managing the processes of pre-production and production:

- quality of the process of managing the techno-technological base k31;

- number of factors considered when evaluating a company's innovation capacity k32;

- quality of the process of managing the manufacture of new products k33;

K4 – integral indicator of the effectiveness of life cycle process management:

- quality of the marketing management process k41;

- number of risks considered by the system when managing the project k42;

- quality of the risk management process k43.

Quantifying the main characteristics of a company that allow achieving global excellence

The first stage of quantitative assessment of a company's global competitiveness is the procedure for analyzing the competitiveness of the products planned for release based on the integral indicator of competitiveness. This model can be used to determine the competitiveness of both finished products and components created for their use in the manufacture of more complex products.

Let us focus in more detail on the calculation of the product innovation index Q. Following the method of solving this problem, we will assume that this indicator is a function of particular indicators of innovation, by which we refer to the key technical characteristics of the product. That is

$$Q = f(q_1, q_2, ..., q_n),$$

where q_i is a particular indicator of product innovation, representing some key technical characteristic. A particular competitiveness indicator q_i is a value that accepts values from the segment [0; 1]. Thus, its value can be found by the formula:

$$q_i = \frac{u_i}{U_i},$$

where u_i is the technical characteristic of a product, and U_i is the same technical characteristic of the market leader or the maximum possible value of the characteristic in accordance with the current level of scientific and technological progress.

The indicator of product innovation Q can be found on the basis of particular indicators of product innovation, taking into account the weighting factors of the importance of indicators of innovation:

$$Q = \sum_{i=1}^{n} \beta_i q_i ,$$

where β_i are the weight coefficients of the particular indicators of product innovation, and

$$\sum_{i=1}^{n} \beta_i = 1.$$

For each product presented or planned to be launched on the market, an objective indicator of the competitiveness of the product is calculated using the following formula:

$$IQ = \left(\frac{Q \cdot S_F}{\frac{S_0}{N} + S_1} \right) \cdot (1 - R) \cdot (1 + F)$$

This formula expresses the numerical index of the competitiveness of the products in question in the market.

The integral indicator of competitiveness IQ can accept values both greater than 1 and less than 1. With an IQ > 1, we can say that the competitiveness of the products presented or planned for withdrawal is higher than the existing level on the market.

The global competitiveness of a company is directly related to the competitiveness of its products. Moreover, a company's competitiveness depends on the entire range of products produced and planned for production. If the integral indicators of the competitiveness of all types of products are known $IQ_1, IQ_2, ..., IQ_N$, where N is the number of types of products, then the integral indicator of the competitiveness of the entire population

$$\widetilde{IQ} = \sum_{i=1}^{N} \omega_i IQ_i,$$

where ω_i is the weighting factor that characterizes the contribution of each type of product to forming of an integral indicator of a company's competitiveness. As a weight factor corresponding to a certain type of product, we will consider the share of revenue from the sale of products on the market in the total revenue of a company:

$$\omega_i = \frac{V_i}{V},$$

where V_i is revenue from the sale of products of the type i, V is the total revenue of the company. Thus,

$$\sum_{i=1}^{N} \omega_i = 1.$$

For the planned production, the forecast values are considered.

As it was noted, the global competitiveness of a company is determined not only by the competitiveness of its products, but also by a number of other factors determined by the capabilities of the company's technology platform:

- integral indicator of the effectiveness of managing the processes of shaping the techno-economic image of the product (K1);
- iintegral indicator of product design process management efficiency (K2);
- iintegral indicator of the effectiveness of the management of the processes of pre-production and production (K3);
- iintegral indicator of the effectiveness of life cycle process management (K4).

To evaluate the listed integral indicators, it is necessary to use estimates of the parameters that determine the functionality of a technology platform. In this case, each integral indicator is a convolution of partial indicators and is determined by the formula:

$$K_i = \sum_{j=1}^{m} \omega_{ij} k_{ij},$$

where i is the ordinal number of the integral indicator, m is the number of particular indicators that form the integral indicator,

$$\sum_{j=1}^{m} \omega_{ij} = 1.$$

In addition, it is necessary to obtain a convolution of the IO of private indicators of the company's competitiveness using the formula:

$$IO = \sum_{j=1}^{n} \omega_j O_j,$$

where n is the number of considered private indicators of the company's competitiveness,

$$\sum_{j=1}^{m} \omega_{ij} = 1.$$

With known values of the competitiveness indicator of the entire set of products IQ and estimates of integrated indicators that determine the technological and functional capabilities of the technology platform K_1, K_2, K_3, K_4, the integrated indicator of the company's global competitiveness will be written as:

$$IQO = w_0 \cdot \widetilde{IQ} + w_1 K_1 + w_2 K_2 + w_3 K_3 + w_4 K_4 + w_5 IO,$$

where w_i are the weighting factors of the company's competitiveness factors. Thus,

$$\sum_{i=0}^{5} w_i = 1.$$

We will consider a company that is globally competitive in the market with an integral indicator of its competitiveness $IQO \geq 1.$

In dynamics, the effectiveness of global competitiveness management can be evaluated as follows. If we evaluate the dynamics in relation to the period of M years, the formula for the dynamic assessment of the global competitiveness of the company takes the form:

$$IQS = \frac{\Delta IQO_t}{\frac{1}{M} \cdot \sum_{i=0}^{M-1} \Delta IQO_{t-i}},$$

where $\Delta IQO_\tau = IQO_\tau - IQO_{\tau-1}$.

The proposed algorithm for assessing the global competitiveness of m allows you to quickly obtain a dimensionless index of global competitiveness.

The successful implementation of projects to create a highly competitive product that could displace existing products or create a new market directly depends on the availability of key competencies and the level of scientific and technological capacity, due to which unique technical, economic and consumer characteristics of new products can be created. Thus, the foundation for achieving global competitive leadership is the competitiveness already formed by a company.

Forecasting the development of a company's technology platform that ensures the achievement of its global competitiveness

In the conditions of intense competition and accelerated transfer of scientific knowledge, the global competitiveness and economic stability of a company is achieved not only by developing existing competencies, but also by creating new radical competencies that can provide high competitive advantages of the developed products due to their uniqueness and the ability to meet future needs. Under these conditions, the main driver for achieving (maintaining) a company's global competitiveness is the intensive development of its technological platform, which makes it possible to create diverse unique products that can create new markets or be dominant in existing ones as a result of the application of radical competencies. Forecasting the development of the technology platform is associated with planning the future values of the parameters that determine the technological and functional capabilities of a company's technology platform. Private indicators presented earlier form a number of integral indicators:

K1 – integral indicator of the effectiveness of managing the processes of shaping techno-economic image of a product;

K2 – integral indicator of the effectiveness of product design process management;

K3 – an integral indicator of the effectiveness of managing the processes of pre-production and production;

K4 – integral indicator of the effectiveness of life cycle process management.

Achieving the measures that allow the development of a technology platform, the generation of radical competencies and products based on them, provides a continuous update of the product line, given the emerging consumer expectations in the market, thereby maintaining long-term competitive leadership in the market, as well as stimulating other market players to progressively develop towards building up the technological reserve and creating innovative products, which in turn determines the development of a technology platform at the industry level.

Achieving and maintaining global competitive leadership is closely related to the effectiveness of managing the processes of increasing global competitiveness. Such management implies setting a forecast trajectory for the development of a company's global competitiveness. It should be based on the possibility of determining, first, the increase in sales of products with high added value due to its intensive demand in the markets, which determines its contribution to the competitiveness of a company, and, secondly, the bar (level) for achieving scientific and technological capacity should be determined, which as an indicator can be used to form a sufficient condition for the readiness of a company's technology platform to release a product with new consumer characteristics based on the intensive application of advanced scientific achievements, including through giving private technical assignments to related parties with competencies to develop unique technical and technological solutions.

In this case the planned (forecast) trajectory of the development of global competitiveness, i.e. the trajectory of the change in time of the integral indicator of a company's global competitiveness can be set. This trajectory is set based on the necessary values of the parameters that determine the technological and functional capabilities of the company's technology platform (private indicators that form the integral coefficients K1, K2, K3, K4 in the introduced designations), which will create radically new products (as well as update existing ones), which will lead to an increase in the competitiveness of the product line (IQ). The planned values of the parameters K1, K2, K3, K4 and IQ determine the forecast value of the global competitiveness indicator IQO, i.e. a new point on the trajectory of a company's global competitiveness development, the achievement of which in the future indicates the achievement (preservation) of the state of global competitive leadership. The correspondence of the real values of the integral indicator of the global competitiveness of a company to the values of the planned development trajectory at any given time indicates the sufficiency of control actions on the scientific and technological capacity and technology platform of the company, expressed in the ability to create radically new products.

The high level of the considered indicators as a whole can provide a company with anticipated appearance of products with high competitive advantages. Consequently, this offers new opportunities both for creating new markets and for increasing sales of products in the existing market, which is the basis for achieving global competitive leadership.

Achieving global leadership is related to its focus on on meeting market needs and maintaining this ability for a long time. Management of a company's global competitiveness is a set of principles, goals, stages, priority areas and mechanisms for achieving leading positions in the industry, which will eventually create completely new technological and consumer markets.

Managing the global competitiveness of high-tech companies as a special model of its functioning necessitates the creation of a fundamentally new innovative system for managing its technological platform: product development, technological and supporting pre-production, production process, sales of finished products, human resources and capital, economy, finance, investments, logistics.

Comprehensive management of achieving global competitiveness of a high-tech company includes the following necessary elements:

– a radical change in the technological basis of the technological platform, providing a technological breakthrough;
– development of intersectoral and cross-industrial cooperation and system integration with a technological breakthrough;
– development of an environment of demand and competition for high-tech products;
– accelerating innovation cycles and promoting the concept of technology leaders;
– increasing production of globally competitive high-tech products and services;
– stimulating the development of radical innovations;
– effective commercialization of advanced developments;
– forming a modern scientific-technical and production-technological environment, infrastructure, economic models, etc., corresponding to the sixth wave of innovation;
– increasing the efficiency of investments and financial returns from the conducted R&D.

The result of achieving global competitiveness of the company is the following permanent components:
– shaping the image of radically new products and promising product lines;
– creation and development of technological and product competence centers;
– conducting applied scientific and technological research of the sixth wave of innovation;
– technical re-equipment for the sixth wave of innovation;
– effective transfer and application of knowledge and technologies of fundamental science and the global information space.

In the context of the external factors of uncertainty, one of the key conditions of competition in the global market may be the development of a technological platform in order to concentrate scientific and technical, production and technical, human and financial resources of an industry and counter the negative effect of intra-industry competition.

The goal of achieving global competitive leadership should be considered as the implementation of measures to develop a company's technology platform, resulting in achieving an economic and techno-logical effect. However, these activities affect the outcome (the ability to create a radically new product) with varying degrees of effectiveness. Therefore, we will consider the following economic and mathematical model of optimal management of global competitive leadership based on the development of a technology platform under resource con-straints.

Let the development plan of a company's technology platform involve various M activities related to the development of scien-tific and technological capacity and competencies. We will assign a number to each event with the number m, which we will denote by Xm. We will interpret this number as follows. If this event is not completed, we assume that

$Xm = 0$.

If the event is completed in full, then we assume that

$Xm = 1$.

Besides, we will consider the values

$0 < Xm < 1$,

which we will interpret as a partial implementation of this event.

Since real measures cannot always be implemented at least par-tially, we will consider the values of Xm with the following constraints:

$Xm \geq vm$,

where the numbers $vm \in [0, 1]$ show the minimum part of the possible implementation of the measure m. If $vm = 1$, then this means that event m must be completed in full, or it will not be performed at all. N

We will assume that N different resources have been allocated for the implementation of measures for the development of the tech-nological platform. Let us introduce numerical values:

$Bm \geq 0$,

which express the volume of each resource.

Since different events consume different types of resources, we will introduce the values:

$aij \geq 0$,

which have the following meaning. The value aij shows what share of the i -th resource is consumed by the j-th event.

Planning measures for the development of a technology platform in conditions of resource constraints consists in choosing such values of Xm, so that the following inequalities are fulfilled:

$$a11 \cdot X1 + a12 \cdot X2 + \ldots + a1M \cdot XM \leq B1,$$
$$a21 \cdot X1 + a22 \cdot X2 + \ldots + a2M \cdot XM \leq B2,$$
$$\ldots \tag{1}$$
$$aN1 \cdot X1 + aN2 \cdot X2 + \ldots + aNM \cdot XM \leq BN.$$

These inequalities reflect the demands linked with general resource constraints. In addition, the following restrictions must be met:

$$v1 \leq X1 \leq 1 \text{ or } X1 = 0,$$
$$v2 \leq X2 \leq 1 \text{ or } X2 = 0,$$
$$\ldots \tag{2}$$
$$vM \leq XM \leq 1 \text{ or } XM = 0.$$

These restrictions reflect the fact that all activities must be completed with at least a fraction of what is feasible, but it is possible that some activities will not be completed at all. By

$$X = (X1, X2, \ldots, XM)T$$

we will denote a column vector of Xm values and call this vector the action plan for the development of a company's technology platform.

We will call plan X feasible if the values of Xm included in X simultaneously satisfy the conditions (1) and (2). The set of all feasible action plans will be denoted by UX

$$X \in UX.$$

We will assume that the set of feasible plans for organizational and technical measures is non-empty:

$$UX \neq \emptyset.$$

In this formalism, the task of optimal planning for the development of a company's technology platform, which is the basis for achieving global competitive leadership, is to choose such an feasible plan of measures $X \in UX$, related to the development of scientific and technological capacity and competencies, which will be most effective for ensuring the considered innovation project. To do this, it is necessary to introduce a criterion that will evaluate the effectiveness of a feasible plan of organizational and technical measures for the development of a technology platform.

As this criterion, we will consider the numerical functional F, given on the set of feasible action plans:

$F: UX \to R.$

Based on the economic sense, we will assume that there is the following condition for the functional effectiveness of organizational and technological measures plans:

$F(X) \geq 0$, for all $X \in UX$.

In addition to writing $F(X)$ we will use the equivalent notation:

$F(X) = F(X1, X2, ..., XM)$.

In addition to the specified condition, this functionality must meet the following conditions:

$F(X1,..., Xm, ..., XM) \leq F(X1,..., X'm, ..., XM)$,

if $Xm \leq X'm$. This condition means that if we implement any measure to a greater extent while maintaining the rest of the measures, then the effectiveness of this action plan will not be worse than the original plan.

As a typical example of the functional effectiveness of measures to build scientific and technological capacity and competencies, we can offer a linear functional that looks like this:

$F(X1, X2, ..., XM) = C1 \cdot X1 + C2 \cdot X2 + ... + CM \cdot XM$,

where the coefficients $Cm > 0$ have economic meaning – the effect of the m th event on the efficiency of the technology platform development.

Another form of the functional for assessing the effectiveness of measures is the multiplicative form:

$F(X1, X2, ..., XM) = K \cdot (X1)\gamma1 \cdot (X2)\gamma2 \cdot ... \cdot (XM)\gamma M$,

where $\gamma m > 0$. It is usually assumed that the following condition is additionally fulfilled:

$0 < \gamma m \leq 1$, $m = 1, 2, ..., M$.

Note that in multiplicative form it is assumed that all feasible plans X satisfy the conditions:

$Xm > 0$,

since otherwise the functional F will be equal to zero. This case describes a situation where the effective development of a technology platform that ensures the achievement of global competitive leader-ship requires the implementation of all measures.

The general scheme of optimal planning of measures for the development of a technology platform consists in solving the following extreme problem:

$$F(X1, X2, \ldots, XM) \rightarrow \max X1, X2, \ldots, XM \qquad (3)$$

We will say that a feasible action plan X^* is optimal if the following condition is met:

$F(X^*) = \max\{F(X): X \in UX\}$.

It can be shown that the set UX is closed and bounded, so problem (3) always has a solution (not necessarily one). Various well-known methods of mathematical programming and optimization theory can be applied to actually calculate the optimal design.

Methods based on the choice of a set of feasible plans

When constructing a model for the optimal planning of measures for the development of a technology platform in conditions of resource constraints, one of the main problems is the choice of a set of feasible plans. In the initial planning of measures, conditions (1) and (2) may lead to the fact that the set of feasible UX plans will be empty, which will indicate that the allocated resources are insufficient to implement all the necessary activities. In this situation, the following methods should be used: In this situation, the following methods should be followed:

1. Elimination of non-critical activities
2. Reducing resource consumption by individual activities
3. Reallocation of resources.

Let us review these methods in detail.

The elimination of non-critical activities allows you to reduce the required resources. Mathematically, this method assumes that action plans are acceptable, which for some actions will have zero values:

$Xm = 0, m \in M'$,

where M' is a subset of the indices of organizational and technical measures that are not critical for the implementation of an innovative project.

The following approach can be used to define this set:

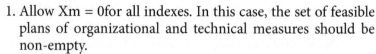

1. Allow Xm = 0for all indexes. In this case, the set of feasible plans of organizational and technical measures should be non-empty.
2. Using this set of UX, find the optimal plan by solving problem (3).
3. Analyzing the optimal action plan X*, find the activities with the minimum values of X*m.
4. Among the activities found with minimal X*m values, there may be non-critical activities.

Another approach for detecting non-critical measures is the functional analysis method for evaluating the effectiveness of plans.

To do this, it is necessary to calculate the partial derivatives of the functional of evaluating the effectiveness of action plans in the implementation of an innovative project:

$$F_m = \frac{\partial F(1,1,...,1)}{\partial X_m}$$

This formula calculates partial derivatives with argument values equal to 1.

Analyzing the values of F1, F2, …, FM, you need to find those values that have the smallest values. If Fm has a small value, then this means that the final functional for assessing the effectiveness of measures is weakly dependent on the value of Xm, therefore, measure m can be excluded from the mandatory measures.

Reducing the resource consumption of individual activities allows to reduce the overall resource requirements, which allows expanding many feasible action plans. In the presented mathematical model, this means that we can reduce the numerical values of the coefficients aij. Since the values of Xm are non-negative, the set of feasible plans designs should increase with decreasing aij values.

Indeed, for coefficients a'ij such that

a'ij ≤ aij,

that always has

a'11 · X1 + a'12 · X2 + … + a'1M · XM ≤ a11 · X1 + a12 · X2 + … + a1M · XM ≤ B1,
a'21 · X1 + a'22 · X2 + … + a'2M · XM ≤ a21 · X1 + a22 · X2 + … + a2M · XM ≤ B2,

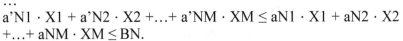
...
a'N1 · X1 + a'N2 · X2 +...+ a'NM · XM ≤ aN1 · X1 + aN2 · X2 +...+ aNM · XM ≤ BN.

Therefore, the set of acceptable action plans for the development of the technology platform, constructed using the coefficients a'ij, which we denote by U'M, satisfies the following inclusion:

UM ⊂ U'M.

Of course, reducing the consumption of resources by each event requires a certain change in organizational and technical measures, but this will to significantly increase the economic efficiency of measures to support innovative projects allow in the future.

Reallocation of resources is another method that allows to optimize the set of feasible action plans for the development of a technology platform. Since various activities require different resources, the initial resource constraints can create a "bottleneck" situation, when one of the resources is scarce, which does not fully implement all the necessary organizational and technical measures.

Resource constraints arise from financial constraints on activities, therefore, it is possible to reallocate resources while maintaining the total amount of financial constraints. To describe this process, we introduce the following notation:

φn = φ(Bn), n = 1, 2, ..., N,

which mean the cost of the n -th resource in the volume Bn.

Thus, the total cost of all considered resources can be expressed by the following formula:

R = φ1 + φ2 + ... + φN.

This value depends on the set of resources

R = R (B1, B2, ..., BN).

We will assume that the value is fixed and cannot be increased, but the Bn values can be changed.

Under the resource reallocation operation, we will consider the representations:

ψ1(B1) = B'1,

ψ2(B2) = B'2,

...

ψN(BN) = B'N.

such that the following resource constraints are met:

$R' = R\psi 1(B1), \psi 2(B2), \ldots \psi N(BN)) \leq R(B1, B2, \ldots, BN) = R.$

These restrictions mean that the total amount of financial restrictions does not increase in the redistribution of resources, therefore, such a redistribution of resources can be considered economically feasible.

Since the processes of scientific and technological development at knowledge-based enterprises are always accompanied by certain economic risks, then with the optimal planning of measures for the development of a technology platform, it is necessary to address the influence of random factors that can have a significant impact on the result of measures. These factors are of particular importance in the context of resource constraints.

Consider two options for the negative impact of random factors:

factors that reduce the economic effect of the implementation of activities;

factors that increase the need for resources;

factors that reduce available resources.

Random factors can cause a decrease in the economic effect of measures to develop a technology platform. According to the developed economic and mathematical model, the functional for assessing the effectiveness of measures should be modified as follows:

$F(X) = F(X1, X2, \ldots, XM) - \xi 1(X1) - \xi 2(X2) - \ldots - \xi M(XM).$

Here ξm (ω, Xm) are random variables that satisfy the conditions with a probability of one:

$\xi m(\omega, \cdot) \geq 0, m = 1, 2, \ldots, M.$

In these random variables, Xm are parameters that determine the distribution of the random variables. We will assume that for all m the following conditions are satisfied, which we formulate in terms of the first two moments (mathematical expectation and variance):

$E[\xi m(\omega, Xm)] \leq E[\xi m(\omega, X'm)]$

and the condition

$D[\xi m(\omega, Xm)] \leq D[\xi m(\omega, X'm)],$

if $Xm \leq X'm$. These conditions mean that with an increase in the value of the implementation of a measure, the mathematical expectation and variance of the corresponding random variables increase.

Random factors that increase the need for resources arise as a result of the fact that many activities in the development of technology platforms may require more resources than previously planned, since innovation processes are always accompanied by the development and implementation of new technologies.

From the standpoint of mathematical model of optimal planning of organizational and technical measures for the implementation of innovative projects, these factors consist in the fact that the aij coefficients must be modified to take these factors into account:

aij $\rightarrow$ aij + χij(ω), i = 1, 2, ..., M; j = 1, 2, ..., N.

Here we consider random variables χij(ω) that satisfy the following conditions:

χij(ω) $\geq$ 0.

This condition shows that the random factors considered can actually increase the need for resources in the implementation of activities.

Random factors that reduce the available resources arise due to the fact that the innovative processes of scientific and technological development, are usually implemented for a long time, therefore, various factors of the economy can reduce the financing of innovative processes and, accordingly, reduce the available resources for relevant activities.

According to the considered mathematical model, to take into account these factors, it is necessary to change the values of Bn as follows:

Bn $\rightarrow$ Bn + ζn(ω),

where the random variables ζn (ω) meet the following conditions:

ζn(ω) $\leq$ 0, n = 1, 2, ..., N.

Since the values of random variables usually do not depend on the chosen plans, to predict their values it is necessary to consider various random factors and risks, which are external factors.

To take these factors into account in the optimal planning of measures for the development of a technology platform in conditions of resource constraints, it is necessary to take into account the possibility of reducing the values of the values of Bn when solving the extreme problem (3). For this, it makes sense to reduce the set of admissible action plans based on constraints (1), where some values of Bn will be reduced taking into account possible risks. Although this may lead to the selection of less effective plans, this will compensate for the possible risks of lack of resources in the implementation of critical activities in the development of the technology platform.

Measures for the development of the technology platform increases the parameters that determine the technological and functional capabilities of a company's technology platform, which leads to an increase in the company's global competitiveness according to the algorithm proposed above. At the same time, the achievement (preservation) of global competitive leadership is ensured in accordance with the built trajectory of the development of global competitiveness.

In practice, it is advisable to establish a corridor of economic sustainability for the trajectory of development of a company's global competitiveness (usually no more than 5-10% of the planned values of the parameters that determine the required dynamics of the development of global competitiveness). This is due to the fact that at certain points in time a company may experience the influence of uncertainty factors that may not allow achieving the required values of the parameters of competitive development.

In the face of risks, through the reallocation of resources or other measures (for example, the creation of a risk fund), it becomes possible to smooth out the negative influence of uncertainty factors on the company's development. In the case of going beyond the corridor boundaries, then a revision of the planning documents is necessary. The market opportunities of a company are determined by the quantitative and qualitative characteristics of its resources and the efficiency of their distribution, the possibility of their additional attraction on favorable terms, the ability of stable economic development based on the intensive development of a technology platform, taking into account the actions of competitors to increase their competitive advantages.

Thus, as research shows, the achievement of global competitiveness and global superiority becomes possible as a result of the dynamic

Sustainable development corridor

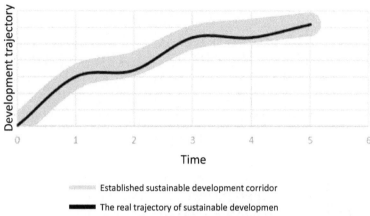

Established sustainable development corridor

The real trajectory of sustainable developmen

Figure 7.7. Corridor for the development trajectory of a company's
global competitiveness

development and increased flexibility of technology platforms, as well as the implementation of methods and measures to manage their development, allowing for the creation of competitive advantages that strengthen positions in a certain market segment or create conditions for entering new ones; the organization of new activities that can generate significant income; creating new markets based on the development of a product that was not previously present on the market.

CHAPTER 8.
SYSTEMATIC APPROACH TO ENSURING TECHNOLOGICAL LEADERSHIP AND ADVANCED DEVELOPMENT OF A COMPANY IN THE CONTEXT OF THE CHALLENGES OF THE XXI CENTURY

8.1. THE MECHANISM FOR MANAGING THE TRANSITION TO TECHNOLOGICAL LEADERSHIP OF A COMPANY BASED ON THE PRODUCTION AND SALE OF RADICALLY NEW PRODUCTS

The mechanism for managing the transition to a company's technological leadership based on the production and sale of radically new products, refers to the set of instruments interacting in dynamics, many of which were described above::

Tools for managing the development of a company's scientific and technological capacity and competencies;

Tools for transforming scientific and technological capacity and competencies into radical properties of new products;

Tools for managing the company's economic growth through the creation of radically new products;

Economic tools for supporting the processes of creating and selling products with high consumer utility;

Tools for the formation of service business models for the sale of products on the market;

Tools for managing a company's advanced development.

Each of the tools includes a set of methods and approaches aimed at assessing, analyzing and managing various aspects of creating high-tech radically new products and achieving technological leadership and advanced company development. These tools are built in the processes of creating radically new products and form a single mechanism for managing the transition to technological leadership. The scheme for constructing such a mechanism is shown in Figure 8.1.

In order to apply in practice the scheme of building a mechanism in a particular company presented in Figure 8.1, it is necessary to know its economic condition.

The economic condition of a company can be different, based on the specifics of their products, technical and technological equipment, type of ownership and belonging to various integrated structures. In this regard, the company's activities should be analyzed taking into account the specifics which allows to develop proposals for effective management of the transition to technological leadership, which is based on the indicators of its current and future economic condition, depending on the economic development of the industry, the country and the global economy. In this regard, a company should be analyzed from the point of view of identifying the real structure of relationships and stable factors that characterize the peculiarity of its functioning and allows to determine the key problems that impede creating conditions for advanced development, and outline ways to solve them.

The economic activity of the company should be analyzed as a comprehensive, phased and element-wise examination.

In a comprehensive form of assessment, all the components that characterize a company's activities are examined, which must be considered by quantifying them. The step-by-step assessment focuses on the main criteria that determine a company's ability to solve its main tasks, achieve economic growth and development. In this case, the problem is reduced to detailing the main criteria that provide a comprehensive assessment. A typical scheme for examining a company's ability for assessing its economic activities is shown in Figure 8.2.

The performance indicators of the company shown in Figure 8.2 represent the various components of a company's scientific and technological capacity in a certain period of time and determine its ability to move to advanced development and achieve global technological leadership.

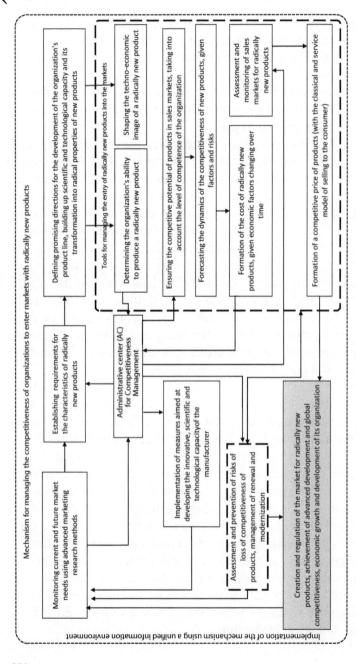

Figure 8.1 Diagram of the mechanism for managing the transition to technological leadership of a company based on the creation of radically new products, taking into account the development of a company and dynamically changing factors and risks

Company capabilities

Organizational	Financial and economic	Production	Personnel	Market and sales	Social	Scientific, technical and innovative
1. Organizational and legal form	1. Income from sales	1. The cost of fixed assets and the degree of their wear and tear	1. The number of employees with the allocation of the main production personnel, managers, specialists and employees	1. The volume of sales of products in value terms and in assortment	1. Structure and value of fixed non-productive assets	1. Number of implemented inventions, rationalization assumptions
2. Organizational structure	2. Non-operating income	2. Capacity utilization rate	2. Employment structure (gender-age, professional, specialty, category, etc.)	2. Main suppliers of raw materials	2. Types and amounts of social payments to employees	2. The number of mastered new technologies, new types of products (works, services)R&D scope
3. Management structure	3. Production costs (cost of production)	3. Provision of material and raw materials and fuel and energy resources	3. The level of wages by groups of workers	3. Main consumers of products	3. Ongoing costs of social and cultural activities	3. Average age of manufactured products
4. Infrastructure	4. Profit distribution	4. The volume and range of products (works, services)L. and area	4. Labor productivity dynamics	4. Main sales markets	4. The cost of maintaining objects of social infrastructure of the organization	4. Competitiveness of manufactured products
5. Cooperation, specialization, concentration of production	5. Profitability	5. Construction in progress cost	5. The level of labor intensity for the main groups of products (works, services)	5. Remains of finished products in the warehouse in value and kind		5. Patent protection of manufactured products and applied technologies
	6. Breakeven point	6. Stocks of unsold inventories	6. Intensity of recruitment turnover, staff turnover	6. Maximum and minimum limit of prices of manufactured products		
	7. Accounts payable and receivable	7.		7. Competitive strategy		
	8. The state of own working capital (availability, growth, surplus or shortage)					
	9. Capital structure					
	10. Share premium					
	11. Financial and operational needs					

Figure 8.2. Scheme for a comprehensive assessment of a company's capacity

The scientific and technological capacity of a company is closely related to the availability of various types of resources, which determines the possibilities and limitations of the company's functioning in various conditions.

All of the above indicators form the competitiveness of a company, and their quantitative assessment is given in [62]. To analyze a company's ability to transition to technological leadership, formed through the use of the tools described above and their regulation through the mechanism presented in Figure 8.1, initial data are used that describe the indicators of the company's economic activity and characterize its capabilities (see Figure 8.2, specific data can be taken from accounting and statistical reports or calculated on their basis) and technical characteristics of products (indicators of financial and economic stability, indicators of production and sales of products, indicators characterizing the state and efficiency of fixed assets, indicators of labor force efficiency, indicators of the efficiency of resource use potential), as well as complex calculated indicators characterizing the company's ability to develop and manufacture radically new products (the level of scientific and technological capacity of the company, its competencies, etc.). Our studies of the patterns of formation of conditions for the transition to advanced development[63] have shown that an important component of assessing a company's ability to achieve technological leadership is information about the technical characteristics of the company's products, which can be obtained from the passports of these products (for already manufactured products) or from the technical specifications for product development. The development and introduction of radically new products to the market can, like any innovative activity, be accompanied by various factors that are usually negative. In addition to purely economic factors that affect the competitiveness of radically new products, uncertainties and risks that affect a company's ability to design, produce and deliver a radically new product to the end user are also of great importance (Table 8.1).

[62] Chursin, A., Makarov, Y. Management of competitiveness: Theory and practice // 2015, Management of Competitiveness: Theory and Practice p. 1–378
[63] Chursin A. Springer

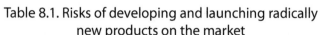

Table 8.1. Risks of developing and launching radically new products on the market

Operational and production and technological risk	Technological failures
	The impossibility of using for technological, commercial, legal, organizational and other reasons in the creation, promotion of the company's products, components, technologies that affect shaping radical properties of products
Legal risks	Restriction of activities, restriction of access to certain information resources, software, etc .; Restricting consumer access to products due to economic restrictions and consumer protection policies
Political risks	Customs restrictions on the import or export of tangible and intangible resources required for the design, manufacture and promotion of radically new products
Personnel risks	Insufficient qualifications of personnel, staff turnover, insufficient labor productivity. Unreasonably high dependence on the competencies of specific individuals (groups of individuals)
Social risks	Rejection of new technologies set in products by major consumer groups.

In order to model and quantitatively describe the control actions related to the use of tools within the mechanism of transition to technological leadership based on entering markets with radically new products, we will consider the economic and mathematical model of this mechanism. When forming a model for ensuring technological leadership, we will rely on a company's competitiveness, a high level of which is a necessary condition for the transition to advanced development. In this regard, we will define an algorithm for forming a quantitative assessment of a company's competitiveness and an algorithm for modeling control actions on the level of competitiveness linked to the use of the above tools.

I. Algorithm for quantitative assessment of a company's competitiveness, given its ability to develop and manufacture a radically new product, taking into account dynamically changing factors and risks[64]

---

[64] Boginsky A. Methodological basis for creating promising high-tech products in the digital transformation. – Talinn: EurAsian Scientific Editions Ltd, 2021 – 265 p.

As the initial data for assessing the competitiveness of products, we have, first, vectors describing the economic indicators of a $P_1, P_2, ..., P_M$. These vectors consist of the economic indicators of a company Pm = (pm1, pm2, ..., pmS). Secondly, we have the vectors Q1, Q2, ..., QM, where each vector Qk is a vector with the technical characteristics of the k--th product type: Qk = (qk1, qk2, ..., qkN).

Note that different types of products may have a different set of technical characteristics, but when forming the model, we can assume that all vectors Qk have the same dimension without loss of generality.

Next, we will assume that all product names are divided into several types of the same type of products Pr1, Pr2, ..., PrL.

In this case, it is assumed that the initial data indicates which products belong to the same type of product, as well as which companies manufacture which products.

In assessing the competitiveness of industrial companies, given the economic indicators of a company and the technical characteristics of the products, the following results are calculated:

1. Objective evaluation of each product in dimensionless (normalized) units.
2. Comparative quantitative characteristics of competitiveness for all pairs of industrial companies.
3. Quantitative characteristics of the competitiveness of each company.

The described economic and mathematical model uses several auxiliary algorithms:

1. Algorithm for normalizing vectors with objective characteristics.
2. Convolution of indicators of objective characteristics of products based on an information feature.
3. Assessment of a company's competitiveness using a game-theoretic approach.

In addition, the model includes various algorithms and procedures for information processing of initial information.

Algorithm for normalizing vectors with objective product characteristics

Each product is represented as a vector with characteristics $Q = (q_1, q_2, ..., q_N)$, where q_n is a separate technical characteristic of the product. This characteristic can be either numerical or qualitative. More generally, this characteristic can be a linguistic variable. In addition, product specifications are generally dimensional. Another problem is the fact that the numerical characteristics of a product can be positive when a higher value of a parameter means better production, or negative when a lower value of a parameter means better production.

To assess the competitiveness of industrial companies, it is necessary to use standardized values of technical characteristics. We will evaluate each production indicator using a finite number of points q_{n0} from zero to 5: $q_{n0} \in \{0, 1, 2, 3, 5\}$.

If the initial parameter has a numerical value q_n, then it can be normalized using the following formula (for parameters whose higher value indicates a better indicator):

$q_{n0} = [5 \cdot (q_n - min) / (max - min)]$,

where min and max are the minimum parameter value among all products and the maximum parameter value, and square brackets are rounding to the nearest integer.

For parameters, a lower value of which indicates a better indicator, you should use the following version of this formula:

$q_{n0} = 5 - [5 \cdot (q_n - min) / (max - min)]$.

For the case of a linguistic variable or for qualitative characteristics, we can use the expert method for normalization.

Thus, after normalization, we will assume that the vectors describing the technical characteristics of a product consist of points of the same scale.

Convolution of objective indicators based on the information principle

To compare vectors with normalized characteristics, it is necessary to convolve these indicators into a single numerical characteristic. The simplest types of convolution are arithmetic averages or geometric averages (for the case of positive values). In addition, when implementing this convolution, weight factors can be taken into account, which will reflect the importance of each product characteristic.

However, in order to assess the competitiveness, it is also necessary to consider the importance of each product characteristic in comparison with other (of the same type) product names. For this we will use the information principle.

Suppose we have some set of products of the same type, which we denote by Pr. This set will contain the vectors $Qm = (qm1, qm2, ..., qmN)$, $m = 1, 2, ..., M$.

The set of these vectors can be represented as a matrix $M \times N$, where each row is the indicators of each product, and each column is the values of the indicators in the entire set of products.

For each column with the number n, we will determine the entropy by the following formula. Assuming that each value of this column is an implementation of some random variable on, which accepts the values

$on \in \{0, 1, 2, 3, 4, 5\}$, we can estimate the probability for each value of this random variable using the following formulas:

$pi = Mi / M$,

where Mi is the number of times when the index n accepts the value $I \in \{0,1,2,3,4,5\}$.

The entropy of a random variable is calculated using the following formula:

$Hn = H[on] = - \sum pi \cdot log2pi$,

where the summation is carried out by i from 0 to 5. As is customary in information theory, we assume that $0 \cdot log20 = 0$.

Thus, for the convolution of the normalized vector with the technical indicators of a product, we will use the following formula:

$Qm = \sum Hn \cdot qmn$,

where the summation is carried out by n from 1 to N.

Therefore, in the convolution of the indicators, we take into account the informational content of each technical characteristic. The more information each characteristic carries, the more weight this characteristic is considered in the convolution. It is possible to use this formula taking into account the weighting factors:

$Qm = \sum an \cdot Hn \cdot qmn$,

where an is the weighting factor for the n-th characteristic.

To obtain an assessment of competitiveness under the conditions of factors and risks, it is necessary to use dynamic models for assessing competitiveness, described in detail in 65.

The proposed approach to assessing the competitiveness of products can be a tool for determining the conformity of products to the criteria formulated above for a radically new product. If the product in question does not meet the criteria of a radically new one due to the application of the above mechanism given the sufficiency of resourcing, a new highly competitive product can be created or the competitive advantages of the existing one can be improved, the sufficiency of which can be assessed by the previously proposed method.

Defining the strategy for the transition to technological leadership based on an analysis of competitiveness and a game-theoretic approach

As a rule, high-tech companies are part of integrated structures that produce a wide range of products, use different management models and have different resources To define the strategy for the transition to technological leadership, it is necessary to identify the company that is most capable of advancing development in terms of producing radically new products of a certain type. To do this, consider the following tool.

Let each company be described by a numerical vector $P = (p1, p2, ..., pG)$. We will assume that the greater the value of each component of this vector, the better the company. Consider a method for comparing each pair of companies.

Consider two companies P and Q. Thus, we have two vectors: $P = (p1, p2, ..., pG)$ and $Q = (q1, q2, ..., qG)$.

We form a square matrix G×G with elements $aij = pi - qj$.

We denote this matrix by $A = \{aij\}$. We will consider this matrix in the context of an antagonistic game, i.e. games of two persons with opposite interests. Recall that the matrix game is implemented as follows. Each player has G strategies at his disposal.

[65] Chursin, A., Makarov, Y. Management of competitiveness: Theory and practice. Springer International Publishing. 2015. Pages 1-378. DOI: 10.1007/978-3-319-16244-7.

Moreover, each player independently chooses one strategy. Suppose that the first player has chosen strategy i, and the second player has chosen strategy j. Then the gain of the first player is determined by the number aij. Accordingly, the payoff of the second player is – aij.

We will be looking at a mixed expansion of this game. As strategies for the transition to technological leadership, we will use random variables that accepts values on a set of strategies. Since the set of strategies is a finite set with G elements, the mixed strategy of the first company is called a random variable ξ, which is given by the vector:

$x = (\xi 1, \xi 2, ..., \xi G), \xi g \geq 0, \xi 1 + \xi 2 + ... + \xi G = 1$.

Similarly, the mixed strategy of the second company is a random variable η, which is given by the vector:

$y = (\eta 1, \eta 2, ..., \eta G), \eta g \geq 0, \eta 1 + \eta 2 + ... + \eta G = 1$.

The gain (expressed in increasing or decreasing the level of competitiveness) of the first company in the case of mixed strategies is a number calculated by the formula: $H(x, y) = \sum \sum aij \cdot \xi i \cdot \eta j$, where the summation occurs by i and by j from 1 to G. Accordingly, the winning number of the second company is $H(x, y)$.

A pair of mixed strategies x * and y * is called an equilibrium situation in the game if for any mixed strategies x and y the following inequalities are satisfied:

$H(x, y^*) \leq H(x^*, y^*) \leq H(x^*, y)$.

In this case, the number $v = H(x^*, y^*)$ is called the price of the game.

According to Von Neumann's theorem, a matrix game always has an equilibrium situation and a game price in mixed strategies.

We will say that company P has a greater ability to transition to technological leadership relative to company Q if the game price $v > 0$.

For the actual calculation of the equilibrium strategies and the price of the game, you can use linear programming methods or iterative algorithms, for example, the well-known Brown-Robinson algorithm, which is also called the effective playing method. This approach allows us to consider the effectiveness of using various tools in the mechanism of managing the transition to technological leadership in terms of their impact on a company's ability to advance development and launch radically new products to the market.

II. Algorithm for managing the transition to technological leadership of companies when creating and selling radically new products, taking into account the development of a company and dynamically changing factors and risks Consider an algorithm for managing the transition to technological leadership of a company, taking into account the dynamics of the economic indicators of its activities and the technical characteristics of the products that arise under the control actions linked to the use of economic instruments. The algorithm is based on the approaches described above to assessing the competitiveness of products, as well as the proposed game-theoretic model for choosing the optimal strategy for the transition to technological leadership of a company. The implementation of this mechanism is carried out in several stages.

Stage 1. Processing of technical indicators of manufactured products.

At this stage, using the described algorithm for normalizing vectors with objective characteristics, we obtain the normalized values of the technical characteristics of the products. As a result, we obtain vectors Qk, the components of which are estimated in points $Qk = \{q10, q20, ..., qN0)$, $qn0 \in \{0, 1, 2, 3, 5\}$.

Stage 2. Convolution of product specifications.

After constructing dimensionless (normalized) vectors of output indicators, it is necessary to carry out convolutions of these indicators based on the information principle. Using the algorithm described above, it is necessary to calculate the information entropy for each product characteristic based on the division of a set of products into sets of the same type of products:

Qm, $m = 1, 2, ..., M$, $Qm \in Pr$,

where Pr is a set of products of the same type.

At this stage, it is possible to use weights that will reflect the importance of each indicator.

Stage 3. Creating a single vector for a company.

Each company under consideration is described by its own vector containing indicators of economic activity. These vectors should be expanded to vectors that should contain components for each product name. Moreover, if a company does not produce any product name, then the corresponding component of the vector is equal to zero, and if a company produces the corresponding product name, then the corresponding component of the vector is equal to the value of the collapsed production indicator. Thus, we obtain vectors Pm = (pm1, pm2, ..., pmG), m = 1, 2, ..., M.

Further, the obtained vectors must be normalized using an appropriate linear transformation pmg = α · pmg + β. This transformation should normalize the values of the components that reflect the indicators of the economic activity of a company. In this case, the choice of constants α and β should be carried out so that the corresponding components of the vector satisfy the conditions pmg ∈ [0, 1], and these indicators should be positive in the sense that a larger value of the indicator means a greater competitiveness of the company. The normalization of the components of the vector Pm that describe the products must be a scale normalization that depends on the numerical values. In this case, all components associated with manufactured products should be normalized to the same α > 0, and the value β = 0.

Stage 4. Creating matrices for the game comparison of companies, taking into account random factors and risks. Pairwise comparison and ranking of companies

After we have received normalized vectors describing each company, given the characteristics of its products, it is necessary to form game matrices for each pair of companies. Consider two companies P and Q. Thus, we have two vectors P = (p1, p2, ..., pG) and Q = (q1, q2, ..., qG). We form a square matrix G×G, denoted by A, with the elements aij = pi – qj + Fij,, where Fij are external factors and risks that affect the comparison of two companies and which can describe various random factors. In the implementation of the model, these factors can be described using random variables, for example, distributed according to the normal law Fij ~ N(m, σ2).

If these factors and risks can be positive for the first and for the second company, then the mathematical expectation parameter is zero: m = 0. If these factors are more favorable to the first company, then m > 0 should be chosen. In the case when the factors are positive for the second company, then you need to choose m < 0.

Using the obtained game matrices for each company, it is necessary to compare the ability of these companies to transition to technological leadership. To do this, using the Brown-Robinson algorithm, we calculate the price of the game for each pair of companies v. Based on the value of this game price (the sign of this value), we rank companies according to their ability to transition to technological leadership. For each company P, we calculate the quantitative characteristic of competitiveness using the following formula:

$$V(P) = \Sigma \, (v(P,Qm) + |v(P,Qm)|) \, / \, 2,$$

where the sum is taken for all companies, and through $v(P, Q)$ for companies Q and P, we consider the price of the game, where company P is considered as the first player, and company Q as the second.

After the numerical characteristic of its ability for technological leadership $V(P)$, is calculated for each company, it is possible to rank all the companies under consideration as follows: P1, P2, …, PM so that

$$V(P1) \geq V(P2) \geq \ldots \geq V(PM).$$

The results of ranking companies in terms of their capacity for technological leadership, given factors and risks, allow us to conclude that the company with the highest index has a greater ability to create a radically new product at a high rate and enter the market with it. Based on this principle, this algorithm allows supporting decision-making on choosing the most effective company capable of creating a certain radically new product, given that it has all the necessary resources.

Stage 5. Simulation of control actions that ensure the growth of a company's ability to technological leadership

The growth of a company's capacity for technological leadership is provided by tools for managing the competitiveness of products offered on the market (in the short term), as well as by improving the overall economic parameters of its activity (in the long term), which means that innovative activities to create unique products (or new markets), provided with sufficient resources, are harmonized with the development of the production system and business processes, accompanied by the economic sustainability of the company.

When applying competitiveness management tools, it is necessary to address the forecast values of the market capacity for radically new products and determine the most effective model for promoting products (including related services) to the market. A tool for assessing and predicting the available market capacity for created products can be used, which is described in detail in our research[66]. This tool allows you to predict the maximum possible market expansion in the future, given dynamically changing market factors.

The proposed game-theoretic approach can be used as the basis for the mechanism for launching radically new products on the market, taking into account dynamically changing factors and risks. Determining the strategy for the transition to technological leadership in the market allows predicting the actions of other players and dynamically changing factors of the economic environment and determining the optimal strategy for selling products. When building such a mechanism, it is necessary to take into account the following provisions:

the mechanism should reflect the scientific, technical and technological component of the development of radically new products, since the costs of pre-production, production and operation depend on their effectiveness;

the mechanism should take into account the costs (and their recovery) for the development and use of production infrastructure and infrastructure for the provision of services in the case of the implementation of the service business model;

the methodological apparatus of the mechanism should provide opportunities for simulating the management of the competitive characteristics of radically new products and their cost in order to maintain a competitive price in the market.

Let us consider an example of using the developed algorithms to determine a company's ability to transition to technological leadership (using the example of two organizations), which allows to focus resources and competencies on one of them that will allow a radically new product to enter the market.

---

[66] Tyulin A. Chursin A. The new Economy of the Product Life Cycle. Innovation and Design in the Digital Era // Springer International Publishing. – 2020. P.400

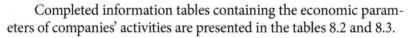

Completed information tables containing the economic parameters of companies' activities are presented in the tables 8.2 and 8.3.

Table 8.2 – Groups of indicators characterizing the economic condition of the company 1

№	Groups of indicators	№	Indicator Name, thousand rubles	Year 2017	2018	2019
	Financial and economic sustainability indicators		Revenues from sales	7 201	7 305	7 839
			Production and sales costs	6 843	6 927	7 275
			Accounts payable	2 075	1 755	2 988
			Receivables	1 344	2 336	182
			Profit	270	215	194
	Indicators of production and sales of products		R&D expenditure	3 409	4 657	6 663
			Cost of sales per ruble (ratio of cost of sales to revenue)	0,90	0,95	0,93

Table 8.3 – Groups of indicators characterizing
the economic condition of the company 2

№	Groups of indicators	№	Indicator Name, thousand rubles	Year		№
	Financial and economic sustainability indicators		Revenues from sales	1 438 928	1 461 630	1 896 404
			Production and sales costs	1 354 867	1 389 477	1 615 957
			Accounts payable	183 391	292 622	645 467
			Receivables	90 619	69 191	43 534
			Profit	1 234	1 491	1 993
	Indicators of production and sales of products		R&D expenditure	13 658	12 908	14 100
			Cost of sales per ruble (ratio of cost of sales to revenue)	0,87	0,95	0,85

Each of the companies produces 5 types of products, and the «Product 1», «Product 2» and «Product 3» of the first company are competitors of the «Product 1», «Product 2» and «Product 3» of the second company, and the «Product 4» and «Product 5» of the first company have no analogues produced by the second company.

Information tables describing the main parameters of the products of the first company are given in tables 8.4 and 8.5. At the same time, parameters 1 and 2 are positive for all types of products, and parameter 3 is negative.

Table 8.4. Description of the products of the first company

№	Product name	q_1	q_2	q_3
1	Product 1	55	350	250
2	Product 2	102	350	320
3	Product 3	140	600	430
4	Product 4	102	800	450
5	Product 5	140	600	540

Table 8.5. Description of the products of the second company

№	Product name	q_1	q_2	q_3
1	Product 1	65	250	200
2	Product 2	104	320	310
3	Product 3	170	500	130
4	Product 4	132	400	150
5	Product 5	240	460	270

Thus, as the initial data, we have vectors describing the economic indicators of the company (P1 corresponds to the first company, and P2 – to the second company):

$$P_1 = \begin{pmatrix} 7\,839 \\ 7\,275 \\ 2\,988 \\ 182 \\ 194 \\ 6\,663 \\ 0,93 \\ 2,75 \\ 20 \\ 18 \end{pmatrix}, \quad P_2 = \begin{pmatrix} 1896\,404 \\ 1615\,957 \\ 645\,467 \\ 43\,534 \\ 1\,993 \\ 14\,100 \\ 0,85 \\ 2,75 \\ 20 \\ 18 \end{pmatrix}$$

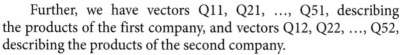
Further, we have vectors Q11, Q21, ..., Q51, describing the products of the first company, and vectors Q12, Q22, ..., Q52, describing the products of the second company.

$$Q_1^1 = \begin{pmatrix} 55 \\ 350 \\ 250 \end{pmatrix}, Q_2^1 = \begin{pmatrix} 102 \\ 350 \\ 320 \end{pmatrix}, Q_3^1 = \begin{pmatrix} 140 \\ 600 \\ 430 \end{pmatrix}, Q_4^1 = \begin{pmatrix} 102 \\ 800 \\ 450 \end{pmatrix}, Q_5^1 = \begin{pmatrix} 140 \\ 600 \\ 540 \end{pmatrix},$$

$$Q_1^2 = \begin{pmatrix} 65 \\ 250 \\ 200 \end{pmatrix}, Q_2^2 = \begin{pmatrix} 104 \\ 320 \\ 310 \end{pmatrix}, Q_3^2 = \begin{pmatrix} 170 \\ 500 \\ 530 \end{pmatrix}, Q_4^2 = \begin{pmatrix} 132 \\ 400 \\ 150 \end{pmatrix}, Q_5^2 = \begin{pmatrix} 240 \\ 460 \\ 270 \end{pmatrix}.$$

Next, we will describe the operation of the algorithm for normalizing vectors with technical characteristics of products, since to assess the company's ability to technological leadership, it is necessary to use normalized values of technical characteristics. We will evaluate each product metric with a finite number of points, for example, from zero to 5, i.e. qn0 ∈ {0, 1, 2, 3, 5}

The first 3 types of products are analogs (in pairs). Therefore, we apply to them the formulas qn0 = [5 · (qn − min) / (max − min)] for positive parameters and qn0 = 5 − [5 · (qn − min) / (max − min)] for negative parameters. Let us demonstrate how the algorithm works using the example of the first pair of products:

$$Q_1^1 = \begin{pmatrix} 55 \\ 350 \\ 250 \end{pmatrix}, Q_1^2 = \begin{pmatrix} 65 \\ 250 \\ 200 \end{pmatrix},$$

$$q_1^1 = 5 \cdot (55 - 55) / (65 - 55) = 0,$$

$$q_1^2 = 5 \cdot (65 - 55) / (65 - 55) = 5,$$

$$q_2^1 = 5 \cdot (350 - 250) / (350 - 250) = 5,$$

$$q_2^2 = 5 \cdot (250 - 250) / (350 - 250) = 0,$$

$$q_3^1 = 5 - 5 \cdot (250 - 200) / (250 - 200) = 0,$$

$$q_3^2 = 5 - 5 \cdot (200 - 200) / (250 - 200) = 5 /$$

$$\widetilde{Q}_1^1 = \begin{pmatrix} 0 \\ 5 \\ 0 \end{pmatrix}, \widetilde{Q}_1^2 = \begin{pmatrix} 5 \\ 0 \\ 5 \end{pmatrix}$$

Similarly, we obtain for other types of products:

$$\widetilde{Q}_2^1 = \begin{pmatrix} 0 \\ 5 \\ 0 \end{pmatrix}, \widetilde{Q}_2^2 = \begin{pmatrix} 5 \\ 0 \\ 5 \end{pmatrix}$$

$$\widetilde{Q}_2^1 = \begin{pmatrix} 0 \\ 5 \\ 5 \end{pmatrix}, \widetilde{Q}_2^2 = \begin{pmatrix} 5 \\ 0 \\ 0 \end{pmatrix}$$

For the obtained pairs of vectors, it is necessary to carry out convolution according to the information principle.

Using the example of the first pair of products, we will form a matrix, the rows of which describe the normalized indicators of both types of products:

$$\begin{pmatrix} 0 & 5 & 0 \\ 5 & 0 & 5 \end{pmatrix}$$

Further, for each column n = 1,2,3, we define the entropy by the formula Hn = H[on] = -Σ pi · log2pi, where the summation is by i from 0 to 5. As is customary in information theory, we assume that 0 · log20 = 0, pi = Mi / M (Mi is the number of times when the indicator n takes the value I ∈ {0,1,2,3,4,5}, M=2 is the number of products of the same type):

H1= -(0.5*(-1)+0.5*(-1))=1;
H2= -(0.5*(-1)+0.5*(-1))=1;
H3= -(0.5*(-1)+0.5*(-1))=1;

The convolution of production indicators, determined by the formula Qm = Σ Hn · qmn, gives the following results:

Q11=5,
Q12=10.

For other types of products, by analogy, we obtain the following results:

Q21=5,
Q22=10.
Q31=10,
Q32=5.

Next, it is necessary to evaluate a company's ability to lead in technology on the basis of a game-theoretic approach. To do this, we will form extended vectors of the company's indicators, supplemented by convolutions of the technical characteristics of the products. For types of products that have no analogues, produced by other companies, zero values must be placed in the extended vector. Extended vectors describing companies are as follows:

$$
P_1 = \begin{pmatrix} 7\,839 \\ 7\,275 \\ 2\,988 \\ 182 \\ 194 \\ 6\,663 \\ 0,93 \\ 2,75 \\ 20 \\ 18 \\ 5 \\ 5 \\ 10 \end{pmatrix}, \quad
P_2 = \begin{pmatrix} 1896\,404 \\ 1615\,957 \\ 645\,467 \\ 43\,534 \\ 1\,993 \\ 14\,100 \\ 0,85 \\ 2,75 \\ 20 \\ 18 \\ 10 \\ 10 \\ 5 \end{pmatrix}
$$

Normalizing these vectors leads to the following result:

$$
P_1 = \begin{pmatrix} 1,0000 \\ 0,9280 \\ 0,3811 \\ 0,0231 \\ 0,0246 \\ 0,8500 \\ 0,0000 \\ 0,0002 \\ 0,0024 \\ 0,0022 \\ 0,0005 \\ 0,0005 \\ 0,0012 \end{pmatrix}, \quad
P_2 = \begin{pmatrix} 1,000000 \\ 0,852116 \\ 0,340363 \\ 0,022956 \\ 0,001050 \\ 0,007435 \\ 0,000000 \\ 0,000001 \\ 0,000010 \\ 0,000009 \\ 0,000005 \\ 0,000005 \\ 0,000002 \end{pmatrix}
$$

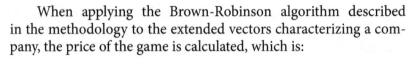

When applying the Brown-Robinson algorithm described in the methodology to the extended vectors characterizing a company, the price of the game is calculated, which is:

$$V(P_1, P_2) \approx -0.79$$

The negative value of the game price indicates that the second company has a greater capacity for technological leadership than the first one. As a result, a decision should be made to concentrate resources on areas that contribute to the development of the company and the effectiveness of creating radically new products and entering global markets.

The analysis of economic performance indicators and technical characteristics of the products allows us to conclude that the efficiency of the second company is achieved due to lower production and sales costs per unit of revenue, as well as since two of the three analog products have better technical characteristics compared to the products of the first company due to the formed radical properties of the products.

Next, we will describe in more detail the nature of the impact of each of the tools in the mechanism of managing the transition to technological leadership of companies based on the production and sale of radically new products and analyze the main aspects of innovative directions for ensuring technological leadership and advanced development of companies associated with the use of these tools in the context of achieving global competitive superiority.

8.2. THE MAIN ASPECTS OF INNOVATIVE AREAS OF TECHNOLOGICAL LEADERSHIP AND ADVANCED DEVELOPMENT OF A COMPANY

The technological leadership of a company means its ability to manufacture and sell products on international markets that surpass not only the products of domestic companies, but also foreign ones. The regulation of the process of achieving the global technological leadership of a company involves the use of a mechanism for managing the transition to the technological leadership of the company based on the manufacture and sale of radically new products, taking into account dynamically changing factors and risks. Appropriate tools aimed at scientific and technological capacity- building of a company make it possible to form the basis necessary for the creation of radically new products (products of advanced development), as well as generating its competitive advantages, were developed and presented above. Their interaction can be described in the form of the following mechanism for managing the achievement of a dominant position of products in the market (Figure 8.3).

The essence of the mechanism presented in Figure 8.3 is that the tools of the mechanism working in a complex contribute to the achievement of product dominance in the market in conditions of a high level of scientific and technological capacity, competencies and resourcing of a company, determined on the basis of the economic and mathematical apparatus described in detail in paragraph 3.1.

The operation of this mechanism must be managed so that when the entire set of tools is applied in practice, a company's activities are sufficiently affected, which is expressed in the timely release of highly competitive products, their renewal and holding (preserving) dominant positions in the market. In this regard, to ensure the effective operation of the mechanism, it is necessary to assess the following areas of the creation and retention of a company's technological leadership:

1) Assessment of a company's ability to form the competitive advantages of new products, allowing it to take a dominant position in the market.

2) Assessment of the effectiveness of the company in the field of updating the product line.

3) Assessment of a company's ability to transition to advanced development and achieve technological leadership.

Taking these assessments into account, as well as obtaining assessments of the scientific and technical capacity and competencies

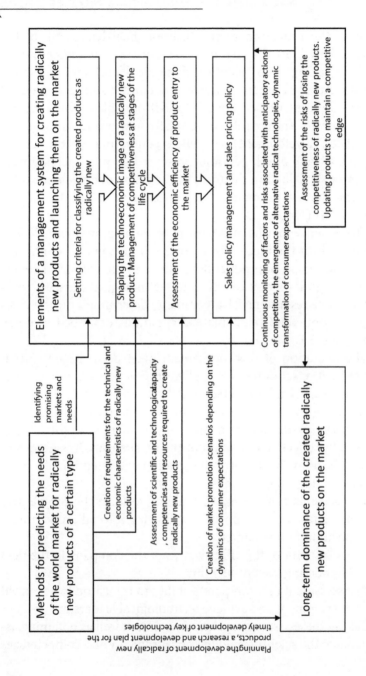

Figure 8.3 Mechanism for managing the achievement of a dominant position of products in the market

of the company, it is proposed to forecast the dynamics of the processes of achieving technological leadership. Modeling the dynamics of the development of scientific and technological capacity, competencies and competitiveness of a company is necessary to understand its ability to form the competitive advantages of new products, which is the basis for various innovative areas of achieving technological leadership. Creating a predictive trajectory of long-term innovative development can serve as an effective mechanism for purposeful regulation of a company's economic activity. In this regard, there is an urgent need to organize an effective system for monitoring its innovative activities in order to provide its management with the necessary information for preparing and making management decisions. This presupposes the development of an appropriate methodological base that reflects the essence and procedure for assessing the innovative potential of various areas of transition to technological leadership. At the same time, we note a number of features of innovative activities that affect the effectiveness of a company's capacity-building.

Thus, a number of features of the innovative activity of a company can be noted, depending on its size (for small and large companies). For example, a holding company that combines the technical, scientific and production competencies of a set of companies has a number of advantages that contribute to increasing its competitiveness due to its own technological platform, expanding sales markets for its products, increasing the profitability of a company through the consolidation of strategic resources, their flexible distribution among subsidiaries. The main economic effects connected with the creation of unified technological platforms on the basis of holdings are:

- the ability to defend the gained positions in the market and expand the sales markets for manufactured and developed products through the consolidation of financial, technical, technological, design and production capabilities;
- organization of a generational change of manufactured products by attracting financial and intellectual capabilities and thereby increasing the competitiveness of the products manufactured by a holding.

- increasing the profitability of a company through the consolidation of strategic resources, their flexible distribution among the participants in rational intra-company pricing, reduction of financial, production, technological and other risks due to their distribution among the members of a holding.

Based on the analysis of the listed effects, it can be concluded that the driver of forming competitive advantages of products is the accumulation of scientific and technological capacity, competencies and resources based on integrated structures and their technological platforms.

An assessment of the economic benefits arising from the merger of high-tech companies on the basis of a single technological platform of a holding allows us to draw an important conclusion about the need to manage these benefits influenced by factors related to such a merger. The management of these factors consists in the implementation of a set of measures aimed at increasing the economic effect from the merger of companies into a holding structure due to the concentration of resources and equal access to all the advantages accumulated on the basis of the technological platform, which makes it possible to effectively involve new technologies in the creation and production of products capable of hold a dominant position in the market. At the same time, it is advisable to conduct a preliminary assessment and further monitoring of a company's innovative capacity.

Above, the issue of the scientific and technological capacity-building of a company was considered, its components were highlighted (various types of resources and factors, including production and technological, financial and economic, intellectual, research and other resources necessary for the implementation of innovative activities), as well as the criteria and methods of their quantitative assessment were defined for each component. On this basis, we will model the impact of the level of a company's scientific and technological capacity on the creation of competitive

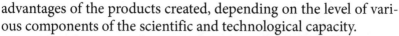
advantages of the products created, depending on the level of various components of the scientific and technological capacity.

Depending on the specific economic situation corresponding to a certain level of scientific and technological capacity, let us consider two situations of achieving competitive advantages of the products being created. According to the first situation, in order to achieve a certain level of competitive advantages of products, it is necessary to master a fundamentally new or basic production technology. The total costs (C) for the implementation of the relevant procedures related to the scientific and technological capacity- building, competencies and the development of technologies are amount to Σ NT = 237 550 c.u. According to the second situation, the company has a scientific and technological capacity and competencies, the level of which allows mastering the technology at a lower cost. The costs in this case are significantly less and amount to Σ IT = 142 780 c.u. Based on the simulation results, we will assess the impact of the capacity of each of the companies on the maximum economic opportunities for the effective implementation of measures to achieve the competitive characteristics of the products being created. To do this, first, we will calculate the level of the financial and economic component of the innovative capacity, for which we will evaluate such particular indicators as the sufficiency of our own working capital, long-term loans and short-term loans for the creating reserves and the normal provision of costs of current production and economic activities (Wc, OC, EΣ). Then, on the basis of the obtained indicators, we find the values that give an estimate of the size of sources to cover production costs, given the possibilities of surplus or shortage of own working capital ($\pm$Wc), as well as attracting long-term ($\pm$OC) and short-term ($\pm$ EΣ) borrowed sources. When analyzing these values, we will also include the costs related to the implementation of two variants of innovative development strategies (Σ NT and Σ IT). This will allow you to evaluate the financial and economic capabilities of a company to achieve competitive advantages of the products.

Table 8.6. Analysis of the scientific and technological capacity of companies

Indicator	Symbol and calculation	Financial and economic indicators	
		Situation 1 (low capacity)	Situation 2 (high capacity)
Sources of own funds	OF	5 724 869	5 724 869
Fixed assets	F	7 436 724	7 436 724
Own working capital	Wc= OF – F	- 1 711 855	-1 711 855
Long-term loans and borrowed funds	BF	3 850 000	3 850 000
Availability of own working capital and long-term loans	OC = Wc + BF	2 138 145	2 138 145
Short-term loans and borrowings	BF	670 000	670 000
The total value of the main sources of formation of stocks and costs	EΣ = OC + BF	2 808 145	2 808 145
Amount of stocks and costs	Z	1 964 273	1 964 273
Surplus (shortage) of own working capital for the formation of inventories and costs	± Ec = Ec – Z	- 3 676 128	- 3 676 128
Surplus (shortage) of own working capital and long-term borrowed sources for the formation of inventories and costs	± OC = OC – Z	+ 173 872	+ 173 872
Surplus (shortage) of the total amount of sources for the formation of inventories and costs	± EΣ = EΣ – Z	+ 843 872	+ 843 872
Three-dimensional indicator of the type of financial strength	S	(0; 1; 1)	(0; 1; 1)
The cost of implementing new technology	Σ NT	237 550	–
the development strategy: improving technology	Σ IT	–	142 780

Surplus (shortage) of own circulating assets for the formation of production costs and development:	new technology	$\pm Ec = Ec - Z - \Sigma\,NT$	- 3 913 676	—
	improving technology	$\pm Ec = Ec - Z - \Sigma\,NT$	—	- 3 818 908
Surplus (shortage) of own circulating assets and long-term borrowed sources for the formation of inventories and costs and development:	Surplus (shortage) of own circulating assets and long-term borrowed sources for the formation of inventories and costs and development:	$\pm Ec = Ec - Z - \Sigma\,IT$	- 63 678	—
		$\pm OC = OC - Z - \Sigma\,IT$	—	+ 31 092
Surplus (shortage) of the total amount of sources for the formation of inventories and costs and development:	Surplus (shortage) of the total amount of sources for the formation of inventories and costs and development:	$\pm E\Sigma = E\Sigma - Z - \Sigma\,NT$	+ 606 322	—
		$\pm E\Sigma = E\Sigma - Z - \Sigma\,IT$	—	+ 701 092
Three-dimensional indicator of the type of innovation sustainability (potential)	Three-dimensional indicator of the type of innovation sustainability (potential)	Three-dimensional indicator of the type of innovation sustainability (potential)	(0; 0; 1)	(0; 1; 1)

The analysis of the scientific and technological capacity allows us to draw the following main conclusions. In the initial situation, a company has normal financial stability and solvency, effectively uses borrowed funds and is characterized by high profitability of production activities. However, if the inventory and costs include the costs of implementing innovative areas to ensure technological leadership, the situation changes.

In particular, if it is necessary to master the basic technology (situation 1), a company may lose its financial stability. This is evidenced by the financial indicator $\pm O_c$. From this we can conclude that the company does not yet have sufficient financial and economic resources to implement the new technology, and it needs to additionally build up its scientific and technological capacity.

The second situation arises due to favorable financial and economic conditions. The costs of engaging improving innovation in the economic turnover are not so high, so the company is able to provide them. In this case, the financial indicators after the introduction of improving innovation show a positive trend, and the company has sufficient innovation and investment opportunities.

Based on the model calculations described above, if in the first situation a company started to develop a new technology without a preliminary assessment of the scientific and technological capacity, it would not have enough funds to complete the project. This could result in a lack of funds to support the current production and economic activities, or lead to a temporary suspension and freezing of the process of creating products. Delaying the timing of the implementation of innovations leads to an increase in work in progress, which is undesirable and is regarded as an irrational use of invested capital. The suspension of an innovation project may also contribute to the development of the risk of delayed commercialization. When products are ready to be launched on the market, they may already be outdated. To avoid such a situation, a mechanism for timely updating the product range is needed, for which a strategy for achieving technological leadership is formed. In this regard, the level of scientific and technological capacity, competencies and competitiveness of a company determines the effectiveness of measures to update its product line.

Assessment of the economic efficiency of new products developed to replace the manufactured ones is carried out not at the stage of their implementation, but at the stage of development in industrial production. Therefore, the effect of the development is inherently potential, it is actually realized only in the application of these products to the consumer. Its value may differ from the value of the effect determined at the development stage, due to different production volumes, more advanced production technology, and other factors.

The change of generations of manufactured products occurs under the condition of a decrease in its consumer value or, if necessary, a decrease in its cost. For this reason, it is necessary to constantly monitor changes in these factors and, if they change, take intensive measures to launch products that are developed instead of manufactured ones, corresponding to the technical and cost characteristics that ensure an increase in production volumes. Under these conditions, the acceleration of the turnover of product generations should be considered as the achievement of an economically feasible increase in market performance on the smallest possible number of manufactured products by identifying and using the potential of the design of the basic sample and the design technology of manufacturing each of its modifications, creating additional competitive advantages.

The acceleration of generational turnover should be achieved by increasing the increase in market performance from product to product and from modification to modification, thereby reducing both the number of modifications and the number of products of each modification required to achieve the required increase in market performance.

In this regard, it is necessary to organize effective management of the activities of high-tech companies, aimed at achieving advanced development as the main stage on the path to technological leadership.

The result of the management of the advanced development of a company is its achievement of technological leadership, which presupposes the following constant components:

- shaping the image of "products of the future" and promising product lines;
- creation and development of technological and product competence centers;
- conducting applied scientific and technological research of the sixth wave of innovation;
- technical re-equipment for the sixth wave of innovation;
- effective transfer and application of knowledge and technologies of fundamental science and the global information space.

Practical approaches to achieving technological leadership can be implemented according to three scenarios of company development: traditional, moderate market and progressive market. However, in the context of external factors of uncertainty, one of the key conditions for the competition in world markets can be effective consolidation of assets in order to concentrate scientific and technical, production and technological, human and financial resources of the industry and counter the negative effect of intra-industry competition. Industrial companies are various corporations, holdings, integrated structures, independent companies. Both between different corporations and within their structure, existing and created production and technological assets, capacities are largely duplicated, the same research and development of new products are carried out in parallel due to distributed budget investments (mainly in technologies of the fourth and fifth waves of innovation) according to the principle of supporting a company's economy in order to solve the problem of breakthrough technological growth and, thereby, the development of scientific and technical competencies and technologies in general slows down. All this negatively affects the ability of high-tech corporations to adequately compete with global players in the world market. These prerequisites determine one of the most important factors when choosing a scenario for the transition to technological leadership – the degree of consolidation of scientific and technological capacity, competencies, resources (assets) in companies, industries and technology platforms, which affects their ability to effectively participate in global global competition.

Scenario I. Traditional (low or medium level of consolidation in the industry, focus on traditional consumers and government customers).

In the traditional scenario, the structure and composition of a company's assets do not change. Intra-industry competition is becoming tougher, both between integrated structures and between public and private companies, as well as large holdings that compete with each other. However, the resistance to competition is weakened due to the negative effect of this very competition – budget resources and company's own funds are "scattered" (small funds are allocated to all assets, which are enough to maintain the current level of production and wage payments, but insufficient for a serious technological and market breakthrough).

Commercial areas are not developing, as the activities of corporations are focused on the state market in the conditions of unconditional fulfillment of state orders.

In addition, there is no factor of international competition due to the priorities for the production of goods for the domestic market and the traditional consumer.

This scenario is the most risky, since companies, in fact, become players in the market of a single buyer (monopsony) and their activities are sensitive to the financial capabilities and needs of the traditional consumer, and internal industry competition does not contribute to the development of key areas and the creation of competitive products that meet the expectations of global consumers.

Scenario II. Moderate market (medium level of consolidation of high-tech industry assets and high degree of market orientation).

All high-tech companies maintain their independence and structure, while continuing to compete with each other and private organizations.

But at the same time, each company creates independent (within its single strategy) market-oriented holdings that have their own technological platform, and develops production and product competence centers. The model of interaction of all organizations of the structure is transformed from competitive into partner: the holdings work by strengthening other holdings with their competencies in cooperation on the basis of a single technological platform.

The company is actively acquiring key competencies by purchasing startups, small innovative organizations and serial factories that are competitors across the entire spectrum of technologies.

Internal competition persists at the first stages of the scenario, gradually decreasing as the centers of competence are built and their competitive advantages are increased. International competition will increase more intensively than in the progressive market scenario, and the holdings will become full-fledged world-class players, competing with leading companies, under the pressure from other organizations entering the global market. The effectiveness of the moderate market scenario of the advanced development of the company is linked to the long-term economic effect of the release of competitive products due to the synergistic effect of the simultaneous achievement of a high level of scientific and technological capacity and competencies in conditions of sufficient resourcing for innovative activities.

Consider the scientific and technological capacity, competencies and resources of a company from the point of view of their non-linear relationship to achieve a long-term economic effect from the creation of competitive advantages of products based on the introduction of innovations caused by the resulting synergistic component as a result of simultaneously high values of these parameters.

Innovation is based on the unique competencies and scientific and technological capacity of a company and its employees

Here the following process arises: competencies-investments-innovations-implementation process-obtaining qualitatively new highly competitive products or radically improving existing products by creating additional competitive advantages. It should be noted that a relatively small amount of investment in innovative products can lead to a significant result – this product will be in demand due to the synergistic effects in a company's economy. Synergistic innovation can occur in both radical and gradual change in products.

Synergetic innovations are characterized by the fact that their creation uses the summing effect of the interaction of two or more factors that form the scientific and technological capacity and competencies of a company (production experience, equipment, technological or marketing competencies), while their effect significantly exceeds the effect of each individual component in the form of their simple sum. Synergistic innovation can rely on end-to-end technologies, technology platforms of companies, which are based on unique technological competencies.

The essence of synergetic innovation is the company's implementation of partial changes that allow it to improve previously mastered products within the established organizational structures and business trends. A competitive technical advantage is created and maintained over the long term, which can lead to long-term market dominance.

The synergistic effect of such innovations is manifested in the fact that innovations become the initial basis for increasing the competitiveness of products, expanding and strengthening market positions, mastering new areas of application of knowledge, in other words, an active means of production. In this case, innovative activity in a short time translates scientific discoveries into practice, and for this reason, a higher level of management of all production processes is achieved. As a result, the company is able to achieve high results at the lowest cost.

To mathematically describe the achieved synergetic effect, the above-mentioned model of the law of advanced satisfaction of prospective needs can be used. According to this dynamic model, the qualitative development of innovative technologies results in the creation and rapid development of new consumer markets, while the development of consumer markets leads to a further increase in financing for the development of key competencies and the creation of innovative technologies. Thus, a spiraling mutual development of new technologies, as well as the acquisition of new key competencies and the creation and development of new consumer markets and the advanced development of the manufacturer arise. The basis of the dynamic model of the law of advanced satisfaction of prospective needs are the following variables:

$EK(t)$ – quantitative assessment of the level of key competencies;

$IP(t)$ – quantitative indicator of scientific and technological capacity;

$Q(t)$ – quantitative indicator of product competitiveness.

The relationship between indicators is described by the following system of differential equations:

$$\begin{cases} \dot{EK}(t) = F_1(EK(t), IP(t), Q(t)), \\ \dot{IP}(t) = F_2(EK(t), IP(t), Q(t)), \\ \dot{Q}(t) = F_3(EK(t), IP(t), Q(t)), \end{cases} \tag{*}$$

The conditions contributing to the achievement of a synergistic effect of a high level of scientific and technological capacity and competencies of a company can be set as follows::

$$F_1(t, EK(t)) = \begin{cases} \beta_i, t > T \\ 0, t < T \end{cases} \quad F_2(t, IP(t)) = \begin{cases} \gamma_i, t > T \\ 0, t < T \end{cases} \tag{**}$$

$$\beta_i \equiv const, \; \gamma_i \equiv const$$

Such assignment of functions describing the dynamics of the levels of scientific and technological capacity and competencies corresponds to the constant high level of these parameters.

To determine a company's ability to develop at a faster pace in this economic and mathematical model, it is necessary to establish a lower limit of competitiveness for those types of products that should ensure its advanced development. Exceeding the lower limit of competitiveness indicates the ability of a company to develop at a faster pace.

Based on the above, using the economic and mathematical model (*), we can plot curves of changes in the competitiveness of products in the conditions of its development at a faster pace as a result of the synergistic effect due to the high level of scientific and technological capacity, competencies and resourcing. To plot the curves according to the economic and mathematical model (*), it is necessary to set the initial level of product competitiveness, as well as the functions of the dynamics of the levels of scientific and technological capacity and competencies (**).

Figure 8. 4 shows a view of solving the system of equations of the model, taking into account the constant management of the scientific and technological capacity, the company's competencies, as well as the competitiveness of released and manufactured products. As the

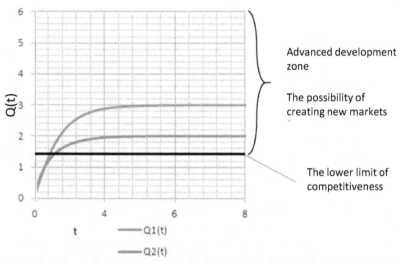

Figure 8.4 The ability of a company to achieve a synergistic effect in the context of a high level of scientific and technological capacity and competencies

* The lower limit of competitiveness is the minimum necessary but insufficient condition for achieving advanced development.

lower limit of the advanced development in the given model situation, the conditional value Q(t) = 1.5 is accepted (in the real situation, the revenue from the sale of products in the market or the share of products in the target market can be considered as the values of Q(t). Competitiveness indicators for two types of products Q1(t) and Q2(t) cross the lower limit of advanced development at times t1 = 1.2 and t2 = 1.5, respectively. Further, the values of the competitiveness indicators Q1(t) and Q2(t) are above the limit of advanced development and stabilize at the level Q1(t) = 3 and Q2(t) = 2 at time t = 5. Thus, for this model example, a conclusion can be drawn about the possibility of a company's development at a faster pace due to the release of the considered types of products, which became possible as a result of the achievement of the level of scientific and technological capacity and competencies of the company. These products, created on the basis of a company's unique competencies with high commercial capacity, will be able to form a new market for high-tech products or occupy a significant segment of an existing

387

market, provided that the company implements advanced development measures.

Scenario III. Progressive market (a high level of consolidation of scientific and technological capacity, competencies and resources of the high-tech industry and a high degree of market orientation).

All high-tech companies position their assets as centers of competence in their field. The model of interaction between all key companies and private organizations on the basis of a single technology platform is of a partnership nature. They work with product and technology profiles and competencies clearly described and approved in their strategies. In this scenario, the most effective solution would be to combine all companies and other organizations of the same industry into a single organizational and economic structure, managed from a single center of the technology platform. Companies can consist of divisions – independent (within the general strategy of the holding) market companies for specific, narrower product market niches. Such companies are active in the M&A market, acquiring key competencies and buying businesses, startups in all technological areas.

In this case, competition among high-tech companies will rapidly decline. However, international competition will increase – the holdings will become full-fledged world-class players. Market key performance indicators (capitalization, market share, operational efficiency, profit, etc.) are set by the holding companies.

Advanced development, accompanied by an increase in scientific and technological capacity, competencies and resources, can lead to an intellectual explosion, as a result of which technologies are created that serve as a base for creating radically new products, as well as production equipment of a new class that changes the existing production paradigm. Thus, an innovative resonance is achieved – an extremely rapid technological progress, consisting in the creation of radically new products based on advanced technologies and means of production in the form of productive, automated and intellectualized machines.

Thus, due to the continuous development of competencies and periodically occurring intellectual explosions, there is a gradual reduction in the number and complexity of work currently carried out at various stages of product creation, which reduces the cost of its development and production and, consequently, the cost of finished products, as well as reduces the risks of going beyond the set cost of the future product created on the basis of new technologies. Thus, new products with high consumer properties become more affordable for a wide range of consumers, which determines the growth of the consumer market.

In order to ensure the growth of the consumer market and the short terms of achieving technological leadership, the law of advanced satisfaction of prospective needs can also be applied, the mathematical interpretation of which is based on the equation (*). If we consider this system from the standpoint of achieving innovative resonance, which is based on the extremely rapid technological progress of a company, then modeling allows to determine the time to achieve innovative resonance and the effect of increasing the competitiveness of products to a level that allows it to be classified as radically new, providing the company with technological leadership in the market.

The spasmodic effect observed during the innovation resonance is defined by the following functions of the system (*), which describe the dynamics of a company's scientific and technological capacity and competencies:

$$F_1(t, EK(t)) = \begin{cases} \beta_i(EK(t)), t \in \Omega \\ 0, t \notin \Omega \end{cases} \quad F_2(t, IP(t)) = \begin{cases} \beta_i(IP(t)), t \in \Omega \\ 0, t \notin \Omega \end{cases} \quad (***)$$

Here $\beta_i > 0$ is the coefficient that determines the nature of the acceleration of the growth rate of scientific and technological capacity and competencies, and

$$\Omega = \bigcup_{i=1}^{p} [t_i, t_i + \Delta_i]$$

dividing a time interval into segments.

In this case, the curves that are the solution to the system of equations for the economic and mathematical model (*), describing the law of advanced satisfaction of promising needs, clearly demonstrate the emergence of innovative resonance with

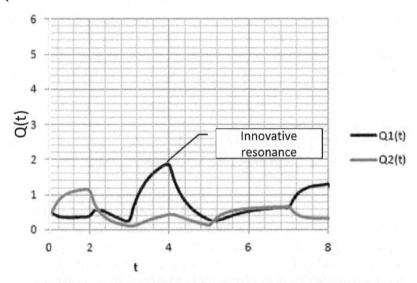

Figure 8.5. Creating innovative resonance in the context of dynamic development of a company's economic characteristics

the simultaneous extremely rapid growth of scientific and technological capacity, competencies and resourcing of a company, which are the basis for creating a radical new products and their launch on the market. To plot curves illustrating the effect of innovation resonance, according to the economic and mathematical model (*), it is necessary to set the initial level of product competitiveness, as well as the functions of the dynamics of the levels of scientific and technological capacity and competencies (***).

Let us describe the process of the emergence of innovative resonance, shown in Fig. 8.5 At the moment of time t = 4, there is an abrupt increase in the competitiveness of products as a result of the simultaneous rapid growth of scientific and technological capacity, competencies and resourcing, determined by the conditions (***) corresponding to a high level of consolidation of scientific and technological capacity, competencies and resources of the high-tech industry, and their achievement of the maximum possible values in the existing economic conditions. The increase in competitiveness gained through the solution of the system (*) indicates the creation of radically new products, due to which a company achieves technological leadership in a short time.

The progressive market scenario involves a more efficient structure, production system, and management system of a company than the moderate market scenario. In addition, the progressive market scenario will require fewer resources and ensure greater competitiveness by consolidating the company's scientific and technological capacity, competencies and resources, creating conditions for the emergence of the innovative resonance, thereby ensuring an accelerated transition to technological leadership.

Choosing one of the considered scenarios, a high-tech company can choose the pace of increasing its presence in many niches, focusing and developing only promising and critical products and technologies, and not "diluting" resources into oversized and underutilized assets.

In order for a high-tech company to achieve technological leadership in the market, it is necessary to form a scenario that focuses on the development of technologies of the sixth wave of innovation. Only in this case, based on new technologies, projects can be launched to create equipment and systems that surpass their world counterparts in their characteristics. Technologies should develop at a faster pace than design and product tasks. Otherwise, companies will always be catching up players – both in traditional markets and in new ones.

8.3. THEORETICAL FOUNDATIONS FOR CREATING OF A UNIFIED METHODOLOGY FOR ENSURING THE ADVANCED DEVELOPMENT OF A COMPANY

It was shown above that a company that strives for advanced development and technological leadership must ensure that its own basic technologies develop faster than its closest competitors. Ensuring the advanced development of a company is a systematic task, the solution of which is to develop a set of theoretical and practical provisions that determine the achievement of global competitive advantage. In our opinion, the methodology of complex activity can be adopted as a theoretical basis for such a systematic approach[67]. One of the complex activities is the creation of radically new products, which is the basis of a company's technological leadership.

When forming a methodology for ensuring the advanced development of a company based on the creation of radically new products, it is necessary to rely on certain patterns that accompany economic activity. These patterns are expressed by classical economic laws. The first group includes laws that have a direct impact on the processes of creating products with high consumer properties: the law of value, the law of demand, the law of supply, the law of increasing marginal costs. The second group includes laws that do not directly affect the competitiveness of products, but are interrelated with the processes of production and consumer behavior, which in turn is decisive in the competition in the market. This includes laws that affect competitiveness through the laws of the first group: the law of diminishing productivity of factors of production, the law of diminishing returns, the law of diminishing marginal utility, the law of optimal consumer behavior, and the law of comparative advantage. Obviously, not all laws affect the production and sale of goods and services in the same way. In addition, there is a strong interaction of these laws with each other. Thus, the laws of diminishing marginal utility and optimal consumer behavior change demand, and demand, as already noted, changes the competitiveness of products. The law of comparative advantage affects the law of value, and the laws of diminishing productivity of factors of production and diminishing returns affect the law of increasing marginal costs.

The methodology for ensuring the company's advanced development based on the creation of radically new products should also be based on new economic laws. Moreover, if the classical laws are mostly based on psychological and retrospective observations and do not take into account various factors of negative impact, then the new ones that function in the digital economy should be described and justified strictly mathematically. Management

---

[67] Belov M.V., Novikov D.A. Structure of methodology of complex activity// Ontology of design. 2017. No. 4 (26).

of the competitiveness of an economic facility, incl. radically new products, should be based on mathematically grounded provisions and axioms, methodological tools for assessing the competitiveness of products, as well as risks and various negative environmental factors. We have described such methodological tools above. The economic laws that expand and concretize the creation of the competitiveness of radically new products are the laws of interaction between the development of competencies and consumer markets and the advanced development of the manufacturer, as well as the law of advanced satisfaction of prospective needs, which is justified above.

The listed laws can be presented as a flowchart that reflects the influence of economic laws on the efficiency of creating radically new products and the sustainable development of a company, as well as the complex relationship and interaction of laws, resulting in the advanced development of the manufacturer.

The flowchart presented in Figure 8.6 illustrates the relationship between economic laws and the processes of managing a company's advanced development, the achievement of the effectiveness of which is a priority task on the way to ensuring its advanced development through creating radically new products.

The created methodology, as shown in Figure 8.6, is influenced by the main economic laws. The methodological apparatus of the created methodology used in the digital economy should be described and justified strictly mathematically and consider the risks and various dynamically changing environmental factors.

Summarizing the results of the study of the processes of development, production and promotion of radically new products, we can conclude that the generation of competitive advantages occurs throughout the entire product life cycle. At each stage, a company's existing competencies are aimed at solving various tasks in order to achieve the target result, which is manifested in the high price and non-price competitiveness of the radically new products being created.

The above production procedures ensure the transformation of scientific and technological capacity and competencies into

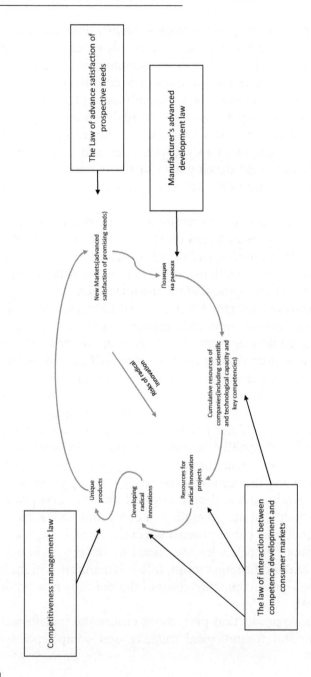

Figure 8.6. The impact of economic laws on ensuring a company's advanced development based on the development of radically new products

a radically new product with given techno-economic characteristics and a competitive price, using the created products with a high technical level.

The main theoretical principle of creating a methodology is the use of a set of laws and axioms developed by the authors, as well as the adaptation of a systematic approach to the creation of effective control actions to ensure the advanced development of a company.

Another principle of creating a methodology is the development of economic mechanisms and methodological tools to ensure the effective application of the methodology in a company's practical activities to regulate the increase of its technical and technological levels and ensure its advanced development based on the creation of radically new products.

Based on the interaction of methodological tools and mechanisms within the proposed methodology, the practical regulation of the process of creation of radically new products is built as follows. Using the methods of forecasting the future needs of the world market, the requirements for radically new characteristics of the products being created are determined (technical characteristics that significantly exceed the competitors' offers available on the market; the first application for more effective solution of existing problems; compliance of price characteristics with the capabilities of the buyer; the ability to meet the current and future needs of buyers, while occupying a high market share (market dominance); the ability to radically transform established patterns of consumer behavior, etc.). The assessment of the characteristics of a radically new product in the future allows to shape its techno-economic image, determine the level of competitiveness both in relation to existing on the market and promising samples, as well as determine a competitive price and plan the necessary research and development for the creation of products.

Based on this analysis, the developed methodology suggests forming a technological roadmap for creating radically new products, which, in particular, sets requirements for the terms of creating the necessary technological solutions, due to which radically new product characteristics are achieved, and also determines the necessary

resources (financial, information, competencies, etc.). When forming a technological roadmap for creating radically new products,
various factors and risks are taken into account, which can increase
the time or cost of product development, as well as change its competitiveness.

The generated technological roadmap goes into the management system for the development of radically new products, which
determines the techno-economic image of the products, given
the need to achieve a high level of competitiveness, as well as to establish its cost at various stages of the life cycle. Within the management system for the development of radically new products, its
price competitiveness is also formed, and the price policy of sales
is set taking into account various risks. It also assesses a company's
ability to create a radically new product and makes the necessary
decisions to develop production competencies.

Gradually implementing the steps described in the methodology, we reach the point of bringing the created radically new products to the markets. The decision to launch radically new products
is made based on a set of numerical parameters (competitiveness,
competitive price, cost at various stages of the life cycle, the level
of risks of loss of competitiveness, the ability to manufactured
the developed product, etc.), determined by the methodological
apparatus of the methodology.

If these numerical parameters are considered insufficient for
management decision-making, the system signals the need to adjust the techno-economic image of the product to achieve high values of competitiveness, price and other estimated indicators. In this
case, the methodology provides for an analysis using the available
tools to determine the values of the parameters that ensure a sufficient change in the techno-economic image based on the involvement of additional competencies, resources or innovations.

The description of the main components of the complex activity in accordance with the proposed methodology allows us to create a complex logical structure, which can be represented as the following graphical model (Figure 8.7), each element of which was
discussed in detail above.

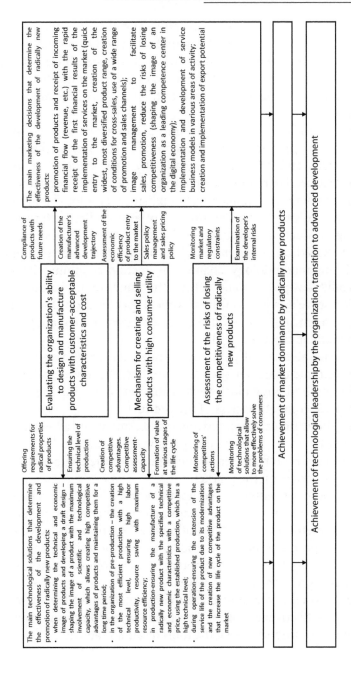

Figure 8.7. Components of activities that confine the methodology for ensuring the advanced development of a company based on the creation of radically new products

Based on the above logical structure and the research results obtained, it is possible to form the main blocks of the methodology, which include the tools and mechanisms discussed above, which allows to calculate and regulate the main economic indicators that are the result of calculations for each of their stages of the methodology being formed.

Based on the list of the main techno-economic parameters that characterize the products, the subsystem for determining the prospective needs and criteria for a radically new product defines the main prospective requirements for it on the part of consumers, as well as restrictions that allow us establish criteria for classifying products as radically new. The process of establishing criteria for classifying products as radically new is described in detail in paragraph 4.1. Based on the identified limitations, the corresponding block of the methodology shapes the techno-economic image of a radically new product and defines the values of its characteristics, which serve as a basis of the technical specifications for product development, and depending on these characteristics, the product development process is built.

The generated set of parameter values corresponding to the techno-economic characteristics of a product is received at the input of the methodology block responsible for managing the price and non-price competitiveness of the product.

Thus, the technical competitiveness assessment unit allows to assess competitiveness based on a comparison of the set of techno-economic parameters transmitted to the input with the characteristics of existing products on the market.

The unit for assessing the competitive price of products based on a given set of techno-economic parameters of the created product and the parameters of competitors allows to determine the competitive price of products and set a pricing policy for selling products in the market and determine the potential sales volume of radically new products given the market capacity,

The tools of the competitiveness management unit allow to evaluate the cost-effectiveness of the development and implementation of radically new products using the tools discussed above.

The output data of the described methodology blocks is received at the input of a company's examination block assessing the readiness to develop a radically new product, where a decision is made on the possibility of developing products with the considered set of techno-economic characteristics. If the numerical parameters received at the input of the examination block are considered insufficient, the tool for assessing a company's readiness to create a product signals the need to achieve a sufficient technical level of production, with a view to ensuring high values of competitiveness, price and other estimated indicators that indicate the possibility of creating conditions for the company to transition to advanced development.

Based on the description of the blocks of the methodology and the above theoretical principles of its construction, it is possible to build a general scheme of the methodology for ensuring the advanced development of a company based on the creation of radically new products (Fig. 8.8).

As can be seen from this scheme, it consists of the tools and mechanisms developed by us earlier, the joint action of which allows to form a sufficient level of scientific and technological capacity and competencies of a company, to master and introduce innovative technologies, to ensure a sufficient technical level of production, etc.

Let us consider the aspects of the practical application of the methodology in terms of the selection of one of the above-described scenarios of a company's advanced development.

The growth of a company's ability to create a radically new product is linked to increasing its scientific and technological capacity and competencies, in particular, improving and optimizing products, creating new technologies, increasing labor productivity through digitalization and automation, introducing intelligent management systems for the company as a large organizational and economic system. Informatization and development of information processing and transmission environments is based on the constant creation and introduction of innovative solutions.

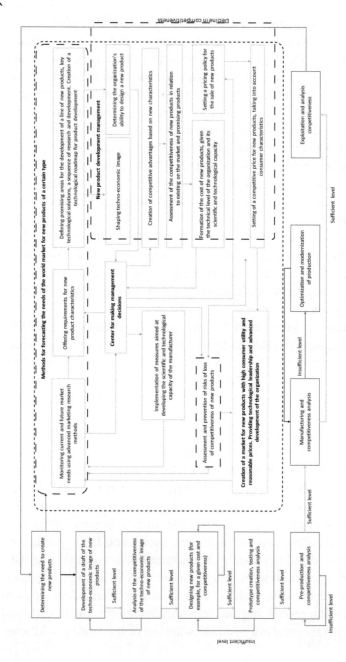

Figure 8.8 Scheme of the methodology for ensuring a company's advanced development based on the creation of radically new products

Naturally, in this case, informatization is considered as a means of increasing competitiveness, and information as a of product or service, the acquisition and use of which increases the efficiency of the company in terms of developing new products. We have a cyclical process: the broad development of informatization contributes to the search, development and introduction of innovative solutions, the generation of new radical competencies (including those reaching the intersectoral level), which allows to shape the techno-economic image of products in accordance with the promising needs of the market and, therefore, to increase competitiveness, which which will increase the volume of sales of products and services.

The above-mentioned cyclical process requires, first of all, industrial companies to use informatization as a tool for creating virtual intersectoral clusters of competencies for effective management and achievement of competitive advantages throughout the entire cycle of design, production, and sales of products, which is possible only with the development of the information infrastructure of large organizational and economic automated systems operating in all areas of a company's activities and contributing to the generation of intersectoral level competencies. Such an infrastructure ensures the creation of popular products using digital production technologies focused on the need to achieve a given level of competitiveness in the market, given the personification of needs, the increasing intellectual potential resulting from the accumulation and synthesis of competencies of companies and society.

The pace of achieving technological leadership depends on the advanced development scenario that can be selected by a company.

The choice of the target scenario is based on the possibility of achieving advanced development by the company using methodological tools that underlie the mechanism for creating and selling products with high consumer utility. This choice can be made using the tables 8.7 and 8.8.

Table 8.7 – Relationship between the level of concentration of company assets and the achievement of global competitive advantage

Market factor	Asset concentration level		
	Low «Traditional» scenario	Average «Moderate market» scenario	High «Progressive market» scenario
Global competitiveness	K – R – C – I –	K+ R + C + I +	K++ R ++ C ++ I +
Traditional consumer market	K– – R – C + I –	K – R + C + I –	K – R + + C + I –

Table 8.8— Selecting a target scenario using methodological tools for managing advanced development

Quantitative indicator	Quantitative value of the indicator
K – competitiveness R – resourcing C – scientific and technological capacity I – readiness to implement the methodology	– – critical value – insufficient value + required value + + sufficient value

Analyzing Table 8.7, we can conclude that only two scenarios provide readiness for advanced development: «Progressive market» and «Moderate market». The «traditional» scenario does not provide the required level of competitiveness, resourcing and scientific and technological capacity (as the main conditions for advanced development). The «Progressive market «scenario assumes a more efficient structure, production system and management system of the company than the «Moderate market» one. Besides, the «Progressive Market» scenario will require greater competitiveness by maximizing the consolidation of scientific and technological capacity, competencies and resources based on a technology platform and eliminating internal competition in the domestic and international markets.

The implementation of the target scenario is provided by the mechanism developed in chapter 7 for managing a company's advanced development based on technology platforms in the current conditions of economic development.

To enter the advanced development mode and ensure global competitiveness in international markets, companies, in addition to offering the best products and technologies, must be cost-effective. To do this, the implemented projects must provide high profitability (at least 15% in projects and more than 7-10% in net profit), and the assets must be loaded by at least 90%. Moreover, in order to withstand global competition, the time frame for creating radically new products should not go beyond the period of the next change in consumer preferences.

The joint application of the proposed methodological tools, which is the basis of the proposed methodology for ensuring the advanced development of a company based on creating radically new products, will help its manufacturer to achieve long-term advanced development due to evolutionary changes resulting from the constant implementation of measures (control actions) to develop scientific and technological capacity and competencies in order to create products with high consumer properties.

At the same time, each wave of innovation naturally changes the organizational structure of the company, bringing new technologies and equipment. Waves of innovation are becoming shorter, which is justified by the acceleration in the field of R&D and the constant improvement of existing labor technologies and production equipment.

From one wave of innovation to a more advanced one, there is a gradual transfer of employee functions to machine complexes, and the directions for improving technology at the onset of the next technological mode are laid on the previous wave. Employees transfer their specific production functions to machine complexes, freeing up their time and energy to perform more important mental work. Production automation is increasing, since not only production functions, but also some production management functions are transferred from employees to automated complexes.

At the same time, the development and accumulation of competencies leads to an intellectual explosion that creates technologies that are the basis for creating radically new products, as well as production equipment of a new class – «ultra-smart machines» that change the existing production paradigm. This fundamentally changes the current wave of innovation. «Ultra-smart machines» begin to create and control the necessary equipment for various purposes and complexity. Thus, an innovative resonance is achieved – an extremely rapid technological progress, as a result of which human labor is completely replaced by machine labor, and the existing machine labor is replaced by more productive, automated and intellectualized machines. This eliminates a number of capital costs related to pre-production from the consumer value chain (the concept of pre-production as such disappears, since all operations are performed by intelligent systems in an automatic or automated mode).

Thus, due to the continuous development of competencies and periodically occurring intellectual explosions, there is a gradual reduction in the number and complexity of work currently carried out at various stages of product creation, which reduces the costs of its development and production and, consequently, the cost of finished products and the risks of going beyond the set cost of the future product created based on new technologies. Thus, new products with high consumer properties become more accessible to a wide range of consumers, which leads to the growth of the consumer market.

For a mathematical description of the achievement of such growth in accordance with the above-mentioned patterns that underlie the law of advanced satisfaction of prospective needs, consider the balance equations describing the cyclical relationship of the level of competence with the growth of consumer markets. Let us use IC(t) to denote the level of financing for increasing key technological competencies for creating innovative technologies at time t. We will consider both continuous time and discrete time variation depending on the problem statement. Using M(t), we denote a generalized indicator of the consumer market, which is created as a result of the release of new products. The first balance equation can be written as follows:

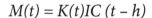

$$M(t) = K(t)IC\ (t - h)$$

Here K(t) is the transition coefficient, the economic meaning of which is that it shows the growth of the consumer market depending on the management, which consists in increasing the financing of the creation of key technological competencies, h > 0 is a time lag, which reflects the fact that the influence of financing of key competencies on the growth of the consumer market is temporarily delayed.

The second balance equation is written as follows:

$$IC(t) = L(t)M(t)$$

Here, L(t) is the coefficient of increase in funds for the development of unique technological competencies, depending on the increase in the consumer market index. This equation is natural, because in an innovative economy, the rapid growth of new markets leads to a sharp increase in the amount of investment in the creation of new technologies to increase the competitiveness of new products.

In these balance equations, we describe a linear situation, although in reality these relations should be written in a non-linear form, since the main coefficients K(t) and L(t) should depend not only on time, but also on the values of IC and M.

By comparing these balance equations, a general balance equation can be derived. From the second balance equation we have:

$$M(t) = \frac{1}{L(t)} IC(t)$$

Then substituting this value M(t) in the first balance equation, we get:

$$\frac{1}{L(t)} IC(t) = K(t)IC(t - h)$$

It is more convenient to write this equation as:

$$IC(t) = L(t)K(t)IC\ (t - h)$$

This is the main linear balance equation for managing the development of key competencies. This is a difference equation, so to define the function IC(t), it is necessary to solve this equation recursively.

Let us consider the economic meaning of this equation and its application in the practical assessment of economic growth as a result of supporting the development of key technological competencies. First of all, we note that this equation establishes the function of financing innovative technologies and competencies, depending on the initial conditions – initial financing. Of course, in a real situation, this financing may depend on management decisions, but then a violation of the balance equations will mean an inefficient investment.

Next, the most important indicator in the balance equation is the condition:

$$L(t)K(t) > 1, t \geq 0$$

Meeting this condition will mean a constant increase in financing for the development of key technological competencies. On the other hand, the violation of this condition shows that there is a constant decline in the financing of the development of key competencies and, accordingly, a decline in the consumer market indices.

Since there is a cycle of growth and decline in consumer markets, the transition coefficients $L(t)$ and $K(t)$ should change their values. A typical situation corresponds to the following conditions for coefficients:

$$L(t) < 1$$

$$K(t) > \frac{1}{L(t)}$$

This situation corresponds to the fact that financing for the development of key competencies is declining, but the growth of consumer markets is quite large. This situation is typical, because even with the constant growth of consumer markets, the financing of innovative technologies can decline. Taking into account the effects of the delay in the growth of consumer markets on the volume of financing for the development of key competencies and technologies, this situation is economically justified.

By adding non-linear components to the model, we explain the cyclical development of consumer markets for new products

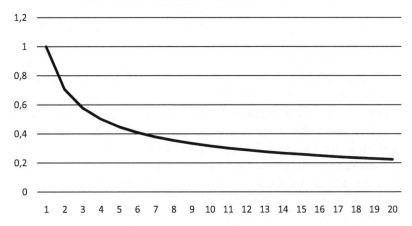

Figure 8.9 Dynamics of the nonlinear growth factor of the consumer market

created through the introduction of innovative technologies. We will consider non-linear models that will reflect the fact of extreme saturation of consumer markets. Indeed, every market has a certain capacity, so its expansion must have limitations, which will be expressed in a nonlinear dependence of the coefficient. K(t). In particular, you can use the following formula for this coefficient:

$$K((t), M(t)) = k_0(t)\left(\frac{1}{1 + M(t)}\right)$$

Here it is assumed that the power exponent satisfies the condition0<a<1. In this formula for the transition coefficient, we see that for limited values of k0(t and for increasing values of M(t), this coefficient decreases, which reflects the marginal utility of the product. A typical view of this coefficient is shown in the following graph (Figure 8.9)

In this case, the model signals the need to update existing products or develop new competitive products that become the main one in the market or create a completely new market.

The obtained regularity allows us to form a new tool of the created methodology, which allows us to determine the point in time when a company's existing product line does not allow the preservation of the advanced development mode. There is a need for an accelerated renewal of the product line and adjusting industrial policy, taking into account forecasting changes in the rate of evolution of technological orders, expressed in the current conditions in the transformation of Kondratieff's long economic waves. Let us consider these processes from the point of view of the dynamics of waves of innovation, which is most relevant for companies that have a long cycle from the moment of determining the image of products to their entry into the market. To do this, we will consider approaches to the evolution of the theory of Kondratieff waves based on the analysis of the results of numerical modeling of the dynamics of balance variables. When modeling, we will use the following initial conditions:

$IC(0) = 1$;
$M(0) = 1$;
$L(t) = 2.5$;
$k0 = 2$;
$a = 0.5$

These values correspond to the stage of rapid growth in the financing of key competencies and, accordingly, the rapid growth of consumer markets (Figure 8.10).

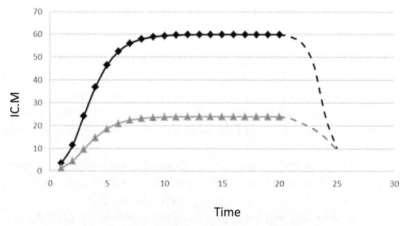

Figure 8.10. Dynamics of balance variables.

The resulting graph shows that at the simulated stage, there is a rapid mutual growth of the balance variables (responsible for managing the development of competencies and market growth), which, after reaching the saturation state, moves to stationary values. The results of this simulation show that when using non-stationary balance coefficients, it is possible to obtain a spiral behavior of the dynamics of balance variables, which will correspond to the modeled pattern of mutual development of competencies and new markets, which is able to transform the phase of the decline of the Kondratieff wave into a close to linear process of maintaining the growth rate of the economy.

Let us consider the results of simulation modeling of economic growth in the case of continuous development of competencies in conditions of sufficient resourcing for these processes. The considered balance model of mutual dependence of the level of management (financing) of the development of key competencies and the growth of consumer markets confirms that there is an objective pattern that describes the spiral growth of consumer markets for high-tech products. The growth of these markets encourages the financing of the development of technological competencies, which is reflected in the balance equations, and the growth of competencies creates new products, which means the creation and development of new consumer markets.

As a result of simulation, taking into account the exit of the indicator of the level of competence in a stationary state, we get the following graph describing the growth of the consumer market (Fig. 8.11).

The graph of the dynamics of the consumer market has a conical shape, which indicates a limit to growth due to the development of competencies in any particular direction. Nevertheless, the early identification of such situations allows to launch the development of new competencies and technologies in a timely manner, which will become the basis for the development of radically new products that meet future needs, and the regulator of new economic growth. Thus, it is possible to avoid serious crises of technology development and prevent a significant economic downturn corresponding to the stage of reduction of Kondratieff waves (see Figure 8.12).

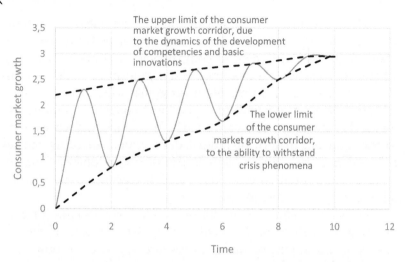

Figure. 8.11. Permanent growth of consumer markets influenced by the development of competencies (no transition to the stage of reduction of the Kondratieff wave)

Long economic wave

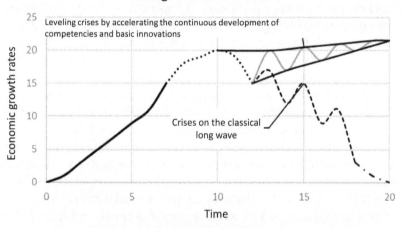

Figure 8.12 – Leveling the Kondratieff wave crises by accelerating the development of competencies and basic innovations

In accordance with the results of the study, it can be concluded that under the influence of modern drivers of economic growth related to the accelerated development of competencies, the change-ability of basic technological innovations, the regulatory effects of a State and the development of knowledge transfer mechanisms through the mechanisms of the global information space, it is possible to avoid crises and the transition of the long economic wave of Kondratieff to the phase of decline due to its transformation into the near-linear process shown in Fig. 8.12 that keeps economic growth at a permanently high level.

The processes discussed above allow company managers, based on the established methodology, to predict a company's entry into the trajectory of advanced development, corresponding to the linear process described above. This is due to the fact that the economic environment is constantly changing (market conditions are changing, new players are emerging, scientific and technological progress is taking place), and in practice it is quite difficult to obtain reliable information about the influence of environmental factors in a timely manner. In this regard, the methodology for ensuring the advanced development of the company should be built in such a way that, based on incomplete information about the environmental factors, timely measures are taken to maintain the technological level of the company and the technical level of production. Contingency creation of the system's flexibility reserve will allow to efficiently react to negative environmental factors at an early stage. As an economic tool, you can use well-known approaches from the practice of risk management, for example, responding to weak signals. This will allow us to take into account the potential trends of the external economic environment in the planning of activities and predict the need for evolutionary and revolutionary changes in a company's product strategy.

411

CONCLUSION

The scientific problems considered in the monograph make it possible to draw the following conclusion. New approaches to ensuring advanced development and sustainability of the company in the conditions of crises and transformation of world economies are considered on the basis of the developed theoretical and methodological provisions and practical recommendations for their implementation.

It is proved that overcoming the crisis phenomena and achieving accelerated economic growth largely depend on the pace and quality of radical competencies, which have become a key driver for ensuring the competitive potential of products and services in the markets. At the same time, it is established that the rates of economic growth and development increase as a result of the spread of competencies to the intersectoral level under the influence of global informatization.

To assess economic growth as a result of the creation of intersectoral radical competencies, a methodological apparatus has been developed, a feature of which is the selection of «useful» data from the entire volume of heterogeneous information and a quantitative assessment of their impact on the rate of economic growth, taking into account the modeling of the impact on it and other key factors. This allowed us to develop a model of the economic development cycle according to the «competencies → industry → personalized needs» scheme.

The economic law of advanced satisfaction of perspective needs has been developed, which became the basis for the formed axiomatic foundations of the theory of advanced development and economic growth of the company, which made it possible to formulate strategic approaches and tools for managing the company's economic growth based on the creation of radically new products.

The formed bases of transformation of scientific and technological capacity and unique technological competencies into a radically new product, decribed in this monograph, provide a detailed description of the chain of its transformation, the process of shaping the characteristics of radically new products under the influence of scientific and technological capacity and unique competencies, as well as methods of managing these processes with a quantitative assessment of various economic parameters that indicate the pace of economic growth and development of the organization.

Practical methods of creating and selling products with high consumer utility are proposed, which form quantitative estimates of the parameters of market segments, the cost of radically new products, taking into account economic factors that change over time, which allowed us to develop the basics of the mechanism for creating and selling products with high consumer utility and measures for its practical implementation.

On the basis of the law of advanced satisfaction of prospective needs, a methodological toolkit for managing the company's sustainable development has been formed based on service models with a description of their essence and mathematical modeling of assessments of their effectiveness in terms of financial results for the company. Service models are proposed as a tool for the transfer of knowledge and competencies to ensure the economic efficiency of the company. Furthermore, a methodological apparatus has been developed for forecasting the company's economic growth as a result of the transition to service models, which allows managers to assess the economic benefits obtained and compare them with planned costs to determine the effect that creates a «cushion» of the company's financial stability.

Mechanisms for managing the advanced development of the company based on technological platforms are proposed as the basis for ensuring economic sustainability. The key components of the company's advanced development mechanism have been formed, which in practice will allow creating specific practice-oriented mechanisms that take into account the peculiarities of individual business structures. This made it possible to draw conclusions and form an algorithm for achieving the company's global competitiveness based on the development of technology platforms.

Moreover, global competitiveness and technological leadership, provided as a result of the company's entry on the path of advanced development, is not a self-organizing process, and the monograph develops a systematic approach to managing the transition to technological leadership of the company based on the production and sale of radically new products, which reflects the main aspects of innovative areas of ensuring technological leadership.

All the presented theoretical and methodological developments allowed us to form the theoretical basis for the development of a unified methodology for ensuring the company's advanced development, which contains a practice-oriented methodological apparatus that allows for the assessment and management of this process.

In general, the scientific and practical significance of this monograph is that it contains:

practical recommendations for organizing the transition to advanced development and sustainability of the company, which are of interest to industrial enterprises, especially high-tech companies, and individual entrepreneurs;

the basics of managing the processes of creating radically new products with high techno-economic characteristics, which will increase the economic stability and positioning of the company in the world market;

modern models and methods of company management, taking into account the advantages of digital technologies, which act as a tool for achieving accelerated economic development;

a mechanism for the transition of high-tech enterprises to a trajectory of advanced development, which can be used in practice in order to achieve global competitive leadership.

BIBLIOGRAPHY

Aldaniyazov K.N. Analysis of actual production self-cost: factors and reserves of its decrease Problems of Economics and Management of Oil and Gas Complex. – 2014. – No. 7. – S. 8- 12.

Artificial Intelligence Index: 2017 Annual Report, http://cdn.aiindex.org/2017-report.pdf

Artyakov V.V., Chursin A.A. Innovation management. methodological tools: textbook / Moscow, 2019. Ser. Higher education: Master

Batkovskiy, A., Leonov, A., Pronin, A., Chursin, A., Nesterov, E. Regulation of the dynamics of creating high-tech products // International Journal of Engineering and Technology(UAE). 2018. Volume 7, Issue 3.14 Special Issue 14, 2018, p. 261-270

Batraeva E.A. Pricing policy of the company. Methods of pricing in a market economy [Electronic resource] / E.A. Batraeva. – Electron. Dan. – Krasnoyarsk: Sib. Feder. un-t, 2013 – 75 p.

Belov M.V., Novikov D.A. Structure of methodology of complex activity// Ontology of design. 2017. No. 4 (26).

Boginsky A. Methodological basis for creating promising high-tech products in the digital transformation. – Talinn: EurAsian Scientific Editions Ltd, 2021 – 265 p.

Boginskiy, A.I., Chursin, A.A., Nesterov, E.A., Tyulin, A.E. Assessing the competitiveness of production of a high-tech corporation to ensure its advanced development // Journal of Advanced Research in Dynamical and Control Systems, 2019, 11(11 Special Issue), p. 73-81

Boginsky A.I., Chursin A.A. Design solutions for optimizing the cost of production // Vestnik mashinostroeniya. 2019.No. 8.p. 74-78.

Boginsky A.I., Chursin A.A. The mechanism for updating the manufactured products // Economics and Management. 2019. No. 3 (147). p. 72-81.

Boginsky A.I., Uchenov A.A., Chursin A.A. Assessment of the needs of companies in support systems for effective management decisions // Microeconomics. 2019. No. 6 (89). p. 22-30.

Boginsky, A.I., Chursin, A.A. Optimizing Product Cost // Russian Engineering Research, 2019, 39(11), p. 940-943

Borodin, R. A. Features of accounting for production costs and calculating the cost of production of auxiliary production / R. A. Borodin. – Moscow: Laboratory of Books, 2011. – 141 p.

Chursin A. A., Davydov V. A., Ozhiganov E. N. Factors and indicators of investment attractiveness of enterprises of space-rocket complex in the current economic conditions. // Defense tech / M.: FSUE "Scientific—technical center "informtekhnika", 2012. No. 6-7. – p. 36-44.

Chursin A., Semenov A., Danilchanka A. Analysis of Innovation Development in the Economy with Exhaustible Resource Sector by First Order Dynamical Systems Application // Nonlinear Phenomena in Complex Systems, vol. 19, no. 3 (2016), pp. 254-270.

Chursin A., Tyulin A. Competence Management and Competitive Product Development: Concept and Implications for Practice. – Heidelberg, Germany: Springer International Publishing, 2018. – 234 p.

Chursin A., Tyulin A., Yudin A. (2016) The Model of Risk Assessment in the Management of Company's Competitiveness, Journal of Applied Economic Sciences, Volume XI, Issue 8, pp. 1781-1790.

Chursin A., Vlasov Y., Makarov Y. Innovation as a basis for competitiveness: theory and practice. Heidelberg, 2016.

Chursin A.A. An integral indicator of the economic efficiency of a complex organizational and economic system // Bulletin of the Moscow University. Series 26: Government audit. 2019. No. 2. p. 114-126.

Chursin A.A. Diversification of issued goods as the basis for stable economic development under the conditions of the cyber economy/ Contributions to Economics. Part 2,2019, p. 39-49

Chursin A.A., Strenalyuk V.V. Synergy Effect in Innovative Activities and its Accounting in the Technological Competencies of an Enterprise // European Research Studies Journal. Volume XXI, Issue 4, 2018. pp. 151-161.

Chursin, A. Competition, innovation and investment (nonlinear synthesis) : monograph / A.Chursin, S. Vasiliev. – M.: Engineering, 2011. – 478 p.

Chursin, A. Problems of competitiveness management in the aerospace industry in modern economic conditions. // Defense tech / M.: FSUE scientific technical center «Informtehnika», 2013. – No. 1.

Chursin, A. Theoretical foundations of competitiveness management. Theory and *practice* / A. A. Chursin. – M.: Spektr, 2012. – 590 p.

Chursin, A., Afanasyev, M. Reform and development of rocket-space industry of Russia (methods, concepts and models): monograph. -M.: Publishing house «Spectrum», 2014. – 451 p.

Chursin, A., Baymuratov, U. Global economy and problems of competitiveness of developing economies. Article. – Reports of the National Academy of Sciences of the Republic of Kazakhstan. – 2010 – №1. – p. 73-80.

Chursin, A., Danilyuk, R., Ostrovskaya, A. Evaluation of the effectiveness of projects in knowledge-intensive industries. // Business in law, Publishing house «Yur – VAK», 2014, No. 4 – P. 148-151.

Chursin, A., Dranayeva, A. Quantitative evaluation of the competitiveness of the organization. Article. -Defense complex to scientific-technical progress in Russia. -2010-No. 2 – P.95-100.

Chursin, A., Drogovoz, P., Sadovskaya, T., Shiboldenkov, V. A linear model of economic and technological shocks in science-intensive industries // Journal of Applied Economic Sciences. 2017. Volume 12, Issue 6, Fall 2017, Pages 1567-1577

Chursin, A., Drogovoz, P., Sadovskaya, T., Shiboldenkov, V. The dynamic model of elements' interaction within system of science-intensive production under unstable macroeconomic conditions // Journal of Applied Economic Sciences. 2017. Volume 12, Issue 5, Fall 2017, Pages 1520-1530

Chursin, A., Ivanov, A. Guidelines for creating a concept of sustainable innovative development of structures with the consolidated capital. Article. – Defensive complex – to scientific and technical progress of Russia. – 2010 – №3 – P.110-117.

Chursin, A., Kokuytseva, T. Innovative economy as the strategic goal of development in crisis and post-crisis conditions. – Bulletin Of The National Academy Of Sciences Of The Republic Of Kazakhstan. – Almaty: The National Academy of Sciences, 2010 – No. 4. P. 80-88.

Chursin, A., Kokuytseva, T. The law of competitiveness. – Problems of modern Economics. – Spb, 2011 – No. 1. P. 43-45.

Chursin, A., Kovkov D., Shamin, R. Approaches to assess the impact of external and internal factors on competitiveness of products of rocket and space industry. // Publishing house «Yur-VAK» , the Journal «Business in law» №1, 2013. – P. 127-131

Chursin, A., Makarov, Y. Management of competitiveness: Theory and practice // 2015, Management of Competitiveness: Theory and Practice p. 1-378

Chursin, A., Makarov, Yu., Baymuratov, U. Investment with innovation: synergy in the competitiveness of the economy / Under the scientific editorship of A.Chursin. – M.:Publishing house «MAKD»: Engineering, 2011. – 496 p.

Chursin, A., Milkovsky, A. The role of information and communication technologies in the management of enterprises. // Business in law, Publishing house «Yur–VAK» 2014, No. 4, P. 123-127.

Chursin, A., Okatyev, N. Approaches to optimization of resources on creation and production of competitive goods. Article. – Directory. Engineering journal, No. 5, 2008 – P. 35-39.

Chursin, A., Sergeev, S. To the question of the mechanism of management of large Russian corporations on the example of the aviation company of holding type, the article of Defense equipment. – 2009 – № 4-5 P. 59-68.

Chursin, A., Shamin, R. Investments and innovations and their role in enhancing the competitiveness of the organization // Defensive complex – to scientific and technical progress of Russia No. 2. – 2011. – p. 83-87.

Chursin, A., Shmakov, E. Economic-mathematical model of optimal allocation of investments in the modernization of technology-intensive enterprises. Business in law, publishing house «Yur-Vak, 2014, no. 3, P. 239-243

Chursin, A., Solovyev, V. The Impact of innovation on mechanisms of competitiveness. / / «Innovation», №3 (173), 2013, P. 60-66

Chursin, A., Tyulin, A. Competence management and competitive product development: Concept and implications for practice. Springer International Publishing. 2018. Pages 1-241. DOI: 10.1007/978-3-319-75085-9

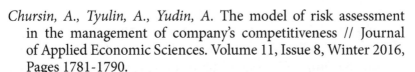

Chursin, A., Tyulin, A., Yudin, A. The model of risk assessment in the management of company's competitiveness // Journal of Applied Economic Sciences. Volume 11, Issue 8, Winter 2016, Pages 1781-1790.

Chursin, A., Vasilyev, S. Competition, innovation and investment (non-linear synthesis). – M.: Engineering, 2011. – 480 p.

Chursin, A., Volkov, V. Some theoretical approaches to evaluating the competitiveness of space-rocket industry when implementing innovative technologies//system analysis, management and navigation: Book of abstracts. -M.: MAI Publishing House, 2012. – P. 133.

Chursin, A.A., Kashirin, A.I., Strenalyuk, V.V., Ostrovskaya, A.A., Kokuytseva, T.V. The approach to detection and application of the company's technological competences to form a business-model // IOP Conference Series: Materials Science and Engineering. 2018. Volume 312, Issue 1. DOI: 10.1088/1757-899X/312/1/012003

Chursin, A.A., Semenov, A.S., Danilchankay, A.V. Analysis of innovation development in the economy with exhaustible resource sector by first order dynamical systems application // Nonlinear Phenomena in Complex Systems. Volume 19, Issue 3, 2016, Pages 254-270.

Chursin, A.A., Shamin, R.V., Fedorova, L.A. The mathematical model of the law on the correlation of unique competencies with the emergence of new consumer markets // 2017, European Research Studies Journal 20(3), p. 39-56

Chursin, A.A., Shamin, R.V., Fedorova, L.A. The mathematical model of the law on the correlation of unique competencies with the emergence of new consumer markets // European Research Studies Journal. 2017. Volume 20, Issue 3, 2017, Pages 39-56.

Chursin, A.A., Shevchenko, V.V. About the possibilities of operational gaming scenario modeling activities of enterprises and corporations // Proceedings of 2017 10th International Conference Management of Large-Scale System Development, MLSD 2017. DOI: 10.1109/MLSD.2017.8109609

Clayton M. Christinsen, Assessing Your Organization's Innovation Capabilities // Leader to Leader. -2001. -№ 21.

Ermakov, V.A., Burmistrova, E.M., Bodin, N.B., Chursin, A.A., Shevereva, E.A. A letter of credit as an instrument to mitigate risks and improve the efficiency of foreign trade transaction // Espacios. 2018. Volume 7, Issue 3.14 Special Issue 14, 2018, Pages 261-270

Falco C.G. Controlling: modern challenges // Modern enterprise and the future of Russia: collection of articles. scientific. Proceedings of the International Forum dedicated to the 85th anniversary of the Department of Economics and Organization of Production of the Moscow State Technical University H.E. Bauman, Moscow, December 5-6, 2014 / Ed. Dr. econ. Sciences, prof. C.G. Falco. M .: NP «Union of controllers». 2014.S. 4-7.

Kim W.C., Mauborgne R. Value Innovation: The Strategic Logic of High Growth // Harvard Business Review. 1997. Vol. 75 (1). P. 102-112.

Kotler F., Trias de Bez F. Lateral marketing. – St. Petersburg, 2009.

Kozoriz N. L. Security issues and access to global information resources. / / Pravo i gosudarstvo, 2013, No. 6, pp. 103-107.

Lifshits A.S. Development of industrial enterprises through the prism of the resource-targeted approach and the theory of limitations // Entrepreneurship. 2014. No. 4. P. 50-59.

Nagirnaya, A.V. The global process of informatization of society: factors of territorial unevenness / A.V. Nagirnaya. – Text: direct, electronic // Young scientist. – 2014. – No. 11 (70). – S. 160-165. – URL:URL: https://moluch.ru/archive/70/12136/ (date of request: 15.04.2020)

Nekipelov A. «We know that we are on the verge of creating a new world financial and economic system» Kuzminov Ya. Viral Revolution: How the Pandemic Will Change Our World (https://www.rbc.ru/opinions/society/27/03/2020/5e7cd7799a79471ed230b774)

Plotnikov A. N., Litoninsky S. N. Analysis of methods for assessing the innovative potential of an enterprise and directions for their improvement // Problems of the modern economy. -2012. – № 7. – c. 248-263.

Porter, M.E. On Competition: trasnl.. from English / M.E. Porter. – M., 2000 .-- 331 p.

Raizberg B.A., Lozovsky L.Sh., Starodubtseva E.B. Modern economic dictionary. 6th ed., Rev. and add. M .: INFRA-M, 2011

Saati T.L. Decision-making. Hierarchy analysis method. – M .: Radio and communication, 1989 . – 316 p.

Selishchev A.S. Microeconomics. – Spb .: Peter, 2003 .—448 p.

Shackelton, R. Total Factor Productivity Growth in Historical Perspective // working Paper 2013-01.-2013.-21 p.

Tellis J.J., Golder P.N., Will and Vision. Saint Petersburg: Stockholm School of Economics in Saint Petersburg, 2005

Tyan E.G. Investigation of the features of the value of an innovative product in consumer perception // Marketing and marketing research. – 2011. – No. 5 (95)

Tyulin A. Chursin A. The new Economy of the Product Life Cycle. Innovation and Design in the Digital Era // Springer International Publishing. – 2020. P.400

Tyulin A.E., Chursin A.A. Fundamentals of managing innovation processes in knowledge-intensive industries (practice). Moscow, 2017.

Tyulin, A. Approaches to measure competitiveness of rocket and space equipment / A.Tyulin, A.Rusinov // Business in law. – 2015. – No. 1. – P. 179-182.

Tyulin, A. Basic principles for the establishment of sectoral centres of competence / A.Tyulin // Resources. Information. Supply. Competition. – 2013. – № 1. – p. 140–143.

Tyulin, A. Benchmarking in the creation of new competences / A.Tyulin // Economics and entrepreneurship. – 2016. – No. 6. – P. 491-497.

Tyulin, A. E. Corporate governance. Methodological tools. Moscow: LLC "SIC INFRA-M", 2019. 216 p.

Tyulin, A. Formation of the conceptual model of sectoral management based on competence centres / A.Tyulin // Russian entrepreneurship. – 2014. – № 9 (255). – P. 4-11.

Tyulin, A. Formation of the mechanism of public-private partnership in integrated business structures / A.Tyulin // In the world of scientific discoveries (economy and innovative education). – 2013. – № 8.1 (44). – P. 199-221.

Tyulin, A. Fundamentals of management of innovation processes in knowledge-intensive industries (practice) / A. Tyulin, A. Chursin. – M., 2016.

Tyulin, A. Fundamentals of management of innovation processes in knowledge-intensive industries (theory) / A. Tyulin, A. Ostrovskaya, A.Chursin. – M., 2015. – 290 p.

Tyulin, A. Improving the competitiveness of the industry on the ba-sis of a *network* of competence centres / A. Tyulin, S. Barash-kov // Science and technology : materials of XXXIV conference devoted to the 90-th anniversary of academician V.P Makeev. Moscow, 10-12 June 2010-2014 vol. 4. -M., 2014. -P. 160-168.

Tyulin, A. Main types of *public*-private partnership / A.Tyulin // materials of the 4-th all-Russia scientific — practical conference with international participation "The regional innovation econ-omy: the nature, the elements, the problems *of* formation". Ulya-novsk, May 2013-Ulyanovsk, 2013 -p 206-208.

Tyulin, A. Marketing analysis of the global market of avion-ics/A. Tyulin//collection of articles of the international sci-entifically-practical Conference on marketing and mass communication in sustainable development of the territory and of the enterprise. Penza, June 2012-Penza, 2012.-p. 72-74.

Tyulin, A. Mechanisms of public-private partnership/A. Tyulin//col-lection of scientific materials of international scientifically-practi-cal conference on the science and education in the modern world. May 31, 2013 in 4 vols. – Vol. II. – Moscow, 2013.– p. 90–91.

Tyulin, A. Methodical approach to assessment and ranking of unique technological competence / A.Tyulin, A.Yudin // Economics and entrepreneurship. – 2015. – No. 12. – Part 2. – P. 681-685.

Tyulin, A. Methodical approach to assessment of influence of innova-tive technologies on the competitiveness / A. Tyulin, A. Yudin // Microeconomics. – 2015. – No. 6. – P. 59-64.

Tyulin, A. Modern development paradigm of rocket and space tech-nology / A.Tyulin // Technologies and services : international forum "Russian innovative technologies and global market." Moscow, November 27, 2015 – M., 2015. – P. 33-40.

Tyulin, A. Network interaction of sectoral competence centres in instrumentation: main elements / A.Tyulin // Collection of materials of II International scientific-practical conference "Fundamental and applied Sciences today." North Charleston, June 2013-North Charleston, 2013. – P. 221-223.

Tyulin, A. Organizational-economic mechanism of functioning of the industry based on *competencies* centres / A. Tyulin// Qual-ity, innovation, education. – 2013. – № 5 (96). – P. 65-69.

Tyulin, A. Organizations participating in integrated structures as competencies centres / A.Tyulin // Academic notes: Economic Sciences/Ulyanovsk State University. – 2013. – No. 30. – P. 44-47.

Tyulin, A. Principles for the establishment of sectoral centres of competence / A.Tyulin // collection of materials of III International scientific-practical conference "Economics and management: analysis of tendencies and prospects of development." Novosibirsk, November 15, 2013 – Novosibirsk, 2013. – P. 298-302.

Tyulin, A. Problems of conceptual competence approach in management: structuring competences / E.Tyulin, E.Rozhkova // Economics and entrepreneurship. – 2013. – № 4 (33). – P. 368-372.

Tyulin, A. Product and technological specifics of aircraft instruments making / A. Tyulin // Academic notes: Economic Sciences/Ulyanovsk State University. 2012. – No. 28 (2). – P. 31-42.

Tyulin, A. Promotion of aircraft instruments making enterprises to the world market / A.Tyulin // collection of scientific papers on materials of International scientifically-practical Conference "Modern issues of education and science." Moscow, December 30, 2012 – M., 2013. -P. 152-153.

Tyulin, A. Proposals for the improvement of the innovative development program of the Corporation based on the selection of the strategy to create new competitive advantages / A. Tyulin // Business in law. – 2016. – No. 3. – P. 40-44.

Tyulin, A. Public-Private partnership: the essence and problems of formation / A.Tyulin // Collection of materials of II International scientific-practical conference "Scientific aspects of innovative research." Samara, June 13, 2013 – Samara, 2013. – P. 65-68.

Tyulin, A. Recommendations on the practical implementation of Open innovation by high-tech Russian companies / A. Tyulin // Microeconomics. – 2016. – No. 3. – P. 55-59.

Tyulin, A. Staffing corporate network of competencies centers in aircraft instrument making / A.Tyulin // Scientific results of 2013: achievements, projects, hypothesis : Compilation of the III International Scientific and Practical Conference materials. Moscow, December 27, 2013., 2013. – P. 218-222.

Tyulin, A. Strategic analysis in aviation engineering/ A.Tyulin, E.Bely // contemporary problems of science and education. – 2012. – No. 3. – P. 25– 32.

Tyulin, A. The core competency of the organizations participating in the integrated structures / A.Tyulin // Problems of economics and management. – 2013. – № 6 (22). – P. 62-65.

Tyulin, A. The development and operation of a branch network of competence centers / A.Tyulin // Economic Science : Scientific and information jornal. -2014. -No. 2 (111). -P. 95-98.

Tyulin, A. The goals and objectives of the innovation development of domestic aircraft engineering / A.Tyulin // collection of articles of the III international scientific-practical conference "Problems of the innovation economy, modernization and technological development." Penza, March 2011 – Penza, 2011. – P. 74-75.

Tyulin, A. The project management process within the corporate network of competence centres / A.Tyulin // collection of materials of International scientific-practical conference "Modern tendencies of development of economy, management and law". Moscow, 22 December 2013 – M., 2013 – P. 177-180.

Tyulin, A. The role of technological and economic factors in the development of sectoral integration / A.Tyulin // collection of materials of the X international scientific-practical conference "Economics and management in XXI century: trends of development." Novosibirsk, November 2013 – Novosibirsk, 2013. – p. 149-154.

Tyulin, A. The selection criteria for the optimal integrated structure of the production system / A.Tyulin // Quality, innovation, education. – 2013. – № 9 (100). – P. 66-71.

Tyulin, A. The technique of a rating estimation of efficiency of use of human capital / A.Tyulin, E.Ozhiganov, V. Korneenko // Economics and entrepreneurship. – 2014. – No. 12. – Part 3.– p. 183-191.

Tyulin, A. Theory and practice of creating and managing competences to enhance the competitiveness of integrated structures / A. Tyulin. – M., 2015. – 312 p.

Tyulin, A., Chursin, A., Yudin, A. Production capacity optimization in cases of a new business line launching in a company //Espacios, 2017

Tyulin, A., Chursin, A., Yudin, A. Production capacity optimization in cases of a new business line launching in a company // Espacios. Volume 38, Issue 62, 2017.

Tyulin, A., Chursin, A., Yudin, A., Grosheva P. Theoretical foundations of the law of managing for advanced development of the organization // Mikroeconomika. 2019. № 1. p. 5-12.

Tyulin, A., Chursin, A.: Fundamentals of management of innovation processes in knowledge intensive industries (practice), Moscow (2016)

Tyulin, A.: Theory and practice of creating and managing competences to enhance the competitiveness of integrated structures, 312 p. Moscow (2015)

Tyulin, A.E. A strategy for implementing the technologies of industry 4.0 and the tools of competency management in the digital economy / Contributions to Economics, 2019, Part 2, p. 291-304.

Tyulin, A.E. Theory and Practice of Competence Management Determining the Competitiveness of Integrated Structures / A.E. Tyulin. – M., 2015.

Vasin L. Directions of reducing the cost of production / L. Vasin. // Economic and Legal Sciences. – 2013. – No. 5. – p. 3-6

Veblen T. Theory of the leisure class. – M .: Progress, 1984 . – 244 p

Veblen T.The Limitations of Marginal Utility/ Voprosy Economici, 2007, no. – Pp. .86-98.

Vlasov Yu.V., Chursin A.A. Assessment of the technical level of production for placing a government order // Microeconomics. 2016. No. 2. p. 17-25.

Vlasov, Y.V., Chursin, A.A. Management of diversificataion system in aerospace industry // Economy of Region. Volume 12, Issue 4, 2016, Pages 1205-1217. DOI: 10.17059/2016-4-21

Vyunova, R.R. Approaches to assessing the innovative potential of an enterprise / R.R. Vyunova // Society: Politics, Economics, Law. – 2015. – No. 2. – P. 35–38.

TABLE OF CONTENTS

Lightning Source UK Ltd.
Milton Keynes UK
UKHW020830171221
395803UK00003B/301